Theory, Culture & Society

Theory, Culture & Society caters for the resurgence of interest in culture within contemporary social science and the humanities. Building on the heritage of classical social theory, the book series examines ways in which this tradition has been reshaped by a new generation of theorists. It will also publish theoretically informed analyses of everyday life, popular culture, and new intellectual movements.

Recent volumes include:

Postmodernity USA
The Crisis of Social Modernism in Postwar America
Anthony Woodiwiss

The New Politics of Class
Social Movements and Cultural Dynamics in Advanced Societies
Klaus Eder

The Body and Social Theory
Chris Shilling

Symbolic Exchange and Death
Jean Baudrillard

Sociology in Question
Pierre Bourdieu

Economies of Signs and Space
Scott Lash and John Urry

Baroque Reason
The Aesthetics of Modernity
Christine Buci-Glucksmann

CONTENTS

ACKNOWLEDGEMENTS

The research and writing for this book began in 1988. Since then, a great many people have been instrumental in helping me to bring it to a conclusion. Here I can thank only those whose role was more direct. Through many stimulating conversations, John Simpson was the author of several key suggestions and criticisms. To Roland Robertson I probably owe the greatest intellectual and practical debt, a fact that may not always be obvious in what follows. I am not sure if there is any important matter having to do with globalization on which I fundamentally disagree with him, except perhaps the nefarious intentions of my erstwhile countrymen. Michel Desjardins and Frank Lechner spent many hours carefully reading and commenting on earlier versions of the theoretical chapters. John Hannigan consistently helped me see matters more broadly than I have a habit of seeing them. Todd Lawson and Ted Hewitt helped me to avoid several pitfalls in some of the case studies, areas in which I am not an expert. Jim Beckford and Karel Dobbelaere provided helpful comments and welcome encouragement for earlier published versions of certain chapters. Stephen Barr and the staff at Sage Publications in London have been admirable in the expeditious and competent way they have transformed this work from incomplete manuscript to quality published product.

Special thanks go to many of my former students, especially those from my 'Religion and Politics' undergraduate course. More than they realized, they gave me the opportunity to hear myself think about the numerous issues involved. From this group, I would like to single out Hamish Telford, Terry Woo, and Gregory Roberts, all of whom have provided me with stimulating insights even after they moved on to graduate studies. My thanks also to the people of the Department for the Study of Religion at the University of Toronto for giving me a peaceful and stimulating academic home these past ten years.

Of course, none of the above is in any way responsible for what use I have made of their inspiration and suggestions in this book.

Most of the material in this book is entirely new. A good portion originated as papers delivered at various conferences; and some has been published previously. Chapter 3 is an expanded and heavily revised version of 'Privatization and the Public Influence of Religion in Global Society', *Theory, Culture and Society*, 7 (2/3) (1990): 373–395. Portions of Chapters 4 and 9 appeared in an earlier version as 'The Global Environment as a Religious Issue: A Sociological Analysis', *Religion*, 22 (1992): 1–19.

INTRODUCTION: RELIGION IN GLOBAL SOCIETY

The Global Metropolis

> There are things that seem not to belong together, except that it is part of the metropolitan experience that such things do not belong together and do live side by side – that you can live upstairs from Khomeini. . . .
>
> I have had the sense of having frequently to reconstruct my life. So that thing about shifting yourself and wondering if there's anything left of the original person or not is something that's very internal to me. It gives me the sense of character as being mutable . . . (Salman Rushdie, quoted in Appignanesi and Maitland, 1990: 8)

On 14 February, 1989, Ayatollah Ruhollah Khomeini issued an edict condemning to death Salman Rushdie for his book, *The Satanic Verses*. Almost immediately, the British author went into hiding with a 24-hour police bodyguard. Hitherto improving diplomatic relations between the Islamic Republic of Iran and various Western nations suffered rupture or serious strain. The incident became the lead item of the world's newspapers and newscasts, calling forth a wide range of comment from notables around the world (see Appignanesi and Maitland, 1990; Pipes, 1990).

At the time of writing, Rushdie is alive and Iran's diplomatic image has recovered somewhat. The affair, however, did not die with Khomeini in June 1989, but resurfaces from time to time as a kind of irritant that seems to point to much more than the fate of a single author. Key aspects of the event are in fact illustrative of the social world we inhabit and the place of religion in it. Among the most striking are the speed with which the affair unfolded, the nearly global range of the response, the deep conflict elicited by a somewhat inaccessible work of modern fiction, and the critical role of a Third World religious leader.

The speed and range are a consequence of today's communication technology, and this in two distinct senses. The power of this technology makes very rapid communication possible over almost unlimited space. Moreover, these media exist nearly everywhere on earth, along with the will and ability to use them. The potential for worldwide communication has been translated into actual practice. We therefore live in a *globalizing* social reality, one in which previously effective barriers to communication no longer exist. In the words of Roland Robertson, one of the leading contributors to a growing social-scientific discussion of globalization, the world is more and more becoming 'a single place' (1987a: 43). Accordingly, if we want to understand the major features of contemporary social life, we have to go beyond local and national factors to situate our analyses in this global context. More pointedly, we must make the primary unit of analysis the global system and not some subunit of it, such as the nation, the state, or the region. The Rushdie affair offers a particularly clear illustration of this notion, but the examples could be multiplied, not least in Middle East developments since the spring of 1989.

Stating the globalization thesis in these simple terms immediately raises some important questions. Why, for instance, has the global social reality developed? What are its underlying structures? How is it given cultural expression: how do major themes and ideas reflect the fact that we live in a globalizing context? I offer answers to these and other related questions in the following chapters. At the moment, however, I want to discuss another critical dimension of globalization, one exemplified in the deeply conflictual nature of the Rushdie affair.

The globalization thesis posits, in the first instance, that social communication links are worldwide and increasingly dense. On perhaps the more obvious level, this means that people, cultures, societies, and civilizations previously more or less isolated from one another are now in regular and almost unavoidable contact. This leads to a twofold result. On the one hand, we see the conflicts that arise as quite diverse and often contradictory cultures clash within the same social unit. On the other hand, globalizing socio-structural and cultural forces furnish a common context that attenuates the differences among these ways of life. The first Rushdie quote above expresses the same idea metaphorically: we live in a global metropolis in which things that do not belong together nevertheless live side by side.

While this twofold result may go some way to explaining the conflict inherent in the global social system, it does not penetrate far enough to the heart of the matter. To do so requires a more multifaceted approach.

Juxtaposition of particular cultures or identities not only brings differences into sharper profile, it makes it much more visible that the diverse ways of living are largely human constructions. In the context of comparison, no single one of them is self-evidently 'correct'. Life-worlds and worldviews appear to a significant extent arbitrary; and as such we can change them. What makes this challenging of identities unavoidable under conditions of globalization, however, is the existence of powerful social structures that ignore or at least recast all group-cultural and personal identities, thus undermining attempts to respond to the situation through renewed communicative isolation. The effort on the part of many people in the world nevertheless to preserve, stabilize, and (re)create particular identities therefore constantly runs counter to this tendency of the global system to relativize them. The resulting conflict, in this case, is then not so much against rival cultures and identities, although people may formulate it as such, as against the corrosiveness of the system itself. It is a response to, as Rushdie puts it, the mutability of character.

But why should mutability be a problem? To some extent, it is a matter of speed. Rapid change is, as I show in subsequent chapters, a feature of globalizing society. It raises the probability of perceived anomie at the personal and group level when too much changes over too short a period of time. On a deeper and more important level, however, speed is less at issue than the direction of change and who controls the change. In broad terms, the problem is one of power, not just meaning. While this observation may apply to a great many social analyses, in the context of globalization, it points to a paradox. One of the central theses that this book defends is that the global system corrodes inherited or constructed cultural and personal identities; yet also encourages the creation and revitalization of particular identities as a way of gaining control over systemic power.[1] It is in the context of this last feature that religion plays one of its significant roles in the development, elaboration, and problematization of the global system.

The Rushdie affair can again serve as point of departure. *The Satanic Verses* is a novel about the mutability of character under globalizing conditions; it is at the same time about religion, in particular Islam. Many Muslims perceive it as an affront to what they hold most sacred and thereby a negation of themselves as actors in global society. The latter phrase is key. The Rushdie affair does more than demonstrate the link between religious faith and particularistic identity. On the whole, outraged Muslims are, in fact, not concerned that Rushdie's book will undermine their faith – all the less so since few devout Muslims will ever read it. What troubles them much more is the notion that they are being asked to surrender the core of that faith – the *immutable sacredness* of the Qur'an – as the price for full inclusion in a global system currently dominated by non-Muslims. Khomeini and many other Muslims equate the relativization of Islam declared by *The Satanic Verses* with the marginalization of Muslims in the overall society. Khomeini's condemnation of Rushdie is therefore part of a much larger Muslim effort to counter inequalities within the global system through the revitalization of Islamic particularity (cf. Appignanesi and Maitland, 1990; Pipes, 1990).

Understanding the Rushdie affair in this way points implicitly to some important aspects of the role of religion in global society. Firstly, even where religion appears as a negative reaction to globalization, this does not mean that religion is simply a regressive force. On the contrary, events like the Rushdie affair, and indeed the Iranian revolution as a whole, indicate that religion can be a proactive force in the sense that it is instrumental in the elaboration and development of globalization: the central thrust is to make Islam and Muslims more determinative in the world system, not to reverse globalization. The intent is to shape the global reality, not to negate it. More generally, religion within the global system can be antisystemic and prosystemic at the same time: it can further globalization in opposing its effects.[2]

Secondly, there is an important sense in which the Rushdie affair is not a religious conflict at all. I am referring here not directly to the fact that it is also about political and economic marginalization, as just outlined. Rather, it is that, from the point of view of Rushdie and his supporters, Muslims and

Islam are not under attack. Rushdie's supporters are equally outraged, but for them matters such as freedom of artistic expression and the sovereignty of states are at the centre of the conflict, not religion. This 'secular' view of the issue is, moreover, an essential part of the Muslim complaint as well. As noted above, for Khomeini and his supporters, the marginalization of Muslims and the marginalization of religion – especially Islam – have been of a piece. This may, at first glance, seem a somewhat obvious equation: after all, if Muslims achieve higher status within the global system, would the religion which identifies them as a group not rise with them? On the level of the global system, however, the short answer to this question is no – or at least, not necessarily. A great many Christians and Jews, for instance, whether nominal or practising, are dominant in world society; but their religious traditions are no less marginalized than Islam. Their most sacred symbols are no more immune from 'blasphemous' treatment than are those of Islam.[3] In other words, the Rushdie affair exemplifies the point that globalization brings with it the relativization of particularistic identities along with the relativization and marginalization of religion as a mode of social communication.

We have then, in sum, a situation in which the revitalization of religion is a way of asserting a particular (group) identity, which in turn is a prime method of competing for power and influence in the global system; but this to a large extent is because religion has an affinity for particularistic identities and because it, like so many groups in our world, has become somewhat marginalized as a consequence of globalization. I elaborate on these matters in the following chapters. Here, however, I must first address a further matter fundamental to the entire analysis. This is the nature and function of religion itself.

Religion as a Mode of Communication

The key to the problem of *The Satanic Verses* for many Muslims is that it represents the larger global pressure towards the relativization of religion and group-cultural identity as the price for fuller inclusion in the global system. They are being asked to bracket who they are and what they hold most sacred. The situation immediately raises the question of what religion is, what allows us to differentiate it from other aspects of human and social life. The question is especially acute in the case of Islam with its characteristic emphasis on the singleness of life under God as a reflection of the singleness of God.

Aside from this practical dimension, defining religion has also been a constant theoretical problem in the scientific study of religion. Introductory texts in the field regularly include discussion of this difficulty. It was at the centre of the classical debate, and definitional diversity underlies current controversies about secularization, privatization, civil religion, and the fate of religion under conditions of modernity. These matters are at the heart of

NOTE

my effort here to assess the role of religion in global society. Some attempt at definition is therefore necessary for what follows, if only to make my assumptions clear.

In keeping with the aims of this study, I restrict the discussion to a sociological perspective. Following Niklas Luhmann, what characterizes the social as distinct especially from the psychological is communication. Social systems consist of communications, that is, situations in which an ego transmits meaningful information to an alter who in turn understands its meaning (Luhmann, 1984b: 30–91, especially 60ff.). Here cannot be the place for a proper justification of this position. Two implications are, however, important. The first is that the elements of social systems are not people but the communication which they engender. Societies are not composed of people even though people are necessary for societies to exist. The social is an emergent reality or, as Durkheim put it, a reality *sui generis* (1933). The second implication is that religion is therefore, sociologically speaking, a certain variety of communication.

Many sociological definitions of religion operate with a basic dichotomy such as profane/sacred (Durkheim), natural/supernatural (Parsons), nomos/cosmos (Berger), and empirical/super-empirical (Robertson). Others speak about religion as dealing with 'ultimate' problems (Yinger) or a 'general . . . uniquely realistic' order of existence (Geertz), implicitly defining it by contrast to a more proximate and equivocal domain.[4] The common thread through most of them is that religion is primarily about something beyond the normal, the everyday, the perceptible; and that somehow this radically other fundamentally conditions human existence.

I prefer to use *immanence/transcendence* to label the central religious dichotomy.[5] What is definitive about this polarity is the holistic nature of the first term. The immanent is the whole world, the whole of perceptible reality, all meaning communicable among human beings. The whole, however, cannot as such be the subject of communication[6] because we cannot distinguish it from anything that it does not encompass. The transcendent, as the polar opposite, serves to give the immanent whole its meaningful context. In this sense, it acts as the condition for the possibility of the immanent. The central religious paradox lies in the fact that the transcendent can only be communicated in immanent terms, and this by definition: communication on the basis of meaning is always immanent, even when the subject of communication is the transcendent. Religion, therefore, operates with sacred symbols, ones which always point radically beyond themselves. It deals simultaneously with the immanent and the transcendent.

While this dichotomy is basic to religion, it does not give a complete picture. Lending meaning to the whole would be of limited importance if it did not address core problems in human life: failure, insecurity, disappointment, in short, the seemingly final indeterminability of the world for human communication in terms of meaning. The social function of religion, in other words, is as much a part of what defines religion as its mode of operation.

Although less central, other polarities associated with religion, such as life/death, good/evil, yin/yang, liberation/suffering, serve to link immanence and transcendence to core human problems. Religion posits the transcendent to give the immanent world meaning; and makes the requisite distinction between the two by further postulating that the transcendent is not subject to the root indeterminacy of the immanent. Hence we have the familiar contrasts between the two realms in terms of, for example finite/infinite, illusion/reality, contingent/necessary, mortal/immortal. From here it is but a small step to assume that the ineffable but absolute is the condition for the possibility of what determinacy exists in the perceptible but ambiguous. The transcendent then becomes a potential solution to those very core problems of life in the immanent world.

A final defining factor remains. To provide meaning, including the meaning of suffering and evil, and further to offer the power to overcome the problem, religion posits the possibility of communication between humans and the transcendent: it treats the transcendent as a social partner. The transcendent partner may be found in a fish, a waterfall, one's 'inner' self, an imperceptible high god, or myriad sacred symbols. The communication may be in the form of speech, ritual, myth, sacred scripture, mystical insight, wisdom, ecstatic trance, or any number of variations and combinations of these. What all have in common is the assumption that the transcendent is a structured reality logically beyond the perceptible and humanly social world; but that it is nevertheless accessible through these special forms of communication.

In sum then, religion is a type of communication based on the immanent/transcendent polarity, which functions to lend meaning to the root indeterminability of all meaningful human communication, and which offers ways of overcoming or at least managing this indeterminability and its consequences.

This way of looking at religion does not overcome the classic problem of including too much or too little when defining religion. It does not answer definitively a question that runs implicitly throughout any analysis of religion, namely, what does and does not count as religion. My justification for defining religion in this way is that it offers certain strategic advantages within the context of the present study, not the least of which is that it leaves open the question of what counts as religion. For the rest, I leave it for the individual reader to judge whether my application of the definition is defensible.

Implicit Meanings in Theories of Globalization

These preliminary remarks about globalization and about religion can form the basis for considering a further intrinsic way that the two are connected. I do this by looking at some implicit meanings in theories about globalization. As already noted, there is a growing social-scientific debate on this topic;

and it is a central purpose of this book to contribute to that debate. I take a more detailed look at some of the principal contributors in the next chapter. The core hypothesis in this discussion is that, increasingly, there is a common social environment shared by all people on earth and that this globality conditions a great deal of what happens here, including how we form theories about it. Any social analysis that ignores this factor is incomplete and misses a key aspect of the human condition in our contemporary world.

Among the several constants informing the globalization discussion is the notion that the situation is new and unique in the history of humanity. Globalization theories assume a salient discontinuity between social life on earth in the past and now or in the future. As such, they include within themselves an extension and reformulation of modernization theories, whether of the Marxian or broadly liberal-functionalist variety. Like these, contributions to the globalization debate speak of a process that is ongoing and incomplete, and also one in which the observed necessarily includes the observer. The result is perceived insecurity in the object of discussion, yielding talk of crisis, open-ended development, and inherent conflict or contradiction in the global system.

As a reflection of these implicit assumptions, some contributors to the debate conceive the fluid situation of the present in terms of a *future stasis*. For example (to anticipate the fuller discussion in Chapter 1), Immanuel Wallerstein analyses the 'world-system', as he calls it, in terms of recurrent cycles and crises which end when the world capitalist system succumbs to its own contradictions – that is, its inability to stabilize – and an entirely different and more or less completely undefined world socialist state takes over (1974b: 415). Chase-Dunn and Rubinson talk about 'ceiling effects' of global expansion with a similar result: a 'change in the fundamental nature of the world system' (1979: 295). Meyer and Hannan, while parting with the Wallersteinians on significant matters, nevertheless also foresee radical change in the future because current patterns will run up against global limits (1979b: 307f.). They follow a more Weberian direction, fearing what seems to be a kind of 'iron cage'[7] as the endpoint of current trends. In each case, the physical limits of the earth determine that the past and present dynamic process of globalization will be negated in the future, yielding to a decidedly undynamic state.

This 'eschatological' dimension of globalization theories is neither fortuitous, nor indicative of some obvious and fatal flaw in the whole undertaking. Rather, it stems from the logical difficulty of conceiving a whole without something to differentiate it from and compare it to. Globalization means, for instance, that we cannot conceive the whole in terms of one of its parts, say the First or Third Worlds, or as a composite system of logically prior nation-states. As I will show in the next chapter, such a strategy breaks down because it cannot justify either logically or empirically the hierarchical ordering that it implies. Then again, the historical uniqueness of the development limits the use of earlier societies as models for conceiving the present. We can detect certain antecedents and similarities between the formation of past civilizations and the current globalizing circumstance.[8] Beyond that, however, they can only tell us what the current social reality is not, not what it is.

The problem, in short, bears a clear resemblance to the religious quest: we posit the transcendent in order that the immanent whole may have meaning. The transcendent, however, is strictly speaking not empirically available, just logically necessary. It is therefore not surprising that some globalization theorists, notably Roland Robertson, regard conceiving the global whole as a highly problematic and contested, but nevertheless central, task of both globalization theory and actors in the global system (Robertson, 1990a; Robertson and Lechner, 1985). As observers and participants, we must also look at the religious dimension of global social reality; and we should expect religion or religion-like phenomena to play a recurrent and key role. Robertson, we might say, takes a more Durkheimian approach to the problem.[9]

The continuities with Marx, Weber, and Durkheim are neither accidental nor representative of a deliberate effort to walk in the footsteps of the great nineteenth-century sociological masters. All three of these thinkers addressed the uniqueness of what, for lack of a better word, we usually call the modern world. If we consider that Marx's sparse writings on religion were but part of his more general critique of ideology, then all three made the analysis of religion a central part of their efforts to understand the transition to the modern world (see Beckford, 1989). Globalization theories are, as I noted above, developments of the fundamental modernization thesis. The latter claims that, at least in the West, radical social changes during the past few centuries have brought about a new type of society. Globalization theories add to this thesis that modernization in the West has directly resulted in the spread of certain vital institutions of Western modernization to the rest of the globe, especially the modern capitalist economy, the nation-state, and scientific rationality in the form of modern technology; and, critically, that this global spread has resulted in a new social unit which is much more than a simple expansion of Western modernity. This assertion of both identity and difference between modernization and globalization brings us back to the central issue of relativization or fluidity of identity. It requires some further comment.

The origin of various globalizing social structures in one part of the globe and their subsequent 'imperialistic' spread everywhere else is another constant in the globalization discussion. It has important empirical and theoretical consequences. Prime among these is that, in one way or another – and the way depends on the specific theoretical approach, the difference between traditional, territorially-limited societies and the modern globalizing system reproduces itself in the contemporary process of globalization. That is, globalization *begins* in all parts of the globe except the West as an exogenous process, meaning that it would not have happened had it not first occurred in the West. In this sense, globalization *is* Western imperialism,

whether economic, political, technological, or broadly cultural. Its dynamism therefore involves a repeated clash of different particular cultures. Yet
because the key globalizing structures originated in the West, this particular
culture often takes on the appearance of a global universal. Historical
examples are the British Empire's styling of its expansion as a 'civilizing'
project, and the more recent equation of the American Way and the Free
World. Hence we also have had liberal development theories which assume
that different cultural areas in the world will modernize to the degree that
they repeat the Western endogenous experience (cf. especially Rostow,
1960).

If globalization were indeed just another word for Western expansion,
then we might be dealing with nothing more than the building of yet another
historical empire, larger but not fundamentally different from others based
in China, the Middle East, or Europe. Globalization, however, is more than
the spread of one historically existing culture at the expense of all others. It is
also the creation of a new global culture with its attendant social structures,
one which increasingly becomes the broader social context of *all* particular
cultures in the world, including those of the West. The spread of the global
social reality is therefore quite as much at the 'expense' of the latter as it is of
non-Western cultures. Globalization theories cannot describe contemporary global society as simply the extension of a particular society and its
culture (that is, as one part becoming the whole) because these also change
dramatically in the process. Equally critically, however, the emergent
'global culture' cannot itself become a new overarching particularism
because it would then be subject to the same relativization as its predecessors.

This idea, that the global social reality 'relativizes' all particular cultures,
including of course the religions that form part of these cultures, has worked
its way into the globalization debate in the form of the following questions
(see Featherstone, 1990): Does globalization mean a progressive homogen-
ization of all cultures so that, two or three centuries from now, only global
culture will exist? Or does globalization merely change the context in which
particular cultures exist, implying transformation but not the disappearance
of separate and recognizable identities? As I indicated above, the answer is,
both. A detailed defence of this response forms part of the argument in
subsequent chapters. For now, let me simply point out its implications for
religion.

It has become a historical and sociological commonplace that traditional
religions, as we know them today, are very closely tied to particular cultures.
In Durkheimian language, they express the wholeness of societies. Therefore, if particular cultures are to survive in altered form in the modern global
context, the religious traditions associated with them will also survive, but
not without themselves facing the serious challenge of the relativized
context. Given that religion deals in absolutes, this adjustment should result
in significant crises within those traditions.

Again, the Rushdie affair is a good example of one sort of response: the particularistic revitalization of a tradition in the face of relativization. Here, as I discuss in greater detail later, the transformation takes the seemingly paradoxical form of insisting that little change is necessary or desirable. Such a 'fundamentalist' response that in essence allows change under the insistence that nothing fundamental is changing is not the only way, however. The religious dimension of globalization itself points to another basic possibility, and that is to reorient a religious tradition towards the global whole and away from the particular culture with which that tradition identified itself in the past. Such a response would not only see relativization as a positive result, but also see in openness to change a prime warrant for the continued authenticity of the tradition. Religion of this sort takes up the values of an emerging global culture. Like the conservative option, it considers it a central religious task to address the problems engendered through globalization, but this time on the basis of relatively indeterminate future possibilities rather than determinate past norms. Such a liberal direction is not a move toward a new 'meta' or world religion so much as an attempt to reformulate the old in the absence of particularity. That, of course, is in its own way paradoxical.

In sum then, there are two formal directions for religion under conditions of globalization, one that approaches the global system from the perspective of a particular, subglobal culture, and one that focuses on global culture as such. While I certainly do not rule out hybrid forms, the pure types point to the paradoxical simultaneity of the universal and the particular, of the transcendent and the immanent, in religion. Implicitly, they also show the paradoxical nature of the global system and the theories about it. These two fundamental religious responses are a central focus of the discussions in the following chapters.

Strategies and Limitations

These general remarks on the nature of globalization and the place of religion therein serve to outline the questions that I address in the following chapters. Before proceeding, however, it seems useful to present a short summary of what the various chapters seek to accomplish. Aside from making the structure of the book explicit, the exercise also sets the stage for taking a brief look at the rather limited aims of my presentation.

The book consists of two sections: Part I (Chapters 1–4) presents the theory, Part II (Chapters 5–9) selected empirical illustrations from the contemporary world.

Chapter 1 examines the work of several principal contributors to the globalization discussion, mainly Immanuel Wallerstein, John W. Meyer, Roland Robertson, and Niklas Luhmann. The chief aim there is to take a critical look at different current theories of what constitutes globalization, what are its characteristic features and problems. There are, of course, other participants in the debate whom I could have profitably included. The purpose, however, is not to offer an exhaustive review of all the scholars involved. It is to demonstrate some of the complexities of the debate by showing how the abstract points presented in this introduction work themselves out quite differently in various theoretical approaches.

These descriptions of the current state of the question are the backdrop, in Chapter 2, for further elaboration of those aspects of globalization that are important for an understanding of the different roles that religion can and does play in the process. A series of analyses centres on various ways in which the global system generates a universal social context that conditions and encourages the operation of both inherited and new particularisms or identities. Specific conceptual pairs that play a vital role are the integration and differentiation of global society, and the inclusion and exclusivity[10] of both individuals and collectivities within that society. Individualism, ethnicity and nationalism are especially relevant here in the context of emerging global values and global culture.

Chapter 3 forms the analytic core of this book. Beginning with a look at the vexed question of the supposed privatization of religion in modern society, I examine the strengths and weaknesses of religion as a social system of communication in the globalizing situation. This then leads into a more detailed analysis of the two very different directions for religion touched upon above. Key operative distinctions here are those between privatized and public religion, pure and applied religion, and liberal and conservative religion.

While Chapter 3 focuses in a very general way on the problems and prospects for religion in global society, Chapter 4 examines the more specific challenges facing those religious actors who wish to make religion publicly and globally influential. The centre of discussion here is the affinity between religion and particularly antisystemic social movements. Religion shares with these its comparatively marginalized status *vis-à-vis* the dominant systems of communication, above all the political and economic. It also shares, for reasons to be analysed, many of the fundamental concerns of these movements.

The five chapters in Part II provide extended illustrations of how the theoretical relations of religion and globalization have become historical reality in the contemporary world. Globalization is a difficult theory to test, and hitherto, historical analyses have been the most fruitful methods of research. Yet, because the theories are fundamentally future-oriented in much of what they predict, both historical and contemporary empirical studies can at best serve as examples of what might eventually be relevant to verify or falsify the theories. The concrete analyses of Part II therefore do not claim to prove the theory, but only to contribute to its fuller presentation. Accordingly, I take more detailed looks at the New Christian Right in the United States, the Latin American liberation-theological movement, the Iranian revolution, contemporary religious Zionism in Israel, and religious environmentalism.

Taken as a whole, these chapters may seem to outline a very ambitious project: a theory of globalization, a theory of religion, a theory of the consequences of globalization for religion, and concrete analyses of five complex and quite different religio-social movements. In a certain sense, those are the aims of this study, but only to a very limited degree. The central question that informs the entire book is the following: What are the abstract possibilities in today's world for religion, as defined above, to be a determinative force in social structures and processes beyond the restricted sphere of voluntary and individual belief and practice? Even more specifically, *what are the possibilities for institutionally specialized or systemic religion in this regard*?

The question of what I call 'public influence' is at the heart of my endeavours here. It acts as a selection mechanism for what I have and have not included. Accordingly, I treat numerous questions important to the globalization debate quite cursorily because they do not directly touch my central concern. Factors such as the status of international law, the role of military forces, and the question of phases of globalization come to mind in this regard. Moreover, where religion is concerned, the focus on publicly influential religion means that I largely ignore a great deal of what counts as religion by almost anyone's standard. This book is not about religion as such in the modern/global world, only about certain restricted manifestations. I only address in a partial and preliminary way the question of what forms religion can or will take in the context of globalized society. That broader issue is not only beyond the scope of the present study, it is probably too vast a project for any single endeavour.

Notes

1 With different emphases, Roland Robertson discusses the features of globalization I am describing here under the headings, relativization of identities, particularization of universalism, and universalization of particularism. Robertson would emphasize that globalization encourages not only diverse particularisms, but also diverse images of 'globality' on the basis of these particularisms. See Robertson, 1992b; Robertson and Chirico, 1985. I discuss Robertson's contribution to the globalization debate in the next chapter.

2 This possibility, of course, does not exclude other roles for religion.

3 On this point, see the discussion of negative responses by Western religious leaders to *The Satanic Verses* in Pipes, 1990: 163–167.

4 See Berger, 1967: 24f.; Durkheim, 1965: 62; Geertz, 1966: 4; Parsons, 1951: 2; Robertson, 1970: 47; Yinger, 1970: 7.

5 This is also the dichotomy used by Niklas Luhmann in his work on religion. See Luhmann, 1977; 1984c; 1985; 1987a; 1989b. My own efforts at definition here owe a sizeable intellectual debt to Luhmann's theorizing. The definition is therefore very Luhmannian, although salient differences prevent a full identification.

6 or the object of consciousness. In restricting myself to a sociological view of religion, I do not of course deny the importance of psychological and theological perspectives for understanding the phenomenon.

7 The reference is to Max Weber's fear, expressed in the concluding pages of *The Protestant Ethic and the Spirit of Capitalism* (1958: 180–183), that the rational spirit of capitalism would lead to an overdetermined, alternativeless society in which nothing new can happen any more.

8 I am thinking above all of the role of the 'world religions' like Buddhism, Christianity, and Islam in the creation of civilizational complexes that overarched and established cultural conditions for communication among otherwise disparate regional societies. None of these was able either to become truly global or to prevent significant 're-territorialization' of societies under their aegis. In Chapter 2 below, I discuss this difference between previous civilizations and current globalization by way of an analysis of the changed meaning of territoriality. For the argument that past patterns do indeed provide important resources for understanding contemporary globalization, see Robertson, 1992b: especially 129ff.

9 I am referring to Durkheim's thesis that religion expresses and maintains the power and meaning of the social whole. See Durkheim, 1965.

10 I choose this word quite deliberately. As I show in Chapter 2, 'exclusion' is not the appropriate term here.

PART I

THEORY AND CONCEPTS

1

FOUR APPROACHES TO GLOBALIZATION

The social-scientific development of globalization as a specific theoretical and empirical theme is relatively recent. Much of the literature has appeared only since the late 1970s and 1980s, although significant seminal contributions date from the decade previous.[1] This is not to say that the process of globalization itself began so recently. It may well be, however, that the emergence of the scientific discussion at this juncture reflects something like a new phase in the process, one which calls for the recasting of inherited theoretical conceptions. Accordingly, globalization theory distinguishes itself from longer established worldwide perspectives in that it takes as its primary unit of social analysis the entire globe, which it treats as a single social system. This changes how we understand various subunits, such as *ethnies*, nations, states, organizations, movements, or religions. These are no longer conceived simply as logically pre-existing social unities which must also take into consideration what is happening in their broader environment. Instead, globalization theory looks at them as social forms that constitute themselves not only with reference to other units, but also – and often more centrally – with reference to an emergent, encompassing whole that has its own distinct social properties.

The global whole, in other words, is more than a collection of juxtaposed particularities, however conceived. It is just as importantly a new and analytically distinct universal that contextualizes the particularities (see Robertson, 1992a; Wallerstein, 1987). The shift in unit of analysis is the root difference between the globalization perspective and others that also look at the whole world, such as international relations, whether of the political, economic, or legal variety. Here, the word international by itself already signals the subglobal primary unit in these vast and highly important fields (cf. Bergesen, 1990).

What does this shift in unit of analysis imply more precisely? To answer this question and carry the discussion further, I turn to an examination of four variants of the globalization approach. Immanuel Wallerstein, John W. Meyer, Roland Robertson, and Niklas Luhmann have been among the more important contributors to the scholarly debate. They are, of course, not the only ones; but my purpose here is not to present a thorough review of the literature. I choose these four because their work crystallizes four distinct but mutually reinforcing directions for conceiving global order,[2] based on analyses of a global economy, a global polity, a global culture,[3] and a global society respectively. Together, their efforts afford us a view of the multidimensional structure and culture of the global system, but also of its inherent ambiguities and even contradictions, characteristics that it is vital to understand if we wish to appreciate the potential roles of religion in that system. Presenting these variants also allows a critical assessment of their relative strengths and weaknesses as a foundation for advancing the globalization debate in general.

Immanuel Wallerstein

The world-system theory of Immanuel Wallerstein[4] has its principal roots in the French *Annales* school of history, especially the work of Fernand Braudel, and in Marxist-derived dependency theory.[5] Both of these approaches emphasize that it is impossible to understand the political and ideological vicissitudes of history without setting these phenomena in their economic and material context. Human history consists as much in the acts of ordinary people as it does in the more visible lives of the great and powerful. What is more, the latter are neither fully aware nor fully in control of the wider contextual forces around them. Far from presenting itself as simple economic determinism, however, Wallerstein's argument is rather one which seeks to analyse the social whole and not just the part played and seen by certain elite actors in it. The reliance on Marxist analysis derives from this concern. Wallerstein quotes Georg Lukács as saying that 'it is not the primacy of economic motives in historical explanation that constitutes the decisive difference between Marxism and bourgeois thought, but the point of view of totality' (1974b: 387).

This Hegelian impulse manifests itself in Wallerstein's typology of social systems. For Wallerstein,

> the defining characteristic of a social system [is] . . . the existence within it of a division of labor, such that the various sectors or areas within are dependent upon economic exchange with others for the smooth and continuous provisioning of the needs of the area. (1974b: 390)

There are three kinds of social system: mini-systems, world-empires, and world-economies. The first combines a single division of labour with a single cultural system. Mini-systems exhibit simple agricultural or hunting and gathering economies and no longer exist because all of them have been absorbed by world-empires or world-economies. World-empires have multiple cultural systems but a single political system within a single division of labour. The great civilizations of the past, such as in China, Egypt, and Rome, are examples of these. World-economies incorporate multiple polities and multiple cultures in a single division of labour. With the development of the modern world-system, world-empires have also ceased to exist, yielding to the development of a single world-economy that, for the first time in history, includes the entire globe.[6]

The deduction of three types of social system is not unique[7] and echoes Hegel's distinction between art, religion, and philosophy as forms of knowledge distinguished by, among other things, their level of completeness. Like Marx, however, Wallerstein replaces philosophy with economy as that which allows description of the totality of a system. He therefore understands the modern global system as first and foremost an economy, specifically a capitalist economy based on market trade and commodification. For Wallerstein, the capitalist world-economy is now the global social context that conditions all other aspects of social life, namely polities and cultures. Other scholars in the globalization debate have asked, as we have to ask, whether the equation of the social and the economic does in fact allow us access to the totality, or whether we are not dealing here with yet another fragment that claims to represent the whole.

A proper answer to this question requires a closer look at how Wallerstein uses his framework and a consideration of his critics. I continue now with the former task.

Wallerstein's extensive empirical analyses deal almost exclusively with the origin and growth of the modern capitalist world-system (see especially Wallerstein 1974a; 1980; 1989). With various antecedents, the story, for Wallerstein, begins in Western European society in the middle of the fifteenth century. Here and for the succeeding centuries, there developed an economy which escaped the tutelage of a single political power and thus the redistributive effects of a world-empire. Capital, or surplus economic value, accumulated in the hands of merchants instead of being siphoned off to support an imperial bureaucracy and its consumption. The capitalist merchants amassed their wealth in towns and cities that largely escaped the domination of the political lords who nominally ruled over the territory in which they existed. From here, they established trade with regions well beyond their territories, especially the Baltic lands and the New World. This trade was not just in luxury goods, as the long-standing trade with the Middle and Far East had been, but predominantly in staples such as wood, grain, and cloth. In this way, far-flung territories definitely not ruled from one political capital became part of a world-economy or single division of labour. From this beginning, the European world-economy has spread to encompass the whole globe.

The key argument that Wallerstein makes about this European world-economy is that it created its own geographical divisions: core, periphery, and semiperiphery (see 1979: 37–48; also Peter Taylor, 1985: 16–18). While not constituting officially recognized political boundaries, these nevertheless conditioned the way in which political units were formed: the new

RELIGION AND GLOBALIZATION

Peter Beyer

SAGE Publications

London · Thousand Oaks · New Delhi

SAGE Publications Ltd
6 Bonhill Street
London EC2A 4PU

SAGE Publications Inc
2455 Teller Road
Thousand Oaks, California 91320

SAGE Publications India Pvt Ltd
32, M-Block Market
Greater Kailash – I
New Delhi 110 048

Published in association with Theory, Culture & Society,
School of Health, Social and Policy Studies, University of
Teesside.

British Library Cataloguing in Publication data

Beyer, Peter
   Religion and Globalization. – (Theory,
   Culture & Society Series)
   I. Title   II. Series
   306.6
   ISBN 0–8039–8916–4
   ISBN 0–8039–8917–2 (pbk)

Library of Congress catalog card number 93–085822

Typeset by Type Study, Scarborough
Printed in Great Britain by The Cromwell Press Ltd,
Broughton Gifford, Melksham, Wiltshire

world-economy led to the rise of modern nation-states. For Wallerstein, a particular region and the nation-states within it are part of the core, semiperiphery, or periphery depending on what position their economies have in the world-system division of labour. Core areas dominate the system. Here is where capital is concentrated. They exhibit a complex variety of economic activities, relatively high wages for workers, and the most sophisticated technologies. Peripheral areas provide cheap staples and raw materials which make core economies possible. Their economies centre on a few primary products, are based on cheap labour, and use relatively simple technologies. Dependency or exploitation defines the relation between the core and the periphery. The semiperiphery, for Wallerstein, is both exploiter of peripheral areas and exploited by the core. It has no unique features associated with it, but rather exhibits a combination of both core and peripheral features. Its function in the world-system is both as a stabilizing buffer between core and periphery, and as the dynamic middle (see Wallerstein, 1979: 95–118).

Semiperipheral areas represent the possibility of upward mobility in the world-system. Their quest for inclusion in the core makes them ideal agents to control the periphery for the core. Thus, for example, Spain controlled Latin America for the core in the early modern period, and Brazil fulfils this function today. Instead of a polar opposition between the interests of core and peripheral countries that would quickly lead to destabilizing conflict, the semiperiphery absorbs some of the blame for exploitation while at the same time making it seem possible to rise in the system without first dismantling it. On the level of the world-economy, it fills the slot of the 'middle class' in Marxist class analysis of national economies. In Wallerstein's world-system analysis, as in dependency theory generally, the various countries of the world have defined positions in a global class structure of nations. The class structure within each of these is not denied, but only contextualized: national class analysis is incomplete except in the context of the world-system, allowing one, for instance, to understand the very different attitudes of working classes in core countries like the United States and peripheral countries like Zaire. In general, we can say that for Wallerstein class is the foundational structural social unit of the world-system.

The geographical categorization of core, semiperiphery, and periphery points to the importance of the nation-state in Wallerstein's world-system theory. Wallerstein agrees with the prevailing scholarly view that the nation-state is a political form unique to the modern world (see Wallerstein, 1974a; 1984b; cf. Bendix, 1977; Gellner, 1983; Giddens, 1987; Smith, 1986). Modern states are therefore fundamentally different from world-empires. The latter constituted their economies by redistributing surplus wealth through such mechanisms as tribute, taxes, confiscation, and plunder. Market trade was a minor part of their economies. Modern states, by contrast, operate within the framework of an overarching economy dominated by market trade. It is the functioning of the market that creates core, semiperiphery, and periphery. States do not control this market, but merely reinforce its operation.

Accordingly, strong states form in core areas to protect the interests of these regions against the semiperiphery and periphery. They serve the interests of the ruling classes of the core but at the cost of redistributing some of the wealth to the lower classes in those areas. States in peripheral regions are correspondingly weaker because their local bourgeoisies have a vested interest in a weak state that cannot threaten their position in the overall capitalist system, and because the powerful states of the core keep them weaker through such measures as war, subversion, diplomacy, and foreign aid. Semiperipheral areas, in keeping with their 'both/and' status, can have either strong or weak states. According to Wallerstein, therefore, nation-states are part of a single logic of the world-economy: they are a dependent function of it and not a countercurrent within it.[8]

The derivative status of sovereign states, for Wallerstein, has its parallel in the domain of culture. What he calls the idea-system of the capitalist world-economy is a way of dealing with the ambiguities and contradictions engendered by this system (1990: 38). At the root of the cultural or ideological problem is the functional requirement of the world-economy to eliminate all social barriers to commodification and the operation of the market, while at the same time assuring the unequal distribution of surplus value essential for the accumulation of capital. Accordingly, the world-system generates both universalistic-egalitarian ideals as well as particular-istic-inegalitarian ones. For example, inasmuch as states are mechanisms to compete for status in the world-system, so the nation is a cultural construct that justifies both a given state's existence and its actual or desired status. Similarly, race is a prime cultural legitimation of the world division of labour into core and periphery; and *ethnie* has a similar role for intra-state divisions of labour that correspond to unequal distribution of benefits. Nationalism, along with *de facto* racism, ethnocentrism, and their gender-based parallel, sexism, are therefore dependent cultural expressions of the world-economy just as much as the universalistic ideals of equality and progress.

Moreover, claims Wallerstein, these historically constructed particular-isms have become such an ineluctable part of the world-system that it becomes almost impossible for antisystemic and class-based movements to avoid crystallizing around them. In other words, the cultural precipitates that serve to cover up the contradictions of the system now unavoidably affect the ways that those contradictions can be countered (see Wallerstein, 1988a). Class conflict – for Wallerstein the actual driving force of history – will today appear most often in the form of ascriptive contests between nations, races, *ethnies*, genders, and indeed, one can assume, religions.

As mentioned in the introduction, the development of the world-system, for Wallerstein, is not a smooth, evolutionary process; nor is it complete. Rather, it is a cyclical affair driven by conflict and contradiction. The conflict is at root class conflict, the struggle between those that benefit from the world-economy and those that, comparatively, do not. Extending Marxist class analysis to the world-system, Wallerstein and dependency theory generally analyse the struggle between states and ethnic groups as class conflicts: the economic divisions of core, periphery, and semiperiphery define the positions of states and ethnic groups in the world-system division of labour. Conflicts between them, while political in form, and cultural in expression, are economic in origin.

Although class conflict is at the root of world-system dynamism, analytically distinct from this are the contradictions inherent in the capitalist mode of production. Chief of these is the requirement of the capitalist system for constant expansion to maintain profit margins. Accumulated capital has to be reinvested and this can only be done if there are new economic opportunities. Hence Wallerstein sees the recurrent 'boom and bust' cycles of modern economic history as a basic characteristic of the world-economy. As each solution to the basic problem reaches the limits of its expansion, a prolonged downturn in the economy results during which new solutions develop, often in different areas. Wallerstein thus incorporates his core/semiperiphery/periphery distinction into the dynamism of the world-system. The whole model is rooted in rigorous, empirical analysis of historical events.

A rough, very much simplified outline of modern world history, according to Wallerstein, proceeds as follows. Between 1450 and 1600, the foundations of the European world-economy formed, based on capitalist agriculture. The core of this system eventually settled around Amsterdam, especially after the failure of the French Valois and Habsburg monarchs to subsume the developing system under a new world-empire. The areas under the control of these rulers became semiperipheral, with the Baltic and New World areas constituting the periphery (see Wallerstein, 1974a). After the initial expansionary phase lasting until around 1600, the system consolidated during the succeeding century and a half under the mercantilist system in which core states built peripheral colonial empires in most areas of the world (see Wallerstein, 1980).

At the end of this period and into the nineteenth century, England became the dominant power of the core on the basis of its industrial revolution. The free trade era sponsored by England during the nineteenth century superseded the mercantilist era, and lasted through two periods of expansion and one of consolidation until about 1870 (see Wallerstein, 1989). The recessionary phase that followed witnessed the rise of contintental powers like Germany and France to challenge British hegemony on the basis of new commodities such as steel and chemicals. An era of renewed expansion was then followed by yet another downturn, one that saw protectionism reassert itself as the European core powers scrambled anew for colonies, predominantly in Africa. World War I inaugurated a period during which the United States emerged as the new dominant core power for the post-World War II expansionary era based on mass consumer machinery, especially the automobile. The new hegemonic power again championed free trade as it sought to penetrate the colonial domains of its predecessors. This latest expansion lasted until the 1960s, yielding to the current recessionary phase of renewed protectionism and instability.[9]

These cycles, for Wallerstein, are not endless. There are, in addition to cycles, also linear trends. Although he does not say so explicitly, logically, there are only three possible trends in his theory: the passages from the dominance of one type of social system to another, from mini-systems to world-empires, from world-empires to a world-economy, and from the world-economy to something else as yet only dimly describable. His most seminal contribution to date (1974a; 1980; 1989) deals with the second of these. The larger part of his other publications on world-system theory deals with the contradictions in the present system that point to its eventual demise. In other words, for Wallerstein, we do not understand the present system adequately unless we realize that its internal contradictions produce not only relatively short-term cyclical crises but also long-term secular crises leading to an entirely new type of system. The fact that we cannot adequately envision this new system does not mean that the trend is not there; rather, the necessity of the new system is a characteristic of the present one.

As I discussed in the introduction, such teleology in globalization theories is characteristic because they attempt to conceive the social whole from a perspective other than that of one of its parts. This operation logically requires something transcendent with which to give the immanent whole definition, and immanent social representatives of the transcendent. Both in the past and in the present, religion, its institutions, its professionals, have fulfilled this function. It is the quintessentially religious task. Wallerstein, like Marx before him, temporalizes the transcendent by projecting it into an indeterminable future social system. The contemporary and immanent mediators of this future system are antisystemic movements, principally socialist ones, and social scientists like himself (cf. Wallerstein 1979: 152–164; 1983). The role of either is to work towards the transformation of the present system and not just to prophesy its eventual destruction.

In this light, Wallerstein criticizes especially most socialist movements for confusing the tactical goal of seizing control of the state with the goal of transforming the system. Accordingly, socialist states have typically become a contributing part of the world-economy, jockeying for position within the global division of labour rather than hastening its undoing. For Wallerstein, seizing control of the state machinery can at best be a first step in the struggle because the state is a dependent function of the world-economy and not an antisystemic institution at all. He therefore calls for what amounts to perpetual struggle on the part of antisystemic movements, struggle that does not cease when interim goals are reached (Wallerstein 1984a: 86–111).[10] He makes an analogous plea for 'reorienting the strategy of social science' (1983: 35), calling upon it to take a holistic view of the modern world-system.

The teleological dimension and the importance of antisystemic movements are therefore understandable within the framework of Wallerstein's theory. They do, however, point to problems attendant upon the equation of economy with the social whole.

Essentially, Wallerstein sees the unity of the global social system in the economy: 'The modern world-system is a capitalist world-economy' (1988b: 584). From this view, he concludes that other aspects of social life, such as the political or cultural, are dependent functions of the economic. But is that all these other aspects are? Are, for instance, nation-states *only* structures for competing in the world-economy? Or would ethnic differences, gender definitions, or racial discrimination disappear if it were not for their function in the world division of labour? Is it, in fact, not entirely possible to turn Wallerstein on his head and analyse the world-economy itself as a dependent function of, say, a world-polity or a world-culture?

Such questions are especially in order when considering antisystemic movements, given their central position in Wallersteinian 'praxis'. Specifically, Wallerstein and his collaborators make clear that these movements appear as a result of the operation of the world-economy (see Arrighi et al., 1989). But they do not and, I suggest, cannot say how these are simply and entirely 'economy'. At the very least, they contain a 'residual' sociality, for instance in the norms, the values, and the moral judgements that the movements embody. To say that these aspects are also economy only because they do not escape economic contextualization is to establish the matter by fiat more than verifiable scientific analysis: where a relation exists, economy is primary – by definition.

The logical insufficiencies of Wallerstein's theory should, of course, lead to empirical insufficiencies. And indeed, many of the critics of Wallerstein centre on the inability of his theory to explain various aspects of the global system, such as strong states in peripheral areas, and countries like Canada and Australia: dependent and resource-based economies that are nevertheless part of the core (cf. Chirot and Hall, 1982: 97–102). These criticisms point to the *relatively* independent role of other social factors in the history of globalization, notably politics, science, education, and group culture. The contribution of John Meyer and his Stanford colleagues to the globalization debate focuses on two of these: politics in the form of the system of nation-states, and education. An examination of their work can show how empirical inadequacies in Wallerstein's theory point to the presence of *at least* two 'logics' in the global social system, an economic one and a political one. Rather than leading to a better conceptualization of the global system, however, this next step in my presentation only brings that problem into sharper focus, preparing the ground for a consideration of both Robertson's and Luhmann's contributions.

John Meyer

The contribution of John Meyer and his Stanford colleagues[11] consists on one level in the application of rigorous quantitative methods to the Wallersteinian world-system model (cf. Chirot and Hall, 1982: 94f.). It therefore accepts many of Wallerstein's ideas, especially as regards the structure of the world-economy. On the level of theoretical understanding of globalization, however, Meyer does more than elaborate the received model: to the basic notion of a world-economy, he adds the analysis of a world-polity, particularly the global system of nation-states. For Meyer, the world-polity is a system that operates parallel to the world-economy and, to a significant degree, is functionally independent of it. Nation-states are not only conditioned by the world-economy: they also condition the operation of that economy in a way that is not reducible to economic forces. In Meyer's words, 'the world political . . . system is linked closely to the rise and expansion of the world commodity economy, but it also operates to restructure and alter this economy, and to transform social life' (1980: 109). This view therefore undermines the basis of the Wallersteinian model because it denies that the global social system is fundamentally a world-economy of which states are but superstructural reflections. The perspective of the economy is not synonymous with the perspective of the whole; it cannot explain the independent power and variation of the system of nation-states.[12]

This critique of Wallerstein has both empirical and theoretical foundations. On the theoretical level, Meyer distinguishes between polity and economy as different systems of social value creation. The economy creates value through commodification, that is, 'through the extraction, production, exchange, and consumption of commodities' (1980: 111). Here the operation of markets and political action are consonant with Wallerstein's theory. Polities, by contrast, create value through collective authority. Besides their role in the commodity economy, they also create value directly, in a non-commodity form, 'through the construction of goals and of invisible commodities, and the direct conferral of value on these ends, the means understood to produce them, and the social units involved' (1980: 112).

What Meyer has in mind here is a large portion of the tertiary sector of the economy, more specifically services whose production and distribution is not regulated by exchange processes and a market, but strictly through the exercise of collective authority. In economic terms, political agents decide that certain services shall be of value and hence worth paying for. They do this quite aside from whether or not sufficient market demand exists and circumvent exchange processes by separating the financing of these services from their distribution. Included are social services of all kinds, such as welfare, social security, education, and legal services. In the modern context, states are the dominant agents of collective authority, but Meyer stresses that the term polity refers also to other such agents, for instance religious and other cultural organizations. The worldwide extension and increasing power of states, however, leads him to focus his concrete analyses on the global system of nation-states.

Theoretically, then, Meyer restricts the term economy to mean commodity economy, thereby enabling him to talk about a functionally independent polity.[13] The distinction requires further theoretical elaboration, above all an analysis of what 'value creation' means. Rather than pursue this task, however, Meyer and his colleagues have relied more on empirical research to validate their theoretical direction. This research has, for instance, undertaken to show that increasingly strong, centralized states have emerged all over the globe. This uniform pattern does not vary according to the world economic status of countries, but rather runs to a large degree counter to what one would expect if individual state structure reflected a country's position in the core, semiperiphery, or periphery of the world-economy. Accordingly, centralized states are strengthening in peripheral countries at a similar rate to those in the higher positions of economic stratification (see Boli-Bennett, 1980; Meyer et al., 1975; Meyer et al., 1979).

Moreover, Meyer points out that the global system of nation-states exhibits an overall structure that largely brackets the vast economic inequalities. With few exceptions, the rationale of states around the world is similar. As illustrated, for instance, in the significant isomorphism of their national constitutions, they have similar goals associated with ideas of 'progress' and 'equality' among citizens and nations.[14] Commensurate with their increasing internal dominance, these states have extremely stable boundaries which, in the case of many Third World countries, are often more or less arbitrary heritages of their colonial pasts. Accordingly, boundary disputes between nations are extremely difficult to resolve. Nation-states, in Meyer's analysis, are very much the prime legitimate actors in the world polity. Internally they are accorded vast powers over their citizens, controlling the legitimate means of violence, the activity of their populations, and the methods favoured to achieve the global ideals of progress and equality. Even the rich, core countries recognize the legitimacy of these internal monopolies in all other countries, regardless of their economic standing.[15] The obverse of this internal sovereignty, for Meyer, is the system of world cultural norms that governs membership in the global system of nation-states. States are the legitimate representatives of their citizens because they pursue the globally legitimated ends of progress and equality. To the extent that they pursue this course within the broad bounds of approved means, they can benefit from external supports ranging from easy access to sophisticated technology and financial aid to international treaties of various kinds.

Conformity to world-polity norms therefore carries with it certain rewards just as too blatant deviance implies corresponding costs. For example, the opening up of China after the early 1970s brought the rewards of diplomatic recognition – including a seat on the United Nations Security Council – and capital investment to assist the Chinese state in its efforts at *rattrapage*. Suppression of political reform movements in 1989 cost the Chinese state some of this international good will, at least for a time. Yet no government seriously considered direct internal interference as punishment for this violation of world-polity political participation norms; and relations with other states have since improved without a change in Chinese internal policy. Similarly, in the crisis leading to the 1991 Gulf war, the sanctions of the United Nations were brought to bear on Saddam Hussein only when he invaded the sovereign state of Kuwait and never as a consequence of his internal policies.

While these remarks do not do justice even to the outline form in which Meyer has thus far presented his globalization theory, they do point to the basis upon which he claims the relative autonomy of a world-system other than the world-economy. Far from constituting a mere contradiction of Wallerstein's theory, however, Meyer's contribution offers a critical complement to it. Meyer does not oppose the world-polity to the world-economy; he sees them as mutually reinforcing modes of value creation. The very goals and inequities that the economy generates are the source of the dominant political norms upon which peripheral states establish themselves. As Meyer puts it, the development of the egalitarian world-polity

> is a kind of dialectical reaction to the rise, and institutional codification, of the world economy. Exchange generates power; the analysis and institutionalization of exchange generates authority. The norms of justice created in the world exchange system also legitimate the rise of the peripheral state. The evolving ideologies – or accounts of progress, or myths of production – of central societies provide legitimacy for the peculiar forms of progress pursued in peripheries. (1980: 135)

The dialectical relationship between the two systems in Meyer's theory can address the anomalous position of antisystemic movements in Wallerstein's theory. The differentiation of the world-polity from the world-economy on the basis of distinct modes of value creation allows the state to become the locus of mobilization against the inequities of the world capitalist system. World political norms defending the internal power monopoly of states even allow more radically antisystemic policies, namely the complete rejection of the cultural ideals of the world-polity and the pursuit of idiosyncratic and isolationist directions as evidenced in Pol Pot's Cambodia and Mao's China. Even these states, however, pursued progress and equality, albeit with means not widely accepted in the world polity. In other words, implicit in Meyer's analysis is that states, especially peripheral states, are fundamentally socialistic. They are antisystemic, but only in the sense that they embody a mode of value creation that largely escapes the operation of the market-driven commodity economy.

Although Meyer does claim that the world-polity is rapidly becoming a more dominant source of value creation than the commodity economy, he does not replace economy with polity as that which fundamentally characterizes a social system. Defining the global system as a whole is not his primary concern as it is with Wallerstein and, as I discuss below, with Robertson and Luhmann. Since, however, Meyer mentions no mode of value creation other than the political and the economic, and since he restricts economy to commodity economy, the idea of polity also seems to function as a kind of residual category subsuming all action except that of the economy. Meyer's correction of Wallerstein may therefore lead to a definition of the global system not as a world-economy but as a world political-economy. Yet the fact that polity and economy are relatively in-dependent modes of value creation points to the logical possibility of other modes. Neither Meyer nor his colleagues pursue this possibility, but their research on education in the world-system offers some evidence that this may be one.

Meyer's empirical contributions to the globalization discussion have always had as a primary focus the rapid development of national educational systems in the post-World War II era. In keeping with his dialectical vision of global value creation, Meyer and his colleagues have tended to treat this growth as an aspect of nation-state dominance in the world-system. This tendency, however, has been somewhat equivocal because their empirical research does not entirely support the hypothesis. States increase their dominance; educational systems grow; but the latter are not a function of the former (see Meyer and Hannan, 1979a; Ramirez and Meyer, 1980). Edu-cational systems do not grow more rapidly in stronger states or even in weaker ones. In the absence of a clear causal connection, Meyer and his col-leagues appeal to the existence of a more general 'world culture' as expla-nation. They write, for instance, that

> Both educational systems and state power are currently expanding in the First, Second, and Third Worlds. This simultaneous development may be an historical accident but seems more likely to reflect the operation of a world culture that legit-imates nation-states and mandates educational expansion as part of the process of building nations based on individual citizenship. (Ramirez and Meyer, 1980: 393)

The relatively independent empirical variation of educational systems does not lead Meyer to the conclusion that there is yet another source of value creation involved here, even though similar independent variation leads to just such a conclusion as concerns the relation of the polity and the economy. The inconsistency again shows the necessity of a more precise analysis of value creation; for it is here that a potential theory of globaliz-ation lies, given the rationale of his critique of Wallerstein. Below, I discuss the extent to which Luhmann's conception of social communication ad-dresses this aspect directly. Here it is sufficient to point out that the inconsis-tency is indicative of the primacy and breadth of political action in Meyer's discussion of globalization, a position further evidenced in his delineation of world culture.

For Meyer, world culture is that which holds the decentralized world polity together. Its carriers are the modernizing intellectuals who act as a sort of international clergy espousing the global myths of progress and tech-nique.[16] As such, he calls them the elites of world *political* culture, people who bridge the gap between the nation and the globe:

> They are members both of their own societies and of a world elite and are pro-tected both by their wider cultural status and by the legitimated international organizational networks in which they participate (i.e., their Church and Orders). (Meyer, 1980: 131)

The religious metaphors are telling. As noted above, Meyer's notion of polity includes more than the state. Religious and cultural processes are also sources of collective authority. Nonetheless, he does not go far in analysing these alternatives to the state. Like the educational systems and the international cultural elites, they are a vital part of global processes, but their precise relation to states and the world commodity economy is left unclear. Meyer therefore makes a substantial contribution to the globalization discussion by undermining the economic monism of the Wallersteinians; but he does so without clearly addressing the problem of how the global whole is then to be conceived. Roland Robertson approaches this question much more directly. It is to his analyses of the global reality that I now turn.

Roland Robertson

More explicitly than others in the debate, Roland Robertson recognizes the great continuity between globalization theory and the efforts of various nineteenth and early twentieth century sociologists to conceive modernity. In doing so, he does not limit himself to one of these, as does Wallerstein. Rather, Robertson focuses on critical questions in the overall classic debate, in particular those concerning the relation between the individual and society under modern conditions, and the importance therein of different forms of sociality, in Toennies's terms, *Gemeinschaft* and *Gesellschaft*.[17]

In the classic discussion, various scholars distinguished pre-modern from modern society in terms of a shift from *Gemeinschaft* or communal to *Gesellschaft* or associative structures. A key manifestation of this change is a greater differentiation of the individual from society which renders the relation between the individual and society problematic (Simmel) or at least radically alters it (Durkheim).[18] This process of modernization takes place within a given society; it is primarily endogenous. For Robertson, globalization repeats the tension between *Gemeinschaft* and *Gesellschaft* across contemporary societies and not just within them. To the intra-societal problem it adds a concomitant inter-societal one (1992a). Moreover, this complication has a parallel effect on the way individuals construct themselves and, in consequence, on how societies respond both to their individuals and to the inter-societal challenge. The core of his argument runs roughly as follows.

Modernization increasingly detaches individual selves from 'primordial' immersion in networks of kinship and locality (*Gemeinschaft*), fostering greater differentiation between self and society (*Gesellschaft*). Life in modern society thereby has two poles of identity, what Robertson calls 'the realm of societal-systemic functionality' and 'the realm of individual and relational . . . being' (Robertson and Chirico, 1985: 234). Globalization complicates this dualism because it sets particular societies in a wider system of societies, resulting in the *relativization* of *both* societies and individuated selves. In a globalized context, the norms and values institutionalized within a particular society face the manifestly different images of the good society presented by other societies in the world. *National societies*, as Robertson calls them, operate in the broader context of a *global system of societies* and this relation has an essential effect on how they constitute themselves. Correspondingly, *individuals* form their personal identities in the knowledge that their society is only one among several actual possibilities. Beyond a person's own bipolar individual–society nexus of identity, there are unmistakably different possibilities for life-in-society, leading to the relativized construction of personal identities with reference to a wider category of *humankind*. These selves, in turn, further intensify the relativized constitution of national identities. Both individuals and national societies act in the context of a relativizing world system of societies whose unity or identity expresses itself in the encompassing notion of humanity.

For Robertson globalization is a process that is bringing about a single social world. This leads to the relativization of all self/society dualisms with reference to an encompassing world-system-of-societies/humankind dualism. Critical for an understanding of Robertson's position, however, is that the latter does not supersede the former:

> In using the term 'globalization' I refer to the overall process by which the entire world becomes increasingly interdependent, so as to yield a 'single place'. We could even go so far as to call the latter a 'world society', as long as we do not suggest by that term that nationally constituted societies are disappearing. (Robertson, 1989a: 8)

National societies continue to exist and are prime actors in the global system of societies as well as prime, but no longer sole, determinants in personal identity. As such, they hold a similar position in this theory to nation-states or national polities in Meyer's work.

Nonetheless, there is an important difference between the two. Whereas Meyer sees a single world culture defining a standard image of the good society based fundamentally on the notion of progress, Robertson disputes the monopoly of this or any other image[19] in the global system. Instead, he points to the empirical presence of conflicting images: not just the somewhat overlapping liberal-democratic and socialist ones, but also others such as those in the Islamic Middle East and in Japan. It is precisely the tension among these images of global society and the concomitant relativization on the level of the individual that results in the formulation of what Robertson calls 'humanitic' or, drawing on Parsons, 'telic' concerns: global discourse on the ends of humanity in the light of the relativization of particularisms. This 'crystallization of global telic concern' (Robertson and Chirico, 1985: 234) is the prime precipitate of globalization.

The conflicting images of the good society, therefore, are not just a matter of empirical disagreement; they are integral to globalization itself. Central to the very idea of globalization is that subunits of the global system can constitute themselves only with reference to this encompassing whole. This is what Robertson means by relativization. But conversely, the global whole becomes a social reality only as it crystallizes out of the attempts of subunits to deal with their relativizing context. Global culture is the product of these efforts. Specifically, national societies, for Robertson, now increasingly constitute themselves in terms of their own particular cultures, histories, traditions; but this inherited matter is only given form through a selective response to the global system of societies, or, what amounts to the same, similar developments in other societies. Globalization thus involves a double and somewhat paradoxical process. Because there is no common and dominant model to which societies can conform, each society creates its own particular image of global order by promoting, even inventing, its own national image of the good society – in short, its own national identity. The global universal or, more precisely, the global concern about the universal only results from the interaction among these images. Hence, Robertson speaks of the simultaneity of, in his words, 'the particularization of universalism (the rendering of the world as a single place) *and* the universalization of particularism (the globalized expectation that societies . . . should have distinct identities)' (1989a: 9).[20]

Although Robertson devotes far less concrete attention to the matter, the role of the individual in globalization is, as I have outlined, theoretically just as important as that of national societies. Moreover, the increased differentiation of self and society under modern conditions means that we cannot see the two simply as different levels of the same analysis. To the degree that individuals escape their particular self–society relation, they can and do increasingly form their identities trans-societally through international non-governmental organizations and social movements, tourism, migration, foreign work, and indeed inter-ethnic and inter-cultural contact within societies. Among the consequences of this relative independence of individuals, Robertson points to conflicts within societies as to what are their respective images, and the valuation and, in his words, 'virtually globewide establishment of various "minority" forms of personal and collective identification' (1992b: 105). The individual pole of the globalization process, in other words, constrains the operation of national societies and the world system of societies quite as much as the reverse.

The constraining tension among individuals, societies and world system of societies, however, only focuses on three of the four poles of globalization in Robertson's theory. The fourth, as indicated, is humankind. Given the concentration of the whole model on images and identities, it is not surprising that this aspect comes to the fore nowhere more clearly than when Robertson actually outlines the possibilities for conceiving global order. Since such conceptions are connected to the parallel importance of intra-societal, national identities, it is also not surprising that here, once again, he inserts the classic tension between *Gemeinschaft* and *Gesellschaft*: 'the *Gemeinschaft–Gesellschaft* theme has itself been globalized – first with respect to images of how societies should be patterned; second, with respect to how the world-as-a-whole should be structured' (1992a: 2f.).

Robertson sees two types each of global *Gemeinschaft* and *Gesellschaft*. A first *Gemeinschaft* image sees the world order as consisting of an agglomerate of closed societal communities, each with its own inherent and more or less incommunicable identity. This conception is the closest to an anti-global global image. It points to the fact that rejection of globalization is as much a logical option under the objective conditions of globalization as various positive responses. Robertson mentions politico-religious 'fundamentalist' views as examples, say in the United States or Iran.

A second *Gemeinschaft* image considers global order possible only to the degree that a single global community is established, a sort of 'global village' or Durkheimian collective consciousness. Such a conception puts the emphasis on harmonization of differences whether through absorption or toleration. Examples are the views espoused by the Roman Catholic church, the contemporary peace movement, and various theologies of liberation.

The two *Gesellschaft* versions roughly parallel these communitarian visions. The first conceives world order as an association of open societies with a large amount of socio-cultural interchange among them. This conception preserves national societies as a central feature of the global system but, unlike the first *Gemeinschaft* view, sees their interrelationship as something that helps them further their own interests and those of the whole. Various liberal nationalisms around the world, such as that found in contemporary Quebec, might serve as examples.

Like the second *Gemeinschaft* conception, the second *Gesellschaft* image places relatively little emphasis on the integrity of national societies, but sees global order as possible only on the basis of deliberate and systematic world organization. There is far less reliance here on cathectic forces to constitute the whole. Examples of this most political of options are the advocates of different forms of world government and the Wallersteinians.[21]

Robertson's typology raises many questions that cannot be addressed here, including the presence of hybrid forms. Of prime concern in the present context, however, is the seeming concentration of religious examples of global conceptions under the *Gemeinschaft* categories. While one cannot conclude that the theory necessarily restricts religious conceptions to the communitarian, there is at least the sense that Robertson's two *Gesellschaft* types correspond to economistic and political models respectively, and reflect, moreover, the dominance of economic and political systems under modern, *Gesellschaft*-like conditions. An examination of Robertson's view of the response of religion to globalizing conditions shows that these appearances are more than accidental.

Corresponding to the two *Gemeinschaft* conceptions of global order, Robertson sees two trends in the religious response to globalization. On the one hand, the traditionally close ties between religions and particular cultures encourages the formulation of national and personal identities *vis-à-vis* the global system in terms of particular religions. This tendency, as indicated, is clearest in the more recent rise of 'fundamentalist' religious movements in countries as diverse as the United States, Iran, India, and Japan. Here, even where such movements do not thematize globality directly, Robertson considers that they have arisen in response to the relativizing constraints introduced by globalization. On the other hand, the crystallization of telic concerns that characterizes globalization also provides a fertile atmosphere for 'world theologies' that address the eschatological implications of an inclusive humanity. Beside explicit examples like that of W. C. Smith (1981), Robertson points to the Roman Catholic church, along with various liberation theologies that have emerged around the world since the 1960s; certain eco-theologies, including the Green movement (see Robertson, 1989b: 15); the Unification church; and Soka Gakkai.[22]

The way that Robertson ties these different kinds of religious movements into his overall globalization theory is instructive. He points out that most of these religious forms are not simply or purely religious, but also centrally political. They are almost invariably involved in 'church-state' or religio-political conflicts. Indeed, Robertson sees in the contemporary proliferation of such tensions empirical evidence of globalization.

How is this so? The relativization of national societies and individuals encourages the search for particularistic identities and for the meaning of the universal whole. This is the dual process of the universalization of particularism and the particularization of universalism already discussed. 'Humanitic' concern, despite its reduction of explicitly *theo*logical reference, centres on the ends of humanity, the ultimate meaning of human existence, the 'deep' issues of human life (see Robertson, 1989b: 14). As such, it is intrinsically religious. Yet, because such concern crystallizes out of the relativization of 'state-centred societies' (Robertson and Chirico, 1985: 236), the problems of globalization are also the internal political problems of nation-states and the global political problems of the world system. More to the point, the relativization characteristic of globalization raises fundamental questions of legitimacy at both the societal and the trans-societal levels. In both arenas, 'civil religious' questions become salient. Hence the global system is witness to both the 'politicization of theology and religion . . . and the "theologization" of politics' (Robertson and Chirico, 1985: 238) as political institutions once again encroach on religious questions and the religious domain, inevitably calling forth a politicized response from religion itself. In Robertson's own words,

> Life has become politicized. In the process that which, according to Durkheim, is most concerned with life – namely, religion . . . – itself acquires political significance. Meaning and power, primordially united, are reunited. (1989b: 20)

With the explicit incorporation of religion and religious questions into the debate, Robertson directly tackles a vital aspect of globalization that Wallerstein and Meyer only address obliquely. In the form of his theoretical model, Robertson acknowledges the impossibility of conceiving the global whole in terms of one of its parts, whether the world economy, the world polity, or a particular society such as that of the West. In addition, while he correctly points to the similarities between globalization and problems of reconciling the particular and the universal in previous civilizational formations (see for example 1991; 1989a), Robertson does not deny the uniqueness of the modern circumstance. Formations of the past are also not adequate for describing the present. Proper conceptualization of the immanent whole requires the transcendent, in this case represented by the notions of humanity and telic concern.

More than this, however, he also shows how this *conceptual* problem has important implications for *acting* in a globalized context, both for national societies and individual selves. It is a problem not only for the scientific observer, but also for the less reflective actor in his or her everyday life-world and for the holders of collective authority. In the terms used in the introduction above, Robertson explicitly incorporates the implicit meanings of globalization into his theory. Wallerstein's insistence on economy as the only essence of globalization blocks a view of the *independent* variation and contribution of other vital aspects, including the political system, the religio-cultural dimension, and individuals. Meyer inserts concepts like value creation and progress at key points in his analysis without analysing them to any large extent. Robertson's strength in this regard allows him to address these matters and thereby make analytic room for empirical events like worldwide religious resurgence, church–state tensions, and various traditionalisms on some other basis than as irrational reaction or false consciousness.

Nonetheless, Robertson does not entirely escape certain analytic insufficiencies. His concept of humanity, for instance, is almost as trans-systemic as Wallerstein's notion of a future socialist system. Humanity is what gives the present global system its 'telos' and hence its definition, but it does not describe the system in terms of what it currently is. Wallerstein, in his extensive analysis of world capitalism, does at least provide such a description, even if we agree with Robertson that it is inadequate. In this regard, Robertson's system of (national) societies, the analytic equivalent of Wallerstein's world-system, receives very little actual elaboration in Robertson's writings. It is a vital component of the globalizing circumstance, but its 'systemicity' remains unclear and largely implicit. Moreover, Robertson's emphasis on national societies and individuals in the world system tends to imply that globalization is primarily an argument about identity and only secondarily a clash of material, structural interests, something that Wallerstein shows is clearly not the case.

To be sure, these apparent gaps in Robertson's theorizing may well be matters of emphasis more than conceptual blind spots. The, up until recently (see 1992b), scattered and largely thematic nature of his numerous contributions indicates that he is concerned to balance the discussion and steer us away from what he considers overly simplistic models of globalization, especially, but not exclusively, those of the Wallersteinians. Accordingly, he concentrates most on matters of culture, on the thematic aspects of the global system, often seeming to assume the contribution of others. In more Marxian language, Robertson seeks to balance the infrastructural bias of the Wallersteinians by emphasizing the equally constitutive role played by ideal, superstructural dimensions.

There is, however, more to Robertson's focus than strategic considerations within the wider globalization discussion. Like Meyer's, Robertson's view of the world system is not simply cultural, but also fundamentally political, a matter of legitimate collective authority. The modern state is central for both of them. What separates the two is Robertson's use of the *Gemeinschaft/Gesellschaft* and particular–universal tensions as constitutive of both modernity and globalization. More precisely, it is Robertson's introduction of the *Gemeinschaft* category into the debate that characterizes his contribution. It is this term that allows him to focus on the relativization of particularisms as the central constitutive impetus of globalization. It is the way that Robertson incorporates this dimension into his analysis that introduces difficulty.

The problem becomes visible if we look more closely at Robertson's concept of national societies. Although these are 'state-centred' and even 'state-run' (Robertson, 1989b: 19), they are not the same thing as nation-states.[23] Robertson does not define these entities. Yet it is clear from his writings that national society is a way of giving conceptual expression to the vital role of social particularisms in the global system. Few if any of us are simply 'citizens of the world'. Most of us also have local or particular roots which greatly influence our social action. Moreover, as Meyer (1980) points out in his analysis of the global polity, nation-states have a great deal of difficulty with non-state particularisms such as that of the Ibo in Nigeria, the Kurds in the Middle East, or First Nations in North America. Robertson is therefore quite correct in avoiding an identification of nation-states with social particularisms in the modern global context. Yet national society stands for both nation-state and social particularism in general. It is both *Gesellschaft* and *Gemeinschaft* and this is precisely what it seems Robertson wishes to convey in the concept. The problem, however, is that states and social particularisms are not coterminous, an empirical fact that Robertson captures precisely in his analysis of religio-political tensions.[24] The term national society tends to obscure this reality, especially when we are told that the global system is a system of such societies. On the basis of Meyer's analysis, this system would be a system of nation-states. But on Robertson's model, it would also have to be a system of social particularisms. The whole notion of social particularism, however, remains largely unanalysed beyond its status as the locus of cathectic *Gemeinschaft*.

There is an ambiguity here that requires further analysis of what we mean by a society and by a global system; for only such an analysis will allow us to put both *Gemeinschaft* and *Gesellschaft* in a broader theoretical context. It is an ambiguity that also leads us again to the question of the relation between social structure and cultural expression that the above comparison between Robertson and Wallerstein pointed to. National society is a concept that ties culture – the thematic aspects of globalization – solidly to globalized political structure; but it thereby lends the political system of states a logical priority analogous to that which Wallerstein gives to the capitalist economic system. Or, to put this slightly differently: whereas for Wallerstein class as the fundamental global building block of the world-system expresses the priority of economy, for Robertson a corresponding cultural base slides into the priority of polity. We must question whether Robertson's implicit monism is any more acceptable than Wallerstein's explicit one.

The problem of the relation between the cultural or thematic aspects of the global system and its structure is a difficult one and central to the theme of this book inasmuch as it points to the role of religion under globalization. Niklas Luhmann's interventions in globalization issues focus precisely on this critical problem. It is to him that I now turn.

Niklas Luhmann

Like John Meyer's, Luhmann's writings on globalization as such are few in number (see especially Luhmann, 1971; 1984a; 1990b), but nonetheless significant because they offer a possible corrective, if not a clear alternative, to the more elaborate Wallersteinian and Robertsonian models. In particular, Luhmann traces the difficulty of thematizing global society, including the theoretical tendency to economic or political monism, to the historical uniqueness and characteristic structures of modern/global society. The problem lies in the object itself and not just in inadequate theory. Unlike Robertson, however, Luhmann begins with the socio-structural as opposed to cultural roots of the dilemma, with very different results.

Although Luhmann's specific contributions to the globalization debate are few, they are prime corollaries of a very complex sociological theory expressed in literally hundreds of publications.[25] We need only concern ourselves with certain key ideas from that theory here.

For Luhmann, the question of globalization already enters through his definition of society. Society is, first of all, a kind of social system. Social systems, in turn, consist of actions but are based on meaningful communication: 'They use communication to constitute and interconnect the events (actions) which build up the systems' (Luhmann, 1990b: 176). Society is the encompassing social system that includes all communication. It is a system of social communication in a very broad sense of that word; and we only reach the boundary of a society when communication ceases to occur. Therefore, for Luhmann, if we want to talk about societ*ies*, there must be a sufficient degree of communicative discontinuity between groups of actors to make the opportunities for communication rare and restricted. Practically, this means above all consistent physical separation and perhaps relatively little overlap in the meaning of acts. The definition almost forces one to conceive the contemporary global social system as a society simply because of the empirical fact that, increasingly, meaningful communication can and often does take place between any two points around the globe.

An important justification for reformulating the social in terms of communication, for Luhmann, is that it allows one to approach the question of society – and, indeed, sociality as such – from a perspective that is independent of any specific kind of social communication, in particular the economic or the political. In Luhmann's own words:

> The theory of social systems, by its own logic, leads to a theory of society. We do not need political or economic, 'civil' or 'capitalistic' referents for a definition of the concept of society. This, of course, does not persuade us to neglect the importance of the modern nation-state or the capitalist economy. On the contrary, it provides us with an independent conceptual framework with which to evaluate these phenomena, their historical conditions, and their far-reaching consequences. (1990b: 176f.)

In the context of the present discussion of globalization theories, then, the concept of communication takes the place of Meyer's notion of 'value creation'. In fact, Luhmann shares with both Wallerstein and Meyer the idea that we have a world society essentially because the fundamental social mode (communication, value creation, economic exchange) now extends continuously around the entire globe. Nonetheless, Luhmann's more abstract starting point allows him to avoid the economic or political reductionisms of Wallerstein, Meyer, or, to a lesser extent, Robertson. The advantage is that Luhmann can, as it were, relieve the capitalist economy and the system of nation-states (or societies) of the analytic burden of having to carry the structure of the global system.

Conceiving the world system as a society based on communication has many consequences for thinking about globalization. Perhaps most centrally, it shifts the theoretical problem away from how disparate parts (societies) can possibly come to form a whole to how the parts (subsystems) have changed so that the whole is now becoming global. Put more in the terms of sociological theory, it changes the problem from one of *integration* to one of *differentiation*.[26] In this respect, Luhmann's strategy is similar to that of Wallerstein.

For Luhmann, as for the other thinkers, modernization and globalization are intimately related. In this case, modern society is a consequence of a change in Western society in the type of inner-societal differentiation that dominates. Unlike, for instance, Spencer, Durkheim, or Parsons, Luhmann sees modernity as characterized not primarily by a quantitative increase in differentiation,[27] but more importantly by a qualitative change in the criterion according to which we form the main divisions of social communication. To conceive the characteristic differentiation of modern society, it is not enough to look to an increase in the division of labour (e.g. Durkheim), an increase in the differentiation of functional subsystems (e.g. Parsons), and/or a shift in dominance of one subsystem over others (e.g. Spencer). These are indeed features of modernity, but they miss the most crucial aspect of the change, which, for Luhmann, is a shift from a dominance of *stratified* differentiation to a dominance of *functional* differentiation (Luhmann, 1982: 229ff). Here the former, pre-modern type is as important for understanding the theoretical problems attendant upon globalization as is the latter, modern type. This is so primarily because functional differentiation makes it much more difficult to thematize modern global society. As a result, many theorists resort to the self-thematization strategies of stratified societies because these had relatively clear self-conceptions. This, in part, is how Luhmann traces the origins of the *Gemeinshaft/Gesellschaft* problem (see Luhmann, 1981; 1990c).

Before going into this matter in greater detail, however, we must have a clearer idea of what Luhmann means by stratified and functionally differentiated societies. A key assumption is the notion that stratification can be a form of subsystem differentiation and not just the unequal distribution of status, wealth, power, and other forms of influence.[28] Stratificatory differentiation forms subsystems on the basis of rank: the question of first order here is to which stratum or status-group an action belongs. It is similar to segmentary or core/periphery differentiation in that each of these assigns primary importance to the group membership of the person acting. It makes a great deal of difference whether such an individual is a member of this clan or that, a noble family or a common one; whether she or he is from the city or the countryside, from this village or that. What is most characteristic of a stratified society, however, is the clear domination of the upper, ruling strata. These not only control much of the political, economic, and other forms of social power, they also define the effective limits of the society. The reach of their communication, fluid and imprecise as it may be, is identical with that boundary. As Wallerstein points out in his concept of world-empire, it is the action of the ruling strata that extends the total division of labour beyond the boundaries of mini-systems. With Weber (1978, I: 302–307), Luhmann would simply add that the status of these upper strata is not reducible to economic or any other strictly functional criterion.

This is not to say that dominance of stratified differentiation excludes the presence and importance of functional distinctions, such as an economic division of labour or specialized institutions like political bureaucracies and religious orders. According to Luhmann, however, these help structure and reinforce the differences between strata, rather than cutting across the primary divisions. In particular, the control of specialized political, legal, military, and religious institutions by the upper strata provides these with the resources to express and maintain their privileged status. Perhaps one of the most structurally consistent examples is the traditional Hindu caste system in which functional role, group membership, and status were highly coordinated (cf. Dumont, 1970).

For Luhmann, then, the gradual and endogenous shift to modernity in Western society has as its central structural feature the reordering of these stratified priorities. Indeed, an extensive literature documents the progressive undermining of status-group centrality and the development of institutional spheres in which action is oriented toward different, functionally specific rationalities.[29] The principle of subsystem formation shifts from the group to which the action belongs to the function it fulfils, that is, what fundamental problem an action addresses. Rather than the traditional nobilities, merchant and peasant strata (systems), we now deal with political, economic, scientific, educational, religious, and other systems.

Again, other types of differentiation are not absent under modern conditions. Segmentation is particularly salient in the geopolitical divisions between states and the religious distinctions of faiths or traditions. Stratification is also a feature of modernity, especially within the economy and in organizations. But both these, along with others such as core/periphery divisions, operate, according to Luhmann, to structure and reinforce the dominant differentiation of functional systems of social communication. Luhmann might therefore point to the analyses of Wallerstein, Meyer, and Robertson as examples of how core/periphery, class divisions, and segmented states are essential structural features of the modern global economic and political systems, but not of global society as a whole.

The development of Western modernity, for Luhmann, certainly involves much more than this single structural factor. The basis of his position, however, is not that a change in the dominant type of differentiation is all that there is to modernity, but rather that this shift holds the key to understanding the multitude of changes that scholars and non-scholars alike have analysed as constitutive of it, including, of course, cultural changes. Among these concomitant changes, the ones that relate most closely to the globalization of modern society are those of greatest concern here. Specifically, the questions to address are these: What is it about a dominance of functional differentiation that leads to the globalization of society? How can one conceive or thematize a global society dominated by functional differentiation? How does Luhmann explain the tendency to economic and political monism in such thematizations? How does Luhmann analyse the role of group identities in global society, what Robertson refers to as the globalization of particularism? And finally, how does Luhmann see the role of religion in global society? Answering these questions in turn will show both the strengths and weaknesses of Luhmann's contribution to the debate.

Only in a relatively early article[30] has Luhmann dealt directly with the question of how globalization devolves from modernization. Here he claims that the most common and least problematic communication with global reach is the sort that displays cognitive or adaptive orientations: scientific and technical communication, trade, news reporting, and travel. Normative, moral, and prescriptive orientations are far less prevalent. What he is suggesting is that globalization is connected with the increased dominance in modern social structures of *learning* as a way of responding to disappointed expectations.

To understand what he means and why this change should lead to globalization, we must start with his notion of expectations. In common with much sociological theory, Luhmann sees expectations as fundamental to social structure. In fact, for Luhmann, social structures consist of expectations. Inasmuch as structure refers to the relatively stable context in which communication can occur, so communication will be impossible without structured expectations. Accordingly, there must be ways of dealing with disappointed expectations. Luhmann sees two fundamental approaches:

norms, and learning (or cognition).[31] The former means for him that we maintain the expectation in spite of the disappointment; the latter that we change the expectation in light of the disappointment.

While all social systems operate with both modalities, historically the normative style has prevailed because it is more easily institutionalized: consensus and collective action are easier if it is clear what the expectations will be after the disappointment. Luhmann claims further that the historical dominance of normatively structured expectations was instrumental in the buildup of the highly complex societies of the pre-modern and even early modern era. The argument here is that a normative emphasis permits greater contrast between social structure and natural events, thus leading to the successful establishment of what, from an evolutionary point of view, are rather unlikely social formations. Such societies, therefore, typically displayed strong normative institutions, especially in the form of religion, law, and politics. They also thought of themselves in corresponding terms as politically constituted, ethically grounded societies, territorially delimited by the reach of those normative structures in the form of upper-strata communication.

For Luhmann, the Western shift from stratified to functional differentiation was at the same time a switch in dominance from the normative to the cognitive mode of responding to disappointed expectations. Just as for types of differentiation, this change did not mean a simple substitution, but rather a reordering: the typically modern norms are those that structure and thereby encourage learning, not those that define the limits of learning. In Weber's terms, normative rationality shifts from ends to means; it is more instrumental.[32] The institutionalization of learning on a normative basis greatly increases the complexity of the society because, in the event of inevitable disappointments, it allows far more possibilities for communication, action, and changes in expectation than does a normative emphasis. If learning is the norm, what is learned is left relatively open. Again, the 'old-style', value-rational or traditional norms do not disappear, but they are relativized in the sense of being denied their previous determinative role in structuring society.

To see how, according to Luhmann, this shift leads to globalization, we must return to his analysis of functional differentiation. The rise of this form means the dominance of social systems that specialize in specific modes of communication. For example, the economy concentrates on money, the political system on power, and the scientific system on truth. As such, they abstract from the hitherto established normative structure of the society as a whole. Differentiated from that structure, they are comparatively free to create many more possibilities for the society than parallel functional institutions could have under the dominance of stratification. Included in those new possibilities, and of central importance here, is the setting of relatively independent boundaries for each system: the extent of the economy need not be and in all likelihood will not be similar to the extent of the polity; and both these will differ from the reach of scientific knowledge.

Unlike in a stratified society, certain subsystems (upper strata) can no longer control the effective boundaries of others and thus claim to define the limits of the society as a whole. Under modern circumstances, says Luhmann, the only boundary that remains possible for the encompassing societal system is then the globe itself (1971: 60f.; 1990b).

The connection with his analysis of expectation structures now becomes apparent. Luhmann speculates that the greater complexity of the modern functional subsystems is only possible on the basis of a primacy of the cognitive mode. In Parsonian terms, their 'upgrading' depends on adaptation (see Parsons, 1971). It is this that allows them to expand in relative disregard of previously determinative system boundaries, eventually limited only by the physical extent of human beings themselves, currently by the globe.[33] Attaching his empirical observation that the sort of communication that has globalized is for the most part cognitively oriented, we come to Luhmann's conclusion that world society is a direct consequence of modernization, the latter understood as the switch to the functional differentiation of the dominant subsystems of society.

Before leaving this topic, I underline a critical aspect of Luhmann's explanation. Functional differentiation and the resultant shift to an adaptive emphasis have globalization as a consequence not because modern systems must expand all around the globe in order to survive, but rather because there is no longer a powerful enough hindrance to this expansion. As Luhmann himself puts it, 'using [functional] differentiation, society becomes a global system. For structural reasons there is no other choice' (1990b: 178).

Luhmann, then, sees globalization as the almost incidental consequence of structural modernization in Western society. This observation leads us to consider the way he analyses the problem of thematizing global and modern society. Like Robertson, Luhmann draws a consistent distinction between what a society is as a social system and thematic representations or images of that society. These images, which Luhmann labels self-descriptions or self-thematizations, reflect the actual structure of a society; but they do so in a selective way. Images of a society are condensed and simplified symbols intended to represent the society within its own processes. Because they are selective, none of them can be complete. Along with the other three thinkers discussed here, Luhmann therefore also speaks of dominant and competing images. Where he differs, however, is on another matter. For Luhmann, the more complex a society is, the more problematic all self-thematizations become. They either become too generalized to guide societal processes – Luhmann's concept of society would be an example – or their selectivity becomes too visible to remain convincing. The unprecedented complexity of global society not only produces competing images of world order, as Robertson puts it; there is also the real question of whether this society can ever develop a univocal and effective 'identity'. Not surprisingly, Luhmann's view of modern global society as dominated by functional differentiation plays a key role in this conclusion.

For Luhmann, stratified societies were less complex than modern society; but it was also, therefore, not as difficult to thematize them effectively. Put simply, the domination of the upper strata allowed these to present and largely enforce the view that they, although tiny minorities, represented the society as a whole. Accordingly, the range of their political, legal, and religious domination defined the boundaries of their society; while the values and purposes embedded in their communication came to be seen as synonymous with those of the society as such. To use the language of Parsons and Robertson, the upper strata determined the telic ends of these societies: this in spite of the fact that much of what happened among the far more populous lower strata may have suggested very different norms and boundaries.

With the shift to a primacy of functional differentiation, Luhmann considers that the old solutions for thematizing society become highly problematic. He suggests two reasons. First, the adaptive upgrading that results from functional specialization means that each subsystem creates an overabundance of possibilities for social action. The tremendous growth during modern times of wealth, state power, technology, and educational facilities all around the world would serve as examples. The greatly increased complexity that this reflects undermines the effectiveness of any self-description for the reasons already mentioned. Second, unlike under stratified differentiation, the relation of societal subsystems under functional differentiation is not structurally hierarchical, making it much more difficult to treat any one of them as the self-evident part that represents the whole. To be sure, Luhmann recognizes that some subsystems, notably the economic and scientific/technological, are more favoured by modern conditions because of the clearly adaptive orientation of their expectation structures. But this at best makes them more potent modes of communication, not the source of clearly self-evident symbols to thematize the whole and its telos.

This last consideration brings us to a final aspect of Luhmann's analysis of globalization before we look at some problems associated with it. Although Luhmann believes that the barriers to a convincing thematization of global society are formidable, he does not deny the importance of self-descriptions in complex social systems. To use Robertson's terms, the matter of humanitic concern or the telic ends of humanity is not trivial. These images are simplified versions of very complex systems that allow the systems to communicate about themselves and thereby set goals (*telos*) and gain some measure of control over their own complexity.

Accordingly, Luhmann's theory expects such self-thematizations to occur in spite of the fact that they are virtually doomed to manifest insufficiency. In general, he sees three sorts of effort in this regard. The first thematizes the global system in terms of what it is *not* (see Luhmann, 1990c). In this category, Luhmann would locate utopian and antisystemic visions of various sorts, ones that comprehend the confusing present by projecting one or more definite futures toward which we are heading. Wallerstein's socialist future fits here as do a variety of prophecies, both religious and secular, both optimistic and pessimistic. A second kind of thematization attempts to revitalize and update the solutions that were characteristic of pre-modern, politically constituted, and regional societies. Here he would place conceptions that see society as a normatively structured system of similarly oriented people. Included are *Gemeinschaft* identities like the ones outlined by Robertson, but also attempts such as that of Robertson to style global society as an international system of societies which, together, constitute the whole by each declaring their identities.[34] Finally, a third strategy uses a specific functional subsystem as the part that represents the whole. Here Luhmann would put especially those notions that see global society as a capitalist system, thereby privileging the economy, and those, such as Robertson's and Meyer's, that give the political system priority. The styling of the global system as a technological one would also find its place here (see for example Ellul, 1964).

All of these strategies are, for Luhmann, inadequate. The first is good for outlining problems, setting goals, and providing motivation for collective action; but it cannot describe what the global system currently is. Such utopian thematizations may therefore include a contrasting description of present society. A common example is the Wallersteinian and Marxist polarity of socialism and capitalism. The second posits incorrectly that we still live in territorially delimited, politically dominated societies. Although the boundaries of states are perhaps obvious modern parallels, there is just too much communication that escapes these limits. Luhmann's criticism here is comparable to Wallerstein's observation that modern states do not control their internal economies so much as participate in a market-driven world-economy that transcends any of their boundaries. On this basis, Luhmann would object to Robertson's description of (one pole of) globalization as a system of societies. This last term focuses the problem at a more local level where convincing thematizations still seem possible; but it is difficult to see how this tack can lead to a global self-description without first abstracting from the national ones. Moreover, and perhaps more importantly, Robertson's analysis does not actually incorporate what Luhmann sees as fundamental to the global system, namely the dominance of functionally differentiated subsystems. Robertson's view is prevailingly politico-cultural and perhaps religio-cultural, referring to functional domains in which normative expectation structures have traditionally prevailed, and which are therefore more likely to be a source of less problematic, pre-modern, pre-global self-thematizations.

This brings us to Luhmann's critique of the third strategy, the one which privileges one of the functional systems for describing the global reality. The lack of a consistent hierarchy among these systems undercuts such self-descriptions. Accordingly, Luhmann would point out that Robertson can only maintain the plausibility of his analysis because he leaves out those systems that cannot be brought under a normatively oriented self-thematization. Robertson would therefore be missing the full depth of the problem because his theory of society is not adequate to what, according to Luhmann, modern global society has actually become.

While Luhmann would criticize both Wallerstein's and Meyer's theories for comparable reasons, I have focused on the interface with Robertson because it opens the door, in turn, to a consideration of the weaknesses in Luhmann's position. In this regard, what I said about Robertson in the previous section also applies to Luhmann. Both focus on certain aspects of the globalization debate while ignoring others. In Luhmann's case, the problem is, if anything, more acute because so many of his publications have potential implications for the debate; yet he has actually done very little of the application. One is therefore left with an underdeveloped contribution which leaves more questions unanswered than it addresses. More specifically, Luhmann has a great deal to say about how Western modernization came about (see especially 1980–1981; 1986; 1989a); but next to nothing about *how* – as opposed to that – this lead to globalization. As I pointed out above, for Luhmann, globalization is almost an incidental consequence of modernization. As a result, his empirical focus is overwhelmingly Western, ignoring the part played in globalization by non-Western parts of the world and the repercussions of their responses on the West. Put differently, Luhmann leaves out precisely what is the heart of Robertson's concern: the interplay of the particular and the universal in the process of globalization. Accordingly, Luhmann does not discuss the role of group identities in global society. And, critically in the present context, the place of religion in global as opposed to Western society barely receives mention.

As with Robertson, such bracketed matters may or may not be indicative of inadequacies in the basic theory of global society that Luhmann represents. Rather than try to decide this matter here, I address this question in the chapters that follow by attempting to develop Luhmann's position in the directions that he has not pursued. This effort will also go some way to showing that the main positions in the globalization debate as I have outlined them are, in fact, not mutually contradictory; but can be integrated to lead to a better understanding of what globalization is and some key roles of religion in it.

Notes

1 Among the earliest clear theoretical formulation is undoubtedly Wallerstein, 1974a. Even earlier precursors are e.g. Luhmann, 1971; Moore, 1966; Nettl and Robertson, 1968: especially 129ff.

2 Simpson (1991) uses the same set of representative authors, but is undecided about whether Luhmann's approach is clearly distinct.

3 Lest the neat parallelism be misleading, Robertson's approach is a 'cultural perspective on globalization' (1992b: 28f.) and not an analysis that assumes the dominance of a single global culture.

4 Wallerstein and world-system theory have many collaborators and adherents who have made substantial contributions both to this variant of globalization theory and to the debate as a whole. Central among these would be Terence Hopkins with whom Wallerstein has

co-authored several works. Among the key sources of world-system literature are the journal *Review*, published by the Fernand Braudel Center at the State University of New York at Binghamton, and several collections of articles under various editors. As examples of the latter, see Bergesen, 1983; Chase-Dunn, 1981.

5 Chirot and Hall, 1982, offer a balanced account of what is new and what is not in Wallerstein's world-system theory.

6 More recently, Wallerstein has made it clear that his scheme does not represent a simple historical progression. Mini-systems have existed at the same time as world-empires and world-economies. Moreover, the modern world-economy is not the first. Its distinguishing feature is that it has avoided disintegration or being absorbed into a world-empire. See Wallerstein, 1987: 317f.

7 There is, of course, the obvious rough parallel with the writings of Marx and Engels. In addition, as will become apparent below, Luhmann works with three fundamental types of society based on different forms of differentiation. The third of these, functional differentiation, also grounds his understanding of modern global society, his logical equivalent of Wallerstein's modern world-system. For another example of this tripartite classification, see Gellner's distinction between pre-agrarian, agrarian, and industrial societies in Gellner, 1983.

8 For a succinct summary, see Wallerstein, 1974b: 402f. Cf. also Peter Taylor, 1985. For a defence of Wallerstein against critics who charge that nation-states form a second logic in addition to that of the world-economy, see Chase-Dunn, 1981. As I discuss below, Meyer and his colleagues at Stanford University take up this criticism, but at a more fundamental level than that of the nation-state.

9 This oversimplified summary is intended only for the purposes of illustration. The analysis of Wallerstein and others in fact follows closely Kondratieff cycles for the 1780–1980 period. There is significant variation in the precise periodizations involved, but the general pattern has a solid following among scholars of international economics. Wallerstein's most detailed work concentrates on the long wave immediately preceding the first Kondratieff cycle. See Wallerstein 1974a for the 'A' phase and 1980 for the 'B' phase. For a succinct summary of the whole model, see Taylor, 1985: 12–21. For discussions of the question of cycles in the world-system model, see Bergesen and Schoenberg, 1980; Bousquet, 1980; P. Weber, 1983. For a detailed analysis of the whole historical period, but critical of Wallerstein's 'economic determinism', see Chirot, 1986.

10 Wallerstein's analysis here would fit well into an understanding of why the Iranian revolution has taken the 'moderate', less antisystemic turn it has since the death of Khomeini. See Chapter 7 below.

11 Chief among these are Michael T. Hannan, John Boli-Bennett, Jacques Delacroix, Francisco Ramirez, and George M. Thomas. I focus specifically on John Meyer here because he has thus far provided the main theoretical impetus of this group. See the contributions by these authors in Bergesen, 1980; Meyer and Hannan, 1979a.

12 The most important presentation of Meyer's theoretical perspective is Meyer, 1980. The following discussion is based substantially on this article.

13 Distinguishing polity from economy on the basis of two different ways of creating value raises Meyer's analysis to a more general level than that of the state. His critique of Wallerstein is therefore more fundamental than others such as Skocpol (1977) and Zolberg (1981), who remain at the more particular level of the state. The latter type of criticism is comparatively ineffective precisely because it lacks a concept more general than either economy or polity, thus allowing Wallerstein's universalizing notion of economy to fill this logical position. Cf. Chase-Dunn, 1981.

14 See Boli-Bennett, 1979. For a study of how the religious particularities of various countries fare in these otherwise similar constitutions, see Markoff and Regan, 1987.

15 For the important distinction, in this context, between state and regime, see Thomas and Meyer, 1980.

16 Compare the views and goals of Christian liberation theologians and Islamic reformers like Iran's Shariati below, Chapters 6 and 7.

17 See Tönnies, 1963. These terms are usually translated as community and society.

Because they have taken on a technical meaning in the sociological discussion of modernization, I, like Robertson, use the German expressions.

18 See Simmel, 1971; Durkheim, 1933.

19 Such as Wallerstein's or that of the antisystemic movements he promotes. See Robertson and Lechner, 1985.

20 In this article, as elsewhere (e.g. 1987c; 1991; 1992b), Robertson sees Japan as perhaps the most paradigmatic model of how the two imply each other: '[Japan's] paradigmatic status is inherent in its . . . history of selective incorporation and syncretization of ideas from other cultures in such a way as to particularize the universal and, so to say, return the product of that process to the world as a uniquely Japanese contribution to the universal' (1992b: 102). Cf. the similar discussion in Chirot, 1986 on the possibility of the Japanese 'corporatist' model as the dominant model of the future.

21 The presentation of this typology is substantially based on Robertson, 1992a. See also 1992b: 78ff.

22 As will become evident in Chapter 3 below, I use a similar dual typology for classifying religious responses to globalization.

23 In his analysis of Robertson's contribution to globalization theory, Simpson (1991) explicitly equates the two, thereby blocking a view of the problem I outline here.

24 Witness the following statements: '. . . globalization involves and promotes *the relativization* of societal and individual (as well as ethnic and civilizational) identities'; and 'As the world becomes a single place, various collectivities – but given the form in which the modern world-system has been made, societies or would-be societies, in particular – are, so to say, called upon to declare their identities' (Robertson, 1989b: 19).

25 It is difficult to say which are the core works, but certainly *Soziale Systeme* (1984b) is one of them. For English language readers, *The Differentiation of Society* (1982) is by now an outdated introduction that must be supplemented at least by *Essays on Self-Reference* (1990a).

26 Luhmann locates this shift not only on the level of society, but also on the level of the theory of society and social systems. The shift from territorial societies to global society accordingly corresponds to a shift in the theory from *identity* to *difference*. Cf. Luhmann, 1982: 133.

27 This formulation is somewhat oversimplified for the sake of presentation. Differentiation is, of course, for all four thinkers mentioned, only one aspect of the shift to modernity. The centrality of the notion of difference in the Luhmannian scheme, however, seems to call for this provisorily simplified formulation if the difference of the Luhmannian model is to be made clear.

28 In addition to running counter to Durkheim and the dominant sociological tradition, conceiving stratification as a form of differentiation is also something absent from Luhmann's own earlier work. See, for instance, Luhmann, 1970: 148, where one can still read, 'Es gibt nur diese beiden Typen', referring to segmentary and functional differentiation as explicitly derived from Durkheim and Parsons.

29 Wallerstein's work is a good example of studies in the development of a functionally differentiated economic system, whereas that of Meyer concentrates on elements of the modern political system. For the development of the scientific system explicitly within the context of the globalization discussion, see Wuthnow, 1987: 265–298. From the literature on the dissolution of status-group loyalties in the process of Western modernization, and its consequences, see Elias, 1978; 1982; Luhmann, 1980–81; 1989a; Nelson, 1969.

30 Luhmann, 1971. The following presentation is based closely on this article.

31 As will become evident shortly, this distinction is somewhat parallel to that between substantive and technical reason, or to Weber's distinction between *Wertrationalität* and *Zweckrationalität*. Such comparisons should not be carried too far, however. Much of the difference between Luhmann and other sociological theorists is in how he defines and uses sociologically familiar concepts like expectations, norms, system, society, differentiation, and many others. Here cannot be the place for discussing the details of these similarities and differences, especially the relationship between Luhmannian and Parsonian theory. Suffice it to say that, even where there are strong parallels, the ways that Luhmann uses such concepts in his

theory make any easy assumption of direct comparability highly problematic. For Luhmann's most thorough presentation of his own conceptual base, see 1984b.

32 The difference between Luhmann and Weber in this matter becomes clear here. Whereas Weber characterized modernity in terms of a shift in the role of norms (ends to means), Luhmann inserts an entirely new category that allows modernity to appear as something more than a potentially dangerous and heartless insufficiency.

33 In his recent work on globalization and modernization, Giddens (1990; 1991) expresses a similar idea when he talks about modernity being characterized by reflexivity and reflexivity being instrumental in globalization. In comparing Luhmann and Giddens on this point, Luhmann's emphasis on learning, it seems to me, gets more to the heart of the matter. It is not so much reflective thinking and action as such that characterizes modernity as the fact that, upon reflection, moderns tend more often to change their expectations, whereas non-moderns put greater emphasis on the normative maintainance of expectations.

34 See the discussion of Robertson above, and also Luhmann, 1975: 57. Here the reference (note 22) is specifically to Nettl and Robertson, 1968.

2
SOCIO-CULTURAL PARTICULARISM IN A GLOBAL SOCIETY

The four theoretical perspectives on globalization discussed in the last chapter are of course not exhaustive of the scholarly debate on the subject. My main purpose in presenting them is to show both the complexity of the issue and how this complexity has thus far resulted in partial or even reductionistic theories. What is of special note in the present context is that only Robertson has gone any distance in incorporating religion into the discussion; and yet his implicit tendency to give the political constitution of society priority leaves him open to Luhmann's charge of inadequate description of what the global system presently is. To gain a better appreciation of the possible roles of religion in this system, then, we must at least add to what Robertson has done thus far.

In this and the following two chapters, I take some steps in this direction. The broad aim of this chapter is to situate socio-cultural particularisms in the global system in a way that avoids giving the political system priority, but without thereby resorting to another functional monism. Accordingly, I work very much on a Luhmannian base for conceiving global society. The importance of this broad task for understanding the roles of religion under globalization is twofold. First, religion has historically been closely tied to various socio-cultural particularisms, various group cultures. The fate of these is therefore going to say a fair amount about the fate of religion in a global society. Second, however, the universalist strains of at least those religions that have come to be known as world religions point to the possibility of a role for religion under globalizing conditions that largely abstracts from socio-cultural particularisms. If our theory of globalization avoids conceiving the global system as primarily political, economic, or even politico-economic, then the door is left open for seeing religion as a relatively independent force. This again points to a Luhmannian base because it effectively means exploring the possibility of a global religious system differentiated out of global society in a manner similar to the economic and political systems. I use such conditional language at this point because, as subsequent chapters show, both the particularistic and universalistic roles of religion in global society are significantly more ambiguous than is the case for other, structurally more favoured modes of communication.

In what follows, I take as my points of departure key features of the theories discussed in the previous chapter. A first section develops a general picture of the genesis and structure of the global system. It begins with an analysis of territoriality in the modern and global systems. The aim here is to examine the relation between social particularism and the modern state. In Robertsonian terms, it is to distinguish the national society and the nation-state in order to get a clearer picture of how and why the particular national content has come to be expressed in the universal state form. On the basis of this analysis, I then go on to a brief consideration of how the European developments led to globalization and what further consequences that expansion has had for Western and non-Western socio-cultural particularisms. In this section, but especially the following ones, I expand Luhmann's contribution to the point where it can incorporate major insights of Robertson, most specifically the continued and revitalized salience of socio-cultural particularisms. The later sections of the chapter approach this task through an examination of social inclusion and exclusivity, and of the relation of culture to structure. In carrying out its tasks, the present chapter develops further many of the points covered in the previous one, but does so with the explicit intention of synthesizing the four perspectives outlined, primarily on a Luhmannian base. Thereupon, Chapters 3 and 4 outline the potential for religion that devolves from this analysis.

The Globalization of Modern Structures

Wallerstein and Luhmann both see globalization as the consequence of expanding functional systems. They differ on a number of other points, of course. One of these is that Wallerstein regards the globalization of the modern world-economy as an internal requirement of capitalism, of its need for perpetual growth. Luhmann, on the other hand, sees globalization as much more accidental, largely because the internal logic of the economic system is for him only one of several logics which, as Meyer stresses, can pull in different directions. A closer examination of their positions, however, reveals that the difference between Wallerstein and Luhmann is not that great; and that a Luhmannian position can actually subsume the important insights of Wallerstein.

The Question of Territoriality

The roughly evolutionary typologies of societies in each case can serve as a point of departure. We note that Wallerstein's distinction between mini-systems, world-empires, and the world-economy parallels the Luhmannian classification of societies dominated by segmentary, stratified, and functional differentiation respectively. What interests us here are the latter two in each case. From a Luhmannian viewpoint, the redistributive nature of world-empire economies corresponds to the fact that, in stratified societies, functional criteria like wealth serve to differentiate strata. The upper strata appropriate a large portion of the wealth produced in the area under their political control in order to demonstrate, promote, and maintain the status of their subgroups. The purpose of empire is the aggrandizement and glorification of the upper status groups. The much more numerous lower status groups hardly count except as material, like land and chattels. To the extent that they benefit at all from the redistribution, it is as loyal servants of the elites; and thus in support of the dominant structures. Moreover, as Wallerstein points out, market-oriented economic activity is quite limited in such societies, reflecting the subordination of functionally oriented economic action to the priorities of the status group.

The priorities of stratified societies also result in a limitation on their territorial extension. Their reproduction depends on the collective action of the quite small upper strata that control so many of the societies' communicative resources, including wealth, military power, writing, and religious symbols. These aristocracies can extend and maintain their influence through the application of these resources. But the dominance of status-group differentiation means that the development of these techniques will be subordinated to considerations of group loyalty and group prestige. As such, their structure is not fertile ground for the development of techniques like capital accumulation and scientific-technological invention to the point where these overcome the physical, temporal, and social barriers to globalization.

The territorial limitation of pre-modern societies is therefore bound up with the failure to develop sufficiently powerful communicative resources (cf. Innis, 1972); and with the tendency of their elites to use what resources there were to create, maintain, and enhance the stratified differentiation. The concentration of communicative resources (surplus!) in the hands of the few made the achievements of these 'high culture' societies possible; but it also set limits to the expansion of those resources. The obverse of this characteristic is the territorially-limited conception that the elites themselves had of their societies. In a real sense, the upper strata define the extent of these societies. As Gellner (1983) has pointed out, the lower status groups not only have very little power, they are also divided into a myriad of small, closed communities that communicate as little with the upper strata as they do with each other. Segmentary differentiation dominates here. Although, using the Luhmannian definition of society, it is difficult to say how far societies extend at this level, the factual range of communication is quite limited just as the members of these lower, most often peasant strata expect such limitation.

For the upper strata, however, matters are different. The reproduction of the stratified system depends on their control over specific territory which includes a number of peasant 'societies'. From their viewpoint, the extent of the society is the extent of elite communication or, in perhaps more familiar terms, elite culture. Among other things, the religion of these elites is a vital societal identifier. In a very Durkheimian sense, their gods (or equivalent) are the symbolic representation of their culture and their prestige. Those who cannot be brought under at least the formal influence of these gods are also those with whom it is formally difficult to communicate: they are the mysterious and distant outsiders, the barbarians, the infidels. Limited communication with these is possible in the form of luxury trade, diplomacy, and through various non-elite contacts; but the dominant relation is isolation or war. The ideological self-definition of stratified societies therefore reinforces and expresses practical limitations on their territorial extent.

The gradual shift to a dominance of functionally differentiated structures beginning in early modern Western society radically recasts the whole notion of territoriality so that it is less and less a delimiter of societies and more and more a matter of functional efficiency.[1] Again, I use Wallerstein's work as a point of departure. A central argument there is that, in sixteenth century Europe, both the French Valois and the Spanish Habsburg monarchies failed in their ambitions to create yet another world-empire encompassing the territory involved in the nascent European world-economy. Their defeat in this effort helped clear the way for the development of a global capitalist economy relatively independent of the redistributive effects of a single political centre. In Luhmannian terms, the functional priorities of an economic system differentiated out of early modern European society emerged victorious over the hierarchical status priorities that had been institutionalized there before. The victory, from this perspective, was one of function over stratification and not simply of economic function over political function. For, as Wallerstein and all other participants in the globalization discussion point out, the development of the global economic system parallels the emergence of a system of states, the dominant institutions of a now global political system that operates in the context of the world-economy and not in negation of it. The relationship between the economic and political systems illustrates the changed meaning of territoriality under modern conditions.

Commodity production for a money economy has been a very powerful way of tying almost all areas of the world into a single communicative network. The political system of states both reinforces and conditions this singleness. On the one hand, all land areas of the globe are by now formally under the jurisdiction of one state or another, creating a continuity of political power that parallels and reinforces that of money. There is only one political system in global society and it is coextensive with the economic system. Wallerstein's division of states into core, periphery, and semi-periphery makes a similar point. On the other hand, as Meyer's corrective of Wallerstein indicates, states also use political power to condition the operation of the commodity economy in their territory. In Meyer's terms, they control a competing but territorially limited source of value creation.

On the basis of this view, a double question arises. Why are states territorially limited and how are the boundaries between them drawn? The answers to this question are, of course, very complex. In the present context, however, a quite skeletal response will be enough.[2] The Wallersteinian answer to the first part is that states are the instruments of competing local bourgeoisies, none of which has been able to eliminate its rivals. This view makes modern territoriality a dependent function of capitalist economic expansion. While it would be unwarranted to deny the relationship, Wallerstein's own analysis points to the insufficiency of such a simple reduction. The Valois and Habsburg monarchies, as examples, were unable to subsume the nascent European world-economy within a single political unit not only because there were rival political centres, but more importantly because the political and administrative apparatus now necessary to accomplish such a task was too unwieldy and costly. The superficial political control characteristic of traditional empires no longer sufficed in the new context of an increasingly powerful and functionally differentiated economy. Or, in Luhmannian terms, the increased complexity of the economic system required a corresponding increase in the complexity of the political system.[3] For reasons of political efficiency, then, the political system became coextensive with the economic system; but to do that it had to be divided into contiguous but separated political units that have since developed into the now global system of sovereign states.

Nonetheless, even if we admit that modern states have territorial limits ultimately for reasons of administrative efficiency and only secondarily for other ones, the second half of the above question still remains. Why are the boundaries where they are? The answers to this question reinforce the idea that state boundaries are above all matters of political function.

Perhaps the most outstanding characteristics of contemporary state boundaries are that they are precise and stable, yet very often arbitrary and disputed. These features are interrelated. In the modern social context, there is a great deal of communication that crosses state boundaries, or at least will do so unless deliberate countermeasures prevent it from happening. A long list includes market trade, mass media, international art and sport, scientific and medical communication, tourism, educational exchange, migration, and 'world' religions. A Canadian, for instance, may have family in China, take a holiday in Thailand, study in Italy, do business with Japan, publish in India, listen to Jamaican music, or pray facing Mecca. Admittedly, most communication is still local; but, effectively, local usually means subnational and therefore not directly reinforcing of state boundaries. Only some communication, namely political and legal communication, is actually oriented to state boundaries.

In this context, these boundaries have to be precise because much else does not stop when political and legal jurisdiction stop. They also have to be stable: people must know which political decisions and which laws apply to them, all the more so as states become stronger and laws more comprehensive. Yet, because ever increasing amounts of communication cross these boundaries, they will in many instances seem somewhat artificial and, in disputed cases, a source of constant or periodic conflict. In short, the precise, stable, often arbitrary, and sometimes conflictual boundaries between states reflect the need to delimit political jurisdictions in an environment where other – notably, but not exclusively, economic – forms of communication crosscut those lines and thereby contradict the political delimitations.

Given this feature of modern territorial limits, the establishment of states within those boundaries is not something simple and automatic. Political and legal communication are matters of authoritative control, of collectively binding decisions and norms. They fulfil necessary functions for any more complex society. Modern political units must establish this collective authority within territorial limits whose legitimacy is not supported by factual limits to communication. The state structures were built up in medieval and early modern Europe in response to developments in other functional areas, most notably the religious, economic, and scientific. Establishing political boundaries was a crucial part of that response, one which, for instance, allowed the state authorities to gain eventual ascendancy over the now overextended religious authorities of the church. But to legitimize these restrictive boundaries required a recasting of the relevant collectivities in a way that both coincided with political capacities and was sufficiently powerful to balance the centrifugal pressures of other modes of communication.

The historic solution in early modern Europe was twofold. The first, absolutism, centred the political unit on a single person, the monarch. The monarch's domain was the state. A parallel and eventually more dominant path developed certain existing ethnic categories into the idea of the nation, a collective actor whose existence required that it have political sovereignty over the territory it inhabited: the nation determined the boundaries of the state and all those included in the state as 'citizens' were to be of the same nation (cf. Bendix, 1977; Gellner, 1983). Ethno-cultural boundaries and political boundaries came to be seen as coincident in a way radically different from previous stratified arrangements, a fact that played no small part in undermining the dominance of the latter. Outside those boundaries and helping to profile the national collectivity were, not barbarians and infidels, but other nations with their own states. In this way, inherited social identifiers and political positions helped modern state machineries to evolve. They used existing cultural material to build up different, functionally oriented structures. To be sure, in France as elsewhere, the strategy allowed only very few of these pre-existing cultural particularities to serve as the justification for nation-states. The rest were marginalized, assimilated, destroyed, or expelled.

These latter incidents point to the fact that religion has often played a critical part in identifying the nation, but not without creating ambiguities and conflict. The close historical relation between religions and socio-cultural particularisms has probably made the attempts to identify nations with single religions inevitable. Nonetheless, the universalism of religions like Buddhism, Christianity, and Islam, combined with the divisions among and within religious traditions, ensured that religions did and still do contradict these political boundaries in many ways. Like political and economic forms, religion is a type of communication susceptible to a fair degree of functional specialization and hence differentiation from particular group cultures. Like other types, therefore, it is not easily subordinated to political priorities. The political attempts to deal with this ambiguity have been numerous, including state-establishment strategies like Anglicanism and Gallicanism, the creation of state religions in early twentieth century Japan and Germany, and 'civil religions' in the United States and Israel. It is probably because of this problem that religion enters Robertson's politically-dominated vision of globalization precisely at this point, namely under the heading of church–state or religio-political tensions. And indeed, the relation of the religious and political subsystems of global society is a major focus in subsequent chapters below.

The crystallization of ethnically defined nations as the basis for state formation proved to be critical for the development of the contemporary global political system of states. The ethnic pattern has so far been the norm, that new states have very often felt constrained to construct an indigenous cultural tradition which could then be the symbolic subject of collective goals, especially in those cases where the boundaries of these states were set by external, colonial powers and expressly designed to crosscut existing ethnic distributions (cf. Smith, 1981; 1986). Moreover, the claims to new, not yet existing states are invariably preceded by the revival, valorization, or creation of such ethnic identities. Again, religion can play a positive or negative role in such attempts.

With this analysis of modern territoriality we thus arrive at an important way that socio-cultural particularisms enter the dominant structures of global society. What I am discussing here is precisely what Robertson calls the coincidence of the universalization of particularisms and the particularization of universalism. My primary justification for approaching the matter in this admittedly indirect and somewhat complex way is to show how this aspect of globalization is best understood, not as what globalization is at root all about, but rather as part of the logic of the modern global political system. The approach has at least two advantages in the present context. First, it allows us to see how social particularisms became the cultural content of functionally oriented forms that brought about globalization, and not just passive recipients of the process whose only choice was accommodation or resistance. Second, it leaves room for group culture to enter the globalization picture in other ways than as the legitimating identities of states. *Ethnies*, group cultures, social particularisms in general, are not simply identical with nationalisms, the latter referring only to those cases in which particularisms become associated with modern state power. Both aspects have implications for understanding religion in global society because of its historically close association with particular cultures. Beyond this connection, however, and as I have noted, viewing globalization as a process dominated by a plurality of differentiated functional systems raises the possibility that there is or can be a functional system for religion. If this is the case, then we should expect the relation of that system to socio-cultural particularisms to be as complex and incomplete as that of the modern global political system.

European Expansion, Globalization, and Westernization

The question of how the European beginnings eventually led to the global society of today is exceedingly complex. Only certain broad features of this expansion are of concern here, features that largely flow from the preceding discussion.

The rise of a market-oriented, capitalist economy centred in early modern Europe made it impossible to reestablish one or more old-style redistributive and politically constituted empires in that part of the world. We understand the implications incompletely, however, if we see this development as simply a triumph of economy over polity. Rather, functional communication was beginning to prevail consistently over status-group communication. To be sure, the shift was not smooth or very sudden. Many transitional forms such as absolutist monarchies and mercantilist empires provided continuity in the midst of change. But key to the whole process was the loosening of various types of functional rationalities from the tutelage of status-based power groups. Pursuit of capital became the primary goal of certain groups, usually based in cities and somewhat outside the influence of the old-style political centres. For various reasons, these new economic power centres could not be or were not brought under centralized control until the political centres themselves came to depend on them as sources of finance for their own increasingly complex administrations and imperial ambitions (see especially Wallerstein, 1974a). But by then political and economic modes of action were already on a more equal footing.

The shift to functional priorities in early modern Western Europe was not just a matter of politics and economics. Religion, centred on the Roman church, had achieved a large measure of independence already by the tenth and eleventh centuries. Especially in the areas of confessional practice and canon law, developments within the church not only established distinct directions for faith, but also spurred the elaboration of secular legal systems and individualistic thought traditions (cf. Luhmann, 1984c; 1989b; Nelson, 1968; 1969). Concomitant with all of this was the advent of a technological revolution based on increasingly differentiated scientific inquiry. Each of these systemic developments was possible only in a societal environment where the others were happening as well. Thus, for instance, the rise of a capitalist economy was dependent on the religious, legal, political, and scientific developments quite as much as the reverse.

The shift to functionally specialized social systems eventually increased Western communicative capacities to an unprecedented extent. Such upgrading meant that Westerners in modern times faced the world with institutionalized techniques and forms of organization that generated more wealth as well as more sophisticated technology, administrative and military apparatus than any of the various other civilizations around the globe.[4] This power superiority along with the cultural ideas and values that were part and parcel of its development is what enabled and drove Western expansion. It is important to underline, however, that this imperial spread was contingent not simply on the upgrading, but equally fundamentally on the ability of each of these functional domains to develop relatively independently of each other while at the same time being highly interdependent with each other. There can be little doubt, for instance, that the search for new capital opportunities was a driving motivation for Western expansion; but so too was the pursuit of political empire, the quest for religious souls, and the thirst for scientific discovery. Each of these expansions followed its own logic. Their histories can and have been written independently. The scientific revolution had no direct territorial referent at all, but was critical for the expansion of trade and empire. The Western market economy extended to various areas not or only minimally under the political control of the European imperial centres, even though the whole enterprise would have failed without their active support. And the Christian missionaries were not always simply agents of imperial and capital expansion, but pursued their own religious agenda that not infrequently conflicted with those of the soldier and the merchant.

From this perspective, then, Western expansion was both a Waller-steinian necessity and a Luhmannian incidental. Western-bred systems did not extend their reach only when and insofar as new capital opportunities required it; and yet the eventually global reach of those systems is inconceivable without that economic expansion. This statement also applies to religion: the virtually worldwide spread of Christian missions during this era was first and foremost a religious development. Worldwide capitalist expansion was a prime condition for its possibility; but the missions were not merely an ideological smokescreen for capitalist advance. They represented the widening of differentiated religious communication in a societal environment that saw parallel developments in other functionally special-ized subsystems. Nonetheless, this religious expansion was specifically Christian in content, thus pointing again to the role of socio-cultural particularism in this globalizing process.

The core of the argument thus far is that Western expansion was a direct result of the shift in European society to a primacy of functionally specialized societal subsystems. The more powerful communicative capacity of these systems enabled their eventual global spread. At the level of social structure, what globalized were primarily these systems of instrumentally oriented communication. At least until the late nineteenth or early twentieth century, however, the expansion of these systems was almost exclusively carried by people who were culturally Westerners. Until that time, it was reasonable for all involved and affected to see the process as the spread of Western socio-cultural particularism, of Western civilization. Adopting Western-bred technique seemed inseparable from becoming a Westerner in all aspects of life. And indeed, to the degree that the culture of the expanding systems had become a part of Western culture in general, globalization did and still does mean Westernization. Nonetheless, given the specialized and instrumental orientation of these functional systems, such identification eventually ran into important limits.

To understand how this was the case, I take up Luhmann's distinction between normatively and cognitively oriented expectation structures. The increased power of the functional systems derives both from their specialization and the prevalence within them of cognitively oriented structures. In Weberian terms, they emphasize instrumental rationality. The clearest examples are the capitalist economy and the scientific system. Even among those systems that operate with collective norms, especially the legal and political systems, the typical structures determine formal procedure, leaving normative content relatively underdetermined and, from the perspective of the system, decidedly changeable.[5] So too in the sphere of religion, the rise of liberal, ecumenical, and now contextual theologies points to expectation structures that stress learning over unchanging norms.[6] In other words, the global spread of the Western-bred systems, while it may have seemed for a time to mean the dissemination of Western normative particularism, was at its core the spread of cognitively oriented structures which undermined the privileged position of such Western 'tradition' not only in the non-Western world, but also in the original heartland where the instrumental systems first rose to prominence.

We arrive hereby at the specific way in which universal and particular interact under globalization. Structurally, we are dealing with instrumental systems whose style allows them to spread all around the globe, not so much in disregard of local and normative socio-cultural particularisms, but largely by subsuming them in these structures. As discussed above, one prime form that this appropriation has taken is in the nation-state division of the political system. Accordingly, towards the latter half of the nineteenth and in the twentieth century, the limits of globalization as Westernization revealed themselves as people of non-Western culture began earnestly to make the functionally systemic instrumentalities their own. The prime examples of this are, of course, the various non-Western nationalisms and corresponding independence movements that arose in Japan, China, South Asia, the Middle East, and then later in virtually all other regions of the globe. Less obvious but, in the present context, critically important examples occurred in the religious sphere as well. Here I refer to a wide range of manifestations from various millenarian movements such as the Boxer rebellion in China to diverse religious reform and revival movements such as Singh Sabha and Arya Samaj in Punjab. Indeed, the conscious identification of 'religions' or 'traditions' in different parts of the world has been as much a part of the formation of a global religious system as, for instance, states have been for the political system (cf. Robertson, 1992b).

These manifestations do not exhaust the role of socio-cultural particularism or normative traditions in the globalization process. Moreover, to this point, the presentation has not said enough about how the particular and the universal, the normative and the cognitive, the traditional and the progressive mesh. We must, therefore, carry the argument further. As a next step, I return to a further analysis of the instrumental systems.

Totalizing Versus Encompassing Systems

In order to understand what globalizing functional systems are, it is equally important to know what they are not: functional differentiation is not the division of social action into so many segments, so many pieces of a pie, each of which focuses on a different function and the sum of which make up the society. Systems are not parts. Functional social systems in particular are much closer to specialized techniques or perspectives. They are ways of communicating; hence the reference to them as instrumental systems.

Further elaboration can use Meyer's analysis of global systems as a point of departure. At a key point in his argument, Meyer (1980) criticizes the notion of a tertiary economy because it is so broad as to imply the commodification of everything that humans do. By definition, it seems, all value creation becomes economic simply because money is involved. He rejects such a broad conception of economy because it apparently denies the independent value-creating power of political decision-making. Instead, his analysis posits the increasing dominance of this political medium in our world. Although Meyer correctly insists on the relative independence of political action, it would be a mistake to think that the use of money by governments is therefore not part of the world economy. Governments buy goods and services. Their commodification consists in this buying and not in how it is decided that these things have economic value. As soon as we assign monetary value to anything, it is thereby already commodified. By the same token, however, as soon as something becomes the subject of collectively binding decision-making processes – including money, prices and other aspects of the economy – it is thereby already politicized. Both instrumentalities are universally applicable and in this sense totalizing. Each conditions the operation of the other without subsuming it. The global system is therefore both a Wallersteinian world-economy and a Meyerian world polity because both address the social totality from the point of view of a particular function. Far from being engaged in some sort of zero-sum competition, they rather reinforce each other's operation and augmentation.

Following a Luhmannian line, however, the analysis cannot stop here. The functional differentiation of modern society leads to more than the development of political and economic systems: global society is more than, as it were, a political economy. The dominance of functional rationality has also led to the development of other subsystems with different functional specializations and different perspectives on the totality. These are not residual or merely analytic categories like 'cultural' or 'social' systems. They are rather more, relatively autonomous systems of communication with their own rationalities, norms, and values.[7] Here cannot be the place for an analysis of all of these. Briefly, there is the scientific system which uses and expands the medium of scientific truth. Without the differentiation of this system and the plethora of technological applications that has flowed from it, modernity and globalization would scarcely have been possible (cf. Wuthnow, 1987: 264–298). There are also the educational, artistic, health, and religious systems, each arguably also vital aspects of globalization. In addition, one could argue for the existence of a familial system and one for news gathering and dissemination.

Each of these subsystems then, whether economic, political, scientific, religious, or other, has its own, relatively independent perspective on the society, and indeed, on the world as a whole. In principle, it should be possible to construct a theory of the modern world system using the communicative techniques of any one of them as a point of departure, especially, in the present context, that of religion. The totalizing potential of these systems points in this direction: just as anything can be commodified or politicized, so anything can become the subject of laws, scientific scrutiny, artistic expression, or religious insight. Anything, as Durkheim said, can be sacred.

Drawing attention to the totalizing potential of these instrumental systems may make it seem that little will escape their reach in a society where they are dominant. If everything, every human action and capability can become the subject of economy, politics, education, religion, or other such spheres, will the totalizing potential not move ever more toward encompassing actuality? Indeed, much critique of modernity focuses on the seemingly inexorable increase in some of these tendencies.[8] There is, however, good reason to reject this view. Precisely because the differentiated functional systems concentrate on specialized means of communication and not, for instance, on the total lives of the people that carry them, they leave a great deal of social communication underdetermined, if not unaffected. From the casual conversation with the neighbour across the fence to the voluntary organization, from social networks to social movements, there is much that escapes these nevertheless dominant systems. These systems are totalizing in the sense that they are applicable to anything in their environment; but they are not thereby all-encompassing. Everything has its price, but not everything is commodified. Everything potentially affects our health, but not everything is medicalized. Different aspects of what remains have been variously called the private sphere, the life-world, or the domain of expressive action.[9] Because a great deal of such 'nondomesticated' communication occurs (cf. Luhmann, 1987b), it is inadequate to think of the dominant functional subsystems as so many pieces of a pie, the whole of which is society.

This feature of the modern societal system yields one of the more common solutions to the problem of conceiving it: namely, seeing the unity of the encompassing system in such non-subsystemic communication. Salient examples of this direction are Robertson's use of the category of humanity to lend unity to his conception of the global system; Habermas's distinction between 'system' and 'life-world', the latter being for him the locus of authentic human communication (cf. Habermas, 1984; 1987); and Wallerstein's location of the unifying push of future socialism in antisystemic movements. Moreover, and critical for the theme of this chapter, here is another important way that socio-cultural particularisms, normative traditions, or systems of solidarity can enter the picture. To pursue this idea, we must examine further the relation between non-subsystemic and subsystemic communication.

Inclusion and Exclusivity

Given the importance that Robertson assigns to socio-cultural particularisms in the process of globalization, his theory is an appropriate place to begin a closer examination of their non-subsystemic manifestations. At the heart of Robertson's perspective are four poles of reference: national societies, the world system of societies, individuals, and humankind. In the first part of this chapter, I have addressed the first two with respect to how particularisms operate there. The second two elements make evident just how important the individual–society relation is to this view of globalization. More precisely, globalization has the specifically *modern* differentiation and relation of the individual and society as one of its prime conditions of possibility. As discussed in the previous chapter, the increased differentiation of self and society is for Robertson at the heart of various key phenomena in the global scene, including the rise of global non-governmental organizations, social movements, inner-societal identity conflicts, and minority forms of personal and collective identification (see above, Chapter 1; Robertson, 1991: 14). The relatively independent individual seems to be the source of much that we are seeking here: non-subsystemic communication in general and socio-cultural particularisms not anchored in a segment of the global political system.

For our purposes, however, pointing to the relation of heightened individuation under modern/global conditions and non-subsystemic forms does not go far enough. We have to probe more deeply into the why and how of this connection, above all in order to gain a better understanding of how religion might fit into the picture. To do this, I turn to an examination of the Parsonian notion of *inclusion* and, more specifically, to a Luhmannian variation on it.

For Parsons, inclusion is an integrative response to evolutionary change. As modern societies become more complex, they have to incorporate a wider variety of differentiated and adaptively upgraded units within their normative structures (1971: 27). The process affects individual members of a society as well. Focusing on the American experience, Parsons calls inclusion 'the process by which previously excluded groups attain full citizenship or membership in the societal community' (cited in Bourricaud, 1981: 211). The Parsonian concept thus points to a realm of social action beyond differentiated units, the societal community, as well as to a relation between the two. It also connects this process to the individual–society relation through the idea of citizenship or membership. Like Robertson's fundamentally Parsonian notion of national society, however, the Parsonian idea of inclusion in a societal community covers up as much as it clarifies. Above all, that which presumably does the inclusion, the societal community, is structurally too vague. Through the idea of citizenship, and like national society, it uses the modern state with its clear boundaries as a surrogate structure, thus obfuscating precisely what I am trying to keep separate here: subsystemic communication, socio-cultural particularity, and non-subsystemic communication. Yet the notion of inclusion, like national society or societal community is not thereby analytically useless; it does, nonetheless, have to be unpacked. For this task, I turn to a Luhmannian approach to inclusion.

Luhmann turns the Parsonian concept of inclusion on its head, both as concerns differentiated units and individuals. Instead of a positively integrative process that balances differentiation, it becomes a negatively conceived term referring to the elimination of structures that negate functional differentiation (see Luhmann, 1977: 232–241, especially 236). The whole notion of social integration receives a rather different cast in this theory. Moreover, cultural particularisms, even 'pluralistic' ones like Parsons's societal communities, are no longer that which does the including, but rather that which, along with individual identities, is included. A Luhmannian notion of inclusion is thereby much more tuned to a global reality because, as functional systems globalize, so does the process of inclusion. To understand this reversed conceptualization better, however, we must look again at the Luhmannian assertion that modern global society is characterized by a dominance of functional differentiation.

For Luhmann, society does not consist of human beings, but of communications. In one form or another, the idea has a long history in Western philosophical and sociological thinking (see, from among many, Simmel, 1971). But this difference between, as Luhmann (1984b: 141ff.) terms it, human consciousness and social communication is not that obvious in a stratified or segmented society. Here human beings are much more completely embedded in one social subsystem and not others: virtually all the actions of an individual are part of one principal subsystem of that society, his or her stratum, village, clan, or other group. Within these units, action can of course be differentiated along other lines. In such circumstances, it makes sense to conceive the relation of the individual and society as one of a part belonging to a whole. With a shift to a primacy of functional differentiation, however, this kind of wholesale allocation becomes very difficult: if much of my communicative action forms elements of, say, the scientific or educational subsystems of society, a great deal does not. Some of it is familial, some economic, and much of it does not contribute directly to the reproduction of any functionally oriented subsystem. Something analogous could be said for the vast majority of people in our world, albeit with lesser or greater involvement in the globalized instrumentalities. This difference between the traditional and the modern has been a constant of sociological thought throughout the nineteenth and twentieth centuries.

Tönnies's distinction between *Gemeinschaft* and *Gesellschaft*, like Durkheim's between mechanical and organic solidarities, are among its most familiar expressions.

The key Luhmannian point with respect to this classic discussion is that the modern way of including the individual in society is not going to be simply a more generalized incorporation into a larger 'stratum', for instance, Parsons's tellingly labelled societal community, that is, *gesellschaftliche Gemeinschaft*. Such a conception does not conceive the difference between the modern and traditional radically enough. The situation calls for an alternative approach. More specifically, if functional and not stratified or segmented subsystems are to be primary, the actions that compose those systems are likely to be significantly more abstracted from the individuals who perform them. Action oriented toward function is, on the whole, concerned less with who a person is and more with what she or he can do.

Conversely, however, this 'impersonality' of functional communication and hence functional systems also means that persons will tend not to be excluded from participation in any given system on the basis of personal attributes, including group membership, that are not functionally relevant. Such negative inclusion is, for instance, typical of modern Bills of Rights, which forbid discrimination on the basis of various personal attributes but say little about what should be the basis of discrimination. They assume that discrimination will take place on the basis of 'merit', that is, according to the selection criteria of the system involved, not those that might operate in that system's environment. Characteristically modern ideals reflect this emphasis. Thus, access to health care should not be influenced by economic status or country of residence, but rather by medical need. Admission and advancement in the educational system should not be influenced by personal criteria (such as ethnicity, gender), but by educational merit. Participation in the political process should not be restricted on the basis of race or creed, but solely by citizenship.[10] And so forth. For the society as a whole, the fact of discrimination is in itself not a problem, but rather a necessity. What is a problem is that such discrimination still very often happens on a basis other than function. This brings us to the question of equality.

A negative formulation of inclusion shows clearly that this structural pressure does not tend towards the actual equality of all human beings; quite the contrary. Inclusion indicates only that discrimination should follow functional criteria, not that everyone should be treated equally.[11] To take an economic example, inclusion means that only the amount of money I have should limit what I can own. It does not mean I will eventually have as much money as anyone else. And in fact, the modern world economy generates and even perpetuates vast inequalities just because it concentrates on the use and expansion of the functionally specific medium of money. Nonetheless, historically, and to a large degree as a direct result of the logic of inclusion, most if not all people in our world have come to see pronounced inequalities as a severe problem in modern global society; especially since the historical rise of instrumental priorities has been conditional upon more or less abandoning the old hierarchical values.

This ambiguity results in two seemingly contradictory directions for addressing the perceived problem. On the one hand are those who consider that the further augmentation of the functional instrumentalities will result in further inclusion of more and more people and hence in a lessening of inequalities. On the other hand, we have those equally convinced that further development of the present systems will only exacerbate inequalities, leading eventually to the collapse of the whole modern global edifice. What these rather radically different viewpoints have in common is that they both emphasize the typically modern and global value of inclusion through progress or, to use a more current term, empowerment. On the basis of the present analysis, however, it is not easy to say which is more correct since the structural reasons for inclusion point in either direction. Indeed, the ambiguity again points to the degree to which a dominance of functional subsystems leaves a great deal underdetermined, more so, perhaps, than in societies dominated by stratified or segmentary differentiation.

Formulating inclusion negatively as the absence of exclusion has correspondingly ambiguous implications for the place of the individual in modern society. If we no longer attribute all the actions of an individual to one subsystem as opposed to others, then individuals will appear in much sharper profile to the dominant features of their social environment. The more elaborate division of labour that accompanies the shift to functional differentiation also increases the variety of life circumstances possible for individuals. The result is the much discussed increase in the individuation of individuals. To the phenomenon of inclusion therefore corresponds a great increase in the *exclusivity* of personal lives, personal identities. Without the necessity of coordinating her or his choices with one dominant subsystem of society, the individual is left 'free' to develop in a larger variety of directions. The inclusion of all individuals in all subsystems therefore has as a direct consequence the greater mutual exclusivity of the same individuals. To deny legitimacy to this exclusivity is just as corrosive of functional dominance as negating inclusion. Moreover, because exclusivity can and does have collective manifestations, modern conditions thereby legitimize group identities, and by extension, socio-cultural particularisms; and this in many more ways than as the national identities of states. Modern society is, in this sense, inherently individualistic but also culturally pluralistic.[12] We value the independent individual and her or his freedom; but we also respect the self-determination of peoples and regret the decline of cultures.

The complementary relation of inclusion and exclusivity has a particularly important bearing on the problem of equality. Inclusion manifests itself in the expectation that most people will benefit from the dominant instrumentalities. When, as is so often the case, this does not happen or at least not to a sufficient degree, then it may be difficult to tell how much the failure is due to a violation of the postulate of inclusion/exclusivity and to what extent it is functionally rational. For example, the fact that the Kurds do not have a Kurdish state is in one sense a denial of their 'political rights', their 'right to self-determination'. But it is in all likelihood also a matter of political functionality for the states in which the Kurds live: not only would these states lose a substantial amount of territory and resources, but an independent Kurdistan would also open the door for further political fragmentation as other group exclusivities like the Armenians and Azerbaijanis sought to follow suit. Similarly, economic discrimination against various ethnic and racial exclusivities around the world is frequently a matter of simple inter-group prejudice; but as scholars such as Bonacich (1972), Hechter (1978), and Wallerstein (see above, Chapter 1) point out, it may also often make economic sense.

The structural source of inclusion thereby favours the equal legitimacy of exclusivities and identities based on them, along with the effort to express this legitimacy in greater access to the benefits of the functional systems for their members. But the functional rationalities of the various instrumental systems also often bring about discrimination against or in favour of certain groups in spite of inclusion. Subsequent chapters show how religion and specifically religious movements can under circumstances respond to this ambiguity in modern globalized structures.

Making the connection between inclusion/exclusivity and identity goes part of the way to understanding how socio-cultural particularisms fit more generally into global society. Identities, following a Luhmannian perspective, are, however, only simplifying self-descriptions (Luhmann, 1982: 324ff; 1984b: 360f). Whether we are talking about personal or social systems, they operate within that system to represent the system as a whole in distinction from its environment (cf. Luhmann, 1984b: 618). They can be instrumental in the control of what happens in the system and therefore the reproduction and change of that system. They are not, however, what constitutes the system as system. To understand the distinction better, I turn to an examination of the relation between the symbolic-expressive elements of social communication, including identities, and the systems in which they operate. This is the relation between culture and structure.[13]

Culture and Structure

I begin by looking more closely at the situation of the individual in modern society. As I have just said, heightened exclusivity means a great increase in the range of possibilities for how individuals constitute themselves in a single global society. In the abstract, the individual person must now select from a greater number of possibilities, and this with the relative certainty that, both locally and globally, other persons will select in a different way. The globalized functional subsystems do not provide the selection criteria for this personal determination in any complete way since they typically address only certain of the individual's actions. Because they are not hierarchically ordered, the subsystems may also push in contradictory directions. For instance, loyalties to one's career may conflict with health considerations, family ties, or political inclinations. These considerations apply to most people and not just those in the First World where the systems are strongest. In fact, they probably apply most to Third World people, especially migrants and elites.[14] The result is often a problem of identity or self-description for individuals, the perception that we are in insufficient control of our personal lives and our social world.

People therefore seek a way of pre-filtering or ordering the choices so that the problem becomes more manageable, so that identity appears less arbitrary (cf. Robertson, 1992b: Chapter 11). There are many possibilities. Identifications may proceed along highly idiosyncratic lines; or they may concentrate on one subsystem as opposed to others: a person may identify herself or himself with a career, as a family member, a member of a political unit, an economic class, or as a religious believer. She or he may also, however, combine specifications from a number of sources in a way that lets self-description vary according to situation or crisis. We can change self-descriptions as our contexts change, interpreting them as, perhaps, stages on life's way or the result of a virtuous ability to learn.[15]

Moreover, and critically for the present analysis, individuals can solve the problem of self-description with group identifications that are not, in the first instance, tied to any of the main functional subsystems. These include identification with a variety of social systemic manifestations, among them the close circle of friends, a multitude of voluntary organizations, and, perhaps most important, ethnic or racial groupings. Any of these, but especially the latter, can be the locus of the socio-cultural particularisms that are of central concern here. Their continued and even increasing salience in global society reflects, among other things, the problem of managing personal identities. To the extent that relativizing forces make themselves felt, individuals seek to orient themselves in our impersonal, global society through identification with a particular group and its specific culture. Those groups that are broadly ethnic in nature mediate a way of life whose character seems beyond individual disposition, even if, as is sometimes the case, they have been more recently invented or reconstructed (cf. Robertson, 1990b). We do not, after all, choose our parents and have little control over our socialization. The culture our parents pass on to us is the way 'we' do things and, through familiarity and trust, it feels right. In a continuously and often rapidly changing societal environment dominated by instrumental norms, such substantively normative cultures can provide continuity, and thus the perception of control and meaningful context.

Collective identities are, moreover, not necessarily just psychological coping strategies. As I have already discussed, inclusion does not lead automatically to significant, let alone equal, benefit from the dominant systems. Collective identities can therefore also be the base upon which to compete in global society, all the more so when the main criterion of a collectivity is inescapable or ascribed, as is the case with race and gender.

Nationalist movements often fit in this context, as do other forms like mutual aid associations, many religious movements, and 'rights' movements for women or racial minorities.

Although *Gemeinschaft*-like self-descriptions thus remain important in contemporary global society, they are far from unproblematic. To be sure, most people in the world today still live their lives to some extent under the aegis of some, often taken-for-granted, group culture. By the same token relatively few do so entirely. It would require a degree of communicative isolation from the power of the dominant subsystems that is at best difficult, even for radical sectarians or geographically isolated peoples. The critical question with regard to these cultural particularisms, however, is not whether or how much they dominate our lives, but how they fit into the dominant structures of global society. To put this another way, group cultures, like all culture, do not exist separately from specific social structures. To exist, they must be the thematic-expressive aspects of social systems. Only then can we speak of group identities that are not simply the observed or imagined aggregate of individual identities.[16] Only then can we know how we 'do' particular group cultures. We have to know how group cultures, and hence group identities, can become expressive of specific social systems in the modern global context.

More traditional sociological approaches to this question would perhaps use the distinction between *Gemeinschaft* and *Gesellschaft* (cf. Robertson, 1992a; and above, Chapter 1) or the parallel concepts of segmentary and functional systems here. The idea that global society contains numerous national societies is, of course, a variant of such an analysis. Strategies of this sort do not, however, get to the heart of the matter. They remain insufficient or at least unconvincing because they remain at the level of observation or self-description. Accordingly, they assume that some version of *Gemeinschaft* persists under conditions of modernity at the level of society as a whole. Whether this is called a national society, a societal community, or something else, the problem of group cultures in global society does not appear radically enough since the theory simply assumes the existence of structures that carry such cultures. The problem can then, at best, reveal itself as one of the relativization of cultures. The term clearly expresses the fact that group cultures are now in a different and perhaps more difficult situation; but it does not tell us enough about the changes that underlie it.

Again, a Luhmannian approach can be helpful here, but it too must go beyond the broad distinction between a dominance of stratified (or segmentary) and functional differentiation. Remaining at this level would mean that group particularisms could only exist at the margins of society as communicatively isolated enclaves, perhaps in the form of radical sectarian groups. Or they would have to become the cultural expression of one of the dominant subsystems, for instance in nation-states or as class identifiers in the economic system. Such a conclusion would be empirically inadequate simply because of the many instances in which group cultures survive and sometimes even thrive without such systemic immersion.

To go beyond the perspective of the dominant instrumental systems, we can begin by adapting a further Luhmannian distinction, that between three types of social system, namely interaction, organization, and society. Briefly, when people communicate with one another directly, usually face-to-face, we are dealing with interaction systems. Organizational systems operate with the distinction between members and non-members along with the rules that determine who is who. Society is the encompassing system in which the other two operate (cf. Luhmann, 1982: 69–89). To this point, it has been the primary focus of the analysis.

I leave aside numerous questions about this typology, such as whether or not it is exhaustive and how one is to conceive the status of subsystems of society. In the present context, it operates primarily to move the analysis of culture away from the level of self-descriptions to the level of social systems. A key aspect of Luhmann's typology is that, as societies become more complex – and modern society is much more complex than previous societies – these three types of social systems become more differentiated from each other. Society becomes less and less organizational, an idea that imposes itself especially if we accept that there is increasingly only one, global society. Further, in both organizations and society, much communication does not take place in interactions; and therefore neither consists simply of interactions. We have here another reason for the perceived 'impersonality' of modern society. Finally, because they no longer have to carry societal functions to such a large extent, interactions develop in comparatively independent directions. This aspect of the development is perhaps most evident in the rise of private, intimate relationships; but it also opens possibilities for broader group-cultural enclaves based on interactions. The total picture means that, in the modern context, we cannot easily transfer findings about one type of system to analyses of the others (cf. Luhmann, 1987b).

Under modern, globalizing conditions, then, group cultures can no longer assume the more undifferentiated situation of the past. More specifically, when we find a culture embodied in interactions, it does not follow automatically that the other types of social system are also going to be carriers of that culture. An illustration may serve to clarify the contrast. Today, interaction among upper-stratum members is no longer critical for reproducing primary societal divisions. Thus, for example, strategic marriages between elite families can no longer be the basis of political alliances, not because there are no more elite families, but because so much more than interaction among the elite carries political functions. Similarly, but in reverse, the culture of interactions can vary a great deal precisely because societal functions are no longer as dependent on them: thus we have cultural pluralism in many areas of the world, but also certain peculiar and stylized types of interaction, such as diplomatic interaction, which still do carry societal, in this case, political functions.

The modern differentiation of interaction and society is important since much of what we mean by group culture in fact refers to interactional settings:[17] not just what language we use but which variant of that language; where we meet and how we talk; the importance and meaning of bodily position and decoration; what food we eat together and how we eat it; and so forth. Accordingly, group culture often manifests itself in the regular interactions of social networks. Such a critical role within interaction systems does not, however, translate automatically into organizational relevance. To be sure, organizations in much of contemporary society provide a vital way of preserving and furthering group cultures. Modern organizations are intermediate forms that allow the systematization of any cultural complex in the form of membership rules. And the rules can make membership contingent on cultural or ethnic characteristics. They can help define what it means to be a member of the group, and make the promotion of the culture their express goal. Yet personal qualification or participation in interaction networks usually does not make one automatically a member. People more often than not belong to organizations voluntarily; and this, of course, includes religious organizations. Organizations can carry group culture and group identity, but they are more than simply an extension of social interaction networks.[18]

Finally, a group culture that manifests itself in interactions and organizations does not thereby already become the culture of societal systems. Given the dominance of functional subsystem differentiation here, for a group culture to be the symbolic expression of society means that it will most likely inform one or more of the principal subsystems; but this means conforming to the functionally specialized norms and values of these systems. Cultures closely associated with past societies or with interaction networks will be significantly transformed if they become embodied in these systems. There is in fact only a limited sense in which the operations of a state, for instance, can be typically Japanese or typically American, because the demands of functional efficiency will temper the traditional cultural style.[19] We arrive here at a key socio-structural reason for the relativization of particularisms in global society, for the difficulty of 'modernizing' without 'westernizing'. It is more than a matter of cultural conflict, of the side-by-side of different worldviews; it is also the structural and cultural recontextualization of any culture dependent on a less complex society with closer entanglement of the three types of social system.

Such change is not the only difficulty, however. There is also the differentiation of these systems themselves. The differences between them make it more likely that group cultures will become relevant in some of these and not others. Earlier in this chapter, I outlined how group cultures in the form of nations and nationalism have been particularly salient in the segmented global political system. Then there is the often close relationship between group culture and art. And, as I discuss in subsequent chapters, religion is another functional sphere that establishes a symbiotic relationship between cultural particularism and functional sphere. On the other hand, it is far less likely that a similar relationship will obtain between group cultures and other subsystems, notably the scientific and economic.

Here is not the place for exploring these different possibilities in greater detail. What is, however, important to underline is that incarnation in one subsystem does not already make a group culture the culture of all the other ones, unless one is willing to identify society with one of its subsystems. In particular, the politicizing of ethnic cultures – or even the political attempt to create them – for the purposes of legitimizing states is not the same as establishing national societies. To be sure, state action can potentially condition all communication within its boundaries: all things can be politicized. Yet to move from this fact to assert that there is therefore a group culture coterminous with society as a whole in a particular state is to confuse the self-conception of a state with what actually happens within its boundaries. It is especially unconvincing to claim that individuals have their identities mediated through the self-conceptions of states; that they are, for instance, members of 'societal communities' where membership is identical with citizenship. Certainly many people will identify themselves primarily as citizens of a particular state; but more, in most cases, will locate their identities in different boundaries, usually within, but increasingly often also beyond, those of the state. Within Canada, for instance, I may be an intense Canadian nationalist deeply devoted to the furtherance of a multicultural, binational country. I may also be a *Québécois* nationalist as dedicated to the independence of *Québec*. More likely, however, my primary identification will be in my personal life, my family, my internationalized profession, the old country, my economic class, my religion, or any number of other places. National concerns may occasionally be the focus of my attention; but more often than not, they will be as fleeting as those of the global economy, nuclear physics, or international sport.

The multidirectional possibilities for embedding a particular group culture in the global societal system are not exhausted after we have looked at the different instrumental subsystems. At the level of society, there is at least one other significant possibility, and that is the social movement. Beside the state, the economic enclave, the legal system, and the religious tradition, an ethnic culture can also become the thematic or expressive aspect of social systems that constitute themselves through mobilization, usually toward specific goals. The most obvious examples are ethno-nationalist movements such as among the Palestinians, the Tamils, the Basques, or the Jews. But the category also includes other ethnic movements not directed toward the forming of a state, such as among American Blacks or the Acadians in Canada. In Chapter 4, I deal somewhat more extensively with the relation between religion and social movements; and therefore leave further discussion of the latter to that chapter. Here, however, the reference to social movements leads us to consider more closely what relevance the various themes of this chapter have for the understanding of religion in global society.

Religion and Socio-cultural Particularism

The upshot of this chapter is that group cultures or socio-cultural particularisms operate in a very much changed socio-structural context in global society. They no longer hold the self-evident position they did in societies dominated by segmentary or hierarchical differentiation. While their position is thus ambiguous and to some extent disadvantaged, they still constitute important phenomena in this modern context. Their most visible manifestation is in nation-states; but these, as I have tried to show, are not the only possibilities for group cultures to become salient forces in our social lives.

The justification for these elaborate analyses has been, on the one hand, to further our theoretical understanding of the process of globalization. On the other hand, however, the place of socio-cultural particularisms has both direct and indirect importance for understanding how religion fits into the global picture. It is to this matter that I now turn.

As already mentioned more than once, historically there has been a close relation between group culture and religion. Bryan Wilson expresses this idea succinctly when he claims that 'the basic function of religion, and the locus of its operation, exists in the community' (1976: 265), by which he means, in the terms I have been using here, that religion is a mode of relating to the world that thrives in traditional, especially segmented societies, and not in modern, instrumentally-dominated society. Therefore, inasmuch as the cultures expressing those 'communitarian' structures of the past are now faced with a very different context, so too is religion. But – and here is the critical point – just as the real or imagined successors to those cultures are now manifesting themselves in different ways, in different social structures, so might we expect religion or, more concretely, religious people to adopt similar strategies: we should expect religious survival and revival to manifest itself in similar ways to group-cultural or ethnic survival and revival. Specifically, under modern, global conditions, to the degree that a religious tradition is seen as part and parcel of a particular group culture, to that degree religion will bear a relation to exclusive identities and to the different types of social system similar to that borne by group cultures. The latter hypothesis applies especially to the political system and social movements.

With religion, however, there is a very significant complicating factor. Unlike group culture, religion is more than an ecology of themes for social communication. It is also a specific way of communicating: religion is not just cultural, it is also (at least potentially) systemic. As such, like political, legal, economic, artistic, and other ways of communicating, it can be and to a large extent is the locus of a differentiated instrumental subsystem of modern global society. The analysis of religion must therefore proceed along a double track, one following its similarity and identification with group culture, another its character as a societal subsystem. Religion, in other words, like the political system, is a social sphere that manifests both the socio-cultural particular and the global universal.

Religion, however, is not politics, because and in spite of the fact that both have been the most frequent subjects of institutional or functional differentiation even in pre-modern societies. The analysis of religion in global society therefore cannot parallel the analysis of politics and the state. In order to sort out the specific way that religion locates itself as both the particular and the universal, I turn in the next chapter to a closer look at systemic religion in global society. To begin that analysis, I focus on the notion of privatization. This concept, unlike the closely related idea of secularization, succinctly expresses the twin fate of religion: a way of communicating that, in one sense, thrives under modern global conditions but, in another sense, carries with it the disprivileged status of a way of relating to the world somehow at odds with modernity. This closer look at the idea of privatization then opens the door to a wider view of the prospects for systemically based, publicly influential religion in global society.

Notes

1 Giddens (1987) offers a related analysis of this shift in the nature of territorial limits by contrasting traditional 'frontiers' with modern 'boundaries'.

2 For more detailed and comprehensive analyses, see, as examples, Bendix, 1977; Elias, 1982; Giddens, 1987; Tilly, 1975; Wallerstein, 1974a.

3 In phrasing the matter this way, I do not imply that the economic developments *caused* the political ones. Indeed, the beginnings of a functionally differentiated political system in medieval European society probably preceded the rise of capitalism and were driven more by developments in the church than in the economy. See Chirot, 1986: 11ff.; Giddens, 1987: 83ff.; Poggi, 1978.

4 See Levenson, 1967 for an instructive comparison with China. Until the fifteenth century, China led Western Europe in technological sophistication and the expansion of trade. The Chinese imperial centre, however, reined in both trends because it feared the rise of rival political (redistributive) centres and because, unlike the European states of a century later, it had no need for the fruits of such developments to maintain its power.

5 Robertson (1989a) makes a similar point when he distinguishes universal form from particular content in national societies. One of my prime purposes here is to dissolve analytically the overly hypostatic notion of national society and recombine its various aspects in a more complex picture that avoids equating the construction of globally contextualized identities with the process of globalization itself.

6 See the discussion of liberation theology in Chapter 6, below.

7 Compare Simmel's similar analysis of 'worlds' of human experience and culture in Simmel, 1959; and Weber's discussion of spheres of value in Weber, 1946.

8 Weber's 'iron cage' argument (Weber, 1958: 181) is perhaps the best-known version. Among the many others, the Frankfurt School, from Adorno to Habermas (Adorno and Horkheimer, 1972; Habermas, 1984; 1987), has engaged in an analogous critique of the increasing hegemony of instrumental rationality. Ellul's scathing critique of 'technique' in general, politics in particular, and even 'religion' is another outstanding example. See Ellul, 1964; 1967; 1983.

9 To a limited extent, the distinction discussed here is the same as the distinction between privatized and public action. This latter dichotomy and its relevance to contemporary religion is the subject of more detailed analysis below in Chapter 3.

10 Thus, to take what seem to be counterexamples, under Israeli law, naturalized citizenship is available to non-Jews; and even South Africa developed the fiction of independent Bantustans to deny South African citizenship to its Black majority.

11 In this context, Wallerstein's analysis of the 'functionality' of gender, ethnic, and racial discrimination in the modern world-economy makes sense. See above, Chapter 1.

12 Compare Lechner's (1989) defence of the idea that globalizing conditions legitimate both institutionalized individualism and institutionalized societalism.

13 What precisely these are and where one ends and the other begins is a subject of somewhat endless debate in sociology. Here cannot be the place for dealing with this matter in detail. How I am using these terms will, I hope, be relatively clear in the section that follows.

14 Recall Rushdie's remark, quoted at the beginning of the Introduction, about the 'mutability of character'.

15 Following Meyer (1987), the idea of a structured life course in modern society helps individuals deal with these changes. In the terms I am using here, this would be a way of controlling the range and change of personal exclusivities so as best to coordinate them with the requirements of the dominant functional subsystems. For a critique of the Luhmannian position on this matter of fluctuating identities as freedom, but from an explicitly theological point of view, see Scholz, 1981.

16 Such group identities are also not simply the product of outside observation. Marx, for instance, was careful to define class as a specific relationship to a mode of production which was then the basis of class identity or consciousness. The looser use of class as for example in the idea of 'lower middle class' is perhaps a useful construct for describing an aspect of a stratification system; but we need more if we are to call it a social system with a specific culture and self-description.

17 Rainer Baum (1980) makes a similar point in referring to the problem of connecting globally homogeneous political systems with particularistic 'styles of communal social interaction' or 'systems of solidarities' (= group-cultural particularisms).

18 The vast literature on ethnicity and the maintenance or loss of ethnic culture and identity, especially in culturally plural countries like the United States and Canada, is of immediate relevance here. For an overview of recent literature, see Yinger, 1985. For an outline of the field, albeit with specific focus on Canada, see Driedger, 1989.

19 This is what I take it Meyer means when he says that modern states operate to a large degree in terms of a world culture. It is the culture of the global political system that is operating here, often overriding local cultural traditions. See above, Chapter 1.

3

SYSTEMIC RELIGION
IN GLOBAL SOCIETY

Privatization and Public Influence of Religion

Since at least the 1960s, many sociologists have put forward the notion that religion, at least in the contemporary Western world, has become increasingly privatized. Most prominently, Talcott Parsons (1960; 1966: 134), Peter Berger (1967: 133f.), Thomas Luckmann (1967: 103), and Robert Bellah (1970a: 43) interpreted secularization in the modern world to mean that traditional religion was now primarily the concern of the individual and had therefore lost much of its 'public' relevance. People were voluntary adherents to a plurality of religions, none of which could claim practically to be binding on any but its own members.

Beyond this core idea, however, there are important variants of the privatization thesis. In particular, Parsons and Bellah relocate 'public' religion in *cultural* forms such as American civil religion or Marxism (see Bellah, 1970b; Parsons, 1974: 203ff). Here privatization characterizes only traditional, systemic religions. By contrast, Berger and Luckmann talk about private and public 'spheres', locating religion only in the former. They have a somewhat different idea of what counts as religion, favouring the systemic or institutionally specialized forms.

Aside from the question of variants, the privatization thesis is also part of the larger secularization debate. Privatization, as such, is not a central item for all participants in this debate. Yet, whether it is Roland Robertson's emphasis on individuation (Robertson, 1977), Bryan Wilson's focus on the loss of community (Wilson, 1976), or Richard Fenn's analysis of the lack of moral unity (Fenn, 1978), the critical core of the privatization thesis is implicitly present: traditional religious forms are no longer definitive for the society as a whole, but can still direct the lives of individuals or subgroups. Equally important, however, is the well-known disagreement among scholars about the meaning and validity of the secularization thesis itself. Does it mean a decline in the salience of religion as a human form of expression (see for example Wilson, 1982)? Does it mean only the compartmentalization or relocation of religion as the privatization thesis suggests? Or is it merely the expression of the cyclical decline of established religions followed by the rise of new or revitalized ones (see for example Stark and Bainbridge, 1985)? The first two positions imply that secularization is a result of the modernization of Western society and therefore unique to that historical process. The third view sees secularization as something that characterizes religion at all times and in all societies, and therefore has little to do with modernization as such.

Here is not the place to discuss these various options in any detail. I have introduced them because they point to ambiguity in the phenomenon, namely the place, importance, and form of religion in the contemporary social world. The privatization thesis has been one way of dealing with this ambiguity, and I believe an instructive one. In this chapter, I use it as the starting point for examining religion in the global context. How can the privatization thesis be used to understand better the role of religion in modern global society? As indicated in the previous chapter, my aim is to show that privatization is not the whole story but rather only a part of it. Specifically, the thesis that I explore here posits that the globalization of society, while structurally favouring privatization in religion, also provides fertile ground for the renewed public influence of religion. By public influence, I mean that one or more religions can become the source of collective obligation, such that deviation from specific religious norms will bring in its wake negative consequences for adherents and non-adherents alike; and collective action in the name of these norms becomes legitimate. In the light of the analyses of the previous chapter, the operative question is of course whether this is possible through functionally oriented, institutionally specialized, subsystemic communication; or whether religion will take the route of socio-cultural particularisms and become an important cultural resource for other types of system and other subsystems.

This thesis depends on a specific analysis of privatization. Therefore, I begin by examining the idea of privatization as it has been used in the contemporary sociological discussion of religion in modern society. I contend that, far from being immediately illuminating, the concept can easily lead to confusion; and that, to a limited extent, a way out of this confusion is offered by Luhmann's analysis of privatization. The Luhmannian distinctions used in this analysis are those between professional and complementary social roles and between religious function and performance. I explain these terms and my adaptation of them later. I argue that, insofar as privatization refers to the rise of pluralistic and voluntary religion among individuals, the basic structures in modern global society encourage it. These structures, however, do not in themselves undermine the possibility of publicly influential religion.

The problem of public influence is then broken up into three interconnected arguments. First I argue that, if institutional religion is to be publicly influential, it is not enough that there be a high level of individual religiosity which adherents then translate into religiously inspired public action. It is also not enough that religious leaders and professionals form and concentrate that religiosity in organizations and movements which institutionalize religion. What is required for publicly influential religion is, at a minimum, that religious leaders have control over a service that is clearly indispensable in today's world as do, for instance, health professionals, political leaders, scientific or business experts. Second, the structures of modern/global society greatly weaken most of the ways that religious leaders have accomplished this before. In this regard, the focal point in this chapter is that a global society has no outsiders who can serve as the social representatives of evil, danger, or chaos. Without these, the forces of order and good also become more difficult to identify *at the level of global society as a whole*, undermining or relativizing, for instance, deontological moral codes and the salience of other-worldly salvation. Third, therefore, religion will have a comparatively difficult time in gaining public influence as a differentiated functional system, that is, at the level of global society as a whole; but such influence will be easier to attain if religious leaders apply traditional religious modalities for the purpose of subsocietal, especially political mobilization in response to the globalization of society. In terms of the question posed above, therefore, privatization applies to religion in global society if we look at it as a functional subsystem; public influence for religion is possible primarily when, like socio-cultural particularisms, it takes on the role of cultural resource for other systems.

The Inherited Privatization Thesis

As already mentioned, scholars have formulated the privatization thesis in various ways. Three such variants are germane to the present discussion: that of Berger and Luckmann, that of Parsons, and that of Luhmann. They each have different contributions to make.

A critical problem for the use of 'public' and 'private' in social theory concerns the question of how the boundary between the two is to be conceived. We do not answer this question but only shift it by talking about private and public 'spheres'. Berger and Luckmann both address this problem by tying the private/public distinction to the individual/society distinction. What is private is a matter primarily for individual disposition while what is public concerns society as a whole or at least a larger segment of society. In addition, the private sphere is manifest in certain institutions and not others. Notably, it manifests itself in religion, the family, and what Luckmann calls 'secondary institutions', that is, intermediate associations that reinforce private, individual identities (Luckmann, 1967: 106; Berger, 1967: 133; 1977: 5ff.). The public sphere, by contrast, is primarily the realm of economic and political institutions that exhibit a high degree of specialization and functional rationalization.

The argument is clear enough, but matters cannot rest here. Privatization refers to the fact that religion is a matter primarily of *individual* disposition. Individual choice, however, is not a characteristic of modernity only when it comes to religion, the family, and voluntary associations (see specifically Berger, 1979: 1–29 on this point). Career choices, economic consumer choices, and political preferences are also matters of individual choice. The private sphere, from this vantage point, is evidently also a vital part of the public sphere. Moreover, if what is specific about the public sphere is functional rationality, then modern religion and families are also not without public traits. Most religious organizations, for instance, conform to the standards of bureaucratic efficiency; and the modern family applies rational technique to everything from child-raising and household finance to saving a marriage. Institutions in the public sphere have privatized features; and those in the private sphere have public ones. Such equivocal references make it difficult to use the public/private distinction in a consistent and clear way. In this form, it is therefore ambiguous and incomplete;[1] but it is not useless.

What Berger and Luckmann attempt to do is to use the single private/public distinction to analyse both a new individual/society relation in modernity and the effect of modern social structures on religion. Central to their argument is that functionally oriented institutional differentiation and a corresponding functional rationalization within these institutional domains have led to the relatively greater isolation of the individual from dominant social structures. I have presented a similar position in the previous chapter. In addition, Berger and Luckmann assert that institutional religion cannot compete in the new structural environment and therefore weakens, leaving the religious task of constructing and guaranteeing holistic meaning systems primarily with the individual and a multitude of voluntary organizations. Taken separately, these two portions of their argument are entirely defensible, and inform the thinking of others in the wider secularization debate (such as Wilson, Fenn, Parsons, and Luhmann). Taken together, they also point out that these various features of modern society are closely connected. Their position[2] is insufficient, however, because the concept of a private sphere implies that there is in fact one institutional sphere, the private one, in which the individual is more solidly embedded than in the public sphere. As I have said above, this implication leads to confusion. If the notion of privatization of religion as a feature of modernity is to be useful, this conceptual ambiguity has to be overcome.

As noted, Parsons offered his own variant of the privatization thesis, one that does not use the concepts of private and public spheres, but retains institutional differentiation and functional rationalization as core attributes of modernity. For Parsons, privatization of traditional, institutional religion is not the result of a discordance between functional rationality and religious 'irrationality'. Rather the religious pluralism of modern society, combined with the necessity of including all the adherents to this plurality of religions in the societal community, precludes any one of the particular, traditional religions from becoming the publicly binding religion. Hence, religious adherence becomes a voluntary, private matter. In tune with Durkheim, however, Parsons believes that the presence of one public religion provides the basic values necessary for the integration of a society. Parsons finds the requisite publicly binding religion in Bellah's concept of civil religion and 'atheistic' rivals such as Marxism (see Bellah, 1970b; Parsons, 1966: 134ff; 1974: 203ff.).

What Parsons has done, essentially, is to distinguish public (civil) and privatized religion on the basis of value generalization. Public religion abstracts from privatized, institutional religions those cultural values that most people in a society can agree on; in the American case, for instance, instrumental activism. The individual operates in public with the general-ized values and keeps the non-generalizable ones of her or his particular tradition to herself or himself. In his variant of the privatization thesis, Parsons thereby avoids the ambiguity in Berger and Luckmann's version. Yet Parsons also introduces a different ambiguity that Berger and Luck-mann avoid.

Much of the contrast between the two variants has to do with divergent concepts of religion, but not in a simple way. For example, Luckmann's definition is at least as functionally oriented and as broad as that of Parsons, and yet Luckmann resists calling highly generalized cultural value patterns religion. The critical issue lies in the problem of generalization. The question is, at what level of generalization do religious values cease to be capable of determining social action without further religious or non-religious specification?[3] Parsons evidently believes that civil religion has not yet reached this point (see 1966: 135f.).[4] Berger (1967: 134) disagrees. He, for instance, confirms the existence of this public religion, but denies its reality. True religion, following Rousseau's discussion of civil religion, is a private matter of the heart; public religion, with its highly generalized and undemanding character, is for Berger at best watery truth.

The key to the disagreement becomes clearer when the above question is rephrased: At what level of generalization does it become difficult or impossible to embody religious values in specialized institutions? Luck-mann's analysis of privatization centres on this matter, on the fate of, as he calls it, 'official' religion in modern society. To the extent that there is a unified religious value system, a 'modern sacred cosmos', it 'no longer rests on institutions specializing in the maintenance and transmission of a sacred universe', or on other 'specialized institutional areas whose main functions are not religious', such as the state or the economic system (Luckmann, 1967: 103). Civil religion has no clear institutional expression in modern society and hence cannot serve as the new public religion that replaces the now privatized religions.[5] What Luckmann is in effect saying is that modern conditions undermine the influence of a specialized religious subsystem of society; religion remains as private (invisible) choice and as religio-culture (cf. Robertson, 1992b: 96).

The difference, therefore, is similar to the basic question that informs this chapter: Can religion assert public influence in global society as societal system or only as cultural resource for other systems? Berger and Luckmann resist counting the latter as public religion. Parsons does not, while he admits systemic privatization. Moreover, the debate has significance for the relation of religion and globalization. Robertson, for instance, essentially adopts the Parsonian stand. His model of globalization sees the 'civil religious' modality as crucial to how 'societies' negotiate their identities in the global field (see especially 1992b: Chapter 5). The state provides critical systemic or institutional support in this enterprise and that fact leads to the 'politicization of theology and religion . . . and the "theologization" of politics' (Robertson and Chirico, 1985: 238). Yet Robertson also recognizes a possible role for systemic religion in these negotiations. The latter sort of religion is the more central focus of the present study. To understand better its relation to the issue of privatization, public influence, and religion as a cultural resource, I turn to Luhmann's contribution to the debate.

A Luhmannian View

In key ways, Luhmann's social theory agrees with that of Parsons, Berger, and Luckmann. All four see functional or institutional differentiation and pluralistic individual identities as basic features of modern society. The institutional spheres, which Luhmann calls functionally differentiated societal subsystems, specialize around specific kinds of actions, for instance, political or economic. Secularization is the consequence of the relative independence of these subsystems from religious norms, values, and justifications. Luhmann, however, goes on to say that, in this socio-structural setting, religion not only retreats somewhat from many important aspects of social life, but also comes under persistent pressure to develop an institutionally specialized subsystem of its own. As with Berger, Luckmann, and Parsons, traditional religion suffers the fate of compartmentalization, but, with Luhmann, in principle not more so than other major functional areas of life, such as the political and economic ones.

The Luhmannian position begins to make a distinct contribution to the privatization debate when one looks at a central structural feature of these societal subsystems: the differentiation of 'professional' and 'complementary' roles (see Luhmann, 1982: 236; Dobbelaere 1985: 381ff.). These roles are critical for structuring the relations of individuals to the main institutional domains. In the communally structured societies of the past, individuals belonged to specific status groups. Such membership largely predetermined access to societal functions: access to wealth, power, knowledge, religious status. To a great extent, it also determined the 'professions' a person could follow, a feature expressed in the older meaning of words like 'estate' or 'station' (cf. Luhmann, 1977: 236ff.). In modern, functionally structured society, this way of determining the access of individuals to societal functions becomes problematic because it negates that dominance of functional differentiation which is so characteristic of modern society. How, for instance, can economic rationality dominate in the economy if, not only the ability to pay, but also group membership, determines who can be a customer?

If functionally specialized subsystems are to be the prime structural features of a society instead of communal status groups, then status-group membership cannot on its own determine access to societal functions. Something else has to do this. Accordingly, modern society has developed what Luhmann calls complementary social roles. As in past societies, an individual usually only occupies one of the specialized professional roles such as doctor, politician, entrepreneur, or priest; but now she or he also occupies an inclusive set of complementary roles such as patient, voter, consumer, or believer, one for each subsystem. These mediate access to the benefits of functions. Since, however, unlike with professional roles, the same person can occupy all these complementary roles, the functional interference implicit in this concentration presents a problem similar to group membership: it threatens the relative independence of the major functional subsystems. It is apparently too much to expect individuals to neutralize this implicit interference themselves in any consistent way. Individual persons do not necessarily divide their consciousness in the same way that society divides its communication.[6] A functional equivalent is therefore found in the statistical neutralization, as it were, of the consequences of this interference. We come to see many of the decisions involved in these complementary roles as a 'private' as opposed to a 'public' matter. Such privatization of decision-making accepts that we sometimes do consume according to religious conviction or cast our vote on the basis of aesthetic criteria; but such overlapping is in principle nobody's business but our own. Hence, the individual pattern of interference becomes more difficult to communicate to others to the point of social – as opposed to personal – significance.

Focusing on complementary roles does not solve the problem of the boundary between the public and the private. The roles themselves are very much public; and it is only the way that an individual combines decisions within those roles that is privatized. For example, the norms associated with being a student are quite clear and public. My decision to study this and not that, to strive for this or that mark, these things are my private affair. Up to a point. Obviously, I must act in some minimally rational way from the point of view of the educational system if I am to continue to benefit from it. Where the line is between the two varies and can easily become a political issue; that is, it can and does become the matter of collectively binding decisions. Yet there remains a range of personal, private decisions whose internal logic need not conform to the priorities of any functional subsystem. My 'lifestyle' or my 'personality' can and do affect how I perform my complementary roles, lending these a measure of legitimate unpredictability, and forming the basis of my 'freedom' and 'equality'. Privatization is evidently another manifestation of the inclusion/exclusivity syndrome discussed in the last chapter.

From the Luhmannian point of view, then, privatization of decision-making is a consequence of central structural features of modern society. In principle, it does not refer more to religion than it does to politics or the economy. The forces of privatization are just as much at work in the 'public' sphere of political action as they are in the 'private' sphere of religion. Especially in Western, First World portions of global society, individuals voluntarily choose their religious convictions and practices as well as their political ideas and actions. These may include membership in a church or party, but need not. A person may vote regularly or may not; she or he may pray or not. Given that few if any observers would claim that such privatization makes politics a minor player in global society, it is therefore insufficient to claim that religious communication must decline in societal (that is, public) importance simply because of the privatization of much complementary role decision-making.

Religious Leadership and Publicly Influential Religion

In the Luhmannian scheme, a corresponding professionalization of public action is as important as the privatization of complementary role decision-making. The much discussed rise of the expert in modern society reflects a socio-structural situation in which professionals become the prime public representatives of societal subsystems. Typical features of professional roles illustrate this capacity. We judge professionals on their ability to perform the function of the specific systems they represent: politicians on their ability to get collectively binding decisions made; business people on their ability to produce marketable goods and services; doctors on their ability to heal illness; priests on their ability to inspire faith. We also expect professionals to follow more or less defined codes of ethics specific to their profession. These codes circumscribe the general limits of professional action and, in particular, seek to prevent the kind of interference that is typical of complementary roles. The private tendencies of a professional should not interfere with the efficient public execution of his or her profession. A teacher should not permit sexual attraction to enter into the teaching and evaluation of a student. A scientist should not allow potential financial gain to influence the results of his or her research. These are examples of 'conflicts of interest' and professionals ought not to fulfil their professional roles when such conflict does in fact occur. The normative rules of professional competence and professional ethics both stress functional, systemic priorities in professional action. They help to differentiate personal identities, including group identities, from what the institutional system does; and so reinforce the relative independence of both the social systems and the individuals involved in them. Nevertheless, real people occupy professional roles. Much more than complementary roles, they concretize the abstract system in human form.

To be sure, societal subsystems do not consist of professional action alone. Privatized, complementary action is still an indispensable part of the system and has its own, far less stringent, norms. Doctors without patients, ministers without believers, politicians without a public, make no sense. Yet, because professionals more closely represent what each system is all about, the public importance of a system rises or falls with the public influence of its professionals.

The meaning of this hypothesis, of course, depends on the meaning of public influence. I have given a brief definition above and treat this topic in greater detail in the section on 'Globalization and Religion' below. Here it is enough to say that public influence refers to the level of importance professional action has outside the narrower audience of fellow professionals and voluntarily associated members of the public. Privatization of religion would then, in a Luhmannian view of the matter, translate into a combination of privatized decision-making in matters of religion *plus* a relative decline in the public influence of the public representatives of the religious system, the professionals or leaders. Admittedly, the organizations and movements that the professionals lead are also implied in this statement. Yet focusing on the leaders has the advantage of providing some real social actors who actually do things. Their actions and attitudes can be examined and compared with those of the general public, religious and otherwise.

An illustration at this point serves to concretize the argument somewhat and provides a transition to the next stage of the discussion. The issue of professional and, therefore, system influence manifested itself well in the controversy, a few years ago, over the possibility of 'cold fusion'. From the narrower viewpoint of science, the work of Professors Stanley Pons and Martin Fleischmann may have been of great significance. It challenged some important prevailing assumptions in the fields of chemistry and physics. Yet what vaulted this issue onto the front pages of the world's newspapers was not the disputed scientific discovery as such, but its potential implications for everyone, including those uninvolved in science. The potential *applications* of this bit of pure scientific research are what gave it its overriding public importance. And by extension, it is such far-reaching applications that lend the scientists and the entire science system their public influence. If 'cold fusion' eventually withstands the onslaught of scientific scrutiny, individuals, corporations, institutions, and countries that ignore or deny the new scientific norm would face possible negative sanctions ranging from loss of prestige to economic downturn. Even though Pons and Fleischmann may well have been wrong, the episode demonstrates the power of the system that they represent as professionals.

The question for religion and religious leaders is, under what circumstances will we all listen to the new revelation or the revival of the old? The answer cannot lie in religion doing what science does, what the economy does, or what any of the other specialized functional spheres do for us. The effectiveness of this specialization, what Parsons called adaptive upgrading, is, after all, one of the key benefits of the socio-structural shift to functional differentiation. The answer must therefore lie within the domain of religion itself. Like science, the economy, or the health system, religion must provide a service that not only supports and enhances the religious faith of its adherents, but also can impose itself by having far-reaching implications outside the strictly religious realm.

Part, but only part, of the answer lies in the strength of the religious institutions themselves. A great deal of social-scientific research has focused on the number of adherents and their degree of involvement in religious organizations and movements as critical measures of religious vitality. Another established research tradition has centred on measuring how 'religious' people are in today's world.[7] Indeed, individual religiosity and organizational strength are essential if systemic religion is to be a viable social force at all. Nevertheless, if the influence of religion is to go beyond the organizations and their immediate adherents, more has to happen. It is in this context that contemporary religio-political and religio-social movements are of particular interest. They are explicit attempts to create the sort of public influence for religion that I am talking about. Whether in Latin America, North America, the Middle East, or elsewhere, these movements and their leaders assert that religious norms and values must to some degree become collectively obligatory, that they go beyond the choices of individuals. These movements imply that religion offers a service that is necessary for everyone, and that is not the same or similar to what is offered, for instance, by the economic sphere or the scientific sphere.

The critical problem, of course, is to know what, sociologically, this essential religious service is. Answers such as 'ultimate meaning' (Parsons, Bellah, Berger) or 'compensators for unavailable rewards' (Stark and Bainbridge) beg the question as to whether and under what social conditions these things are essential. These needs are in any case easily enough filled through privatized religion. Claiming that religion integrates societies, as does the Durkheimian tradition in sociology, makes the empirically unwarranted assumption that religion necessarily performs this task. I address this issue in some detail in the section on 'Globalization and Religion' below. Before proceeding to this task, however, I want to introduce a further Luhmannian distinction that plays an important role in subsequent arguments because it separates two different and yet closely related aspects of what I have called the religious service: the purely religious aspect and the implications this service might have for other, non-religious social action. This distinction is already implicit in many of the preceding arguments about the possibility for public influence of religion in modern society.

Function and Performance

As noted, for Luhmann, the central structural feature of modern and global society is differentiation on the basis of function. Institutional spheres cluster around particular kinds of social communication or action on the basis of relatively autonomous functional instrumentalities. These subsystems include polity, law, economy, science, religion, education, art, health, and the family. The autonomy that each of them exhibits is real enough, but it is heavily conditioned by the fact that the other systems are also operating in the same social milieu. The above discussion of complementary and professional roles outlined a central structural feature of this 'both autonomous and conditioned'. One important logical deduction from this theoretical position is that there is a difference between how a subsystem relates to the society as a whole and how it relates to other social systems, especially other subsystems. Luhmann analyses the former in terms of *function* and the latter in terms of *performance*. In the present context, function refers to 'pure' religious communication, variously called the aspect of devotion and worship,[8] the cure of souls, the search for enlightenment or salvation. Function is the pure, 'sacred' communication involving the transcendent and the aspect that religious institutions claim for themselves, the basis of their autonomy in modern society. Religious performance, by contrast, occurs when religion is 'applied' to problems generated in other systems but not solved there, or simply not addressed elsewhere (cf. Luhmann, 1977: 54ff.; 1982: 238–242). Examples of such problems are economic poverty, political oppression, familial estrangement, environmental degradation, or personal identity. Through performance relations, religion establishes its importance for the 'profane' aspects of life; but in the process, non-religious concerns impinge upon pure religiousness, demonstrating the fact that other societal concerns condition the autonomy of religious action.

Function and performance are more than analytic categories dependent on Luhmannian theory for their importance. A real tension exists between the two. Historically, various religious institutions have sought to effect a clear separation between them. In Weber's terms, ascetic and mystic rejections of the world have sought to eliminate mundane demands from the purely sacred realm.[9] The medieval church considered the ascetic monk on a surer road to salvation than those immersed in profane life; the elder Hindu, having completed his duty of raising his family, retired to the forest for the proper pursuit of religious goals. Nevertheless, function and performance are also inseparable and mutually reinforcing. Indeed, it is only in modern society and in the leisured upper strata of some traditional societies that the two become clearly differentiated at all. Buddhism, for instance, only became a widespread and mass religion as it compromised its religious purity and made itself suitable for life in the everyday world. In modern times, the practical Catholic orders involved in education, social welfare, and health care were instrumental in allowing the Roman church to maintain its influence in predominantly Catholic areas such as Latin America, Quebec, and the Netherlands (see, for example, Beyer, 1989; Coleman, 1979; Levine, 1981; Mainwaring, 1986).

This last example illustrates the critical importance of performance relations for religion in the modern world. As the example of Pons and Fleischmann from the science system implies, the *functional* problem of religion in the modern world is actually a *performance* problem. Therefore, if 'pure' religion is at a disadvantage in modern global society, if there is pressure toward the increasing privatization of religion, then the solution lies in finding effective religious 'applications', not in more religious commitment and practice.

But why should religion be at such a disadvantage? Why is performance a problem? The answers to these questions are certainly not simple; yet a key aspect is the peculiarity of the religious function itself. Here I refer to the holism of religion, its effort to determine the whole of existence through the possibility of communication with a posited transcendent. In the terms used in the previous chapter, religion is a mode of communication that styles itself as at once totalizing *and* encompassing. This encompassing holism leads to at least two distinct but interrelated problems under modern, globalizing conditions. On the one hand, it runs counter to the specialized and instrumental pattern of the other dominant functional systems. More concretely, the major applications dominated by religious experts in the past – for example collective knowledge, writing, higher education, healing – have largely been upgraded and taken over by the experts of other functional domains. Religion's general applicability in societies without a primacy of functional system differentiation turns out, under modern structural conditions, to be a disadvantage. On the other hand, holism lends itself well to the establishment, maintenance, and regulation of clear social boundaries. But as I have argued above, especially in the discussion on territoriality, modern conditions produce a variety of mutually crosscutting boundaries that is difficult or impossible to coordinate, religiously or otherwise, except at the level of the globe itself.

These two dimensions require further elaboration. I leave a more detailed discussion of the first to the following chapter. Here I concentrate on the second because it addresses very directly the problematic relation between religion as a mode of communication and the modern globalization of society.

Globalization and Religion

Further consideration can begin with a brief look at the role morality plays in the relation between religious function and performance. In the past as in the present, most religious traditions – and certainly the 'world' religions – have linked religious communication and social problems through moral codes.[10] The moralization of religion, or the development of a religious ethic, has allowed the interpretation of social and other problems as consequences of sin, ignorance, or similar contravention of religious norms. Conforming to these norms then becomes the solution to the problems, whether they concern health, economy, social conflict, personal happiness, or a whole host of others.[11]

Establishing religious performance through moral codes is, however, strictly dependent for its effectiveness on social structures that favour morality as a privileged form of social regulation. This obtains primarily in societies, such as segmented or hierarchical ones, in which communal and solidary group formations dominate social structure. The frequently heard lament that today's society is becoming increasingly immoral or amoral points to the fact that modern, global circumstances do not favour morality in this way. As examples, business people put profit and market share ahead of moral considerations. Politicians lie, mislead, and otherwise compromise their principles in order to get and maintain power. Scientists engage in research with insufficient care for the moral dilemmas their discoveries can create. And the sheer plurality of moral outlooks encourages the bracketing of moral considerations in a great deal of communication. Yet religious leaders continue to talk about moral or ethical failings in an effort to assert the practical relevance of the religious modality. We can therefore assume that the privatization and loss of public influence of religion are closely connected with the similar fate of morality. The decline in the central regulatory role of morality has everything to do with the functional problems of religion in modern society.

The common fate of morality and religion under modern and global circumstances is, of course, directly related to the propensity for both social forms to intertwine with particular group cultures. The ambiguous status of socio-cultural particularisms under globalization thereby applies to morality and religion. Morality tends toward such attachment because it is a mode of social regulation that is very interaction-based (cf. Luhmann, 1978; 1987b). The less interaction networks carry major social functions, the more will moral codes be subject to the pluralization characteristic of privatized domains. The question then becomes whether religion can really hope to escape this outcome to become a functionally specialized societal subsystem like the others and thereby thrive under globalization. Can it divorce itself from the particular and the communal?

Continuing along the lines of Luhmannian theory, the characteristic communication of each modern functional subsystem revolves around a central dichotomy that is also the focus of professionalization (cf. Luhmann, 1977: 193ff.). These dichotomies consist of a positive term and its negative opposite. Thus, for instance, the world of science operates with true/false, the economy with owning/not owning, art with beautiful/ugly (or, perhaps, inspiring/uninspiring). In religion, immanence/transcendence takes this place (see Luhmann, 1977: 46; 1987a). In the introduction, I structured my definition of religion around this dichotomy. To repeat some of what I said there: in comparison with other functional domains, the situation for religion is complicated by its holistic view. Just as religious commitment implies the whole person, so the religious dichotomy uses the whole of perceptible reality as its positive term, immanence. In other words, the total world that, for instance, science approaches with the difference between true and false statements, religion subsumes under that which is immanent. However, since the whole cannot as such be the topic of communication – that is, it does not distinguish itself from anything that is not itself – the transcendent functions to give it definition. But, as every major religious tradition shows only too clearly, the transcendent is not anything that can be talked about except in immanant terms. Hence religion always deals with the simultaneity of immanence and transcendence, as in the Middle Eastern concept of divine creation or the Hindu concept of *maya*.

The only historically stable solution to this fundamental religious problem (or, as some would say, mystery) is to specify the transcendent in terms of immanent categories, especially, it seems, those that structure social groups and social relationships (cf. Douglas, 1970; 1975; Durkheim, 1965: 462ff.). People, in other words, come to imagine transcendent cosmic order in terms of the rules that govern their everyday lives and vice versa. Bad things then happen to them to the degree that they fail to live up to the ethical and ritualistic requirements of the cosmos through their social relationships (cf. Berger, 1967: 24ff.; Weber, 1978: 529ff.). This close association of social and cosmic rules obtains in oral societies, in traditional societies, and in modern global society, albeit in critically different ways. It also holds regardless of whether one is talking about conservative or transformative religion. The key point is that the transcendent cosmic order, however conceived, is *ipso facto* universally applicable. Since human beings have no choice but to express this universal order in terms of a particular social order, that social order becomes the battleground between ideal and real, expectation and disappointment, good and evil. Religion and its quest for 'salvation' (harmony, enlightenment, happiness) are then what life is at root all about. The problem of religious influence arises only when religion tries to encompass too many lives that are manifestly 'about' different things, resulting in a level of generalization that makes practical application difficult.

Historical and anthropological data show that there are many different ways to structure social existence, and hence many different constructions of cosmic order. This variety does not present great problems as long as communication between societies is restricted and internal variety is limited. Where this did not prove to be possible, older societies solved the problem by emphasizing the differences and hence the boundaries between social groups. Differences in religious expression, including the behaviour that this implied, were one of the principal ways of drawing or maintaining these boundaries. Using terms more suited to the modern context, one can say that to be a member of a particular societal group was to be an adherent of that group's religion.

More complex older societies ordered along hierarchical principles, more often than not, still identified religious membership and social group membership; but the dominant status groups, in an effort to bolster and express their control over a greater social diversity, usually attempted to style their religion as definitive for the society as a whole, often in the form of an overarching cosmology that made the norms and values of the upper strata, including their moral code, the presumptive standard for all behaviour. This did not exclude the religion of the lower strata, but rather specifically allowed for it, for instance through a distinction between great and little traditions or between religion and superstition. The overarching religious ideologies did not have to penetrate to the popular strata, only to claim relevance for these as well (cf. Abercrombie et al., 1980; Wilson, 1982). Group membership and its defining norms were thus still intimately related to cosmic order, but now the group was defined in a more complex way with one religion declaring itself binding for a far wider variety of actual life-worlds.

The resulting pressure towards abstraction[12] and generalization of the moral code produced more unified and hierarchical cosmologies, first in the form of hierarchical pantheons with the good gods at the top, then increasingly in the form of monotheistic or henotheistic views. These either identified the morally good with the transcendent as in the Abrahamic religions, and thereby more thoroughly moralized religion; or they posited a 'transmoral' realm beyond good and evil as in the Tao, Brahman, or Nirvana. The esoteric, mystical, and socially elitist nature of these latter concepts indicates that too great an abstraction from specific group moral rules yields a religion with limited influence in the larger society (cf. Stark and Bainbridge, 1987: 113–115). Here, moreover, as in the ascetic and mystical movements of the West, religious function and performance were becoming clearly differentiated for the first time, foreshadowing the problem of religion in modern society.

The close association between moral codes, group membership, and religion in pre-modern societies did not, of course, solve the problem of inter-group or inter-societal conflict. But it could help to structure it. In situations where one societal group threatened another, or where there was simply competition, the enemy could be interpreted as the embodiment of evil, as the negation of the correct relationship between social order and the transcendent that one's own group represented. In justifying the conflict, religion promoted the survival or expansion of the group and its culture. This specific application of religion is one that is quite obviously not only still possible in contemporary global society; the legitimacy of group exclusivities combined with the great amount of communication that challenges the self-evidence of these identities encourages it.

To illustrate what I have said thus far, and carry the argument further, I turn to an example from traditional Christian theology.[13] Here, a personal, good God represents the unity of the immanent/transcendent distinction through his creation. The characteristics of this unity are relevant for human beings through moral behaviour that Christians conceived in terms of the affirmation or denial of the fundamental immanent/transcendent relation: that is, God and his rule over creation. The possibility of affirmation or denial is represented in the first instance by the possibility of salvation or damnation, both dependent again on the quality of individual behaviour. The individual soul, the personalization of this overall quality (however determined), stands before judgement on the basis of its moral character, being finally and irrevocably determined in its character as a personally good or evil soul by this judgement.

To personify the possibility of denial or evil, the devil embodies evil not simply as immoral behaviour but as the denial of the dependence of the immanent on the transcendent and thus its unity and thus God. The key to the viability of the entire picture is the assumption that we can expect everyone to live more or less by the same moral code. Anyone who does not, for whatever reason, acknowledge and live by this code denies God and invites chaos, death, or failure. Such a person is the morally and religiously other; and can legitimately be seen as an apostate, an outcast, the one beyond the pale. To concretize and make visible this possibility Christian society had not only artistic images of the devil, but also true outsiders, whether Jews, barbarians, or Saracens, all of whom were from time to time the objects of violent persecution or war. To the extent that such outsiders had the opportunity to become insiders, they could be 'saved' not simply by abstract morally good behaviour, but only by religious conversion (cf. Luhmann, 1987a).

The consistent characterization of the transcendent as source and guarantor of the group's moral norms made it possible to give Satan this unequivocal, personal presence.[14] And Satan was essential to show the importance of God and salvation. The religious leaders of traditional Christian society could represent threats to the group as outside threats, whether by actual outsiders or by their imputed moral counterparts within the society. By tying the pure religious goal of salvation to a particular social order in this way, they also helped to assure the relevance of religious norms and hence their own influence.

At this point, it is important to emphasize that defining and guaranteeing group boundaries or communal solidarity was not the only or perhaps even the major way that religion asserted its public influence in pre-modern societies. Nonetheless, as long as the primary internal differentiations of societies ran along group lines, it was one key way. The societal shift to the primacy of functional differentiation, insofar as it resulted in the formation of global society, undermined this symbiosis, at least on the level of that global society. As I have argued, the autonomy of functionally specific rationalities runs counter to a priority of communal group boundaries. The resultant globalizing tendencies of society have radically altered the conditions under which the moralizing solution is still possible because the societal group now includes everyone. The situation of religion at the level of global society alters correspondingly.

To begin, the person who used to be the unequivocal outsider is now often literally my neighbour, whether I approve or not. This is what Rushdie called the metropolitan experience (see above, p.1). The outside/inside distinction readily at hand for reinforcing the internal moral codes of communal, and hence territorial, societies becomes at least difficult to maintain over the long run in a world of virtually instant global communication, itself a consequence of functional specialization. Not only, for example, does the leader of the 'evil empire' reveal himself to be less than totally evil when met face to face; more important, it is increasingly difficult not to meet with him, not for moral reasons, but for primarily political and economic ones. In the process, morality has lost its central structural position: the decadent and unjust West can be made to pay dearly for its oil, but economically, a sizeable portion of the petrodollars must be reinvested in the West.[15]

Translated into more theological language, the globalization of society does not lead to the death of God, as some Western theologians of the 1960s asserted. God is still in his heaven and his will still rules the world; but the visage of the devil is becoming increasingly indistinct. The result is that God can still be loved, but it is more difficult to fear him. He is still there, but does he make a difference? Is salvation still essential; or will it become the privatized proclivity of a minority, similar and not superior to other leisure pursuits? On the global level, the problem of specifying the transcendent and thus giving the central religious dichotomy meaningful definition and applicability must be addressed anew.

I do not wish to assert, with this analysis, that evil is disappearing from the face of the earth. Far from it. What is happening is that structural changes in, and the globalization of, modern society have made it more difficult than it used to be to personify this evil, to attach it to a self-evident social correlate. The morally other is less easily negated as the outsider or interloper. With this development the old solution to the problem of specifying the transcendent has been undermined, although, I stress again, only on the level of society as a whole. The conditions and implications of using the old solution have been altered. Religion, and, in the current context, religious professionals are therefore faced with a fundamental choice, even dilemma: whether to address the contemporary problem of religious influence without the old solution or by reasserting it.

Each of these two paths has its attendant problems. In what follows, I call them the conservative and liberal options. The first would correspond to the reassertion of the reality of the devil and the second to the acquiescence in his dissolution. Using the distinction as a point of departure, I want now to examine how contemporary developments in global religion reflect the structural tendencies outlined thus far. In the process, I again take up the various themes introduced above, but specifically the notion that, regardless of which option is taken, public influence for religion will be found in the direction of religious performance; while action concentrating on religious function will continue, with certain exceptions, to be the domain of privatized, highly pluralistic religiosity.

Privatized Function and Public Performance

The liberal option addresses the central problem of the determination of the transcendent only in a very abstract fashion: there is evil in the world, but it cannot be consistently and clearly localized or personified. It is a limitation in all of us, in all our social structures. It is especially not to be found in the fact of pluralism, including religious pluralism. If anything, the opposite is true: intolerance and particularistic ascription are a prime source of evil.[16]

Religious professionals and adherents with this attitude tend to be ecumenical and tolerant. They see comparable possibilities for enlightenment and salvation in their tradition and in other religions. They are also polite. The central theological problem of this option, as critics (such as Berger, 1979; Kelley, 1972) point out, is that it makes few really *religious* demands: it conveys little specifically religious information that would make a difference in how people choose, or that people could not get from non-religious sources.

Professional responses to this dilemma under the liberal option reflect the difference between function and performance outlined above. In terms of function, the tendency is to orient the organization toward helping services, including the celebration of important life passages and, of course, the 'cure of souls' for those who feel the need (cf. Bibby, 1987 for excellent Canadian data). This response accommodates itself to what the private adherents evidently want. Function concentrates on private choices. God is preached as benevolent and not wrathful: his only real request is that people imitate his attitude in their relations with others. Evil exists but it is a negative deficiency to be filled and not a positive presence to be destroyed. Moreover, religious leaders with this ecumenical attitude have picked up the universalistic orientations of elitist strains in the major world religions: the possibility of enlightenment for all, the possibility of wisdom for all, the possibility of salvation for all. Now, however, as part of the globalization process, everyone is included, and not just upper strata virtuosi with the leisure for such functional specialization. The combination of pluralism and inclusion excludes very few from the virtually automatic benefits of the religious function.

Religious leaders and organizations that follow the liberal option therefore have difficulty in specifying both the benefits and the requirements of religion in functional or 'pure' form. This indeterminacy has led them to a reliance on performance relations to reestablish the importance of religion and hence the influence of the religious system. Here, often globally oriented issues ranging from gay liberation to political oppression are providing the opportunity to show that religion leads to benefits and demands that are far from insignificant.[17]

To repeat, the view of performance I am using sees it as the attempt by one system to solve problems that are generated elsewhere in the societal environment but not solved there. As such, the problems addressed by religious performance are not religious problems at all, at least not directly. The solutions, therefore, while religiously inspired, will tend to take on the characteristics of the target system: economic solutions to economic problems, political solutions to political problems, and so forth.[18] The deliberate attempt to conform to this structurally encouraged pattern is characteristic of the liberal option inasmuch as it correlates with the basic structure of modern society. There is the conviction that educational problems are not going to be solved by adherence to the traditional faith; that health problems are not going to be solved by meditation, political problems not by the correct execution of rituals.

Instead, the liberal option returns to the communitarian past of religion to define its 'application' as that which is concerned for the community as a whole. In this modern case, however, humanity as a whole is the community and the religious task is to work for the fuller inclusion of all people in the benefits of this global community.[19] Hence religious leaders of this direction style the problems of global society in corresponding terms: conflict among various sectors of the world community is the result in large part of the marginalization of some (often the majority) from systemic benefits like 'adequate' income, political participation, health care, education, and so forth. Yet, the notion of a global community is very general and very vague, including as it does a vast variety of group cultures and individual lifestyles. The styling of the applied religion in terms of a global community in fact reflects the benign functional message of the liberal option. Combined with the respect for the independence of other systems, notably the political, this may work against such activity being recognized as specifically *religious* communication, as something that religion does for us. While this is a problem, it does not mean that such religious activity cannot be effective.

An example may help to illustrate this point. I treat the liberation theological movement in Latin America extensively in Chapter 6. Here I anticipate certain aspects of the arguments presented there.

Generally, liberation theologians (and their First World parallels) represent the liberal option.[20] They are concerned with justice and peace, values that point to the egalitarian inclusion of those marginalized from the benefits of modern institutions. This 'preferential option for the poor' rejects traditional religious interpretations in favour of a contextual theology that uses present experience as the basis for finding the correct religious understanding. Liberation theologians do not present one particular group culture and its religion as being closer to the divine will than others. While the alleged opposition of the 'poor' and 'capitalism' sometimes comes close to being an opposition between good and evil, these religious leaders generally criticize the latter for its creation of vast, global inequalities and not for being an alien worldview destructive of the true and good order that their own group represents. Accordingly, they also do not discourage religious pluralism.

The critics of liberation theology accuse them of having lost the specifically religious (for example, Ratzinger) or of offering economic and political solutions that do not accord with economic and political realities (for example, Novak) (cf. Berryman, 1987: 179–200; McGovern, 1989). One attack is in terms of function, the other in terms of performance. In fact, liberation theology places primary emphasis on religious performance. While 'pure' religious belief and practice are important, they are so only to the extent that they contribute to the alleviation of social ills, leading to an emphasis on *praxis*. Essentially, liberation theologians respond to the privatization of religion by seeking a revitalization of the religious function in religious performances, particularly in the political realm. Sin becomes primarily social and the principal religious demand is for social justice (see G. Baum, 1975: 193ff.).

Seeking to establish religious influence by linking function and performance is, of course, not new or unusual. As discussed above, all religious traditions have historically done this. In modern circumstances, however, function and performance are more clearly distinguishable because we use function as a central way of dividing social action. Therefore, if working for social justice is going to be a recognized *religious* performance, then its necessary connection with religious *function* must be apparent, just as the necessary connection between Einstein's pure scientific endeavours and the building of the atomic bomb is apparent. The criticisms of liberation theology, that it is neither good religion nor good economics, indicate a problem here. And in fact, liberation theologians have relied heavily on non-religious interpretations like dependency theory and Marxist analysis to understand the problems, and prefer explicitly political courses of action.[21] The connection with the theology is clearly visible in the writings of its proponents; but it is anything but necessary. In this light, it should not be surprising that liberation theologians have sometimes been tempted to address the problem through an increasingly 'Manichaean' opposition of the poor and capitalism, with socialism, the group culture of the poor, as the vaguely defined, communitarian goal.

I do not want to suggest with this analysis that liberation theology is not legitimate theology. If anything, the opposite is true. The issue here is rather the position of religion in global society and how the problem of privatization reflects this position. Liberation theologians are attempting to establish public influence for religion in the face of privatization. They are doing this through religious performances that concentrate on political involvement although they do not go so far as to advocate the legislation of religious norms. One can argue, as does Phillip Berryman (1984), that they have been somewhat successful in this endeavour (but see Mainwaring, 1989). Yet, whether this strategy can lead to a reestablishment of the public influence of religious communication in general in our society is still an open question.

While performance relations under the liberal option thus offer a possibility for religion to break out of its privatized functional ghetto and back onto the political stage especially, the possibilities are limited. In addition to problems just touched upon in the example of liberation theology, the pluralism permitted on the level of function implies an equal pluralism on the level of performance. Therefore, to the extent that religious leaders, such as those in North American liberal Protestant churches, can control their organizational levers and take a unified public stand on issues, to that extent they risk losing an appreciable portion of their adherents, regardless of the particular stand taken (cf. Bibby, 1987; Hadden, 1970). Mobilization becomes a serious and constant problem in this respect. In the absence of additional, non-religious measures (especially direct political involvement)[22], religious leaders are left with the kind of persuasion that in the Christian tradition is called evangelization: reliance on voluntaristic, privatized decision-making with its attendant fissiparous pluralism.

In spite of this difficulty on the part of the liberal option, its religious cosmos does correlate with the structural tendencies of a global society, as the above argument has outlined. To the degree that global society continues to become a more solid reality, the liberal option might be seen as the trend of the future. In the meantime and at least for the foreseeable future, however, it is not the only possible direction.

The conservative option (the reassertion of the tradition in spite of modernity), far from being merely a throwback correlating with bygone social structures, is in fact the one that is making religion most visible in today's world. It is a vital aspect of globalization and not a negation of it. Given the direction of the preceding analysis, this claim requires a bit of explanation.

For privatized faith, the conservative option implies a reassertion of the traditional view of transcendence, often explicitly as a normative response to a society ('the world') that is seemingly heading in a different and evil direction. The present analysis would confirm this impression: the conservative option has fewer problems with transcendence but finds itself in conflict with dominant trends in global social structure. Globalization and the social forces bringing it about are themselves a critical part of the problem to which religion has an answer. Nevertheless, religious leaders and professionals who orient their organizations to privatized, committed religiosity with a conservative perspective are basically offering a variation on the liberal functional response: accommodation to individual proclivities in matters of religion but with a holistic emphasis that can but need not result in sectarian organization. Conservative religion, from this point of view, only contradicts modern social structures to the extent that it emphasizes individual, personal holism in the face of differentiated (and hence impersonal) social structures. It concentrates on religious function and tends toward privatization, with the difference that the religious selections more often include the element of holistic commitment and concentration on community solidarity. Conservative religion on the level of function responds to some of the possible disparities between the structure of personal systems and the societal system. It therefore reflects modern structures rather than negating them.

I want to make a similar argument with respect to the performance response under the conservative option: what seems to be running against globalization and modernity is actually better seen as reflective of it, albeit in a very different way when compared with the liberal option. To explain this requires a short digression.

Globalization, as I have tried to show in previous chapters, does not mean the inevitable, evolutionary progress toward a global spread of Western modernity. Such developmentalism is inadequate not only because the empirical facts negate the proposition, but also because, from the theoretical point of view, globalization should have as profound effects on the formerly territorial societies of the West as it is having on other formerly territorial civilizations around the world. Up until the middle of the twentieth century, the West may well have believed that its successful imperial expansion of the previous four centuries was essentially a one-way street. Today this illusion is rapidly revealing itself as what it is.

The resistance to, or perhaps better, digestion of globalization in various parts of the contemporary world has given rise to movements informed by the conservative religious option: above all political mobilization as the service (performance) of the religious faith. Whether the complaint is 'Westoxication' in the Middle East or the difficulty of 'making America great again', the problem is similar. In the West, former 'outsiders' (the Soviets, the Japanese, the Arabs et al.) are undermining the long-standing political, economic, and general cultural dominance of the West. The West can rely less and less on its economic, political (especially military), and scientific might to assure the continued hegemony of its culture. On the homefront, the functional differentiation that is such a key aspect of globalization continues to bring about rapid change in the old core structures: the family, morality, and religion. In the non-West, in spite of increased political independence and/or economic power in many areas, Western cultural patterns still seem to be becoming increasingly dominant. What appears to some in the West as moral, economic, and political decline of their own culture, appears to many in the non-West simply as continued Western cultural, economic, and political imperialism. With its clear ties to communal group cultures, both in the past and still largely in the present, religion is an obvious candidate for structuring a response to both.

Many of the religio-political movements that have sprung up in recent decades all around the world reflect this development. In the West, for example, the New Christian Right in the United States has battled to restore the old Western dominance. Traditional Christian moral values, combined with an emphasis on free enterprise and vigorous defence against Communism, would restore America as the great nation God intended it to be. In the non-West various Islamic movements from Indonesia to North Africa, for instance, are attempting to build concrete paths toward the long desired separation of modernization from Westernization; or, as in the case of some factions in republican Iran, toward the rejection of modernization as an intrinsically infidel product. I give both the American and Iranian case extended treatment in Part II. In many of these instances, and certainly in the ones just mentioned as examples, the religious leaders consciously adopt the conservative option. Whether it is the 'Evil Empire' or the 'Great American Satan', the reappearance of the devil as that which gives definition to the transcendent signals a return to a traditional way of making religion capable of communicating publicly essential information. Far from being a mere yearning for imagined bygone days, such reassertion is a logical outcome of a globalization that has generated and continues to generate fundamental conflicts among different regions of the world.

When political and economic responses to these conflicts fail, religious performance may be able to fill the breach. Since the adherents to the various religions around the world are still by and large localized, leaders can often express regional conflicts and disparities in religious terms.[23] Here, the conservative option, grounded as it is in traditional, communally oriented societies, offers distinct advantages. Its solution to the problem of transcendence allows an approximate dichotomization of the world into the religiously pure and impure, into us and them. Such a clear religious message can, under the correct conditions, lead to successful mobilization of entire populations. Politicization on this religious basis then becomes a way for regions to assert themselves in the face of globalization and its consequences. Hitherto, the most visible examples of such conservative religious performance movements, in the Islamic Middle East and in the Sikh Punjab, have occurred after prolonged, unsuccessful political attempts to address problems attendant upon modernization and in the wake of significant increases in regional wealth (cf. Esposito, 1987; Keddie, 1980; Leaf, 1985; Telford, 1992; Wallace, 1986; 1988).

This combination of factors is probably not accidental. The modernization that correlates with globalization is not simply benevolent, let alone egalitarian. It destroys as well as creates. The attempt to gain some transcendent perspective on this historical process is understandable, especially when immanent techniques such as purely political nationalism, socialism, open-door capitalism, secularized education,[24] and even economic progress all seem to fail. If the necessary definition of the transcendent means applying the religious correlates of bygone social structures to the very different divisions of today, then this only indicates that contemporary structures do not offer a self-evident alternative.

Religious movements grounded in the conservative option contrast with their liberal counterparts in a number of ways. Critical among these is the conservative notion that the public influence of religion should be supported by law. Important religious norms should be enshrined in legislation; they should not have to rely on a 'demonstration effect' for their influence. The conservative religious leaders lay great stress on a particular group-cultural moral code as the manifestation of divine will. In a global social environment that is generally corrosive of group cultural boundaries and that therefore encourages religio-moral pluralism, there is little hope that one cultural outlook will prevail on the basis of its own unique merits.

The alternative is to gain control over a limited territory dominated by the particular culture and then control pluralism within it. This has certainly been the goal of the New Christian Right in the United States, Sikh extremists in Punjab, the politicized neo-orthodox camp in Israel, and Islamic fundamentalists in the Middle East. Given the problems of territorial boundaries, the coextension of legal and political systems, and the fact that the nation-state has already provided a locus of institutionalization for socio-cultural particularisms under globalizing/modernizing conditions, it is not surprising that such efforts should so often be (ultra-)nationalist in ideology or effect. This difference between the liberal and conservative options in fact emphasizes the degree to which the latter uses and reinforces the segmentary and territorial differentiation within the modern global political system of states. It is another example of how the conservative direction within global religion is reflective of the structures of global society and not just a reaction against these.

Indeed, what I have been calling the conservative performance option for religion in the modern world does not at first glance seem to accord well with a primacy of instrumental, functional differentiation. One of the more explicit aims of many of the movements under scrutiny is to dedifferentiate many functional areas, mainly religion and politics, but also religion and the family, religion and education, religion and economy, among others. However, dedifferentiation in the absence of an alternative structural base, such as was provided by hierarchical status-group differentiation in older societies, is still a response to problems of globalization in terms of a primacy of function. Religious movements like the Iranian revolution want to solve overall societal problems by giving the religious system and its values first place among the various functional spheres. Like economic dominance in the nineteenth century West or political dominance in the People's Republic of China, a strategy which attempts to combat the effects of functional dominance under the banner of the religious system can perhaps best be seen as a critical accommodative response to a globalism in which function dominates.[25] It may stem the tide of modernization and some of the more disruptive consequences of globalization for quite some time in particular regions, perhaps even until the global system collapses under the weight of its own internally generated problems. But it does not negate the fundamental structure of global society.

Conclusions

In sum, regardless of whether the functional dilemma regarding the basic religious dichotomy is solved in a liberal or conservative direction, religion in the modern world takes on a privatized or a public face depending on whether one is looking at religious function or religious performance. It is, therefore, not simply a matter of greater or lesser privatization. Privatized religion continues to develop in a myriad of pluralistic directions across the full range of religious possibilities from supererogatory asceticism to eudaemonistic liberality, from committed sectarianism to piecemeal *brico-lage*. For the leaders and their organizations, religion seems to be going in one of two directions: concentration on ministering to private religious choices or entering the public, especially political, arena. The latter direction itself contains two possibilities: an ecumenical one that looks to the global problems generated by a global, functionally differentiated society; and a particularistic one that champions the cultural distinctiveness of one region through a reappropriation of traditional religious antagonistic categories. Both represent possibilities for publicly influential religion that are direct consequences of the globalization of a society that encourages increasing privatization.

Although it may seem that the liberal direction is significantly more problematic – more susceptible to privatization – than the conservative one, this is not necessarily the case. If the conservative option has an advantage, then it is its attachment to the same socio-cultural particularisms that inform so many modern states. What conservative religious movements sometimes succeed in doing is making religio-cultural themes the stuff of politics and law. As such they supply religion as a cultural resource for the political and legal systems. But as is theoretically the case with all performance applications, we should expect that the functional exigencies of these latter systems will significantly transform the religion. The power of modern functional systems rests in their instrumental specialization. To the degree that religious goods come to be cultural content within those systems, they can be expected to take on the appropriate form. Religious laws, for instance, will in form look like any other law, and will be susceptible to interpretation, amendment, and repeal like any other law. And we can expect politicized religious issues to be treated like other issues: the stuff of expediency, compromise, brokerage, and the shifting sands of competing interests. The liberal performance direction, by contrast, usually does not seek to enshrine religious issues in law and political decision-making. Its problem, as indicated above, is to establish its contribution as specifically religious.

I take up the further elaboration of these two directions in Part II. There three examples of the conservative option (from the United States, Israel, and Iran) and two of the liberal option (religious environmentalism and the Latin Amerian liberation theological movement) are explored in greater detail. The aim is both to elaborate and illustrate the general observations of this and the previous chapter. Before proceeding to that task, however, some important aspects of how religion operates in a globalizing society have yet to be discussed. Of the many questions that remain, two are the subject of the following chapter. First, we must look further at the specific disadvantages of the religious modality under modern globalizing conditions: aside from the question of boundaries, what else stands in the way of specifying the religious function in practical and effective ways? What else prevents the instrumentalization of religion? On the basis of this analysis, I then look at how a thus disadvantaged modality like religion can bridge the gap between privatized function and public performance. In this capacity, I explore the critical role of a particular kind of social system, namely social movements. Social movements provide the general form in which religious cultural resources can impinge upon an inner-societal environment dominated by much more powerful instrumental subsystems. The extended examples of Part II also serve to illustrate these matters.

Notes

1 Karel Dobbelaere (1984; 1985) offers a more elaborate critique of Berger and Luckmann along precisely the lines I have mentioned here, including a comparison of their position with that of Luhmann.

2 By using the singular here, I do not wish to deny the important differences between Berger and Luckmann, especially with regard to their differing prognoses for modern society. Compare, for instance, Luckmann, 1967; and Berger et al., 1973.

3 Cf. Luckmann's consistent use of the term '*au sérieux*' to express this notion in 1967: 77ff.

4 At least for the United States. Parsons (1966) concentrates on this country, although he does claim more general applicability for the analysis. This fact raises the possibility that the theoretical divergence between Parsons and, say, Luckmann (or Luhmann, for that matter) is at bottom a difference in empirical focus: America vs. Europe. Parsons may be correct for the United States and Luckmann for Europe. Although here cannot be the place for it, the argument is worth pursuing, especially because it would illustrate the varied effects of globalization in different parts of the world. The discussion in the text seeks to abstract from such particularities.

5 Stark and Bainbridge (1985: especially 366ff.), who certainly cannot be accused of a European bias, arrive at a similar conclusion on the basis of empirical evidence. Their research shows that religious beliefs without institutional backing have little effect on social action.

6 Berger (1979; Berger et al., 1973) and, recently, Dobbelaere (1988) have argued persuasively that such correspondence happens to a large extent even in modern, functionally differentiated society. It is, however, the inconsistency and incompleteness of such correspondence that is at issue here.

7 The literature is vast. As recent representative examples in the North American context, see Bibby, 1987; Roof and McKinney, 1987; Stark and Bainbridge, 1985.

8 Cf., in particular, Parsons's similar analysis with regard to the rise of Christianity in 1957: 393ff.

9 To some degree, the Luhmannian distinction between function and performance as it applies to religion is parallel to Weber's distinction between other-worldly and this-worldly aspects of religion. See above all Weber, 1946.

10 A complete analysis at this point would, of course, have to deal with the often equally important role of religious ritual here, perhaps using Weber's distinction between ritualistic and ethical salvation (1978: 529ff.). I bracket consideration of religious performance through ritual in this discussion because, with minor exceptions such as the Transcendental Meditation movement and privatized beliefs in the direct efficacy of various rituals for solving social problems, few religious leaders, organizations, or movements in the contemporary world consider ritual a possibility for asserting public religious influence. As will become evident especially in Part II, moralizing efforts, by contrast, are in the forefront in this regard.

11 A fuller discussion of this matter would have to include the different ways of enforcing religio-moral codes, including the role of religious law in the Abrahamic traditions. This latter issue arises quite explicitly in the case of the Iranian revolution. See Chapter 7 below and especially Arjomand, 1988.

12 The invention of writing undoubtedly also contributed significantly to this pressure for abstraction.

13 With relatively minor changes, the following example also describes the dominant scheme in the Islamic tradition.

14 For the obverse of this argument, that God loses his personal presence in the modern circumstance, see Dobbelaere, 1988: 93.

15 With the result that moral differences are reduced, for instance, to the privatized stipulation that Saudi-backed racing-car drivers must toast their victories with orange juice instead of champagne!

16 A dramatic and graphic illustration of this option and its opposite appears in the 1986 Granada television documentary, *The Sword of Islam*. The film begins with Terry Waite asserting that 'true Islam' is tolerant and respectful of human rights, painting a picture of Islam

that seems more consistent with liberal Protestantism than with the militant Islam of the film's subjects, al-Jihad in Egypt and Hizb Allah (Waite's apparent kidnappers) in Lebanon.

17 This point becomes especially important in religious environmentalism, for which see below, Chapter 9.

18 For examples, this time from Roman Catholic leaders in the United States and Canada, see the documents in Baum and Cameron, 1984: 3–18; and in O'Brien and Shannon, 1977: 518–537.

19 See, for example, the concern for world community in more recent papal documents such as John XXIII's *Pacem in Terris*, and Paul VI's *Populorum Progressio* (both are reprinted in O'Brien and Shannon, 1977).

20 The liberation theology literature is quite large. A useful summary is Berryman, 1987. Representative samples from around the world are in Ferm, 1986.

21 The reliance on outside 'ideologies' and the direct political involvement are two of the central points on which the more conservative Roman Catholic hierarchy in Latin America opposes those who act on liberation theological principles. The fear on the part of these bishops is that the church will be compromised and lose its independence both from the point of view of its religious message and its ability to put that message into practice. For the clear manifestation of this conflict in Nicaragua, see Berryman, 1984: 226ff.; Bradstock, 1987.

22 Even here, the divergent selectivities of the religious and political systems may neutralize the religiously inspired efforts. Salient examples are the New Christian Right in the United States and Soka Gakkai in Japan. See, for example, Roof, 1986; Shupe, 1986; Chapter 5 below.

23 That the strategy breaks down and is even counterproductive when such correspondence between religion and territory does not obtain has been evidenced in, among other places, Lebanon. See Norton, 1987.

24 It cannot be without significance that both the typical member of al-Jihad in Egypt and the typical follower of Bhindranwale in the Punjab are and were comparatively well educated youths from the lower-middle and middle economic classes. See Nayar and Singh, 1984: 23; and Ibrahim, 1986: 355.

25 The strategy of giving priority to religious communication for the purpose of halting modernity was followed successfully in Quebec for almost a century. Eventually, however, in this instance, the religiously controlled structures set up to stem the tide provided some of the foundations for the rapid modernization of Quebec after World War II. See Beyer, 1989.

4

RELIGION AND SOCIAL MOVEMENTS
IN GLOBAL SOCIETY

Thus far, I have approached the possible responses of religion and religious actors to globalization primarily in terms of theoretical distinctions between function/performance and liberal/conservative options. This is only a first general step in analysing what is a highly complex relation and multifarious empirical reality. To carry the inquiry further, this chapter again takes up the idea that religion under modern/global structural conditions has certain disadvantages when compared, say, to political, economic, or scientific communication. This assessment, however, is set in the larger purpose of looking at the very key role that social movements as social systems play in bridging the gap between privatized function and publicly influential performance. Besides contributing a few more bricks for the abstract understanding of religion and globalization, the exercise has two main purposes. It aims at showing how religion can become a wider cultural resource that operates somewhat independently of its institutionalization within a functional subsystem for religion, and can thus escape or even take advantage of its functional disadvantages. It also provides a transition to the closer empirical examination of specific religio-social movements in Part II.

To repeat briefly what has been said before: modernization and globalization have had ambiguous, and not simply negative, results for religion. Institutionalized and special communication with a posited transcendent has certainly not disappeared or become irrelevant. Various events around the world show that it can still have a significant impact. Yet in most regions, we have witnessed the greater or lesser depriviledging of traditionally religious concerns, symbols, and professionals. We cannot say with any certainty what will happen in the future, but the trend today seems to be towards privatized pluralism in religion with a few, albeit very visible, exceptions.

My main thesis here is that we should expect religiously-based social movements focused on what I will call the 'residual' problems of globalizing systems to be a persistent and prevalent response of religion – leaders, organizations, adherents – to this circumstance. Such movement involvement counters the tendency for religion to become a privatized mode of communication by applying it as a cultural resource (cf. Beckford, 1989) to serve mobilization directed at problems which are not inherently religious. These are performance-oriented religio-social movements.

Empirical research and theoretical reflection on social movements have a fairly long history within the social sciences. In particular, social movement perspectives have informed a great deal of research on religion, more recently new religious movements of the 1960s and 1970s, and religio-political movements such as the New Christian Right in the United States.[1] As the latter example indicates, one of the important features that emerges from this literature is the frequency with which religion makes its presence felt in the world order and responds to globalization precisely in the form of religious or religiously motivated social movements.[2] What is, however, surprising is the relative neglect of religion as a salient factor in the study of what have come to be called the *new* social movements (such as peace, anti-nuclear, feminist, ecological): this in spite of the fact that religious actors and organizations are often directly involved.[3] Still, even here, recent work by James Beckford (1989; 1990) and John Hannigan (1990; 1991) has begun to pay direct attention to the possible connections.

The new social movements are of distinct importance in the present context because they represent a significant performance direction for the liberal religious option in particular. While conservative religious outlooks gravitate more toward religio-political movements, liberal ones seem to favour the type of aims and strategy associated with new social movements. The latter, moreover, like the globalization discussion, are a relatively recent concern. In this case, it could not have been otherwise because the movements themselves did not begin to appear before the mid-1960s.[4] And the clear theoretical delineation of these movements and their possible significance had to await the last decade (see for example Habermas, 1981; Melucci, 1985; Offe, 1985; Touraine, 1981; 1985). Whereas the globaliz-ation perspective differs from 'international' perspectives in the primary unit of analysis, the new social movements discussion posits a new phase in contemporary society of which the movements are a symptom. Differences exist, in this regard, as to what is new about the movements as compared with 'old', especially labour movements. Most descriptions, however, focus on a shift from politico-economic issues of inclusion in the benefits of industrial society to more cultural concerns with the quality of life and the image of the good society (Beckford, 1989; Hannigan, 1990; Klandermans and Tarrow, 1988). This new and different focus, I suggest, has much to do with the more positively global perspective of most new social movements, and, by extension, of the liberal religious option.

To explore these issues and connections more fully, the following analysis is divided into two parts. First, I return to a further consideration of the consequences globalization has had for religion as a mode of social communication. The main purpose in this section is to demonstrate that the ambiguous situation of religion under conditions of modernization/ globalization has its roots in structural and cultural features of modern globalizing society as these relate to the way that religion typically operates. Second, I look at some of the features of social movements that make them suitable socio-structural vehicles for religion to respond to its situation. The whole analysis sets the stage for Part II, in which I flesh out the various theoretical arguments of this and previous chapters by examining concrete contemporary examples of religiously-based social movements.

Performance Religion in Global Society: A Second Look

Reprise: Global Structures and Cultural Values

The basic globalization hypothesis with which I am working can be restated briefly. Globalization is a direct consequence of modernization. The epochal transformation of social structures and ideas that began in Western Europe has had as one of its most important consequences the spread of key aspects of modernity to encompass the entire globe, above all a world capitalist economy, the political system of sovereign states, the worldwide scientific-technological, health, education, and perhaps news media systems. They represent differentiated means of specialized, instrumental communication which have a strong tendency to coopt, undermine, and otherwise challenge previously existing group-cultural and personal boundaries, including those of the initial, European carriers.

Historically, these functionally specialized social systems began their rise to prominence in early modern Western Europe. There they gradually replaced the established community-group and status-group structures as the dominant systems of the society. One of the important consequences has been a significant increase in the individuation of persons as no one or even all of the newly dominant subsystems of society encompasses all aspects of their lives. The reverse side of this individuation, however, is the 'impersonality' of the systems: each of these centres on a different means of communication and not directly on the persons involved. Thus, for instance, the world capitalist economy operates in terms of money, the global political system in terms of bureaucratically organized power, the scientific system in terms of verifiable truth, and so forth. Moreover, the instrumental orientation of these systems gears them toward constant increase of their specific means, yielding such cultural values as progress, efficiency, and technical rationality.

If this view is accepted, then modernity results simultaneously in the increased individuation of persons and the increased impersonal power of the overarching social systems. This combination points to a further critical aspect of the entire picture. Precisely because the differentiated functional systems concentrate on specialized means of communication and not on the total lives of the people that carry them, they leave a great deal of social communication underdetermined, if not unaffected. There are various terms available that refer to this domain: private sphere, life-world, the domain of expressive action, and others. None of these terms is entirely adequate; but whatever we call it, social movements belong predominantly here. Far from being unimportant residuals, therefore, this domain is in fact where much of social life takes place.

Moreover, its underdetermination by the dominant systems points to the extensive variation that becomes possible in this area of social reality. As I have argued in previous chapters, the distinction, say, between private/public, life-world/system, or expressive/instrumental is a basis of both individual diversity and the modern individualistic ideal, as well as the cultural legitimacy of plural collective identities. Along with individuation on the personal level comes a corresponding individuation on the group level, leading, among other things, to the continued but recontextualized salience under modernity and globalization of ethnic, geographic, and other group particularisms (cf. Lechner, 1989).

These structural changes also have their cultural expression. I have already mentioned the ideals of progress and technical rationality that were an indispensable part of the rise of the instrumental systems. On the individual side, the ideals of the French Revolution, liberty, equality, and fraternity, played a corresponding role. The two sets of ideals are, moreover, closely related.

In early modern Western society, as functional communication began to challenge status-group communication for dominance, the old social boundaries had to be challenged. In particular this meant that the social prerogatives of the nobility and the cognitive/normative ascendancy of the church had to be dismantled and replaced by the abstract rule of monied capital, positive law, and the scientific method. The personal freedom espoused by the bourgeoisie and the Enlightenment intelligentsia was at the same time the freedom of capital, the state, and rational inquiry. Equality meant the removal of status-group membership as a criterion of discrimination: henceforth only personal ability in manipulating the rising instrumentalities should serve in this role. The result would not be chaos, but rational progress. Indeed, the intimate link between personal freedom and equality on the one hand, and progress on the other, shows that all these fundamental values were but different aspects of the same overall development.

In the third of its core values, fraternity, the French Revolution expressed a further key value attendant upon modernization and globalization. Like freedom and equality, fraternity pointed to the removal of old status-group barriers and the inclusion of all in the presumed benefits of the rising instrumentalities. But fraternity also had a group or communal component. As noted above, the rise in dominance of the functional structures meant the increase of individuation. It also left room for the continued but recontextualized salience of group identities, especially through the political system in the form of the nation-state and nationalism. Indeed, without the fraternal ideal of the nation, the modern state as the prevailing subunit of an autonomous and global political system would probably not have been possible.

As has been and is presently the case with globalization, the process of modernization in the West was, of course, not smooth or inevitable; nor did it go unchallenged. Various antisystemic movements arose, for instance, among those who wished to restore the old aristocratic society or those who sought to prevent their own marginalization through the new techniques. Yet, historically, these and others like them were unable to prevent the eventual ascendancy of the functional systems, and of the values that were an essential aspect of their rise. More important, in the present context, the power of these systems enabled their eventual global spread. They now have profound influence on the overwhelming majority of our lives and on the non-human world around us. Among the many results are vast inequalities among people in terms of wealth, power, and life chances; exacerbated cultural conflicts as people of very different outlooks find themselves living in the same society; greatly accelerated population growth; and the significant alteration of the physical environment.

One consequence of the imperial and global extension of the Western-bred systems and their core values is that the diffusion of the core values, especially equality and progress (and their variations like dignity, empowerment, identity), has gradually become a notable symptom of this globalization.[5] That is to say, it has not just been the dominant Westerners who have come to espouse these values, but also a sizeable portion of the indigenous elites in most areas of the world as these have become incorporated into the global system. One critical consequence has been that the great inequalities generated within the same system have come to be seen by many as a negation of those values and a failing of the global system, and this by people in both the advantaged core and the disadvantaged peripheral regions. Put slightly differently, the global system has built into it inherent contradictions between systemic effects and systemic values.[6] While it would be unwarranted to conclude from this the inevitable demise of the system, the tension does augment the dynamism of a system that is already oriented towards constant increase and hence constant change. It favours action intended to redress inequalities rather than acceptance of their legitimacy. Such action, therefore, is antisystemic and prosystemic at the same time. We should distinguish it, at least analytically, from more purely antisystemic action which rejects both the structures and the cultural values of the global system, often in favour of particularistic and communicatively delimited groups (such as sects, 'fundamentalisms') that focus on problems of personal and collective identity.

The Role of Religion

I start from the premise that, to situate religion in the globalizing context, we have to ask whether or not religion is or can be a functionally oriented subsystem. Elements of this approach can be found in those versions of the stillpowerful secularization thesis that stress the consequences of functional or institutional differentiation for religion (see, for instance, Parsons, 1966; Berger, 1967; Luhmann, 1977; Wilson, 1982). Following Luhmann's variation on this thesis, religion under conditions of modernity has faced the challenge of structuring religious communication in a way that, in fact, more or less parallels similar structures in other systems. On this model, doing so means focusing it around a bipolar code with one positive value-pole and its negative counterpart. In religion, immanence/transcendence takes this place (see Luhmann, 1989b), and the functional challenge for religion under modern conditions derives from the holistic character of the first term combined with the empirically unavailable character of the second.

Religion, under modern and global conditions, forms a differentiated functional subsystem to the extent that the type of communication peculiar to it operates recursively and thus in relative independence of other types. Concretely, this means that the people involved – especially professionals and leaders – structure their religious communication around the immanent/ transcendent polarity. A prayer, a meditation, a ritual act gains its meaning in the first order with reference to this duality. As I outlined in the Introduction, the primary function of such recursive religious communication is to lend meaning to the root indeterminability of all meaningful human communication, and to offer ways of overcoming or at least managing this indeterminability and its consequences.

Like other functional spheres, therefore, religion is potentially applicable to everything. Just as anything can be commodified or politicized, so anything, as Durkheim stated, can be sacralized. What distinguishes religion from the others, however, is that it deals specifically with the overall conditions for the possibility of any communication; that is, it gives immanence as a whole its meaning. It thematizes those conditions, styling them as a special type of 'divine' communication accessible only in religiously controlled ways such as revelation, myth, ritual, mystical experience, and so forth. Yet, because religion is also about what is actually beyond all human communication, functional differentiation aimed at the creation of a specialized system of purely religious communication runs the risk of making religion generally relevant in all situations, but specifically relevant in comparatively few.

In pre-modern societies, this functional peculiarity was often an advantage; today it is far less so. Put more concretely, before the ascendancy of such functionally specialized social systems as for economic production, political decision-making, scientific explanation, or academic education, religious modalities provided essential and often professional support for a large portion of communication in these domains. Religious ritual and prescription were indispensable for the good hunt or harvest, the successful military campaign, the maintenance of health, and the continued rule of the realm. Religious specialists played important roles in these matters and as teachers, scribes, and general sources of knowledge and wisdom. In many areas, they offered social welfare services, mediated disputes, administered law, provided community leadership, and smoothed the way for trade. With the development of instrumentally specialized systems, however, religious approaches to these problems and functions have largely been displaced, marginalized, or privatized in most areas as these become enmeshed in the global system.[7] In addition, the global spread of these systems has often brought with it anti-religiousness and anti-clericalism as part of the delegitimation of the old and the promotion of the new.

The response of religion to these developments has been quite varied. In the West, beginning in the later Middle Ages, Christianity went a long way to making religion a differentiated functional subsystem centred specifically around faith as a mode of communication distinct above all from scientific truth (natural reason). The Roman Catholic church in particular complemented this process through organizational elaboration that paralleled the emergence of increasingly autonomous legal and political systems. Later, both Protestant and Roman Catholic churches fostered a budding educational system, for a long time establishing this as at root a religious responsibility. In general, the Christian churches latched on to European imperial expansion, styling religion as the necessary holistic essence of the 'civilizing' project: along with the merchant and the soldier came the missionary.

Ultimately, however, the Christian attempt to respond by making religion a functional subsystem with public influence comparable to the others failed. It foundered on the increasing autonomy or, from the point of view of religion, secularization of the other systems. As these developed their instrumental specializations, religion and the churches were, so to speak, thrown back onto 'faith alone'. The Roman Catholic church responded to a large degree by sacralizing and further elaborating the organization. But, as with its Protestant siblings, the long-term result in most areas was progressive privatization of religious communication. In other words, religion became increasingly a matter of concern primarily to voluntary adherents, witness to which, perhaps more than anything else, is the increasing or continuing diversity of religion while other, more powerful modes of communication as in science, health, education, politics, law, and economy have become globally more homogeneous.

A related critical aspect of religion's systemic fate centres on the historical results of globalization itself. As long as Westerners could conceive the process as more or less the expansion of their particular culture, the carriers of the Christian religious system were able to respecify the religious function as an indispensable part of the project. Hence the tremendous worldwide missionary effort. With the progressive relativization of particular group cultures, however, especially after World War II, this vision became problematic for the larger part of the Christian leadership as ever more non-Western areas appropriated some or all of the major globalizing instrumentalities (modern state, economy, education, science/technology, health care) while rejecting a great many of the various non-systemic facets of Western cultural particularism, including, more often than not, its dominant religious culture. The holistic perspective of any religious tradition made it difficult if not impossible to separate the universal and inclusive aspect of Christianity from the many ways it is bound into that particularism.[8] Nonetheless, as with the other systems, non-Western areas did by and large adopt the systemic *form* of religion, even where it had not existed clearly before. Thus the 'discovery' or assertion of such religions as Hinduism or Native North American religious traditions accompanied Western imperial expansion quite as much as the parallel crystallization of non-Western nations.

If we accept this description, then one of the core problems of religion in modernity is that its way of relating to the world is too broadly-based to allow the sort of instrumental specialization typical of functional subsystems like economy, polity, or science. It is precisely the highly selective nature of the specializations that makes these systems so effective, allowing them to spread around the globe in relative disregard for pre-existing cultural boundaries. Religion has not been able to follow suit because its general applicability has historically tied it closely to these identities.

In light of religion's functional peculiarity, it is then unlikely that we are going to see the development of a global religious system like the world capitalist economy or the system of sovereign states, at least not during the current phase of globalization. This does not mean, however, that no global religious system is possible or that religious communication will shrink to the realms of pious public platitudes and the private concerns of a minority. The holistic starting point of religion points to these, but also to other possibilities, above all conservative, anti-global, particularistic, and often politicized 'fundamentalisms'; and liberal religion that seeks to address the severe problems engendered by the global system, but on the basis of the prevailing global values and not in opposition to them.

To understand how a disadvantaged modality has advantages under modern global conditions, I return to the fact that the dominant instrumental systems are not all-encompassing. As I noted above, these systems are effective, globalizing, and totalizing; but there is much that they exclude. Among these are the meaning or thematization of the social whole, the 'private sphere' or 'life-world', and many problematic effects of their own operation. Now, within the meaning of the word, immanence, religion includes all those matters about which the other functional systems communicate, plus all that they leave out. It is the one mode of communication that is in principle both totalizing and encompassing. Religion can and to some degree does serve as a system specializing in what, from the perspective of the dominant functional systems, are residual matters. Religion's view, under modern and globalizing conditions, is therefore typically 'antisystemic' in the sense that religious adherents, professionals, and leaders tend to see their communication as essential because it addresses the problems that the dominant systems either leave out or create without solving.

I stress, however, that 'antisystemic' may mean against the dominant structures and values of emerging global society, but need not. As noted in the above discussion of the tension between systemic values and systemic effects, communication in this society can be antisystemic and prosystemic at the same time. This also applies to religion, especially (but not exclusively) what I am calling liberal religion. More precisely, given the functional peculiarities of religion and the structural characteristics of global society, we should expect the emergence of a relatively prominent form of religion that sees among its central religious tasks 'antisystemic' action based on central 'prosystemic' values, yielding a somewhat ambiguous attitude to the global social system.[9] In addition, of course, there will be the less ambiguous, more purely antisystemic and conservative kind of religion; although even here, rejection of a single global society usually does not extend to denial of core values, especially progress and equality.[10]

A final point before I move on to the role of social movements as structural mediators in this circumstance. Although religion has affinity for what I have just called residual[11] matters, social communication outside the dominant systems is not simply therefore religious. The respecification problem is not solved by default. Nonetheless, the affinity does make it likely that communication about residual matters such as personal or collective identity, thematization of global society, and the various problematic effects of the dominant systems will quite often take on seemingly religious forms even when it is not what most observers would call religion. The sociology of religion abounds in examples such as analyses of Marxism as religion (for instance Parsons, 1974), the vexed civil religion debate (see Mathisen, 1989), and, central for the current context, the observed similarities between religion and new social movements (Beckford, 1989: 129ff.; Hannigan, 1990; 1991). Such manifestations, I suggest, are virtually religious: that is, they are religious by virtue of the affinity between religious holism and residual matters.

Religion and Social Movements

In short, the modern and global context carries negative implications for religion as a mode of communication, but also new potential. A more powerful global subsystem for religion seems unlikely, and yet emerging global society is anything but a stable, harmonious, cohesive system in rough equilibrium. In spite of their ever increasing power, the dominant instrumentalities leave vast areas of social life underdetermined and create serious problems that they do not solve: everything from problems of personal or group identity and ecological threats to increasing disparities in wealth, power, and life chances both within and between regions. The question for religion and its carriers is, how to take advantage of this situation; or more in the language I am using here, to what extent can residual matters and the religious modality be linked concretely? As argued at the end of the last section, the link is clear in terms of abstract function. The problem is rather a practical one: it is structural more than ideological.

The major instrumental systems owe their globalizing influence to their special modes of communication such as money, political power, or scientific truth. In the West, the Christian religion attempted to follow suit by developing faith as a parallel such mode; but this effort has had only partial success and has not been substantially repeated in other religious traditions. In most parts of the world – but certainly not all – religion has in consequence become a domain of voluntary activity on a level with other privatized pursuits. Without the possibility of forming a strong functional societal subsystem, religious leaders and adherents have had to resort to other kinds of social system to maintain – and where possible expand – religious communication. The most common such systems have been interaction-based social networks, and organizations defined by offices and the formal distinction between members and non-members. In the social movement, however, religion has the possibility of informing a system that largely escapes the demands of functional specialization while at the same time avoiding the restrictive characteristics of interactions and organizations.[12]

The problem of defining social movements and distinguishing them from other forms, especially organizations, is a long-standing one in the literature and here cannot be the place to give it a full airing. One of the more important common threads, however, is the notion that social movements are somehow non-conventional, outside or beyond currently normal institutional bounds. Accordingly, various conceptions have located them in the realms of deviance, social problems, and antisystemic directions in society.[13] Even a practical approach such as resource mobilization theory assumes the constant presence of 'grievances' or 'strains' as the motivational base of social movements.[14] A related recurring feature is the instability, evanescence, or fragility of social movements. Like Weber's charisma, they must routinize or institutionalize to avoid disappearing. And just as charisma was for Weber a key element in social change, so many observers regard social movements as similarly connected.[15] What unites all these and various other possible defining aspects is, of course, that social movements move: at the heart of any proper conception must be the notion of mobilization.[16] Precisely what would not happen if things were left to their normal, institutional, or systemic course: this is what social movements are all about. As such, they exist only through constant mobilization until they disappear either by simply fading or by becoming institutionalized themselves.[17]

These few common features in most discussions of social movements already point to their possible role in the question of religion and what I am here calling the residual matters of the dominant global systems.

The reproduction of religious communication through religious organizations and interaction-based social networks alone cannot counter the privatizing trend embedded in globalizing modernity. Even religious movements or social movements informed by a predominantly religious ideology and concerned before all else with the expansion of religious faith and practice will not counter this tendency except perhaps temporarily and locally. New religious movements, the New Age movements, and probably the greater part of CEB-based movements in Latin and North America would fall into this category. All of these – organizations, networks, and religious movements – can, however, serve as a resource base for wider social movements, especially the new social movements that focus on both local and global peace, environmental, and social justice issues; and regional, often 'fundamentalist' religio-political movements that seek to reverse the relativization of cultural particularisms attendant upon globalization. Notwithstanding vast differences, these movements have two common characteristics vital for the present context. First, they mobilize around what I am here calling the residual problems of global society and are, from this perspective therefore, antisystemic. Second, they seek to address those problems by influencing the operation of the dominant instrumental systems, all the way to actually becoming institutionalized within those systems, especially, but not exclusively, the political and legal systems. Such movements may, but need not be, 'dedifferentiating' in their goals. The specific role of religion varies a great deal. But in all cases, the aim is to apply this modality to otherwise non-religious problems through means other than the straightforward reproduction and expansion of religious communication, the latter being the typical technique of the more dominant subsystems.[18] Religiously-based social movements therefore constitute distinct possibilities for bridging the gap between privatized religious function and publicly influential religious performance.

Resorting to antisystemic social movement formation as a way of bringing religious influence to bear outside the privatized, voluntary realm does, of course, have its problems. Chief among these is undoubtedly what we may call the danger of 'cooptation', the loss of the specifically religious in the process of respecifying the religious. Consisting as they do of mobilization, social movements are inherently fragile and thus either disappear as systems or become institutionalized in other forms. Given the dominance in global society of functionally oriented subsystems, this means practically that social movements frequently seek the institutionalization of their goals and themes in one or more of these. While, from one point of view, such institutionalization would seem to be the very measure of success insofar as gaining public influence for religion is concerned, subjecting religious goods to the norms and values of other functional subsystems does run the risk of, for instance, changing religious truth into political expediency. To be sure, this is an age-old problem for religion. But it is one exacerbated in the modern/global era precisely because of the greater differentiation of functional spheres and the attendant intensification of their specializations. To avoid these problems, religio-social movements can, of course, institutionalize in voluntary organizations or localized social networks; but this path, from the point of view of religion, does not counter privatization.

A related potential problem is that the identification of a social movement with a particular religion may be decisive in leading to the failure of that movement just because it thereby violates the universalistic norms of the global system. Corresponding to this basic problem are others, including increasing rifts between social movement and existing institutional concerns, especially through a distancing of sections of the religious leadership and the 'grass roots'. All these problems indicate that pursuing this strategy is no guarantee of success in solving the 'problem of religion in modern society' (Luckmann, 1967). Indeed, the marginality and fragility of most social movements already point to a low success rate. As long as the residual matters persist, however, social movements in all likelihood will continue to emerge along with the possibility of applying religious resources in aid of their mobilization.

Conclusions

The possible symbiosis of religion, social movements, and 'residual' problems in global society allows us to pull several of the theoretical strands of the last chapters together. The historical affinity of religion to socio-cultural particularisms has a great deal to do with the normative and holistic style of this mode of communication. Among the more persistent residual problems attendant upon globalization are those pertaining to the relativization of personal and group identities, the mutability of character, as Rushdie put it. Religion can and does respond here, either in a privatized form or as part of a larger social movement seeking wider public influence.

Identity concerns are, however, only part of this portion of the picture. Socio-cultural particularisms are more than loci of meaning in our world; they are also bases of power, of competition for the benefits of global society. The global instrumental systems do not tend automatically towards equality. Instead the global system generates the expectation of equality while creating the reality of vast inequalities. The defence of socio-cultural particularisms therefore becomes a way of claiming or protecting a greater share of wealth, power, knowledge, health, and general prestige. Given the power of the political and legal systems in global society, movements with such goals are likely to be nationalist or subnationalist in nature. In some circumstances, religion has been and continues to be an important resource for such movements, yielding religio-political movements in places as diverse as Ireland, Israel, Iran, India, and Japan. Because of their emphasis on socio-cultural particularisms, such religious movements often display the conservative option with its typical stress on the relativizing forces of globalization as prime manifestations of evil in the world.

In encouraging the legitimation and equality of socio-cultural exclusivities, the global system of course also produces great pressure toward inclusion, toward universal culture. When global society as such is the unit of reference for religious actors, residual problems appear in a different light. Inequalities and identity are still at issue, but now from a global rather than a sectional point of view. For religion, the whole is all of humanity, and even all of existence, rather than a particular segment of it. This typically liberal perspective also sees different problems such as the peaceable coexistence of diversity and the negative consequences of altering the natural environment. Social movements oriented in this direction, especially many of the new social movements, can avail themselves of liberal religious resources. Religio-social movements of this stripe are likely to be less concerned with controlling political and legal powers, with seeing particular religious precepts embodied within these systems because they do not see relativization and pluralism as a problem.

In actual practice, of course, few religio-social movements are going to conform exactly to either one of these more or less ideal-typical directions. The two are, however, sufficiently different that we should expect quite a number of movements that clearly manifest one much more than the other. To carry the theoretical model to this more concrete and empirical level, however, requires a shift away from the abstract and theoretical into the realm of specific contemporary illustrations.

Notes

1 The term 'movement' in New Religious Movements already points to this fact. See, as representative of a vast literature, Barker, 1983; 1991; Robbins, 1988. For examples from the literature on the NCR, see Bruce, 1988; Liebman and Wuthnow, 1983; and Wald et al., 1989. For a related approach to Gush Emunim in Israel, see Weisburd, 1989. The New Christian Right and Gush Emunim are subjects of more detailed analysis below, Chapters 5 and 8.

2 As further examples, see Zald and McCarthy, 1987; Lechner, 1987.

3 See for example the studies of the Dutch peace movement by Kriesi, 1988; and Schennink, 1988.

4 See, for example, Robert Bellah's discussion of the 1964 Free Speech Movement in Berkeley and its debt to the American Civil Rights Movement in Bellah, 1976.

5 As I outlined in Chapter 1, Meyer and Hannan (1979a) and Meyer (1980) see the global extension of these values as a key element of global culture with which they explain, in part, the integration of the world system.

6 I dealt with this problem briefly in Chapter 2 above.

7 A related analysis to the one I am presenting here is, of course, embedded in the prevailing secularization thesis. See B. Wilson, 1985. The problem also echoes in the discussion about whether the function of religion is primarily to provide meaning or whether we must also speak about religion necessarily furnishing power. See Beckford, 1987; McGuire, 1983.

8 In this context, see the current discussion about Christianity's failure to 'inculturate' in non-Western areas as seen, for instance in Küng and Ching, 1989: especially 252ff.

9 The prime example in Part II is religious environmentalism. See Chapter 9.

10 I discuss this point in greater and more concrete detail in the section on the Iranian revolution in Chapter 7 below.

11 Since I use this term quite often in what follows, let me stress at this point that 'residual' here does not mean 'of secondary importance'. Rather, as stated above, it refers to matters that the dominant functional instrumentalities leave out.

12 See the discussion of interactions, organizations, and social systems above, Chapter 2. Cf. also Luhmann, 1982: 69–89.

13 For the religio-political movements that are the focus of Part II, this flavour of social movements comes out most strikingly in Weisburd's treatment of Gush Emunim. See Weisburd, 1989.

14 A good summary statement is in Ahlemeyer, 1989.

15 Thus, to take one example among many, John Wilson defines social movements as 'a conscious, collective, organized attempt to bring about or resist change in the social order by non-institutionalized means' (1973: 8).

16 For a recent effort to define social movements in terms of 'mobilizing communication',

see Ahlemeyer, 1989. This explicitly Luhmannian approach to social movements significantly informs my analysis here. See also Bergmann, 1987; Luhmann, 1984b: 488ff.

17 This creative feature of social movement is probably at the root of Alain Touraine's attempt to make social movements the core of all sociology. See Touraine, 1981.

18 A small corrective is in order here. The application of religious resources to social movements whose aim is not purely religious is not unique to the modern globalizing context, just as social movements themselves are not. It is only the context that is unique.

PART II
CASE STUDIES

RELIGION IN GLOBAL SOCIETY: FIVE CONTEMPORARY CASES

The great diversity of religious forms and contexts in today's global society offers a corresponding variety of cases that could illustrate and thereby develop the main theoretical points outlined thus far. I limit myself to five examples primarily for reasons of space. The case studies rely mostly on secondary sources, except in the case of religious environmentalism where the secondary literature is as yet far too sparse. My purpose is not, therefore, to break new ground in the detailed analysis of the different movements: those already thoroughly familiar with one or more of them will find little that is new empirically. The intention is rather to show how quite diverse manifestations of religion in our world reflect the global context in which they operate. For this, the current state of research is usually sufficient.

The reader may legitimately ask, why these five and not any of a host of others? The reasons are both practical and theoretical. On the practical side, the secondary literature[1] on the New Christian Right, the Islamic revolution in Iran, the liberation theological movement in Latin America, and religious parties and movements in Israel is sufficiently voluminous to make the task I set myself here relatively straightforward. The same cannot be said for other areas where religious actors are attempting to reestablish or preserve public religious influence. Hindu religio-nationalism in India, the Sikh version in Punjab, and Tibetan Buddhism are just three examples in which the paucity of reliable literature is most likely due to the recent nature of developments or to political difficulties.[2] Nonetheless, I have included one subject on which there is relatively little analytical literature, religious environmentalism. Its inclusion points to the weightier theoretical principles of selection.

The first of these concerns the matter of publicly influential religion. I have restricted my choices to examples in which the carriers of religion try to bring it to bear at the level of other globally extended functional systems, specifically in the form of 'prophetic' applications that seek to condition the operation of these systems. There is no shortage of possibilities in this category. I have avoided the myriad instances of more purely functionally oriented religion because, while often of great importance in contemporary society, their focus is on the reproduction and expansion of religious communication as such, not on the direct conditioning of the dominant global systems. Their influence on the latter is more indirect, making them less suitable for illustrating and developing the core issue of public influence in a globalized society.

The choice of religious environmentalism derives from the wish to illustrate in a roughly balanced way the differences between the conservative and liberal options as outlined especially in Chapter 3. The New Christian Right in the United States, the Islamic revolution in Iran, and, to the largest extent, religious Zionism in Israel are of the conservative variety. The liberation theological movement is an example of the liberal religious option, although not always unambiguously. For balance, a further liberal example is called for. Religious environmentalism suggests itself because it is more than another manifestation of the 'social justice' orientation of liberal religious actors, as are liberation theological directions. As I show in Chapter 9, ecological issues are typically liberal religious ones, but they exist in a certain tension with a social justice emphasis. The two liberal examples therefore show different aspects of the liberal position in the context of globalization, much as the three other studies do for the conservative option.

Finally, there is the matter of geographical and religio-cultural representation. For both conservative and liberal directions, I have chosen examples from the First and the Third Worlds. In a global society, either option should be globally possible. In addition, I have tried to include examples from as many world-religious traditions as possible, but here practical considerations prevented a completely satisfactory sampling. In particular, it would have been more elegant to include fewer examples from the Abrahamic faiths (essentially, all five are from these three traditions) and more from Eastern religious traditions. In this regard, it is unfortunate that the literature on the Hindu, Sikh, and Buddhist examples just mentioned is not more voluminous and reliable. The one clear possibility for redressing the balance that I did not choose is Soka Gakkai in Japan.[3] Here, the American and Iranian examples serve to illustrate most of the key points I would have tried to make with an analysis of this movement. And the Japanese case would have had to replace the New Christian Right (First World, conservative), a decision that seems to me unwise given that the vast majority of readers of this book will be English-speaking Westerners. Whether one deems this reasoning sufficient or not, those familiar with any of the many possible examples that I have not included should see echoes of these in the following five studies.

Notes

1 I am limited in my research to works published in English, German, and French.

2 The most up-to-date, reasonably reliable study on the Bharatiya Janata Party in India is

Andersen and Damle, 1987. The research here does not go much beyond the early 1980s and does not anticipate the recent success of that party. There is a great deal of literature on the Sikh situation, but much of it is polemical, unacceptably biased, questionable in terms of scholarship, or simply does not address the religious dimension in any depth. Among the better examples, see Brass, 1988; Kapur, 1986; Nayar and Singh, 1984; Telford, 1992; Tully and Jacob, 1985; Wallace, 1986; 1988. From the few works on the Tibetan situation, none of them particularly up-to-date, see Burman, 1979; Michael, 1982.

3 Representative studies in English include Brannen, 1968; Dator, 1969; Metraux, 1988. See also Shupe, 1986.

5

THE NEW CHRISTIAN RIGHT
IN THE UNITED STATES

In the late 1970s and throughout much of the 1980s, Americans witnessed the rise to public prominence of a conservative religio-political movement often called the New Christian Right (NCR). With its roots in American evangelical Protestantism, the movement captured widespread media attention and may well have had a significant impact on the course of American politics during the last decade. Pat Robertson, one of the leaders of this movement, made an ultimately unsuccessful bid for the Republican presidential nomination for the 1988 presidential election. In 1986, as yet undefeated, he wrote that

> Great segments of the American electorate are awaking to a new sense of patriotism and political concern. Led by evangelical Christians determined to bring about a new era of spiritual and political renewal, more people will vote and vote wisely than in any other presidential election in the nation's history. (P. Robertson, 1986: 296)

In a country where church and state are constitutionally separated, the aim of the New Christian Right was to establish traditional Christian religion as a dominant force in all spheres of society, including the political.

As a religious phenomenon and as a social movement, the New Christian Right in the United States provides excellent illustration of the theoretical conclusions at issue here. It mobilized institutional religious resources in order to recover public influence for religion by directly conditioning the operation of major instrumental systems, especially the political, legal, and educational. A nationalist and clearly conservative movement, it sought to limit the inclusive tendencies of the global system by asserting the exclusive validity of a particular group culture. This American example shows that the residual problem of relativized identities, so much at the heart of Roland Robertson's analyses of globalization, is one that occurs in all regions of global society, not just the historically colonial Third World areas. It also reveals how such ethno-cultural defence is often a way of competing for power in the major global systems.

The New Christian Right offers one of the clearer examples in contemporary global society of the affinity between applied, performance religion and the social movement. In this form, the NCR used existing institutional religious resources and developed some powerful new ones to mobilize its supporters in pursuit of the direct public influence for religion that would not have occurred through the straightforward reproduction and expansion of religious communication. This combination of old and new resources concerns both the form and the content of the movement. In addition to the already established denominational and independent church structure, for example, the NCR added the mobilizing potential of televangelism and computerized mailing lists. And to the older Fundamentalism, it added new issues like abortion and homosexuality, the theological lionizing of private enterprise capitalism, and above all, the threat of secular humanism.

Most of the scholarly literature on the New Christian Right pays close attention to its character as a social movement and its roots in American history.[1] Very few studies, however, pay any attention to the way that this movement reflects the global context. That is, of course, my primary purpose here. But in doing so, my aim is not to negate other analyses that ignore this. It is rather to show that adding consideration of the global context enhances our understanding of the NCR. Accordingly, the following analysis looks at the NCR historically and as a social movement, but seeks to show that these dimensions contain responses to the structural and thematic aspects of globalization. To this end, two questions guide the discussion, namely, why the movement occurred when it did and in the form that it did; and, above all, why the issues for the movement were what they were.

The New Christian Right and American Fundamentalism

Most of the literature on the New Christian Right stresses the extent to which the movement is rooted in American evangelical Protestantism, the dominant religious tradition in American history. Some approaches, such as the 'Great Awakenings' theory of William McLoughlin (1978), would see the contemporary movement as another in a series of religious resurgences stretching back to the beginning of American history (cf. Hammond, 1983). The many points of continuity, however, between current politicized conservative religion and American Fundamentalism in the first decades of this century[2] suggest that the tracing of historical roots is best limited to these two phenomena.

At the level of symbolic issues, perhaps the most significant link between early twentieth century Fundamentalism and the New Christian Right is the opposition to Darwinian evolution. This may seem a strange and incidental item of ideological continuity; but, considering the amount of effort that representatives of both movements expended in fighting the legitimacy of evolutionary theory, one should suspect that the issue stands implicitly for much else. The famous Scopes trial of 1925 is generally acknowledged as a critical turning point that signalled a decline in the public influence of Fundamentalism and its leaders. In this trial, liberal opponents of anti-evolution laws passed by many states challenged a Tennessee version by having John Scopes, a teacher, deliberately break the law. Although the state of Tennessee and its prosecuting attorney, Fundamentalist leader William Jennings Bryan, won the case, the liberal press won the public relations battle by portraying Bryan and his supporters as irrational and ignorant. In the 1980s, New Christian Rightists spearheaded campaigns to legalize the teaching of 'creationism' in the public schools and restrict the teaching of scientific evolution. After a number of unsuccessful court cases, the effort continues (see Bruce, 1988: 114–123; Jorstad, 1987: 54–58; Morris, 1984). Although proponents present 'creationism' as a scientific alternative to evolution and not as religious doctrine, the issue is still the same as it was in the 1920s: scientific rationalism vs. a belief in the literal authority of the Bible.

The pivotal position of evolutionary theory in these two movements points to a whole constellation of issues. The prime opponents for the early twentieth century Fundamentalists were the 'modernist', liberal leaders in the principal denominations of the time. For the Fundamentalists, the cardinal error of these representatives of the 'New Christianity' was their use and approval of biblical higher criticism. This technique did not approach the sacred Christian scriptures from the standpoint of faith: that what was written there was the inspired word of God. Rather, higher criticism used the rational methods of science to judge the foundations of the religious tradition. Darwinian evolution was a particularly blatant example of the corrosive effect of this non-religious rationality. In contradicting the Genesis account of creation, it denied more than the literal word of the Bible. It removed God as the direct agent of the human and natural world. With his sovereignty thus undermined, God's moral law was no longer written into the very fibre of his creation. Darwinism literally claimed to find the Kantian divorce of pure and practical reason etched in stone.

Nevertheless, it would be a mistake to see this conflict as simply one of religion against science. Fundamentalist leaders like Bryan were not against science. They were against the too strong differentiation of scientific and religious rationalities and the effective subordination of the latter to the former. Therefore, evolutionism was wrong because it was bad science, not because it applied scientific method. Similarly, in the contemporary battle over 'creationism', evolution is still considered to be questionable science that 'creation science' can challenge. The argument in each case is not against the influence of science, but against the compartmentalization of religion and the decline in religious influence.

The Fundamentalist opposition to the liberal Social Gospel showed a similar logic. In what Moberg (1972) has called the 'Great Reversal', conservative American Protestants in the 1920s came to reject social concern as a valid outgrowth of their religious convictions. Before this time, Fundamentalists had not taken this extreme position. The critical part that the Social Gospel played in liberal, modernist Protestantism, however, brought about an identification of social commitment with liberalism. Liberals, it seemed, not only saw working toward the alleviation of social ills as the consequence of faith; they further judged the faith on its ability to inspire social action. In the words of one Fundamentalist, John Horsch, the Social Gospel taught that 'education and sanitation take the place of personal regeneration and the Holy Spirit. True spiritual Christianity is denied' (quoted in Marsden, 1980: 255, n.31). The opposition here between personal evangelism and social concern is not simply the expression of sectarian and premillennial rejection of a sinful world. It points further to the fear that liberal Christianity undermines functionally independent, 'pure' religion in favour of residual religious performances that answer only educational, health, and other non-religious systemic needs. As with the relation to science, the problem here is that liberals subordinate religious rationality to the rationality of other institutional spheres.

The contemporary New Christian Right has inherited the problem of social concern in a significantly altered form. In the wake of the Great Depression and Roosevelt's New Deal, many social welfare concerns became the target of government activity. Today's religious rightists oppose not so much the involvement of Christians in solving social ills, as liberal definitions of what those ills are and 'big government' attempts to legislate solutions to these liberal-defined ills. For conservative religious leaders like Jerry Falwell, the welfare state and 'New Deal socialism' are not solutions to social problems, but rather part of the problem. Moral regeneration on biblical grounds and disciplined personal lifestyle are the solutions to problems of drugs, crime, and moral decay. The 'pure' religious emphasis of the early Fundamentalists has not been lost; contemporary religious rightism has rather recaptured the earlier, nineteenth century evangelical unity of function and performance through a reassertion of the religious moral code as the solution to non-religious problems. Again, the issue is not one of denying the relative autonomy of non-religious spheres, but one of asserting religious influence on them through religious performance.

Status Politics and American Fundamentalism

The influence of religion in comparison to other institutional spheres has not been an isolated, abstract concern of religious rightists in America. Other issues, notably the radical anti-Communism of both New Christian Rightists and their Fundamentalist forebears point to the broader context of status, nation, and global society that informs their movements.

One of the more widespread scholarly interpretations of social movements like the New Christian Right focuses on status politics. According to this view, people who support such moral reform movements do so in defence of their particular lifestyle and worldview, and to promote the social status of those who embody them (cf. Harper and Leicht, 1984; Hunter, 1983: 102–119; Lipset and Rabb, 1978; Simpson, 1983; Wald et al., 1989). While there are significant variations of this theory (cf. Bruce, 1988: 1–24), all style the New Christian Right as the representative movement of an identifiable group within the United States. Applied to the contemporary movement, the argument has certain problems, as I discuss below. Its logic is clearer in the case of early twentieth century Fundamentalism.

Until the latter half of the nineteenth century, the United States was religiously pluralistic in law, but not in fact. The first amendment to the American constitution recognized no officially established religion; but the country was, in fact, overwhelmingly Protestant. The influx of large numbers of Catholic and Jewish immigrants during that time, however, undermined this *de facto* hegemony. Moreover, these decades also saw the rapid industrialization of the American economy with an attendant urbanization of the population and all the modern problems that these changes implied. The fact that so many of the new immigrants settled in the urban areas only served to underscore the interconnectedness of these transformations. The response of the Protestant churches and especially their leaders was twofold. Most prominent were those who accepted the changed situation. Under the title of the 'New Christianity', these leaders wanted to take the churches in a liberal direction that included an ecumenical acceptance of different churches and religions, including, to a limited extent, Catholics and Jews.

The forebears of the New Christian Right were born as a reaction to this New Christianity. Leaders of the movement that would eventually be called Fundamentalism rejected the heavy involvement of the New Christianity in the values and rationality of the modernizing urban life. Fundamentalist leaders like Arno C. Gaebelein and Billy Sunday emphasized personal, individual salvation as the key to Christianity, in contrast to the socially oriented Social Gospel emphasis of their opponents. They rejected the ecumenical and accommodating attitude of the liberals, emphasizing instead the duty of every Christian to evangelize for the faith, to battle other religions – and hence other cultures – as false and dangerous. In addition, personal lifestyle was to be frugal, abstaining and hardworking. Not the plural lifestyles encouraged by the urban and cosmopolitan environment, but the traditional and morally uniform lifestyle of the farm and the frontier were the Christian ideal. Founding this traditional morality was the Bible, but not the liberal Bible accessible only through complex hermeneutics. Rather the Bible was the plain dealing book of God, literally inspired and literally true. Not only was everything in the Bible beyond the questioning of scholarly rationality, it was also easy to understand, as plain as the nose on your face. Not the sophistication and tolerance of the North Eastern liberal, but the down home common sense and righteousness of the small town and rural American was the road to salvation.

Looked at in this way, conservative Protestantism of the time therefore reflected a sense of status decline on the part of those, predominantly in rural and small town America, who felt that the modernizing world was no longer operating according to their cultural norms. Indeed, the strong premillennial current in the Fundamentalist movement supports the notion that it tended toward a retreat from and rejection of the world, emphasizing sectarian features of the Protestant tradition to define and defend an ethnic

culture of predominantly Anglo-Saxon heritage. Nonetheless, Fundamentalism also had a strong activist side. Several of its leaders maintained
that their Christianity was the necessary foundation of civilization in general
and of the American nation in particular. And nowhere was this offensive
side of status politics clearer than in the attitude to the American
involvement in World War I.

Until the United States entered the war in 1917, many Fundamentalist
leaders were opposed to such involvement and to the war itself. From that
time on, however, these same leaders vied with the liberals in demonstrating
patriotism and support for the war effort. Far from showing inconsistency,
this shift actually represented a politicization of Fundamentalism that was to
continue in the immediate postwar period. The terms of Fundamentalist
defence of American involvement in the war are instructive.

It was perhaps a happy accident of history that the prime representative of
everything that was wrong with the New Christianity, higher biblical
criticism and its removal of certainty, was an intellectual product of German
scholarship of the nineteenth century. Accordingly, Fundamentalist leaders
came to see World War I as a battle between German rationalism and
American Christianity. The German attitude to the Bible was the centre-
piece of a wider phenomenon that was at the heart of everything that was
wrong with modernity. Could it be any accident, then, that this destroyer of
God's ordained order should have led the German nation into the abyss of
militarism and social disorder, the direct result of which was World War I?
The conflict between the United States and Germany took on epic
proportions as a classic battle of good versus evil. In this battle, the liberals
on the homefront were representatives of the evil enemy, perhaps duped,
perhaps conscious allies, but nevertheless the seed of the evil without in the
Lord's vineyard.

What this episode shows is that early twentieth century Fundamentalism
was already to a significant extent a response to globalization. The United
States was feeling the effects of globalizing systems like the industrial
capitalist economy, positivistic science, and the system of sovereign states.
Their development brought with it the relativizing challenge of real cultural
'strangers'. In this situation, Fundamentalism recreated and reasserted a
particular American group-cultural exclusivity as uniquely valid. It based
that claim on a religion whose God sanctified the culture and battled
insidious evil within the nation, but evil with its source in real outsiders.
Contemporary New Christian Rightists carry on this view but change the
enemies to Communism without and secular humanism within.

The period immediately after the war was in some senses a golden time
for the Fundamentalists. Their greatest political victory came in the form
of Prohibition in America. Although the outlawing of alcohol had the support of most liberals as well, it was a cornerstone for Fundamentalist interpretations of social problems. It was the kind of personal moral issue
whose political institutionalization vindicated the Fundamentalists' version
of Christianity, their idea of social order, their group culture. In John

Simpson's words, Prohibition 'symbolized a status triumph of rural Protestant Americans over the Eastern upper classes, the Catholic and Jewish immigrants and the urbanized middle classes' (1983: 199).

Even though this establishment of religious influence was shortlived, ending with the repeal of Prohibition in 1933, it illustrates the close connection in the modern context between ethnic group culture, politicization of religion, and the personal symbolization of evil. Once the liberal modernists of the New Christianity had been identified with the external threat of Germany, the boundaries between true Christian America and the others could be drawn with far greater confidence. Modernism was not an alternative direction for the nation; it was foreign and evil, a threat to civilization, Christianity, and America. What was clearly a status conflict among competing elites was for a time successfully styled as a choice between good and evil, us and them, order and chaos, or simply God and Satan.

The politicization of Fundamentalism during this time illustrates clearly that the difference between religious liberals and conservatives cannot be reduced to a difference between concentration on applied religion and pure religion respectively. We do not understand 'liberal' and 'conservative' adequately if we conceive of them simply as the alternatives of accommodation and resistance to modernity. Rather, the difference centres around the way these alternatives render the transcendent in immanent terms. Both the New Christian Rightists and their Fundamentalist forebears have sought to identify a particular group and its culture as the expression of the divine will, as the potentially closest approximation to the transcendent good that is possible in the immanent realm. To counter the evident manifestations of evil or sin within the purportedly good group, they have seen the clearer embodiment of evil in an external group, whose evil interests are represented internally by the rightists' liberal opponents. This strategy identified the cultural and status interests of an important subculture in the United States with the interests of the American nation as a whole and with God's will.

Liberal religious leaders, on the other hand, have increasingly, as the century wore on, looked to all of humanity as the privileged group of God's concern. Recently, one group of more liberal American church leaders expressed their opposition to the contemporary rightist agenda in the following terms:

> We do not simply disagree with [the religious right's] stance on particular items on their agenda; we find their selection of issues to be theologically and ethically inadequate. An agenda identified by Christian believers ought to reflect *God's concern for the whole world*. . . . Our study of the biblical witness convinces us that the God of the prophets and of Jesus calls the people of God to work for peace and things that make for peace, to seek justice for the poor, and to care for the created order. (quoted in Roof and McKinney, 1987: 188; my italics)[3]

The evidently global perspective shown here seeks not to exclude those that deviate from some culturally specific set of religious norms, but to include them through pluralistic conciliation and egalitarian action.

Status Politics and the Status of America

Applying status politics arguments to the contemporary New Christian Right presents certain difficulties; not because there is no longer an identifiable group defending and promoting its cultural norms and values, but because the global context of this struggle has become far more immediate since the time of the Fundamentalists. In the current situation, the United States, as a political segment of global society, is experiencing not only a furtherance of the internal consequences of modern structures, but also a 'status' crisis as a nation in the world system.[4] While Fundamentalists and Evangelicals have, if anything, improved their relative status in comparison to other groups within the United States (see Jorstad, 1981; Roof and McKinney, 1987: 107ff.; Simpson, 1985), the global status of the United States in its role as economic and political superpower has been successfully challenged in the last three decades by global actors as diverse as Japan and the USSR, Vietnam and Iran, the EEC and OPEC, to name but the most significant. The platform of the New Christian Right reflects this situation quite clearly.

In their explanations of the rise of the New Christian Right, both Simpson and Hammond point to the failure of the New Deal welfare state to solve the problems of modern America. Hammond writes that

> the current crisis of legitimacy is not the same as gave rise to Fundamentalism in the 1920's. . . . Today what we despair over is quite different. We have lost faith in Keynesian economics, in the United States as a world policeman, and in the good faith of government legislators. City life has brought not utopia but the jungle again. . . . The Social Gospel proved no more adequate a guide to the Kingdom than did the New Deal. (1983: 222)

Simpson says much the same, emphasizing the extent to which Evangelical/ Fundamentalist Protestantism 'provided a strong source for a sense of cultural continuity' (1983: 202) in a time of disconcerting events like Vietnam and race riots in American cities.

While these interpretations correctly locate the rise of the New Christian Right in the peculiar conditions of post-1960 American society, the negative indicators listed by both authors as proof of a crisis in American modernity point to much wider phenomena than the shattered optimism of an individual country. Aside from the manifestly internal events like presidential assassination, urban blight, racial tension, and persistent poverty, Simpson and Hammond also mention Vietnam, the Iran hostage crisis, and a general failure on the part of the United States to develop a workable foreign policy. The juxtaposition of these external factors with the internal ones is not fortuitous. Since the globalization of society is a consequence of modernity, internal crises associated with modernity are more than likely going to be at least partial reflections of major developments in global society, especially when the country concerned is as permeated by global structures as is the United States. The platform of the New Christian Right illustrates this global connectivity quite well.

A first, quick acquaintance with the issues championed by the New Christian Right reveals a somewhat odd combination of personal moral issues, geopolitical issues, and economic issues. Opposition to the inclusion of homosexuals is placed alongside anti-Communism, and both of these are paired with an explicit espousal of individualistic *laissez-faire* capitalism. While the writings of the movement trace them all to a fundamental moral and biblical message, the highly selective nature of these issues and their resemblance to the platform of the secular right in America indicate that there is more at issue than the reassertion of pure religious norms and values.

The message of the New Christian Right is a call to religious revival, moral regeneration, and the resurgence of the American nation. Jerry Falwell, as a prime example, states that 'America needs the impact of a genuine spiritual revival led by Bible-believing pastors'; that 'moral cancers . . . are causing our society to rot from within'; and that Americans 'have the opportunity to rebuild America to the greatness it once had as a leader among leaders in the world' (1981: 217, 188, 186). The three ideas are, of course, strictly related. Religious revival is the essential prerequisite of moral regeneration which in turn will cause the United States to recover its leadership role in the world. Simpson quotes the Rev. Adrian Rodgers, one-time head of the Southern Baptist Convention, to illustrate this syllogism: 'The scream of the great American eagle has become the twitter of a frightened sparrow. America must be reborn again or join the graveyard of the nations' (1983: 202).

Pat Robertson, in his book, *America's Dates with Destiny* (1986), presents one of the more systematic expositions of the basic Christian Rightist message. Claiming that liberals have sought to eliminate the 'central role of America's Judeo-Christian heritage in the founding and later history of the nation' (1986: 15), Robertson presents his own version. In the spirit of early twentieth century Fundamentalism, he sees American history until the late nineteenth century as an essentially positive story of discovery. The twentieth century, by contrast, Robertson sees as a time of decline and loss until the rise of the New Christian Right in the 1980s. World War I and American involvement in it were the result of the 'pulling up of the nation's spiritual roots, the disregard of its Judeo-Christian heritage' (182). In contrast to the uniquely American cast that populates his times of discovery, he traces this subsequent apostasy to the influence mostly of foreigners like Darwin, Marx, Nietzsche, Einstein, and Freud. Subsequent indicators of decline include the founding of the American Civil Liberties Union, Roosevelt's New Deal, the spread of Communist regimes after World War II, and Johnson's 'Great Society'. The nadir of the downward spiral are for Robertson two external events: the American military defeat in Vietnam and the Iranian hostage crisis.

With the April 1980 'Washington for Jesus' rally, however, the nation began to turn around. Robertson calls it 'the beginning of a spiritual revolution' (282). Ronald Reagan's inauguration is the next hopeful sign. Political renewal, a 'return to our conservative roots', was already happening in response to the beginnings of spiritual renewal. And Robertson already sees some concrete results. Outlining the problems the United States was facing at the time of the 1981 inauguration, he writes:

> Abroad, America had become the world's laughingstock. The defeat in Vietnam; . . . the Soviet's recent invasion of Afghanistan; and the loss of Angola, Mozambique, Ethiopia, South Yemen, and Nicaragua to Communists left the United States looking powerless and afraid. The Soviets were expanding their atheist-Marxist sphere of influence around the globe with impunity. And in Teheran, fifty-two American hostages were spending their 444th day in captivity. The new president had promised to end this era of Soviet expansionism and to bring the captives home.

The author then relates that the Iranian hostages were released that same inauguration day and attributes their freedom to the beginning of the new era:

> Apparently, the Ayatollah Khomeini and his terrorist friends sensed a new mood in Washington. The president had promised 'an era of renewal', and on his first day in office, at least one tyrant half a world away took him seriously. (1986: 284)

Most New Christian Right leaders share the 'cosmic' logic apparent in Robertson's interpretation of American history. It is what binds the varied issues of their platform into a consistent whole. This general insight does not, however, clarify the relation between specific issues, for example, homosexuality and anti-Communism; nor does it show sufficiently how these reflect the globalization of society.

One of the points of contrast between New Christian Rightists and their Fundamentalist forebears is that the former do not stress pure religious issues nearly as much. Leaders like Falwell reach out to conservatives in other faiths, particularly Catholics, Jews, and Mormons. Accordingly, spreading Evangelical faith and being 'born again' are not explicit aims of the movement as they were for early twentieth century Fundamentalists. While Falwell, Robertson, and other New Christian Right leaders often speak of a 'Christian' America founded on 'Christian' principles, they use the word more as a synonym for 'moral' than, for example, 'Evangelical' or 'Fundamentalist'. Far from betraying a lukewarm commitment on their part to their particular branch of Christianity, this ecumenical attitude indicates that the emphasis of the movement is on religious performance rather than religious function. Therefore, what constitutes spiritual renewal is left comparatively vague and implicit. Specific moral issues, by contrast, are at the heart of the New Christian Right platform.

The most important moral issues for the New Christian Right all concern the control of the body, above all sexual control. Abortion, homosexuality, and pornography are the most obvious ones, but others are directly related. Critical among these latter are the character of the family and education. The connections can be described as follows: Religion or God determines what proper (sexual) use of the body is. Correct education inculcates this bodily propriety into the next generation. But the family is the core social institution upon which all else depends. A family is ordered properly, is healthy and strong, to the extent that it embodies and fosters correct bodily behaviour. When families are thus ordered, the health and strength of society and of the nation follow. Falwell puts it like this:

> The family is the God-ordained institution of the marriage of one man and one woman together for a lifetime with their . . . children. The family is the fundamental building block and basic unit of our society, and its continued health is a prerequisite for a healthy and prosperous nation. No nation has ever been stronger than the families within it. America's families are its strength, and they symbolize the miracle of America. (1981: 204)

At one level, the New Christian Right is espousing a 'politics of virility' here: sexual discipline is the basis of moral discipline, which in turn is a prerequisite for national discipline (cf. Simpson, 1987). If the United States is to regain its dominance in the world, its families must maintain a structure that consistently yields individuals motivated to channel their energies for the sake of their nation and not in pursuit of sensual pleasure (cf. Swanson, 1986). Families, therefore, exist to foster necessary bodily control.

There is, however, another dimension to this relation. Besides families, other social institutions also exist that can exercise control over the body. In particular, schools, governments, and health institutions fulfil this function in contemporary society (cf. Foucault, 1978). Yet the New Christian Right insists that the family cannot be replaced in this regard. On the contrary, attempting to replace it is at the heart of the problem with modernity.

What the family represents for the New Christian Right is an authority structure beyond the disposition of modern functional rationality. Leaders of the movement reject the development of the modern family as an institution that exists to reinforce pluralistic, individual lifestyles; and they especially reject the relative decline of the family as the primary locus of child socialization. They express this rejection most clearly in their characterization and criticism of those whom they call the *secular humanists*. While secular humanism does function as a convenient label for all that is wrong with contemporary America and the world, it also has a more specific and instructive meaning. It refers to a view of the world, allegedly dominant among the New Christian Right's opponents, which is not 'God-centred'. For Falwell, '[secular] humanism has its origin in man's attempts to place human wisdom above divine revelation' (1981: 199). Pat Robertson also traces the decline of twentieth century America to the movement that put 'man at the center of the universe' (1986: 175).

By contrast, the traditional family favoured by the New Christian Right is founded on 'Judeo-Christian principles'. It is therefore uniquely qualified to raise children in the correct way. Again, in Falwell's words,

> The most important function performed by the family is the rearing and character formation of children, a function it was uniquely created to perform and for which no remotely adequate substitute has been found. The family is the best and most efficient 'department of health, education, and welfare'. (1981: 206)

As this statement hints, the secular humanist enemies are to be found especially in those public, often governmental institutions which seek to apply instrumentally rational techniques in those areas the New Christian Right insists are the responsibility of the family. These institutions include, above all, the public school system, government bureaucracies like the Department of Health, Education, Welfare; but also private organizations such as Planned Parenthood, the National Educational Association, and the National Organization of Women. All of these seek to supplant divine authority by insisting that humans can and should make their own decisions on the basis of informed choices. These include 'lifestyle' choices, opening the door for all those sexual variations that are so abhorrent to the New Christian Right.

In Weberian terms, New Christian Right leaders decry the supplanting of traditional authority with rational-legal authority and value-rational with instrumental action. Indeed, the defence of the traditional family is at heart a defence of a specific lifestyle, a specific worldview, a specific culture, legitimated with reference to American Evangelical Christianity in a society dominated by instrumental systems. The God of the New Christian Right prescribes a particular pattern of behaviour and outlook; he does not justify this pattern to human beings any more than a parent justifies various protective prohibitions to a child. Humans stray from the appointed path at their own risk. For their own good, they must simply accept it as the best way.

Bodily discipline for the New Christian Right is therefore only indirectly a prerequisite for national power. Between these two is the traditional family as the social incarnation of religious truth. What is needed for national power and health is above all for Americans to accept the unity of the transcendent Christian God and his immanent creation. Americans express their acceptance by adhering to the moral code that is the manifestation of God's sovereignty over the world. Moreover, this moral code is culturally specific, like all moral codes. For the New Christian Right, the closest approximation to this divinely sanctioned culture is the American one; but not the one that is dominant at present. Rather New Christian Rightists see twentieth century Evangelical/Fundamentalist culture in that role. Although not dominant at present, it is the correct one that Americans abandoned when they substituted modern, human-centred rationality towards the end of the last century. If they are to recover the greatness that was once theirs, Americans must return to this cultural outlook and its characteristic institutions: the family, the church, and Christian schools. Correspondingly, they must restrict the independent power of modern instrumentalities, especially the bureaucratic state, academic education, and positivistic science.

Evidently, as with all revivalist movements, the New Christian Right sees traditional American culture very much through the prism of its own time. Whether the United States was ever dominated by the culture its leaders describe may be doubted. What is certain, however, is that their cultural vision is a reflection of the contemporary culture of their own status group: white, predominantly Southern, rural and small town, middle to lower middle class, less affluent, less educated Americans (see Hunter, 1983: 49ff.; Shupe and Stacey, 1982: 15ff.; Simpson, 1983) who are nevertheless benefiting from a current rise in status as a result of economic and demographic changes in the United States (see Egerton, 1974; Shibley, 1991; but also Shortridge, 1977). Accordingly, the New Christian Right emphasizes not only the sexual and religious norms of this group, but also espouses untrammelled free enterprise, a low social welfare role for government, and the removal of policies like affirmative action, all of which threaten to compromise its members' further status elevation.

Spiritual renewal and moral regeneration through reestablishment of traditional bodily discipline are, however, only part of the picture. Although the status politics of the New Christian Right are the expression of status competition between groups within the United States for power and influence, the status of the United States as a nation-state within global society is equally at issue. New Christian Right leaders want to 'make America great again', indicating not just a threat to American greatness, but the successful erosion of that greatness as well.

Some indicators of this global decline have already been mentioned: the defeat in Vietnam, the Iran hostage crisis, other foreign policy failures in the Middle East and Central America. These, however, are only some of the more visible signs of a decline in American world dominance over the past decades. These external crises are not, any more than the real internal problems such as poverty and drug abuse, artificial phenomena manufactured by the NCR leaders for the sake of their own status advance. The decline of American influence, especially after its unchallenged dominance in the immediate post-World War II decades, is very real and extends beyond the issue of military prowess. A detailed analysis of this decline is well beyond the scope of this book. To show the connections between the global fate of the United States and the New Christian Right's link between moral decline, secular humanism, and the spread of Communism, a brief presentation is, however, necessary.

Although the United States still has the largest national economy in the world, its hegemonic position has been challenged in recent decades, above all by the European Community and Japan. Key symptoms of this change are the problems encountered using the US dollar as the international monetary standard, the severe American trade deficit of the 1980s and 1990s, and the recurrent protectionist sentiment within the United States (cf. Wallerstein, 1974b). Militarily, America is still the most powerful state in global society. Yet the use of this power in the world scene is more and more subject to political restrictions. The unsurpassed military might of the United States may be justified as a deterrent in some cases, but more often than not its use proves highly risky if not always entirely counterproductive. The loss of the war in Vietnam, the failed attempt to rescue the hostages in Iran, the destruction of the US Marine barracks in Beirut, even the continued power of Saddam Hussein in Iraq after the Gulf war: all illustrate that the role of the military in foreign affairs is severely limited in a global political system that depends on the sovereignty of states within often recognizably artificial boundaries, and where a nation's international image is a critical aspect of its international influence.

This state of affairs itself already shows the degree to which no nation can be so dominant in the world system of today that it can simply exert force wherever its interests demand (see Meyer, 1980). Certainly the 1991 Gulf war and the end of the Cold War in favour of the United States may seem to belie this analysis. Yet, if one considers the careful and multilateral ways in which American governments have proceeded through these events, then the notion that they represent a revival of US hegemony appears significantly less obvious. In any case, during the heyday of the NCR between 1978 and 1985, these 'successes' had not yet happened.

The implication of the foregoing is that American global decline is not just a cyclical affair in which one imperial power fades to make room for the rise of the next one. In addition to economic and political cycles, we are also witnessing the increasing development of global societal structures (cf. Bergesen, 1980; Meyer and Hannan, 1979a). As the example of the ambiguity of military power illustrates, decline of American hegemony is not so much an absolute loss of power; it is a reflection of changes in the way states can use their power, especially outside their boundaries.

Within the terms of this theoretical outlook, the fundamental problem that the New Christian Right is facing is more than a decline in the global influence of specifically American culture. It is also the declining influence of that culture in America. For the movement's leaders, global decline and moral turpitude are two sides of the same coin. So, from the present theoretical viewpoint, the increasing development of the American state as part of the global system of formally analogous states, the further ramification of the world economy, the independent spread of similar educational systems, the increasing world-dominance of the scientific outlook, and other important global developments in health, communication, technology, and environmental concerns all are manifestations of the increasing strength of functionally rationalized and differentiated systems on a global basis. Group culture, in this system, is either privatized or politicized. The New Christian Right resists the former by pursuing the latter. Its complaints about the spread and dominance of secular humanism, moral decay, and turning away from the Christian Evangelical/ Fundamentalist God are all part of this global picture.

The most critical confirmation of this analysis is the very clear association that New Christian Right leaders draw between secular humanism, the domestic 'atheistic' attitude, and international Communism, the external and unequivocal incarnation of the godless evil towards which the secular humanists are leading America. Accordingly, Tim LaHaye, another prominent New Christian Right leader, identifies the basic tenets of secular humanism as atheism, evolution, amorality, autonomy of man, and one-world socialism (LaHaye, 1980). And Jerry Falwell approvingly quotes his colleague Mel Gabler to the effect that humanist education promotes, among other things, 'situation ethics, self-centredness, evolution, the neglect or negation of Christianity, sexual freedom, . . . and international-ism' (Falwell, 1981: 199; cf. also Bruce, 1988: 77). LaHaye's choice of words may be especially revealing: socialism is a threat at least in part because it claims that there is or ought to be only one world. Given that this one world evidently contains a great plurality of different group cultures, different religions, switching to the 'global community' as a primary unit of identification relativizes and privatizes American culture both around the globe and in the United States.

New Christian Rightists define the line between the American culture to be defended and the encroaching global system in religious terms: Chris-tianity vs. atheism; amoral secular humanism vs. moral America; the free world vs. Communism. The domestic threat and the international threat of decline and relativization meld in this last opposition. New Christian Right leaders, but especially Jerry Falwell, therefore saw no contradiction in defending America internationally, whether through increased defence spending or through support of 'Christian' governments beleaguered by Communist, one-world opponents, as in Israel, South Africa, or the Philippines. Communism, instead of the exceedingly complex phenomenon that it has been in the world system, becomes rather a catch-all for manifest evil in the world, manifest evil that threatens the manifest good and its manifest destiny.

The New Christian Right as a Religio-social Movement

The New Christian Right did not happen spontaneously simply as a reflection of prevailing social conditions. The founders, leaders, and activists had to crystallize the conditions into clear issues and then bring people to act on the basis of these interpretations. They had to mobilize resources. Embedded in this assertion is the idea that the NCR would not have happened without some *extra*-ordinary effort. The routine functioning of religious and political institutions by itself would not have produced it. This, of course, is a defining feature of any social movement. Its added significance here is that the religious actors involved did not, indeed could not, rely on the straightforward reproduction and expansion of religious communication alone in their attempt to assert public religious influence. By contrast, Pons and Fleischmann merely had to claim the discovery of cold fusion for the world to beat a path to their door. And in the early 1980s, Lee Iacocca could engineer the massive government bailout of the Chrysler Corporation on the basis of the economic consequences alone.

To create a viable social movement, NCR activists had to address several interconnected but analytically separable problems. First, they had to generate issues in such a way as to combine already established religious interpretations with newly perceived problems. The link between 'old time religion' and 'making America great again' had to be framed in a fashion that would be convincing to the potential supporters of the movement, ultimately Falwell's 'moral majority', but more immediately American Fundamentalists and Evangelicals. In this chapter, I have already devoted considerable space to a discussion of this aspect. Beyond such 'diagnostic framing', however, movement leaders also had to devise a programme of action that would eventually solve the problems thus interpreted. In the case of the NCR, this 'prognostic framing'[5] advocated above all direct political action at all levels, from the local school board to presidential elections. The final task was then to bring potential supporters to act on the basis of the interpretations thus provided.

A detailed presentation of how or how well the NCR accomplished these mobilization tasks is beyond my scope here. Others have in any case devoted considerable attention to this aspect.[6] What is, however, important for the present context is the extent to which globalizing systems provide both possibilities and constraints for the success of religio-social movements like the New Christian Right. It is a central thesis of this book that modern globalizing circumstances deliver both. How does the current case illustrate this notion?

As a social system, the New Christian Right operates primarily within a number of functional subsystems, but without doubt the most central are the religious and the political.[7] The religious system of global society has as one of its more notable characteristics a great pluralism of forms and styles. I have argued that this feature distinguishes religion from the more dominant subsystems like science and economy, and that it is a consequence of the holistic starting point of religion. Religion in the United States is typically very pluralistic, even though most of that pluralism consists of variations on a Christian theme. The situation has helped and hindered the NCR as a social movement.

On the positive side, the United States has a large percentage of fairly conservative Christians, the bulk of them Evangelicals (including Pentecostals) and Fundamentalists. Their number has been growing steadily in the post-World War II period. Beyond such explicitly religious identification, probably in the neighbourhood of 30–40 percent of the entire population shares in the NCR's consensus on most key socio-moral issues.[8] To help mobilize this group of potential supporters, the movement had an array of cultural and organizational resources at its disposal. These included a large number of independent, mostly Baptist churches which were the primary source of NCR leadership. Tim LaHaye, Greg Dixon, and Jerry Falwell are well-known examples of ministers who built up large 'super' churches as their base of operation. Moreover, most of these leaders were already members of both informal networks and more formal national organizations such as the Baptist Bible Fellowship (Liebman, 1983). Country-wide communication among the leadership therefore did not have to be built from the ground up; nor did it require taking over an existing denomination, even though NCR supporters have had some success in this regard with the Southern Baptist Convention (see Ammerman, 1990). In addition, the development of religious broadcasting and computerized direct mail built on earlier urban revivalism. In combination, they gave the issues and the leaders a broader audience, and provided the key to financing the movement (see Frankl, 1987; Hadden, 1987; Hadden and Swann, 1981; Hoover, 1988).

Balancing these advantages, however, were religious factors that stood in the way of mobilization. Although the NCR targeted primarily Evangelicals and Fundamentalists, it also tried to expand its appeals beyond this core constituency, and succeeded to some extent at the level of leadership (for example, Richard Viguerie, Paul Weyrich). Nonetheless, the movement remained for the most part a creature of conservative Protestantism. The advantage of growing out of a vibrant religious subculture was also a weakness in a pluralistic and privatized religious context. To reach effectively beyond its relatively inelastic core group, it would have had to play down the root religious factors or at least compartmentalize them. Either strategy would have run counter to the NCR's holistic and particularistic view of what the problems and the solutions were (cf. Bruce, 1988: 126–146). Given the large number of conservative Protestants, this may not have been that much of a problem. Like other religious groups, however, this branch of American Protestantism is not homogeneous in its attitudes. Many held similar socio-moral attitudes, but refused to support the NCR's course of action. And those who were mobilized tended to be Fundamentalists and Evangelicals with stronger religious identifications, making compromise for the sake of expanding the movement even within the core group not only ideologically, but also practically, risky.[9]

The situation shows both the strengths and weaknesses of the modern religious system. On the one hand, NCR activists had considerable religious resources at their disposal which they combined creatively with the latest globalizing technologies to achieve substantial mobilization. On the other hand, dependence on those resources, especially the voluntary adherents of their core constituency, restricted the movement even to a minority of those who might have been expected to support it. To move beyond this stage, the NCR had to mobilize non-religious resources and modify or compromise its aims. To be sure, this is a dilemma faced by most social movements, religious or not. It also illustrates the typical problems of reconciling the demands of pure function and applied performance. Religion is not different in this regard from other functional modes of social communication. What is different is that religious leaders should have to resort to social movement strategies to apply religion in a non-privatized way; and that they have relatively few resources at their disposal from other, already established performances such as political legitimation, education, social welfare, or knowledge production. This problem is well illustrated in the ambiguous outcome of NCR involvement in the political system of the United States.

As in religion, so in politics, American culture celebrates pluralism. The much more homogeneous structures of the political system, however, its more uniform norms, funnel that pluralism in very consistent ways. Specifically, the political process centres around competition among interest groups, whether this be in political parties, elections, or the actual functioning of government. The American political system thereby puts a premium on the ability of interests to organize and mobilize resources. This feature has played no small part in the rise of the New Christian Right.[10] It means that the political system resonates with social movement strategies for effecting social change: one does not have to mobilize a majority or already be part of the established elite to be politically successful. Moreover, American political culture incorporates a much-discussed, quasi-religious nationalism (civil religion) that facilitates the linking of religious information and interpretations to public policy formation in spite of the fact that religion and the state are constitutionally separated (see especially Bellah, 1970b; 1975).

It is just because of such political and cultural advantages, combined with considerable religious resources, that the only very limited success of the NCR is so significant in the present context. To be sure, the Equal Rights Amendment was not ratified, there have been small but significant moves favouring the NCR's position on abortion, and conservative forces have won some local school battles centring on matters like sex education and textbooks. Overall, however, the NCR's moral issues agenda has not been institutionalized in the political and legal structures of the country. What has happened is that conservative Christianity has reasserted its status as a legitimate interest within the American polity – perhaps especially at the grass-roots level of the Republican Party – a minority position that, like other minorities, cannot be easily ignored. In the theoretical terms developed in previous chapters, the NCR as a social movement has succeeded in having the exclusivity it represents included more solidly in some of the dominant instrumental systems in the United States, but not to the exclusion of other pluralistic and privatized worldviews and lifestyles. The NCR has had only very limited success in making conservative Protestantism more publicly influential in the sense I am using that concept here: with occasional and local exceptions, one can generally ignore what happens in the religious system without adverse consequences.

Conclusions

The rise and decline of the New Christian Right as a social movement is then instructive from several angles. Given the resources at its disposal, certain features of the American political system, and the situation of the United States in the late 1970s and early 1980s, such a movement was relatively easy to create. These very advantages, however, also stood in the way of institutionalizing the movement solidly in the communication of various instrumental systems, especially the political, legal, and educational. If the American system favours interest group mobilization, then anything the New Christian Right can do, its opponents might also do. More importantly, perhaps, the fact that the key NCR resources were religious by itself limited the extent of its success. Religious pluralism and the compartmentalization of the religious system are institutionalized in the American political and legal systems, and in most variations of American culture. A particularistic and explicitly holistic movement like the NCR contradicts these tendencies.

Among the many illustrations of this fact is the fate of Pat Robertson's run for the Republican presidential nomination. The campaign featured impressive organization and mobilization of resources, but it failed to a large degree because Robertson was first and foremost a religious leader. The small minority that supported him did so because of this fact. Most voters, however, apparently rejected him for the same reason: he might impose his religious particularism on those that did not share it; and being a religious leader made him, if anything, unsuitable for political office (see Bruce, 1988: 129–131; Johnson et al., 1989: 394–397; Jorstad, 1987: 249–255). Even though religion in the United States is quite strong as a privatized system, religious leaders have difficulty translating that strength into public influence. And like other systemic experts, as soon as they step outside their sphere, they are judged by the criteria of other systems: in spite and because of being grounded in religion, Pat Robertson failed as a politician and creationism failed as science.

Although these typically American cultural and structural factors go some way to explaining the fate of the New Christian Right, the conditions of its rise and, if not fall, then levelling also correspond to the global developments discussed above. Inasmuch as the rise of the NCR was at least to a certain degree a response to the status decline of the United States in the global system, so we should suspect that the waning of this movement has to do with the perceived arrest of that decline. Put slightly differently, while the partial success of the NCR in the 1980s cannot be denied, the immersion of the United States in global society leaves this movement subject to developments within that society. In particular, the economic boom under Reagan with its unabashedly triumphal capitalist rhetoric, combined with mid-1980s loosening of Eastern European socialism, indicated that the enemy of the New Christian Right was not as formidable or intractable as the latter's ideology would have it. The relativization of American global superpower status has its parallel in the similar, but much more precipitous and dramatic, fate of the Soviet Union. The dire necessity for moral regeneration attenuates without the clear presence of identifiable satanic forces both within and outside the nation. Unlike liberal religious directions, a conservative movement like the New Christian Right depends on such real presence of evil to lend its message the urgency requisite for public influence. Without this factor, conservative religion may continue to provide powerful resources for social movements, but the religious content itself offers little distinct advantage.

It may seem far-fetched to claim that a period of economic boom and the favourable outcome of the Cold War for the Americans were instrumental in bringing about the relative fading of the New Christian Right in the United States. To be sure, other factors were probably at least as important, as I have discussed above. Yet the degree to which the New Christian Right has been an attempt to defend American group culture against the relativization inherent in the development of global society leaves it vulnerable precisely to external events. The United States is deeply involved in the major subsystems of global society. Only with great sacrifice and considerable difficulty could it choose the isolationist path of early revolutionary Iran, Maoist China, or even Ne Win's Burma (cf. Arjomand, 1988; Chirot, 1986; Steinberg, 1990). Defending any defined version of American group culture against the compromises of the global social system therefore becomes possible only when there is a perceived decline in American status in the world *and* the bipolarity between superpowers locked in a perpetual Cold War persists.[11] Attenuation of the latter in particular makes the distinction between the 'free world' and 'Communism' significantly less clear. A message of moral regeneration loses some of its plausibility just as much as Ronald Reagan's Strategic Defense Initiative.

Accordingly, since 1985, not only did Reagan become somewhat of a dove in his relations with the Soviet Union, but Jerry Falwell and Pat Robertson retired peacefully from the national political scene. The foray into public performance religion had not proved entirely satisfactory. As if admitting this, in his 1986 autobiography, Falwell declares that it was time to return to the pure religious task:

> For the past seven years I had given most of my time to political causes associated with the renewal of our nation's spirit and the change of her political and moral direction. Those years as chairman of the Moral Majority had taken a tremendous toll on my ministries at Thomas Road Baptist Church. Looking back, I felt that my decision to enter into the political arena had been right and necessary. But looking to the future, I knew that God wanted me to return to the basics of my own spiritual journey. (1986: 388)

He concludes his work with the somewhat melancholy statement that 'God has promised that the evildoers who cause suffering "shall soon be cut down . . . and wither". And I hang on to that promise like a sailor hangs on to a life preserver while floating on a stormy sea' (446).

Notes

1 The relevant literature is probably best divided into works that deal with the contemporary movement explicitly, and those that provide the necessary historical context. As examples of the former, see Bromley and Shupe, 1984; Bruce, 1988; Hill and Owen, 1982; Jorstad, 1987; Liebman and Wuthnow, 1983. From the latter, see Hunter, 1983; Marsden, 1980; 1983; McLoughlin, 1978.

2 I note here a pattern that repeats itself for each of the case studies of this chapter and the following three (5–8). The contemporary movement in each case has a significant antecedent movement during what Robertson (1992b) calls the 'take-off' period of globalization and what for Wallerstein (1984a) is the peak of the long wave previous to the current one. Thus American Fundamentalism parallels the New Christian Right, social Catholicism parallels liberation theology, the Constitutional revolution the Iranian revolution, and (religious) Zionism contemporary religious Zionism.

3 Note that the contrast is between conservative personal moral issues and what amounts to 'Justice, Peace, and the Integrity of Creation', for which see Chapter 9 below.

4 Wallerstein (1976), for instance, speaks of phases of globalization with certain identifiable characteristics. The phase we are in now has as one of its defining features the end of American world hegemony.

5 The terms are those of Snow and Benford, 1988.

6 To date, perhaps the most self-conscious social movement analysis of the New Christian Right is Bruce, 1988.

7 Other important connections are with the systems for art, health, education, news media, and the family; but given the centrality for the New Christian Right of mobilizing religious resources to affect political decisions, these latter would seem to be primary.

8 This figure varies according to what and how one measures. For various estimates, see Ammerman, 1987; Hunter, 1983; Simpson, 1983; Yinger and Cutler, 1983.

9 On the difficulties of mobilizing the core constituency, see Shupe and Stacey, 1982; Wilcox, 1989. According to the latter study, NCR support (measured as Moral Majority support) in 1983 stood at about 25 percent of Evangelicals.

10 Simpson and MacLeod, 1985, and Bruce 1988: 68–76 both make this point by comparing the American situation to the Canadian and British political systems respectively.

11 Although in the context of a different argument, John Simpson (1987) also makes the connection between American superpower status and the rise of the New Christian Right.

6

THE LIBERATION THEOLOGICAL MOVEMENT IN LATIN AMERICA

The Global Juncture

The discussion of Latin American liberation theology can begin by noting that its origins date from the same decade as most new social movements and the globalization debate itself, namely the later 1960s to early 1970s. Both Roland Robertson and Immanuel Wallerstein style this period as the beginning of the most recent phase in the globalization process or in the world-system. Among the defining features of this phase, they see a heightened awareness of globalization, enhanced concern with humanity as a species-community, and the inclusion of the Third World (Robertson, 1990b: 27); or upheaval in the realm of antisystemic movements and decline in American global hegemony (Wallerstein, 1988b). Without attempting to defend the periodization as such, the listed symptoms are of the sort that ought to be manifest in liberal religion[1] because it typically affirms globalization and global values, and addresses residual problems on that basis.

The dominant religious tradition out of which Latin American liberation theology and its attendant movement developed, Roman Catholic Christianity, is a case in point. Since the 1960s, it has been subject to major upheavals. The pontificate of John XXIII and the Second Vatican Council marked, among other things, a decisive turn on the part of this church away from a prevailing Eurocentric and conservative attitude toward an explicitly global and largely liberal perspective. These features are well marked in the papal social encyclicals of that decade and in key documents of the Council. There the concerns shift toward affirmation of inclusive human rights, the problems of a marginalized Third World, the desirability of working toward world community, and an ecumenical tolerance in the interests of pursuing those goals.[2] This shifting emphasis at the core of the Roman church was instrumental in the appearance and rise of the Latin American liberation theological movement.

What happened in the 1960s was not, however, a simple and straight-forward embracing of a liberal religious option. During its long history of dealing with the modernizing and globalizing context, the Roman church had generally adopted a significantly more conservative frame of reference deeply suspicious of structures and ideas that tended to marginalize its influence. That earlier period provided significant antecedents for the events of the 1960s, in terms of both ideology and practical strategy.

In the late eighteenth and during the nineteenth century, the Roman Catholic church reacted to the destruction of the traditional European alliance of throne and altar by further asserting the independence of the organization, even to the point of sacralizing it in the doctrine of papal infallibility. By the end of the nineteenth century, this response had proven inadequate for maintaining religious influence, thus spawning official social Catholicism. A new strategy developed on this basis in the decades following: the Roman church set in motion various interconnected social movements, all of which were to use the Catholic religious organization as their practical and ideological resource base. Social Catholicism addressed the many residual problems of modernization by developing Roman Catholic versions of non-religious social movements. These centred on social movement organizations with direct or indirect links to the hierarchy. Important examples were Catholic labour unions and Catholic Action groups. The latter, especially, were conceived as direct extensions of episcopal authority and consisted of organized groups of 'militants' (that is, mobilizers) whose task was to spread the Catholic social movement within their milieu or constituency.[3]

Beginning with the pontificate of Pius XI, the church also envisioned the extension of the labour movement in the form of corporatism, an attempt to institutionalize social Catholicism in the capitalist economic system and the modern state.[4] Correspondingly, in the political system, the movement led to the formation of Catholic political parties, some of which came to power during the post-World War II period in countries like Germany, Italy, Chile, and Brazil. All these social movement efforts were in addition to the continued role of Catholic social welfare, health, and educational institutions.

Like the latter, social Catholicism was a movement aimed at enhancing the practical performance of the religious system. Its goal was to solve problems like the plight of the industrial worker and what it saw as the chaos and conflict inherent in modernity. The root of these problems lay in moral failings, above all, the greed of the rich and the envy of the poor. Reestablishing religious influence by 're-Christianizing' society was therefore the prime solution. This idea of making society Christian again points to the particularistic and hence conservative nature of this movement. As an ideology, social Catholicism was antisystemic in that it traced modern problems to the religiously unconditioned operation of the capitalist economic and state-based political systems, that is, to the functional independence of the dominant instrumental systems. This is an attitude we might expect from any performance-oriented religious movement, liberal or conservative. In addition, however, social Catholicism rejected key modern and global values, especially social equality and its adjunct, pluralistic inclusion. Thus, even though the Roman church was a worldwide organization, it was at that time not liberally oriented in the sense that it insisted on the exclusive validity of (Roman Catholic) Christianity and saw the source of modern problems in the abandonment of that particularism. In the 1960s, the church severely muted this particularism, opening the way for religious approaches that interpreted the faith in harmony with typically modern and global values. Latin American liberation theology was one of the more significant outcomes.

It would, however, be inaccurate to see liberation theology simply as the Latin American reflection of the Second Vatican Council. In the decades before the 1960s, social Catholicism in Latin America looked much as it did in other parts of the world. Yet important differences in the local context provided fertile ground for certain developments that eventually led to a more radical version of the church's subsequent liberal turn. Unlike many other areas in which the Roman church claimed a sizeable portion of the population, Latin America formed part of the peripheral, Third World in the global system. The majority of the people were and still are quite poor and powerless. Moreover, it was precisely among this large group that, in many countries, the official hierarchical church had historically had the least direct influence.

The period after the Great Depression brought to Latin America the sort of accelerated industrialization and urbanization that in the late nineteenth century had spawned social Catholicism in Europe. Vast numbers of rural people were now more visible. From the perspective of many Catholic church leaders, they were also religiously vulnerable to the attractions of Protestants, spiritist groups, and Communists. A significant portion of this elite began to see the Roman church as weak and in dire need of new ways to reach the poor and dislocated masses. As part of this analysis, many of them developed a greater concern for the general economic development of Latin American countries, the lack of which they saw as a root cause of all the problems. Although Brazil provides perhaps the best example of this tendency (see Mainwaring, 1986), the general concern was widespread among other Latin American Catholic leaders.

The actions taken in the light of this new understanding were at once distinctively Latin American and indicative of how much that region was already woven into global society. On the regional level, the 1950s saw the formation for the first time in Latin American history of national and international bishops' councils.[5] Their intended purpose was to allow coordination of actions and sharing of information across hitherto isolated dioceses and between the churches of the different Latin American countries. In this way, the church could address the religious and developmental problems of the continent more effectively. At the same time, region-wide meetings of Latin American specialized Catholic Action groups provided the occasion for similar directions among lay Catholic youth. These also began to see the religious problems of their church in their socio-economic context; and, although they still saw the goal as a 'new Christendom' in Latin America, that vision already showed more liberal trends such as a more positive attitude to Protestants (see Cleary, 1985: 3–6).

These internal developments were, however, only part of a larger picture in which external factors also played a key role. In response to the perceived crisis of the Latin American church and to the blockage of missions in other parts of the world, large numbers of foreign Catholic missionaries came to the continent during the 1950s and 1960s. These not only relieved the chronic shortage of clergy in most of the countries, they also brought with them different ideas that challenged more established Latin American ecclesiastical patterns. Somewhat in reverse, many young Latin American clerics went to European schools for graduate studies. There they often absorbed those new theological currents that were instrumental in bringing about the liberal changes of Vatican II. This group includes several of the leading lights of subsequent Latin American liberation theology, most notably Hugo Assmann, Leonardo Boff, Gustavo Gutiérrez, and Juan Luis Segundo (Cleary, 1985: 77–81).

On perhaps a somewhat obvious level, these two factors simply exemplify the long-standing trans-national character of the Roman Catholic church (cf. Vallier, 1972), and as such were not new in the post-World War II situation. What they also represent, however, is an intensification of linkages with the worldwide church. Inasmuch as developments like the Latin American Bishops Conference (CELAM) and the national bishops' bodies meant a strengthening of organizational ties and communicative links within the Latin American church, these were in important respects the internal manifestations of a more global process. That increase, in turn, both in the Latin American and in the larger church, happened in the broader context of parallel intensifications in other instrumental systems and in other respects. As already mentioned, Latin America was during this period undergoing pronounced economic growth and change, this during a general period of post-war expansion in the global economic system. Accompanying demographic shifts along with technological developments such as regularly scheduled air travel increased the communicative possibilities within Latin America and with the rest of the world. The Cuban revolution combined with the subsequent Alliance for Progress intensified the entanglement of Latin America within the prevailing East/West bifurcation of the global political system. All this in a continent that had the longest history of incorporation into global systems of all the areas in what was now beginning to be called the Third World. The Latin American liberation theological movement has been, in other words, an aspect of and response to the accelerated globalization of the post-World War II era.

Greater communicative linkage in the context of globalization did not by itself already imply the liberal religious directions that this occasioned in both the Latin American and the worldwide Catholic church. Although liberal religion resonates positively with globalizing structures and ideas, the comparative disadvantages of religion under modern/global conditions make conservative directions just as likely. Which option or mix of options appears in any given case will depend on a number of factors, including those specific to the local context. The rise of liberation theology in Latin America illustrates this contingency.

The Appropriation of Resources

In the immediate post-war decade, the prevailing view among Latin American Catholic church leaders and activists was that both their church and secular society were in a state of crisis. The social Catholic ideals and developments of that decade were to address both aspects by working toward the construction of a 'new Christendom'. Function and performance were seen as two sides of the same coin here. To function better, the church had to perform better, but also vice versa. At that point, the prevailing tone was both liberal and conservative. With the subsequent rise and success of liberation theological movements, however, we see a shift in priority toward good performance as the condition for good function.[6] This represented a decidedly liberal orientation. As already noted, a prime event that made this possible was Vatican II which, among other things, put the received way of delivering functional religious communication into question. Roman Catholics, both professional and lay, were asked to reexamine virtually everything about the way they *did* their religion. The resulting fluidity and uncertainty was, in the first instance, a window of opportunity for liberal views – those embodying typically modern/global orientations – because it was precisely the perceived inadequacy of the hitherto dominant conservative orientation that Pope John XXIII, with substantial support, had called the Council to address. In the early 1960s, a great many Roman Catholics around the world were prepared to learn.

In Latin America, as elsewhere, the direction of Vatican II thus left the field open for liberal proponents to appropriate both old and new Catholic organizational resources, and to implant radically revised versions of the social Catholic ideology. Key figures in this development were change-oriented bishops in various countries, central among whom were undoubtedly Manuel Larraín of Chile and Dom Helder Camara of Brazil. This relatively small group of bishops had been instrumental in the founding and strengthening of CELAM and the various national conferences. Some of them, notably Cardinal Silva of Chile, had been vocal reformers at the Council. For about a decade after Vatican II, they faced little opposition in putting sizeable organizational resources at the disposal of the new direction. The best example of that trend was the second general conference of CELAM held in Medellín, Colombia in 1968.

The Medellín conference was called to apply the results of Vatican II to the Latin American situation. It formulated something close to official policy for the Latin American church of that time; and it was dominated by precisely those who produced the first wave of liberation theology, the progressive bishops and their radically liberal advisors. The concluding documents approved the basic impulses of subsequent liberation theology, above all that authentic Christian belief and practice must contribute to egalitarian progress in Latin America; and that the region's problems in that regard had much to do with its marginal position in the global system.[7]

The years following Medellín were in a real sense the 'take-off' period for the Latin American liberation theological movement.[8] CELAM provided important and expanding resources for several years until more conservative bishops took over after 1972. Religious orders such as the Jesuits, Dominicans, and Maryknollers became more and more involved in the cause. Liberation theologians were driving forces in various priest groups like Golconda in Colombia, ONIS in Peru, and 'Priests for the Third World' in Argentina. Several of the more prominent liberation theologians formed or led research and training institutes which promoted liberation theological directions. The core founding works on liberation theology were published during this time.[9] Numerous periodicals and international conferences provided public platforms for the dissemination of liberation ideas. And sympathetic bishops used the resources at their disposal to put the ideas into practice at the diocesan and national levels.[10] Equally as important however, the post-Medellín decade also saw the proliferation throughout Latin America of basic ecclesial communities (CEBs). These small, grass-roots religious organizations extended the movement beyond the elites and the professionals to the powerless people themselves.

Perhaps even more than the Medellín conference and the theology itself, CEBs have transcended their role as social manifestations of the movement to become a primary symbol of its goals. Here, those people who demonstrated in their poverty and powerlessness the disparity between modern, global values and modern, global effects would begin to rectify the situation through a renewed religious message of liberation and new religious community. They were at the core of 'a new way of being church' on the way to creating a new society (see L. Boff, 1986; McGovern, 1989: 197ff.). The fact that the reality of the CEBs and their actual influence lived up to their symbolic stature only infrequently says much about the liberation theological movement itself. It also points to the typical characteristics and difficulties of liberal religion in global society. It is to these matters that I now turn.

Liberation Theology as Liberal Performance Theology

After more than twenty years of development, there are now a great many respected Latin American liberation theologians; and the theology as a whole has undergone some notable changes when compared with its formative years.[11] Some basic characteristics are, however, quite consistent; and they offer valuable insight into the nature of the movement. A brief summary follows.

Liberation theologians see a close connection between the problems of religion in the modern world and what I am calling the residual problems of the global system. The argument runs as follows: the fact that there are so many poor and otherwise marginalized people in our world is morally and religiously unacceptable. Their condition is not a matter of fate, providence, or due to the moral failings of the poor. It is a state of oppression that results from the unjust social structures of modern, global society. The Christian religious message is fundamentally one of liberation; and in the current historical context, this means, in the first instance, working toward the alleviation of the oppression by way of changing the institutional structures that are its cause. Hitherto, most Christians, including those dominant in the Roman Catholic church, have cast the Christian message in far too individualistic and other-worldly terms, with the result that oppressive structures are ignored and thus wittingly or unwittingly supported.

Giving Christianity back its liberating power requires a conversion. The structures, including very critically the church itself, must change to serve those whom they now oppress. Rather than being run by and for the dominant, the church must become the church of the poor, in the sense that its message, its rituals, and its organizational structures empower them to be the agents of their own liberation. The task of the privileged Christian is to act in solidarity with the poor and in their service. As part and parcel of turning around the church, Christians must work toward a corresponding revolutionizing of political, economic, and other social structures. Liberation theology itself is a critical reflection on this practical task. Like its architects, its purpose is to facilitate the empowerment of the poor through the Christian message, not to dictate timeless truths for the sake of an individualistic, other-worldly salvation.

Even such a brief summary statement already points to several features of the Latin American liberation theological movement that are germane to my purposes here. To begin, at the core of its interpretation is a liberal religious attitude. Liberation theology explicitly espouses key modern/ global values, especially with its stress on inclusive equality and progress, and understands these values to be at the heart of authentic Christianity.[12] Although it tends to be strongly antisystemic in its view of certain globalized social structures, notably the capitalist economic system, that critique usually centres on the failure of the global system to live up to those goals (see for example Gutiérrez, 1988: 49ff.). Like much liberal religion, it is prosystemic and antisystemic at the same time. In tune with its liberal character, liberation theology is also religiously and culturally tolerant, in no way portraying Christianity or a certain version of it as the only true religion or even as the only best way of knowing the transcendent.[13] Perhaps the clearest evidence of this aspect is the strong representation of Protestants, the erstwhile religious opponents, in the movement from its inception,[14] and the virtually total absence of claims to want to make Latin American society Christian again. Liberation theologians want religion to be publicly influential, but they do not insist on a particular religion.

A further characteristic of liberation theology is its performance orientation. Although functional questions are not ignored or irrelevant, they are treated in the imperative context of addressing non-religious problems on a religious basis. The theology, after all, is to be in the practical service of the

movement and its goals. In their succinct introductory work, Leonardo and
Clodovis Boff put the matter like this:

> How are we to be Christians in a world of destitution and injustice? There can only
> be one answer: we can be followers of Jesus and true Christians only by making
> common cause with the poor and working out the gospel of liberation . . . The
> Christian base communities, Bible societies, groups for popular evangelization,
> [and other movement manifestations] have all shown themselves to have more
> than a purely religious and ecclesial significance, and to be powerful factors for
> mobilization and dynamos of liberating action. . . . (1987: 7)

Liberation theologians also see the functional problems of religion as
rooted in lack of performance. In the words of the same authors,

> Commitment to the liberation of the millions of the oppressed of our world
> restores to the gospel the credibility it had at the beginning . . . The eternal
> salvation [God and Christ] offer is mediated by the historical liberations that
> dignify the children of God and render credible the coming utopia of the kingdom
> of freedom, justice, love, and peace, the kingdom of God in the midst of
> humankind. (1987: 8f.)

One of the more significant consequences of this 'praxis' orientation is the
central role that social and historical analyses play in the theology. In a way
which is reminiscent of the older Catholic Action motto, 'see-judge-act',
liberationists often begin their arguments with a sociological explanation of
poverty and marginalization, which then serves as the basis for theological
reflection and finally prescriptions for concrete action (see C. Boff, 1987; L.
and C. Boff, 1987: 23–42). Where the Catholic thought of the former era put
corporatist or personalist philosophies, however, Latin American liberation
theologians have consistently relied on social analyses of Marxist inspiration. Until relatively recently, various versions of dependency theory held
a dominant place in this regard, undoubtedly because they offered an
explanation at once of the marginalized position of the poor in Latin
America and the peripheral status of Third World countries in the global
economic system. Dependency theory identified how both local and global
social structures produced the unjust situation. It is in this aspect of the
movement's ideological frame that its global orientation comes out most
clearly. In fact, the social analyses of liberationists have, as one might guess,
a decidedly Wallersteinian flavour. They usually lack the scientific sophistication of this type of globalization theory; but then sociology is here in the
service of a theology, which itself is in the service of a social movement. The
eschatological and practical dimensions take precedent.

Liberation theology elaborates a religious 'option for the poor'. It
consciously favours the 'have-nots' over the 'haves'. Aside from displaying
the modern global value of inclusion and a religious concentration on
residual problems, this bias also contains an evident exclusivity, one that
resonates with class analysis for understanding the basic social structures of a
society, and with a critique of modern capitalism as the source of modern
global problems. Indeed, even though liberation theologians now stan-
dardly recognize other forms of marginalization (such as race, gender), they

tend to consider class divisions as the main form. Thus for example, in the relatively recent work already cited, Leonardo and Clodovis Boff express the matter as follows:

> in a class-divided society, class struggles – which are a fact and an ethical demonstration of the presence of the injustice condemned by God and the church – are the main sort of struggle. They bring antagonistic groups, whose basic interests are irreconcilable, face to face . . . Although exploiting bosses and exploited workers can never finally be reconciled (so long as the former remain exploiters and the latter exploited), blacks can be reconciled with whites, indigenes with nonindigenes, and women with men. (1987: 29f.)

Since this is combined with a critique of capitalism that also stresses the global division between the rich North and the poor South, one may well wonder if liberation theology does not lean in the direction of conservative religion. Such an interpretation might point to how capitalism operates as a synonym for evil in our world, evil whose primary incarnations are the United States externally and the dominant Latin American elites internally. A Christian socialism (or utopian equivalent), founded on the original Christian message and built up in the wake of revolution in Latin America, would be the alternative society that represents the good. Looked at in this way, the vision of the Latin American liberation theological movement would appear as a kind of inverse New Christian Rightism, similar in form, although differing in content. Communism and capitalism would change places as the evil and good respectively; instead of the United States, Latin America would become the privileged place where the divinely willed order is to be constructed in opposition to a predatory global system. To achieve these goals, social action at all levels would be imbued with religious principles.[15]

Although interpreting Latin American liberation theology as at least a conservative-leaning religious ideology is possible, it would be seriously misleading in key respects. In the first instance, it would be to ignore the diversity among liberation theologians. While some, such as Hugo Assmann and the Chilean Christians for Socialism, leaned in this direction in earlier stages of the movement, others, like Gustavo Gutiérrez and Leonardo Boff, have from the beginning taken less dualistic positions.[16] Of greater importance, however, is that most liberation theologians have changed their views over the past twenty or so years. And here it is not simply the fact of change itself that is indicative of a fundamentally liberal character, so much as the idea that liberation theology is open to change in principle. In the Luhmannian terms discussed in Chapter 1, liberationists approach the world as much with a learning as with a normative perspective. For some of them, in fact, the normative aspects of Christianity are primarily guidelines for learning. At root, therefore, they are in tune with one of the more basic characteristics of modernity that has led to globalization. This assertion requires some further elaboration and illustration.

To recall what I have said earlier, a liberal religious attitude is not one that necessarily 'stays out of politics' or any other functionally differentiated domain. The attempt to have an impact in other spheres – in general, to have public influence – displays a performance orientation, the wish to apply the religious modality effectively to matters that are not purely religious. The distinction between liberal and conservative religion is not to be confused with those between function and performance (pure/applied) or privatized and public.[17] Instead, what distinguishes liberal religion is its positive resonance with the core values and orientations of modernity and globalization: egalitarian and inclusive progress on the basis of an adaptive, cognitive style. Conservative religion, by contrast, insists on a predominantly normative, past-oriented framework and thus on a particular and exclusive religio-cultural tradition.

The source of the seemingly conservative quality in liberation theology is its antisystemicity: concentration on residual problems provokes the condemnation of the systems that generate them. From the religious perspective, whatever and whoever represents those systems becomes the embodiment of evil. Given the location of Latin American liberation theologians in a comparatively poor region of the world system, and in light of the practical orientation of their theology toward solving the problems of Latin America specifically, the bifurcation of the world into geographically concentrated evil 'haves' and good 'have-nots' becomes a logically enticing interpretation. Hence the attraction of even some of the more extreme versions of dependency theory when that theory and Marxist views in general still enjoyed a fair bit of broader credibility, especially in Latin America (cf. McGovern, 1989: 156ff.; Sigmund, 1990: 182–184). Such antisystemicity, carried far enough, can lead to a position that bears some similarity to a conservative exclusivism and its claim to normative absolutes.

Although there is thus definitely ambiguity within Latin American liberation theology, overall I would argue that its tendencies have been liberal because of its consistent espousal of central global values and its propensity to learn. The latter feature is not accidental but rather something close to a constitutive principle for liberation theology. Evidence for this assertion is not hard to find. In his foundational work, Gutiérrez elaborates on what he means when he claims that theology must be critical reflection on praxis:

> As critical reflection on society and the Church, theology is an understanding which both grows and, in a certain sense, changes. If the commitment of the Christian community in fact takes different forms throughout history, the understanding which accompanies the vicissitudes of this commitment will be constantly renewed and will take untrodden paths. A theology which has as its points of reference only 'truths' which have been established once and for all . . . can be only static and, in the long run, sterile. (1988: 10)

Moreover, a key moment in this theological task is a scientific analysis of the concrete historical situation. Here, although Latin American liberation theologians have tended to favour Marxist and dependency theories, these are usually seen as tools that can be changed if they prove inadequate. To continue with Gutiérrez, even in the early 1970s, when he was more committed to such approaches, he did not find them entirely satisfactory (see for example 1988: 53). By the late 1980s we can read statements such as this:

> The tools used in this analysis [of the situation in Latin America] vary with time and according to their proven effectiveness for gaining knowledge of the social reality and finding solutions for social problems. Science is by its nature critical of its own presuppositions and achievements; it moves on to new interpretive hypotheses. It is clear, for example, that the theory of dependence, which was so extensively used in the early years of our encounter with the Latin American world, is now an inadequate tool. (1988: xxiv)[18]

For Gutiérrez, at least, we can conclude that, as times and circumstances change, as insights change, so does liberation theology. More generally, these thinkers can claim to be true to the constant Christian faith while remaining open for change in almost everything the theology implies concretely. The basic normative values, encapsulated in the word liberation, do not change; but these need to be variably specified in concrete historical situations.

Among the various key figures, it is perhaps Juan Luis Segundo who elaborates most clearly this relation between normativity and learning in liberation theology. In one of his more seminal works, Segundo presents authentic Christianity as a critical conjunction of 'faith' structured by values, and 'ideology' or the means by which faith values are pursued concretely. Finding the appropriate ideology in each situation is a practical task that involves learning at its very core. The normative values that structure faith are more than anything a basis for learning. These values are expressed in traditions, in dogmas, in revelation; but these are not so much what is to be believed as guidelines for learning. In Segundo's words,

> revelation, the object of faith, [does] not teach us prefabricated things, recipes, or modes of conduct: i.e., ideologies. Instead it [teaches] us how to learn, how to create ideologies or accept ideologies created by others insofar as they [force] values 'to come to terms with' historical reality. (1984: 130)

Elsewhere, he expresses the matter as follows: 'How, then, can Christian tradition be simultaneously normative and liberative . . .? Certainly not by offering us an inherited set of ready-made answers. It must assume tradition to be a process of *learning to learn*' (1984: 338; emphasis in original). To the degree that Segundo here reflects the position of liberation theologians as a group, he displays just how positively this religious orientation resonates with the modern values and communicative modes that have brought about globalization.

To be sure, this interpretation of liberation theology as fundamentally liberal might be challenged on the basis of other quotations from other theologians and other books. The decisive evidence in this case, however, would be whether liberation theology *has* learned. Certainly many of its contributors have changed their positions in the light of criticisms and evolving situations. To some degree such change is probably simple submission to the more conservative wind blowing from Rome. But it is certainly not entirely so. If the temptation toward an isolationist and religio-cultural exclusivist position was or is there, the movement does not seem to have followed that impetus thus far.

The Role of Basic Ecclesial Communities (CEBs)

From its inception, a practical orientation has been central to Latin American liberation theology. It sees itself as the intellectual dimension of a religio-social movement whose aim is to help solve pressing residual problems. That performance emphasis led, for instance, to its criticism of European political theology of the 1960s as still too abstract because it did little toward concrete liberation in the present (see C. Boff, 1987: 195–197; Gutiérrez, 1988: 123–130). Political theologians talked about the perform-ance implications of religious function, but did not actually carry them out. By contrast, the Latin American liberation theology movement has seen itself as one that acts simultaneously upon the church as religious system and upon society at large. It seeks to mediate a new church and a new society at the same time. In pursuit of these goals, various organizations and activities have embodied the movement; but the most central ones have been those associated with mobilization of the poor. Here the basic ecclesial communi-ties (CEBs) occupy a key position.

The basic ecclesial communities are in one sense a fruit of efforts by the Roman Catholic church to reach the mass of the Latin American population that had become so much more visible in the post-World War II era. The shortage of priests made reliance on the established parish structure ineffective. During the 1950s and 1960s, attempts in various Latin American countries to find a different approach drew significantly on the experience and structures of Catholic Action, most notably specialized Catholic Action and the revivalistic Cursillo movement (see Cleary, 1985: 3–8; Berryman, 1987: 64–68). By the late 1960s, CEBs had emerged as the most widely accepted solution. They were small groups of Catholics, usually in rural and suburban slum areas of Latin America, who met regularly for religious discussion and reflection. The idea was that they would be formed and initially led by priests, members of religious orders, or trained lay pastoral workers; but that eventually the members themselves would keep the CEBs going and even help to form new ones, thus spreading the movement. CEBs therefore combined the specialized Catholic Action characteristic of being a milieu-specific training ground for lay religious 'militants' or activists, with the Cursillo emphasis on developing greater commitment to Christian religion. Like these earlier movement organizations, they also promised to create new resources, expanding religious communication rather than just redirecting it.

Virtually from their inception, however, CEBs were conceived as something more than practical ways of enhancing religious function. They emerged and took root in Latin America at the same time as liberation theology, becoming a distinct organizational form as part of that movement. Many of the elite promoters of the CEBs saw in them a way of enlisting the poor for the liberationist cause: CEBs would be places where the poor would deepen their understanding of the religious tradition, but they would do this as part of a larger process of 'conscientization'. That is, through their faith, they would come to realize that their situation was one of oppression and injustice; that the Christian message was primarily for their sake and enjoined them to change their condition through political and social action.

Like their antecedent, specialized Catholic Action, CEBs have thus been oriented toward both function and performance. They were intended both to strengthen the church and to be a basis for changing society. Yet, unlike the older organizations, CEBs have figured much larger in the identity or self-conception of the movement as a whole. I mean this in two senses. On the practical side, if one were to ask what the liberation theological movement most centrally does in pursuit of its goals, then its answer might well ring, 'conscientization'. Translated into social movement terms, this is precisely 'mobilization'. To the extent that the movement has actually mobilized the poor in Latin America, this has happened primarily through CEBs, or at least small grass-roots organizations that look and function like them, even when under a different name. At least as important as this practical dimension, however, is their identifying position within Latin American liberation theology itself. Here they appear as the structural incarnation – I use this word advisedly – of several core themes. They are the poor becoming the agents of their own liberation, empowering themselves to begin to create the new church 'from below' and also the new society. CEBs are ecclesial structures but they are fundamentally performance-oriented. As such, they promise to lend the poor power and dignity as the basis for building an inclusive, egalitarian, and progressive society.[19] Although some liberation theologians have been critical of CEBs as they have developed concretely, the centrality of the ideal itself is generally not in doubt (see Hewitt, 1990).

CEBs thus have a pivotal position in the Latin American liberation theological movement. Ideally they are at the heart of how the movement proposes to get the religious system to perform. In this role they raise two very much interrelated questions that will advance the discussion at this point. On the one hand, movement participants put CEBs forth as a legitimate, institutional expression of the religious system, particularly the Roman Catholic church organization, while at the same time regarding them as a challenge to that system. They thus raise the question of the relation between two social systems: the differentiated religious system and the social movement. The Latin American liberation theological movement's relation to the religious system is in fact more than one of the appropriation of religious resources for the sake of the movement. It also seeks to alter the religious system as such, to become institutionalized in that system in order to make it more effective both in terms of function and performance. With the same stroke, the movement, especially through the CEBs, seeks to solve residual problems of the global system as they are manifest in Latin America. This aspect raises the question of whether the movement is able to generate public influence for the religious system. Both are questions of efficacy. Significantly, they are also the two points at which most critics of the movement have directed their assessments.[20]

The further examination of these two questions requires a more concrete focus than Latin America as a whole. Accordingly, in what follows, I restrict my view primarily to two countries, Brazil and Nicaragua. Although the liberation theological movement has a presence in most Latin American countries, scholarly discussion has in fact centred more around these two. The reasons are fairly straightforward. Brazil is the largest country in Latin America; a very significant number of its bishops has been sympathetic to the liberationist cause; it boasts the most CEBs and is the country where these first became widespread. In brief, the liberationist movement has been at its most developed in Brazil. In Nicaragua, the movement was heavily involved in the revolution of 1979, and in the Sandinista regime that followed. For many members of the movement, the Nicaraguan revolution was an opportunity to build the new society and the new church. It was a crucible which might permit the institutionalization of the movement and its goals in the various structures of a sovereign state. If successful, it would act as a model for the rest of Latin America and perhaps the Third World in general. Nicaragua, at least during the 1980s, represented the possibilities of the movement.

The Social Movement and the Religious System

In Chapter 3, I argued that the core problem of religion as a way of communicating in modern society has to do more with performance than function; and that performance for religion in the context of powerful, instrumentally specialized systems is somewhat problematic because of the holistic scope of religious communication. In Chapter 4, I then argued that this circumstance makes it likely that attempts to bring religion to bear on especially residual problems will often take the form of social movements. These use the resources of the religious system, but differentiate themselves from that system largely through the separate mobilization of people around performance issues. The combination of performance orientation and differentiation raises the question of how the institutionalized and primarily functionally oriented religious system will respond to the social movement, and vice versa.

In the earlier social Catholic movements, the potential problems inherent in this relation were addressed in various ways. Catholic Action was to be a direct lay extension of the episcopal office; efforts such as labour unions and cooperatives had their chaplains for guidance; and Catholic political parties were to apply official Catholic social teaching, but were otherwise largely independent. Even here, however, relations between the movement organizations and the hierarchy were not always smooth. In the post-World War II era, and especially in the 1960s, these relations often became much more conflictual or tenuous. Perhaps the clearest example in Latin America during this time was the conflict between the Brazilian bishops and the JUC, specialized Catholic Action groups for university youth. Here the hierarchy eventually proscribed the wayward organization. At the heart of this conflict was not simply the degree of JUC radicalism, but the fact that the youth movement eschewed episcopal authority and criticized ecclesiastical authority structures, largely because these were not similarly oriented toward performance.[21] The recursive logic and performance agenda of the movement had taken precedence over the functional priorities of the religious system as represented by the Catholic hierarchy. The episode foreshadowed later relations between church authorities and the liberation theological movement.

Before looking at that topic more closely, however, a word about certain peculiarities of the Roman Catholic church as representative of the global religious system: within a system that is internally segmented according to religions and subdivisions of these, the Roman Catholic church is undoubtedly that segment in which organization and social system have become most closely identified. Following a process that began in the Middle Ages, and in direct response to the concurrent emergence of the European, then global, state system, the Roman Catholic church has progressively developed and guarded its independence. It did this by elaborating itself as an administrative apparatus roughly parallel to the surrounding political states, but one whose function was primarily to reproduce religious communication, to guard, transmit, and even expand the 'deposit of faith'. Put differently, the Roman church became a kind of functionally specialized state, complete with legal system, external diplomacy, and bureaucracy, yet without specific territorial limits and a military. As such, the Roman Catholic church has consistently claimed to represent the religious system in the way that governmental organizations represent the political system. And, at least since the later nineteenth century, a critical aspect of defending this parallel yet independent existence has been to insist that the church's mission is primarily religious.[22] The combination of features greatly affected how the Roman Catholic hierarchy and the liberationists in Latin America responded to one another. The result is a particularly clear example of the ambiguous relation in the modern context between a religious system centred on function and a social movement bent on performance.

Previous discussion has shown that, in the fluid atmosphere of the first post-Vatican II decade, liberationists were able to enlist key church resources in the cause, most especially CELAM and certain national bishops' conferences. After 1972, however, movement opponents within the church managed gradually to halt and even reverse such appropriation. While it is perhaps tempting to see this story as a simple battle between anti- and prosystemic forces in the church, a closer inquiry reveals that divergent systemic interests were also very much at play. How this can be the case becomes clear when one looks at the Nicaraguan situation after the 1979 revolution.

When Anastasio Somoza's regime fell in 1979, few church people regretted its passing; but church people were by no means unanimous in their support for the dominant partner among the opposition forces, the Sandinista Front for National Liberation (FSLN). Some sided with both the Sandinistas and their idea of an explicitly socialist revolution. The bulk of these were from among the liberationist elite and the Nicaraguan CEBs.[23] Others, led by the small corps of Nicaraguan bishops, initially suspended judgement of the FSLN, but went into more and more definite opposition as the 1980s progressed. A great many held attitudes somewhere in between these two groups (see P. Williams, 1989: 65–78). It is the two more extreme segments that are of interest here.

As elsewhere in Latin America, the later 1960s and the 1970s saw the growth of the liberation theological movement in Nicaragua. For instance, radical priests like Uriel Molina and the two Cardenal brothers, Ernesto and Fernando, spurred the process of conscientization among the urban poor and among university students. Religious orders like the Maryknoll sisters in Managua and the Capuchins in rural areas helped in the formation of CEBs and in the training of peasants as mobilizing 'Delegates of the Word'.

By the time of the revolution, this grass-roots and elite mobilization was not only thriving, but actively involved with the revolutionary opposition forces. In fact, since the late 1960s, the FSLN had been cultivating links with the religious liberationist movement, with the CEBs, with local priests, and with the leaders. At the time of Somoza's overthrow, the practical and ideological ties between the two movements were sufficiently strong that the high degree of direct involvement by liberationists in the subsequent revolutionary regime is not at all surprising (see Dodson and O'Shaughnessy, 1990; Foroohar, 1989; Williams, 1989). Most prominently, religious leaders like Ernesto and Fernando Cardenal, Miguel D'Escoto, and Edgard Parrales accepted and kept important government positions. They did this, however, not primarily as representatives of the church, but as participants in a revolutionary process. Their liberation movement was religious, to be sure. Yet its aim was to work for the practical progress and equality of Nicaraguans through radical social change. Only through performance would renewed spirituality or function come about. For most movement militants, the functional independence of religion from the political system was of quite secondary concern when compared with the need to get involved in the political process that would bring about progressive change.

For most Nicaraguan bishops, on the other hand, the order of priority was rather different. Led by the Archbishop of Managua, Miguel Obando y Bravo, this group regarded itself as the legitimate representative of the Roman Catholic church and to that extent of the religious system. With few exceptions, its members held ambiguous views about the liberationist movement in their country and distrusted the FSLN because of its Marxist socialist orientation. Involved in both attitudes was the fear that neither of these would ultimately serve the interests of the church, and thus of religion.

Unlike in other countries such as Brazil, bishops were not in the forefront of liberationist mobilization in Nicaragua. The 'progressive' or 'popular' movement in the church here developed much more independently of episcopal authority and encouragement, with the result that its activity could appear more easily to challenge episcopal claims to represent the interests of religion (cf. Mainwaring and Wilde, 1989: 19–20; Van Vugt, 1991: 33ff.). Under different circumstances, this potential conflict may never have become acute. That it did has much to do with the fact that the movement got heavily involved in the Sandinista regime.

What most of the Nicaraguan bishops suspected or feared was that the Sandinistas were Communists in the mould of Fidel Castro. In particular the more extreme among them, like Archbishop Obando and Bishop Pablo Vega, were convinced that the FSLN's aim was to set up a totalitarian socialist state such as existed in Cuba, one in which the influence of religion and the church would be minimized or at best harnessed in the service of the Marxist state ideology. Accordingly, the Sandinistas were not to be trusted; their seeming overtures to the church and its leaders were to be regarded as tactical, intended to deflect opposition until it was too late.[24] Moreover, the direct collaboration of many liberationists with the Sandinistas assisted the latter in their nefarious intentions by dividing the church and seeming to lend them religious legitimacy.

The bishops and their clerical supporters were not unanimous in the degree to which they held this view. They also differed on tactics, not all of them convinced that Obando's confrontational and often overtly political style of opposition was the most productive route to follow. What they shared, however, and what set them apart from the liberationists, was a concern that identification with the Sandinista-dominated revolution would lead to the weakening of religion. The positive achievements of the revolution which were paramount for the performance-oriented liberationists were less important than guarding the functional integrity and independence of the church. In tune with the long-standing opposition of the Roman Catholic church to Marxist-Leninist socialism, this group feared the centralized control of communicative resources in the hands of the state, more specifically in the hands of the Sandinista party and its organizations. To participate in the Sandinista regime, its programmes and organizations, was therefore to risk transferring religious authority to these organs. The political leaders would usurp the power of the religious leaders, resulting in the conflation of political and religious authority. If the revolution did progress toward state-centred totalitarian structures, then the church would lose its independence. It was therefore important that the church maintain a critical distance from the regime.

In their interpretation of the situation, the Nicaraguan bishops had the full support of the Vatican and Pope John Paul II. During his much discussed visit to Nicaragua in 1983, the Pope berated the prominent priests who occupied political positions and was heavily critical of the progressive church movement. Both were for him, as they were for the bishops and their allies in the church, a threat to church unity and authority. As if to underscore the order of priorities, in his homilies the Pope almost completely ignored the economic and political difficulties of Nicaragua, problems which for the revolutionaries and the liberationists were of the first importance. In the words of François Houtart, a European liberation theologian,

> John-Paul II had a twofold vision of the situation in Nicaragua: on the one hand, he saw a political regime moving quickly toward an anti-religious Marxist socialism; on the other hand, the church would only be capable of standing in the way of this process if it were solidly structured along doctrinal and organizational lines. (Houtart, 1989: 333; my translation)

The entire thrust of the Pope's concern was, in other words, the exact opposite of the liberationists: here performance was possible only on a solid functional base, not the other way around.

Those siding with the progressive religious movement of course did not share the apprehensions or priorities of the Vatican and the Nicaraguan bishops. Where the latter saw attempts to coopt the church on the part of the Sandinistas, the former saw a sincere wish to cooperate combined with respect for religion as a practical, transformative force. My point in discussing the matter is not to help decide which viewpoint is correct, but to show the differing emphases of the two systems and their representatives. Although the tension between these two stands has been particularly sharp in the charged atmosphere of revolutionary Nicaragua, the analysis is, I believe, applicable to the general Latin American situation. Whether in Nicaragua, Colombia, Brazil, or several other countries, the liberation theological movement operates in terms of a different logic when compared with the institutionalized Roman Catholic hierarchy. Functionally oriented 'raison d'église' (Coleman, 1989) can be and often is in conflict with a performance-oriented 'option for the poor', no matter how much proponents of either view claim that they are not. In this respect, the example of Roman Catholicism in Latin America is analogous to that of conservative Protestantism in the United States. The New Christian Right's difficulty in mobilizing more than a minority even of its core constituency is also indicative of this tension between function and performance.

The problem of competing orientations between movement and religious system is, however, only one part of the picture. The larger question is whether even an unequivocal performance orientation can actually lend liberal religion a public influence that it did not have before. It is to this matter that I now turn, again concentrating on the Nicaraguan, but now also on the Brazilian, situation.

The Question of Public Influence

As already mentioned, one of the clearer differences between the liberation theological movement in Nicaragua and in Brazil is that a large number of the bishops in Brazil actively promoted the movement whereas such support was the exception in Nicaragua. As the previous section has shown, the Nicaraguan hierarchy was relatively uninvolved in the growth of the movement before the overthrow of Somoza; and, in the case of some bishops, notably Obando and Vega, increasingly opposed it under the Sandinista regime. By contrast, the 'option for the poor' still receives a fair amount of official support from the Brazilian hierarchy, in spite of a noticeable cooling of the ardour in recent years (Hewitt, 1989; 1990; 1991: 91ff.). Conflict between religious system representatives and movement activists has accordingly not been nearly as severe in Brazil. One might conclude, therefore, that the liberation theological movement in Brazil will have been far stronger and more effective than in Nicaragua. The actual historical trajectories of the movement in the two countries, however, have been remarkably similar. With or without hierarchical support, the movements were at their strongest when authoritarian regimes restricted political involvement; and weakened precisely when these atmospheres changed through revolution or eased through political liberalization. Although the dampening policies of various domestic bishops and the Vatican under John Paul II certainly played a role, this parallelism also points to the more general problem of liberal religious performance – and hence public influence – under modern/global conditions. I look more closely at Brazil first.

A common observation in the literature on the Latin American Catholic church since World War II is that the Brazilian hierarchy has been among the most progressive of all the national leadership groups (see, for example, Adriance, 1986; Bruneau, 1974; Mainwaring, 1986; Mainwaring and Wilde, 1989). Before Vatican II and the advent of the liberation theological movement, however, this tendency was comparatively limited. It did not, for instance, prevent a large number of Brazil's bishops from welcoming the military coup of 1964. The much more marked radicalization of the Brazilian National Bishops Conference (CNBB) under the subsequent twenty-year military regime therefore had its roots only partly in the post-war national developments. The effects of a repressive authoritarian regime and, independently, the rising liberationist ambience that pervaded most of Latin America during these decades were additional vital factors.[25] I have already devoted considerable space to the latter. Here I focus on the contribution of the former.

Above, I noted that the ecclesiastical search for new ways of reaching the Brazilian masses in the post-war period was in large part an attempt to renew the influence of the institution in a changed social and historical context (see Bruneau, 1985; cf. Azevedo, 1987: 39ff.; Hewitt, 1991: 19ff.). In the spirit of official Catholic social teaching, many church leaders and activist professionals came to the conclusion that this religious goal had to include concern with broader social issues like land reform, mass literacy, and overall economic development. The military coup of 1964, along with Vatican II, eventually contributed significantly to the radicalization of these efforts. Especially after 1967, the new government pursued policies centred on two core objectives: the concentration of political power in military hands and rapid, capital-intensive economic development focused around the exploitation of the Amazon basin. To a large extent, it met with success. The military government oversaw rapid overall growth in the Brazilian economy during the next few years and made meaningful political participation or opposition very difficult.

Economic growth, however, did not mean equitable distribution of the benefits. In fact the gap between the well off minority and the poor majority widened; many of the poor even experienced a worsening of their living conditions. Government success thereby exacerbated rather than alleviated the problems of precisely those people the church was trying to reach, the marginalized peasants and urban migrants, and made political efforts at redress difficult to impossible. The experience of working among these disadvantaged groups helped to convince many church activists to take up their cause, putting them in a position of clear opposition to the rulers. Yet, given the authoritarian priorities of the latter, this concretized 'option for the poor' only brought the same repressive techniques to bear on the church activists as had already been applied to those who dared continue secular opposition.

Nonetheless, the military leaders were not as ruthless and thorough with the church because, at least in part, they saw themselves as defending Christian culture against the onslaught of Communism. The upshot was that, although the liberationist or popular segments of the church suffered harassment, imprisonment, and even occasionally death as a result of their oppositional activities, the church organizations benefited from the relative tolerance of the government and thus presented one of the few possibilities for any kind of political opposition in the country. That beginning during the worst years of the military's repressive tactics blossomed after 1974 in an atmosphere of gradual political liberalization. As the government slowly and haltingly eased its rigid policies, the opportunities for political participation and popular organization increased. It was precisely at this time that the liberationist impulse in the Brazilian church attained a level of consolidation that allowed it to take full advantage of this opening.[26] From 1974 to the early 1980s, the popular church organizations experienced their greatest growth (see Mainwaring, 1986: 145–181).

While the military government's policies were certainly not the only thing that affected popular church growth, they did make a contribution. Somewhat ironically, this factor becomes clearer when we look at developments in the 1980s. From the early part of that decade, the church's liberationist organizations ceased to grow at their previous rapid pace and eventually, as the decade wore on and formal democratic institutions were fully restored after 1985, entered a period of decline. This decline, again, had much to do with the more conservative wind blowing from Rome after the accession of John Paul II; but it also had to do with the changed political climate in Brazil. On the one hand, lay activists who joined popular church organizations and were conscientized there in the 1970s and early 1980s could now just as easily opt for secular social and political action organizations which not only had the church's blessing (or at least did not receive its condemnation), but were also free from the more strictly religious priorities attendant upon church control (see Mainwaring, 1986: 182ff.; Hewitt, 1991: 88f). On the other hand, the reopening of the political arena to broad participation exposed the religiously motivated church activist directly to the realities of liberal democratic party politics with its characteristic compromises unsuited to ethical absolutes. Such experience bred a certain disillusionment with political process and a retreat to more strictly religious concerns on the part of many a liberationist activist (Mainwaring, 1989: 176–183).

Indeed, in the mid to late 1980s, the institutional church as a whole swung from a clear emphasis on social and political action to one that again stressed religious priorities: the main problem for the church in the 1980s again appeared to be rapidly growing Protestant groups and Brazilian spiritist groups like Umbanda and Candomblé. Moreover, as Hewitt (1989) makes clear, the way in which the Brazilian bishops increasingly tried to exert their influence reverted to the older tactics of directly soliciting the support of political elites rather than going the circuitous movement route represented by popular church organizations like the CEBs. Without the extreme situation of an authoritarian dictatorship that severely restricted access to functionally specialized political institutions, the option of resorting to the ethically-based performance resources of the religious system for addressing the pronounced social and economic problems seemed less necessary or even appropriate.

What the Brazilian developments show is that the liberal religious option, which tends to respect differentiated spheres as well as the tolerant inclusion of plural worldviews, may have difficulty in gaining public influence even when it informs strong social movements.[27] Addressing residual problems on the basis of religious norms and priorities is for this approach a performance that religion and religious institutions can offer. But if it seems that other institutions with more instrumental functional specialization – notably, although not necessarily, the political – are capable of addressing those problems more effectively, then we should expect a tendency to leave the problems to those institutions, or at least to operate in them in terms of *their* norms and priorities. The alternative is to switch to a more sectarian and conservative mode, the temptation to which in the case of liberationists I discussed above.

Thus, even when the religious movement succeeds in significant mobilization, as it did in the Brazilian case, that mobilization tends to get siphoned off when other more secular possibilities once again become open. At the most, religiously-based mobilization will become only one interest group among several, seeking allies among the secular groups as opportunity and expendiency suggest, thereby depriving such mobilization even further of its explicitly religious content. Like a number of the efforts that the church spawned in Brazil, the successful mobilization efforts become secularized, leaving the church again with its voluntary flock of adherents and the rest of society only indirectly touched. What is specifically liberal here, however, is that the religious actors will in general welcome this outcome: the point is and was to help solve certain pressing problems, not to enforce particular religious norms.

The case of Nicaragua is different in detail but similar in outcome. There the liberationist movement also reached its peak in the 1970s, leading up to the successful overthrow of Somoza. As already discussed, the CEBs and popular church organs were heavily involved in the opposition front led by the Sandinistas. Many in the popular church organizations were also clear supporters of the subsequent revolutionary regime. Nonetheless, within a short period after the overthrow, we witness the same redifferentiaton of religious and political action. The CEBs especially began to lose many of their activists as these joined secular Sandinista organizations or became otherwise heavily involved in government-sponsored programmes and activities (see Williams, 1989: 54ff.). Left essentially with their more purely religious identity and purpose, the strength of the liberationist social movement organizations declined not only because the Nicaraguan hierarchy opposed them, but also because the church organizations were less effective places to be for the purposes of contributing to social change and political action. As in Brazil, a successful mobilization did not lead to any lasting public influence of religious leaders and norms except insofar as these could be and were accommodated in secular political and social organizations, programmes, and values.

The critical linking factor in both cases is the liberality of the Brazilian and Nicaraguan church leaders and also many of the activists. The priorities for public influence of both movements during their heyday was the implementation of global norms of inclusion, progress, and equality, not the particularistic cultural and religious priorities of a conservatively oriented movement. As such, the pursuit of those global values followed the more effective lines of functionally specialized political action when this became readily available in both countries. Moreover, a quite significant number of church leaders and activists, but above all many bishops, approved of this development because they felt that functional religious priorities could be pursued better away from the powerful influence of political institutions. Function and performance parted ways once again as the global structures and global cultural values reasserted the logic of functional system differentiation and hence the assignment of collective decision-making and action to the institutions designed to specialize in the production of these, namely the political. Religious institutions have not disappeared or even weakened as a result, but neither have they attained that public influence that may have seemed, for some, just over the horizon during the heady days of the 1970s and early 1980s.

Perhaps as a final illustration of the tendency, liberation theologians have themselves largely abandoned the quest for direct and effective public influence, leaving the ideas of Christian-inspired revolution to the mistaken optimism of the past and concentrating instead on their own specialized realm of religious action, CEB spirituality (see McGovern, 1989).

Conclusions

The rise and history of the Latin American liberation theological movement illustrates a number of the characteristics of liberal performance religion in the modern/global societal context. What is perhaps most significant for my purposes here, however, is the degree to which globalized values and globalized structures have conditioned this movement. There seems little doubt that the theology itself is an expression of the values and that the severe problems the movement has sought to address are direct consequences of the powerful operation of the globalized instrumental systems, above all the capitalist economy and the system of sovereign states. Moreover, the rise and subsequent decline of the movement has had much to do with internal responses of the religious system – here especially but not exclusively the Roman Catholic church – to that same modern/global context.

What stands out in all this is the tremendous amount of activity on a religious basis that has, with hindsight, had rather meagre results. The reasons for that outcome, I suggest, go beyond the false optimism and faulty social analyses of liberationists, attitudes that perhaps led to the expectation of relatively rapid solutions to weighty residual problems. They also exceed the dampening effect of a conservative hierarchy with its 'raison d'église' (Coleman, 1989). More fundamentally at issue are the prosystemic orientation of liberal religious actors, and, in general, the functional characteristics of religion as a differentiated mode of communication in modern/global society. The degree to which these are or are not a problem specific to liberal religion can be seen by comparing the fate of the Latin American liberation theological movement with that of the theocratically oriented Iranian revolution. Although the differences are striking, so too are the similarities.

Notes

1 The previous chapter, of course, discussed how the conservative New Christian Right manifested the latter Wallersteinian symptom.

2 See especially the encyclicals, 'Pacem in Terris' (1963) by John XXIII and 'Populorum Progressio' (1967) by Paul VI; and the conciliar document 'Gaudium et Spes' (1965). Published in Walsh and Davies, 1984.

3 I am referring here primarily to specialized Catholic Action groups along the Franco-Belgian model, rather than a host of other movement organizations that also fell under the heading of Catholic Action. See Poggi, 1967.

4 Ironically, corporatism, or the construction of encompassing organizations along the lines of different industries and professions as a way of obviating economic class conflict, has not been done on an explicitly religious basis in those countries, such as Italy, the Soviet Union, and Japan, where it has been carried the farthest.

5 Between 1952 and 1959, national councils formed in Brazil, Mexico, Bolivia, Peru, Colombia, Chile, Ecuador, Paraguay, Venezuela, and Argentina. The Latin American Episcopal Council (CELAM) met for the first time in 1955. See Cleary, 1985; Smith, 1991.

6 I elaborate this point below.

7 The Medellín conference published numerous concluding documents, but the historically most important and most cited are those on 'Justice' and 'Peace'. See O'Brien and Shannon, 1977: 547–572.

8 Various of the key social movement organizations and mobilizing events are the subject of most analyses of the liberation theological movement. To date, however, the only study that offers a focused sociological treatment from a social movement/resource mobilization perspective is Smith, 1991. On post-Medellín mobilization, see especially pp.165ff. in this work.

9 These would certainly include Alves, 1969; L. Boff, 1978; Dussel, 1981; Gutiérrez, 1988; and Miranda, 1974. These were all first published in their original-language versions between 1969 and 1972. Note that Alves, like a not insignificant number of Latin American liberation theologians, is a Protestant. I discuss this aspect of the movement further below.

10 The Brazilian church offers the best examples of this aspect of the mobilization. See Bruneau, 1974; Mainwaring, 1986.

11 There are by now numerous general works on Latin American liberation theology itself. Among the more sympathetic introductions, see Berryman, 1987; L. and C. Boff, 1987; McGovern, 1989; Nuñez, 1985; Sigmund, 1990. McGovern and Sigmund also explicitly deal with changes in liberation theology over time.

12 For perhaps a classic statement of the relation between these values and the Christian message in liberation theology, see Gutiérrez, 1988, Chapter 9, especially pp. 100–105.

13 To take but one rather clear example, Juan Luis Segundo writes, 'I fully admit that authentic types of religious faith can exist outside Christianity' (1984: 334f.), and goes on to assert that his focus on Christianity is justified 'if only for practical reasons', that is, because it happens to be the dominant religion in the region with which he is concerned, namely Latin America.

14 See, as examples, the work of Rubem Alves (1969), José Míguez Bonino (1975), and Julio de Santa Ana (1981).

15 Elements of such an interpretation can be found in the work of various critics such as Garrett, 1986; 1988a; 1988b; Roth, 1988; although not with quite the sharp formulation I am using here. R. Robertson, 1986; 1987b, suggests that the conflation of religion and politics evident in Latin American liberation theology might qualify it as a type of 'fundamentalism', a common term for what I am here calling conservative religion that seeks public influence. See note 17 below.

16 See Assmann, 1976; L. Boff, 1978; Eagleson, 1975; Gutiérrez, 1988. For a general discussion of the contrasts, both between different theologians and over time, see McGovern, 1989.

17 Accordingly, to the extent that my use of the term 'conservative' here is synonymous with 'fundamentalist', I would have to disagree with R. Robertson when he claims that liberation theology is *fundamentalistic* to the extent that it advocates the conflation of the political and religious realms' (1986: 90f.). Insisting that religious insight and values be incorporated in political decision-making and action is, as such, no more conflation of realms than would be the claim that economic criteria ought to be thus influential. However, rather than try to decide when one does or does not have conflation of realms, a clearer strategy is to define fundamentalism or conservatism more along the lines suggested in the text. Following either strategy, liberation theology would not qualify.

18 For a further and significantly earlier critical stance on dependency theory on the part of another liberation theologian, see L. Boff, 1979: 77f. See McGovern, 1989: especially 136f., 229f.; Sigmund, 1990: 178–180, for general discussions of such changes among liberation theologians.

19 On the position of CEBs in the movement, see, from a fairly extensive literature, Bruneau, 1981; Cleary, 1985: 104–124; various contributions in Levine, 1986; McGovern, 1989: 197–212; Torres and Eagleson, 1982; Van Vugt, 1991.

20 For a balanced treatment of these, see McGovern, 1989; Sigmund, 1990: especially Chapters 8 and 9.

21 See de Kadt, 1970; Mainwaring, 1986. For analyses of the sometimes troubled relations between Christian Democratic political parties and church authorities in Latin America, see B. Smith, 1982; Lynch, 1991.

22 For a more detailed version of this argument, under the heading of *raison d'église*, see Coleman, 1989.

23 I do not mean to imply here or elsewhere in this chapter that CEB membership is somehow synonymous with a liberationist perspective. In fact, there is a fair amount of conflict *within* CEBs as to their proper orientation, a conflict that often parallels the larger battle between the liberationist elite and the more conservative hierarchy.

24 Not surprisingly, quite a number of authors who show some or a great deal of sympathy for the revolution and the liberationist cause tend not to take this level of distrust seriously, with the result that Obando and Vega in particular appear more or less as simple counterrevolutionaries, bent on stopping meaningful change in the interests of pre-revolutionary elites. See, as examples in varying degrees, Dodson and O'Shaughnessy, 1990; Foroohar, 1989; O'Shaughnessy and Serra, 1986. The literature that does bring forth episcopal motivation more clearly, again not surprisingly, tends to share the distrust. See, e.g. Francou, 1988; Langguth, 1989. Among the more balanced analyses, see Bradstock, 1987; Williams, 1989.

25 That Brazilian radicalization was also not just a response to the repressive policies of the military regime becomes clear when one looks at parallel developments in Chile, whose hierarchy had a similar progressive reputation. There significant radicalization occurred, not just after Pinochet's coup of 1973, but also before under Christian Democratic and Socialist regimes. See B. Smith, 1982.

26 Compare the similar increase of religious mobilization in Iran immediately after the Shah lifted somewhat his suppression of organized political opposition in 1977. See below, Chapter 7.

27 I am of course assuming that the movement has been strong. For recent doubts that this was ever actually the case, see Hewitt, 1992 with further references.

7

THE ISLAMIC REVOLUTION IN IRAN

The central aim of this study is to examine the possible roles of religion under conditions of globalization, and more specifically to assess the chances for public religious influence in this society. Without doubt, the creation and development of the Islamic Republic of Iran after 1979 stands as the most outstanding contemporary event in this regard. Here we have religious professionals taking over and transforming the political and legal structures of a sizeable country, directing its economy, and generally controlling such vital areas as artistic expression, news media, and education. The outlook of this institutionalized religio-political movement has been clearly conserva-tive; its ideology, action, and aims directed against the global operation of modern instrumental systems. Its leaders have insisted that Iran must reassert its particular religious culture, namely Iranian Twelver Shi'ism, against what they have often called 'global arrogance', most notably attributed to the embodiment of evil in the world, the Great American Satan. The revolution has also claimed to be for the benefit quite specifically of the 'disinherited', indicating that religious performance solutions to residual problems are very much at issue. In brief, the Islamic revolution demonstrates rather unequivocally how public religious influence through religious performance is possible in today's globalizing society; and this as a direct response to globalization.

The relevance of the Iranian Republic to my endeavours here, however, goes beyond the straightforward illustration of some of the main theoretical points. As with the other movements that I examine in these chapters, the developments that have taken place in Iran since the overthrow of the Shah in 1979 allow clarification, qualification, and elaboration of the theoretical starting points discussed in Part I. The Islamic revolution did give immense public influence to the mullahs. As the authoritative carriers of Islam, they were now in positions to enforce the precepts and practices of their religion, to promote its specific values, and to protect the integrity of Iranian cultural particularism. But most people in Iran and a sizeable portion of the clerics themselves expected more than this. The revolution should also bring material benefits to the people. It should fulfil the expectations that the Shah's policies had raised but not satisfied for the majority. The Iranian revolution, in other words, was also about progress and equality. While the concomitant global value of relativizing and tolerant inclusion was decidedly rejected, the pursuit of progress and equality acted as a counterbalance to the Shi'a particularism, eventually steering the revolution toward accommo-dation within global systems and enhancing their operation within Iran.

Put somewhat differently, the Islamic revolution could make Islam obligatory in Iran; but the Islamic solutions to residual problems, as elsewhere in the Muslim world, had to meet the criteria of the dominant instrumental systems, the influence of which in Iran was precisely what a great many pious revolutionaries had originally conceived to be the problem. The Islamic revolution therefore shows the limits of religious performance in global society, all the more so because it has been such a resounding success. In the process, the consummately anti-global revolution has almost paradoxically demonstrated itself to be part and parcel of the furthering of globalization. Conservative religious responses are part of the process of globalization as much as liberal ones.

The further analysis of both the successes and limits of the Iranian revolution as a religious response to globalization takes the following course. A first section looks briefly at how Iran became incorporated into global systems during the last two centuries and how certain developments among the Shi'a clerics of Iran paralleled that process. This is followed by an examination of how the revolution came about and how the radical *ulama* managed to win the post-revolutionary power struggle in relatively short order. Both these sections set the stage for consideration of the struggle between revolutionary religious purism and incorporative globalizing pragmatism in the fourteen-year history of the Islamic Republic, a battle that, at present, is leaning decidedly in favour of the performance-oriented pragmatists. A final section examines the degree to which we are dealing here with the peculiarities of religious function as compared with the pressures of globalization as such.

Iran, the Global System, and the Shi'a Clerical Sodality

The incorporation of Iran into the European-centred globalizing systems began in the nineteenth century (see Keddie, 1980; 1981: 40ff.). Under the rival influence of chiefly Russia and Great Britain, Iranian economic production gradually shifted toward greater involvement in international trade. Landowners devoted increasing portions of the limited cultivable land to cash crops such as cotton, tobacco, silk, and opium. Cheaper imports of manufactured goods from industrialized countries undermined many local handicraft industries and shifted emphasis to others, notably carpets. Nonetheless, compared to countries such as Egypt and Turkey, Iran's entanglement in the global economy remained quite minor until well into the twentieth century. In part this was because the rivalry between colonial powers tended to dampen development rather than encourage it; in part Iran's geography made trade and political centralization more difficult. Another very significant factor was the patrimonial political system that prevailed in Iran until Reza Shah Pahlavi's reforms after 1925.

During the nineteenth century, Iran's was still very much a traditional state, and a rather weak one at that. The Qajar shahs in Tehran ruled nominally over the entire country, but they did not have at their disposal anything like a modern state bureaucracy, army, legal or taxation system. Iran has very few navigable rivers and there were practically no roads. Much political control rested in the hands of local tribal chiefs, landowners, and religious leaders. The state left them alone so long as they did not threaten rebellion and the requisite taxes and tributes continued to flow into Qajar coffers.

Corresponding to this meagre level of control, the shahs and their ministers were able to muster relatively few resources for developing the country in a modern sense. Indeed, until near the end of the century, those who benefited from the patrimonial structures, including many religious leaders, blocked most efforts at fiscal, legal, and military reform the government did make. In consequence, the spread of globalizing processes into Iran during the nineteenth century was both quite limited and largely in the hands of non-Iranians and non-Muslims.

Partly because of Iran's political and economic weakness, the nineteenth century also witnessed unique and far-reaching developments among Shi'a religious leaders. In contrast to the situation during the Safavid dynasty (1501–1722) and the chaotic period of the eighteenth century, under the Qajars, the Shi'a *ulama* (religious scholars) managed to attain a level of independence from political authorities combined with increased influence over the mass of the Iranian population that eventually proved critical in the revolutionary period of the late twentieth century.

The achievement of clerical independence had several aspects. Its theological roots lay in the Twelver Shi'a notion that ultimate religious and political authority rested with the Hidden Imam, the messianic successor to Muhammad who would only return at the end of history. During the later eighteenth and the nineteenth century, the leading Twelver *ulama* consolidated the idea that, in the absence of the Hidden Imam, religious authority rested with the *mujtahids*, those prominent Shi'a clerics qualified to derive religious norms through independent reasoning (*ijtihad*) on the basis of tradition. The Imam's political authority, by contrast, they conceived as being delegated to the secular rulers, in this case, the Qajar shahs. That delegation, however, was sharply limited in the sense that, unlike with the Safavids and the Sunni notion of caliphate, the Qajars were neither granted nor did they claim direct religious legitimation. Since the *ulama* conceived Iranian society as Shi'a and thus as above all a religious collectivity, this meant that ultimate communal leadership devolved to those with final religious authority, namely the Shi'a clerics and more centrally the *mujtahids* among them (Arjomand, 1984: 221ff., 253).

Lending substance to this theological differentiation of religious and political authority were a number of other developments. The *mujtahids* achieved significant economic independence from the rulers by successfully claiming a share of religious taxes and endowments; and because they had the long-standing option of locating in the Shi'a holy cities of Iraq, outside the easy fiscal and political reach of the secular Iranian rulers. The *ulama* also strengthened the religious courts, in part by restricting their operation to matters of traditional religious jurisdiction like personal and inheritance laws, leaving criminal and other matters to the state tribunals. A crucial element in this process was a corresponding decline in the rival influence of the *qadis*, the religious judges appointed by the state, and the hereditary religious notables, the *sayyids*. Perhaps most important for future events, however, the clerics consolidated and increased their influence among the mass of Iranian Shi'is. Building on a trend begun in Safavid times, the *ulama* stressed elements of popular religiosity like shrine pilgrimages, processions, and passion plays, notably those commemorating the deaths of Ali and Hussein. Moreover, as part of the overall development of their authority, they emphasized the notion that ordinary Shi'is were not competent to interpret the religious tradition on their own, but had to rely on a leading *mujtahid* as their 'source of imitation'. Finally, the Qajars cooperated by helping the Shi'a *ulama* to suppress Sufism as a competing focus of popular religious influence.

Although the nineteenth century thus gave the Shi'a clerics a virtual monopoly on religious influence in Iran, that power had practical limits and was to some degree conditional on its apolitical nature. The popular religion that the mullahs (a general term for clerics of all ranks) represented was decidedly other-worldly; the *mujtahids* with the greatest reputations were also those who made a point of rejecting not only political patronage but also involvement. And it was really only the *mujtahids* who enjoyed independence, the majority of the *ulama* having to rely on state-controlled appointments or the voluntary patronage of their followers. Moreover, by the end of the century, the number of *mujtahids* had itself increased markedly. This inflation lead to hierarchical gradations among the top religious authorities, but such ranking was informal and based on the number and position of the followers a given *mujtahid* had. The implicit competition for scarce resources gave the followers a certain leverage over the *mujtahids*. Indeed, the Shi'a leadership was largely acephalous, with no formal organization such as exists in the Roman Catholic church to concentrate its influence in a practical way. As a result, the differentiation and consolidation of religious authority in nineteenth century Iran did not amount to direct political power for the *ulama*. Their political interventions with the state typically took the route of communal action, that is, social movement mobilization under religious leadership. They exercised a great deal of public influence, but mostly at the local level; action at the 'national' level was irregular and uncoordinated.

Relative independence from state tutelage combined with the acephalous and decentralized character of religious authority put the Iranian *ulama* in a potentially contradictory position. On the one hand, they were considered, both by themselves and, it seems, by the average Iranian to be the final legitimate guardians of Shi'a society: throughout this period, they in fact acted as mediators between the state and its subjects. On the other hand, the *ulama* were without regular means of exercising their influence in the country as a whole. This ambiguity mattered relatively little as long as the Iranian state was still the weak and traditionally patrimonial creature that it was during the Qajar period: the capacities of modern state machinery were not there to challenge the decentralized and local hold the clerics (and local secular leaders) had over the lives of most Iranian Muslims. Not surprisingly, therefore, the weakness of the *ulama's* position became much more visible precisely to the extent that they faced the powerful challenge of the dominant global systems as these increasingly manifested themselves in the late nineteenth and twentieth centuries.

Although one could draw on earlier examples of such clerical response to the encroachment of Western modernity,[1] the clearer and more consequential instances begin in the two decades around the turn of the century. Here the Tobacco Protest of 1891–2 and the Constitutional revolution of 1905–6 show both the mobilizing potential of the *ulama* and their inability to appear as a unified force to protect their interests. The first event was one of several instances of indigenous Iranian opposition to the degree of European control of the economic incorporation of Iran. The Qajar Shah of the time, Nasir al-Din, had granted a number of concessions to British and Russian nationals, largely in an attempt to enhance the fiscal position of his government so that it could increase centralized political control in Iran. When tobacco became the subject of one of these in 1891, Iranian opposition forces mounted an effective boycott of tobacco products, bringing about the cancellation of the concession. Of pivotal importance in the success of this movement was the action of the leading *mujtahid* of the time, Mirza Hasan Shirazi, who was prevailed upon to issue a ruling banning tobacco as long as the concession remained in effect. The fact that Shirazi had to be coaxed into action shows both the reluctance of many of the most prominent clerics to get involved in political matters, and their ability to mobilize the masses once they did so. The Tobacco Protest was in important respects much more of a secular nationalist response than it was a religious one. Successfully making it a religious issue, however, was critical for the success of the movement.

On the matter of granting Iran its first modern constitution and democratically elected assembly, the *ulama* were much more sharply divided. Among the leading *mujtahids* there were those, notably Shaikh Fazlallah Nuri, who distrusted this type of reform because it seemed to undermine the authority of the religious class over the people. It would secularize the political and legal systems of the country, leaving them to develop free of religious tutelage. Others, such as Sayyid Abdallah Bihbihani and Sayyid Muhammad Tabataba'i, felt that the monarchy was largely responsible for selling out Iranian and Muslim interests to the Western powers, and that popular institutions would be more susceptible to national/Muslim control and thus to clerical control. Both sides saw rising Western influence as the core of the problem. With the formal success of the revolution, Fazlallah's assessment proved the more accurate. The irony of the situation was that *mujtahid* support in the early stages was critical for lending legitimacy to the establishment of key modern political and legal institutions in Iran (see Martin, 1989).

Seventy years later, under dramatically different circumstances but for analogous reasons, the *ulama* would repeat this midwife function. For the Constitutional revolution showed not only that a rising group of modernizing Iranian nationalists was beginning to espouse global values and challenge traditional forms of authority, but, more important, that, in resisting Western/global incorporation, Iranians of very divergent interests were actively developing global institutions within their country. The idea that this could be done in a specifically Islamic way, and consistent with the Shari'a and clerical power, continued to entice many a religious leader for the remainder of the century.

Both the Tobacco Protest and the Constitutional revolution were thus manifestations of Iranian attempts to build more powerful and centralized political structures in response to the European-controlled spread of globalizing systems. Such development generally worked against clerical influence because the reforms it introduced tended to supplant the judicial, mediating, and community leadership roles that comprised the core of *ulama* religious performance. A dramatic example of this relation occurred under Reza Shah Pahlavi. From his base in the Russian-led Cossack Brigade, the only effective military force in Iran at the time, Reza Khan led a successful coup against the last of the Qajar shahs. In 1925, with the approval of the leading *ulama*, who still believed monarchy was more conducive to religious influence, he had the constitutional assembly, the *majles*, declare him shah.

What followed, however, was not a return to the nineteenth century division between religious and political authorities, but the deliberate and extensive development of centralized political authority in virtual disregard for the wishes of the clerical leaders. Once again the *ulama* had helped smooth modernizing reform only to be shunted aside in the aftermath. Ruthlessly suppressing all opposition, Reza Shah built up the military, instituted legal and fiscal reforms, set up a National Bank, created a modern state bureaucracy, vastly improved transport and communication, and encouraged indigenous industry, often under state support or control. His policies created a small but significant urban and modernizing middle class centred in the military, the state bureaucracy, and various professions (see Abrahamian, 1982; Keddie, 1981; Salehi, 1988).

Ideologically, Reza Shah considered Islam and the *ulama* a largely regressive force to be discouraged; he tried to appeal more to the pre-Islamic Iranian past than to Islam and the Shari'a. Several of his policies were aimed directly at clerical influence. Following trends begun under his constitutionalist predecessors, he devoted funds to the beginnings of a modern educational system, and greatly increased the presence and power of secular law courts. In both cases, he was striking at the heart of how the clergy exercised influence in society and also how many of them earned their living. One of his more well-known measures was to legislate Western dress for

Iranians, banning the Islamic veil for women and traditional dress for men. Although many clerics and students of religion were exempt from these regulations, determination of such clerical status was in the hands of state agencies. The undermining of public religious power was in fact only part of Reza Shah's general aim of greater incorporation of Iran into the modern world, but with the express purpose of giving himself and Iranians greater control over the process: he was in key respects a typical nationalist modernizer.

Where Reza Shah did not succeed was in spreading the modernization process effectively to the vast majority of Iranians who still lived and worked on the land, and to important traditional sectors, especially the *ulama* and their allies, the merchants and guilds of the urban bazaars. The peasants, the clerics, the shopkeepers, and the artisans benefited relatively little from the changes. Given the near dictatorial powers of the Shah, the *ulama* could do little to counteract his policies; but they remained largely in implicit opposition, their influence among important groups in Iranian society more or less intact.

The patterns set in the first half of the century continued after World War II. While global political pre-eminence shifted to the United States and the Soviet Union, Iranian nationalists carried on the effort to develop the country along modern lines. That process accelerated significantly in the 1960s under the second Pahlavi, Muhammed Reza Shah. Among the more significant changes, he implemented significant land reform, vastly increased the size and sophistication of the armed forces and the state bureaucracy, further developed the economic infrastructure, encouraged modern industry, introduced literacy and health campaigns, enhanced the secular education system, and set up the beginnings of a social welfare net. The direction of these reforms was thus continuous with what Reza Shah had pursued earlier; but whereas British military intervention forced the father to resign in 1941, a domestic and eventually theocratic revolution ended the rule of the son. Changes in global and national circumstances were one important factor in the difference of outcome. Developments among the clerical caste and in Iranian Islam were of equal importance. It is to an examination of these conditions of theocracy that I now turn.

The Iranian Revolution and Theocratic Triumph

An analysis of the causes of the revolution can begin by looking at the consequences of the Shah's reforms for various sectors of the Iranian population. On the matter of land reform, the changes introduced had the effect of undermining the traditional dominance of the large landowners over the largely landless peasantry. The move enhanced the centralization of authority in that it eliminated the former as an important social and political force in Iran, substituting the state. The latter, however, did not gain proportionately. The amount of land actually transferred was insufficient to take care of anything more than a fraction of the rural population, the Shah's policies being at least as interested in promoting modern mechanized farming. Combined with the attraction of the booming cities, above all Tehran, the result was a mass migration of people to the urban areas (Hooglund, 1982). There they encountered the classic problems of cultural dislocation and the fact that the urban economy could not hope to absorb them all. The migrants thus constituted a restive force with a large amount of mobilizing potential (Kazemi, 1980). In this regard, their traditional and still strong identification with Shi'ism and its clergy proved to be vital. It was from among these recent urbanites that the radical clerics drew their mass support base, and the revolution its most ardent defenders.

The expansion of modern industry, the military, and the civil service had analogous, ambiguous results. On the one hand, it increased the size of the Iranian middle and modern working classes, groups that benefited from the modernizing process and thus could be expected to identify with its goals and values. On the other hand, the dictatorial character of the Shah's regime effectively froze these same people out of meaningful political participation. Interpreting disagreement as disloyalty, the Shah tried to crush all opposition; but succeeded only in undermining his support in this vital sector of the population. The increase in the military and administrative capacities of the Pahlavi state was not matched by comparable development of political organization and legal structures. By the late 1970s, large numbers of people had come to the conclusion that the monarchy had to go precisely because it violated democratic values. In addition, and of equal importance, these and most other Iranians saw the Shah as a puppet of Western interests and thus one who violated the cardinal nationalist value of indigenous control of the country.

The Shah's economic strategy likewise met with important successes, but showed critical imbalances. Its accelerated pace was to a large extent made possible by oil revenues, especially after 1973. While Iran therefore had a ready source of financial capital to undertake its own industrialization and economic development, the country could not as easily and as quickly produce the requisite economic integration and human expertise. Although post-secondary enrolments increased dramatically, they were not enough to supply the burgeoning industries; and industrial inputs from raw materials to advanced technologies had to be imported. Dependence on foreign sources for vital goods, services, and expertise was not the only problem. Other aspects of government policy exacerbated the uneven distribution of wealth, making it seem that the Shah's revolution was for the benefit of foreigners and the privileged few, not the mass of Iranians (see Abrahamian, 1982, Bashiriyeh, 1984; Farhi, 1990).

With these factors, a number of others combined to create an explosive situation in the late 1970s. The billions poured into the Iranian economy created development, but also inflation, by 1975 at a rate of about 27 percent per year (Abrahamian, 1982: 497). A contributing factor, above all in major centres like Tehran, was the army of very well-paid foreign advisors and experts who drove up the prices, in particular of housing and even basic foodstuffs. Such inflation frustrated the rising expectations of the modern middle classes. In addition, the lifestyles of the Westerners offended the cultural sensibilities of a great many Iranians. The fact that a large portion of those Iranians who benefited most from the Shah's system seemed to imitate these Western ways reinforced the notion that the whole process was but a worsening of Iran's domination by colonial powers. At the same time, the Shah intensified his hold on political power: in 1975, he abolished even the semblance of party democracy by establishing a single party, the Rastakhiz or Resurrection Party. All those not interested in joining were invited to leave the country or attract the attention of the Shah's ruthless secret police, SAVAK.

What resulted was in effect a rough polarization of effective power centres: the traditional landowning elite had lost its influence through the Shah's reforms; the now much larger, educated middle class had little opportunity to spawn a secular national elite with solid links among average Iranians. The Shah, with the military and a small circle of the very wealthy to support him, controlled the state apparatus, but had little broad legitimacy. The *ulama*, by contrast, shut out of direct influence on the state, maintained their communal leadership role among the traditional bazaar merchants, the artisan guilds, the recently urbanized working and lower classes, and among the rural masses.

Even here, however, the Shah continued and elaborated the policies of his father in an effort to undermine clerical influence. He greatly expanded the secular education system, simultaneously seeking to control theological education both in the traditional seminaries and in new, rival theological faculties in the secular universities (see Akhavi, 1980; Fischer, 1980). He solidified government control over religious endowments. And he created a country-wide literacy corps and even a religious corps in an attempt to supplant the clerics directly in their traditional roles. Such a frontal attack could not but rouse the opposition of a clerical estate whose prevailing mood had been rather more quiescent and apolitical.

It is worth emphasizing that the Shah took the more blatant measures such as enforcing Rastakhiz and sending out the religious corps precisely at the time when serious faults were beginning to show in his economic and political policies. The inflation of the mid-1970s was symptomatic of the imbalances in the former; and his repressive techniques made him the target of American President Carter's campaign to improve human rights in countries allied to the United States. Given that the Shah cultivated his international image as an enlightened modernizer and was solidly tied into the American sphere of influence, it is perhaps not surprising that he actually reacted to this criticism. Accordingly, at roughly the same time in 1977, the Shah's government relaxed slightly its repression of political opposition and took measures to curb inflation.

These measures seemed to appease important segments of the middle classes. They also generated recession in precisely those sectors where the great mass of Iranians worked; and, as part of the response, the goverment attacked the traditional bazaar merchants as responsible for the price rises. Put briefly, fighting inflation heightened discontent precisely among those Iranians who were more likely to see the *ulama* as their leaders. The latter took advantage of the more liberal political climate and escalated the mobilization against the Shah from the tens of thousands in the middle classes to the hundreds of thousands and even millions in the lower classes. The spiral of protest eventually shut down most vital sectors of the government and economy with strikes; and the Shah's military reached a point where it refused to massacre more unarmed Iranians. When his lack of power matched his lack of popular legitimacy, the Shah had to leave. Then the question became, who would take over?

To understand the theocratic turn of the Iranian revolution, it is probably most important to recall the traditional influence of the *ulama* among the general Shi'a population. In general, this was not a secularizing society at the individual level. For a great many Iranians, especially in the bazaars, the guilds, the countryside, and among the recently urbanized masses, Islam was still a central part of their lives and the Islamic clergy the natural community leaders. As well, the *ulama* had the organizational network of the country's mosques through which they could reach the people for the purposes of political mobilization. The critical question, however, is why and how the clerics managed to take over the revolution and the state. What explains the successful transition from a group that, in the past, had occasionally roused itself to direct opposition to the state but had then always retreated, to one that now saw it necessary to take over the state and crush all secular opposition? The Shah's anti-clerical policies mentioned above are only a small part of the answer. The erosion of traditional clerical positions had after all been going on since the Constitutional revolution. More critical were developments among the *ulama* themselves and among the secular (as opposed to clerical) nationalists who lost in the post-revolutionary power struggle.

In the post-war period, secular, non-religious nationalism had two streams of representation: the monarchy, and the liberal democrats who reached their greatest prominence in the early 1950s under Mohammed Mossadeq and the National Front. The Shah clearly gained the upper hand by the 1960s and his subsequent autocratic policies made it difficult for the National Front or any successor organizations to remain a viable political force. Even had such continuity been possible, the Western-style moderniz-ation that the democrats embodied had become too closely identified with the Shah. Without some indigenous modification or expression, this ideology amounted to 'Westoxication' (*gharbzadegi*; see Al-e Ahmad, 1982), the uncritical mimicking of things Western at the expense of the authentically Iranian. The Shah's attempt to address this need by linking his modernization programme with the pre-Islamic Iranian past merely elimin-ated that heritage as a legitimate possibility. The kind of oppositional discourse that could gain legitimacy in the Iran of the 1970s had to be different. Only two possibilities presented themselves, the Marxist or the Islamic. The organizations representing the former not only suffered the brunt of the Shah's repressive apparatus, they also carried the hue of foreignness, and thus lacked authenticity in their purer form. That left Islam as the only viable option, albeit in different variants.

Oppositional Islamic discourse in Iran took quite a number of forms. To describe even the main ones in any detail is beyond my purpose here. Three do, however, stand out because they were instrumental in mobilizing significant segments of the population or played key roles after the Shah's overthrow. Their most well-known representatives were Ali Shariati, Mehdi Bazargan, and Ayatollah Khomeini respectively. Aside from their concrete historical importance, they also show how the distinction between liberal and conservative religion manifested itself in the Iranian context, and the close relation between public religious influence and the performance power of the professionals.

Although Ali Shariati died in 1977, his effect on predominantly the burgeoning population of young, secularly educated Iranians was enormous. Like other Islamic reformers before him, he traced an Islamic way of appropriating modernity without becoming Westernized. For Shariati, Shi'a Islam was a dynamic, revolutionary way of life that eschewed conservatism and backward-looking tradition in favour of progressive change leading to justice and equality. As such, it was the authentically Iranian way of approaching the modern world: not derivative of Western ideologies, but a different and better way. While Shariati used the vocabulary of traditional Shi'a Islam and the ideas of leftist Western social science, he criticized the practitioners of both in crucial respects. On the one hand, he accused Marxists of focusing overly on economic class conflict and not enough on the imperialist, including cultural, domination of the Third World by the West. His vision of Islam saw national cultural integrity as a prime condition for revolutionary progress. In this respect, he stressed the context of globalization over that of more local modernization. On the other hand, Shariati disparaged the apolitical and conservative *ulama* of Iran because they negated the progressive dynamism of Islam as he saw it, and thereby perpetuated injustice and oppression rather than working to change them. He spoke of two types of Islam, a conservative one identified with the clerics and a progressive one carried by intellectuals like himself.[2] Here the emphasis was on cultural modernization as the core issue.

In form, Shariati's ideology amounted to an Islamic liberation theology, and thus a decidedly liberal religious option. He laid the same stress on progress, equality, and action on behalf of the poor and exploited. Islam was for him a formula for change. Correspondingly, he looked upon the established religious authorities as too conservative and thus a witting or unwitting supporter of the unacceptable status quo. His use of social-scientific and Marxist analysis could serve as another parallel. The key point in the context of the Iranian revolution, however, is that Shariati held great appeal for a vital sector of the Iranian population: the young, secularly educated who were nonetheless largely from traditional Shi'a backgrounds. He was instrumental in their mobilization against the regime because he gave them a way of claiming full inclusion in the global system on the basis of what they perceived to be their own authentic exclusivity, and not at its expense.[3] His progressive and liberal interpretation of Islam was vital for establishing the link between Iranian cultural particularity and modern global universality.

The role of Shariati in the Iranian revolution demonstrates the mobilization power of liberal religion, but also shows with far greater clarity than does the Latin American liberation theological case how the liberal option bears an ambiguous relation to the possibility of public religious influence. Shariati saved some of his sharpest criticism for the religious professionals, going so far as to suggest that the new elite carriers of revolutionary Islam would be the intellectuals, not the clergy. Religion's influence might in such a case tend to become broadly cultural, perhaps moving in the direction of an Islamic civil religion. The clergy would lose their claim to be the authoritative mediators of the tradition. Nonetheless, Shariati was not anti-clerical in principle. He admitted the possibility of progressive *ulama*; and, in particular, admired the political activism of Ayatollah Khomeini. His followers therefore had no difficulty in accepting the latter's unifying leadership of the revolutionary Islamic movement after Shariati died. What they and most other secular Islamic revolutionaries did not adequately realize, however, was that Khomeini and his circle were operating with a view of Islam that contradicted theirs precisely on the matter of clerical authority.

Mehdi Bazargan represented the Islamic wing of the old National Front. His was a liberal nationalism with a strong Islamic component. The Liberation Movement of Iran (LMI), of which he was one of the most prominent leaders, had its roots and much of its appeal in the traditional sectors such as the urban bazaars, and among modern technical professions like engineers. Along with his influential clerical ally, Ayatollah Mahmud Taleqani, Bazargan stressed the importance of integrating Islam into all aspects of society, including a central role for the *ulama* in interpreting Islamic law and precepts. His movement occupied a middle ground between the laicized Islamic radicalism of Shariati and the conservative 'fundamentalism' of Khomeini. Like the former, Bazargan insisted that Islam was conducive to the modernization of Iranian society; but like the latter, he saw an indispensable role for the clergy in implementing Islam. Continuing the Christian parallel, Bazargan's movement probably came close to a kind of Islamic Christian Democracy, liberal but not as radical as liberation theology.[4]

Not surprisingly, Bazargan and his allies had little trouble cooperating with other Islamic oppositional groups, above all Khomeini and his followers. The kind of professional influence foreseen by the latter, however, went significantly beyond what even the LMI envisaged, and indeed constituted the central issue in the post-revolutionary power struggle. *Ulama* involvement in Iranian politics at various levels was nothing new in Iran: aside from playing key roles in everything from the Tobacco Protest to the National Front government of the early 1950s, clerics regularly sat as members of the legislative assembly, the Majles. The 1906 Constitution even provided for a council of religious leaders to ensure the Islamic nature of government legislation, a provision that, notably, was never properly implemented. Not satisfied with these precedents, Khomeini developed the notion that the *ulama* should rule directly. More pointedly, the leading *mujtahids*, and preferably the most prominent among these, should exercise direct and supreme political authority. Through his doctrine of *velayat e-faqih*, or rule of the jurist, Khomeini wished to abolish the *de facto* differentiation of religious and political authority that had character- ized Iranian Shi'ism since at least the eighteenth century. Negating the tendency of the leading *mujtahids* to be among the most apolitical, supreme religious authority and supreme political authority were to be invested in the same person. Only then would Islam, Shi'ism, and Iran be able to thrive and counter the nefarious influence of the West.[5] He could hardly have made a clearer assertion of the close relation between public influence, perform- ance, and professional authority.

Leaving aside the profound theological implications of Khomeini's innovation, the questions that concern us here are why Khomeini and his considerable clerical following considered such a change necessary and why they succeeded in putting the principle into practice. As regards the former, the argument put forth by Hamid Enayat (1983) seems fairly convincing. Since the late nineteenth century, the *ulama* had been losing their positions of practical public influence under various modernizing regimes. Yet, as I outlined above, they also played key roles in the various transitions towards a modern state, demonstrating their pivotal position as community leaders and sources of authority. Before 1979, however, their temporary secular allies always succeeded in excluding the *ulama* from meaningful power after the event, and usually continued the erosion of their performance positions in education, law, and the political arena. Khomeini and other clerical notables like Ayatollah Morteza Motahhari intended to reverse that pattern; their theological innovations gave the Islamic justification for that strategy (Rahnema and Nomani, 1990: 38–51). Explicit in their reinterpre- tations was that the interests of Iran and of Islam were identical with those of the professional representatives of the religious system, the *ulama*. In that sense, they took a similar position to the conservative Catholic hierarchy when faced with the challenge of the liberation theologians.

Turning to the question of why Khomeini and his clerical faction succeeded, two aspects were probably central. Ideologically, Khomeini shared a number of positions with his secular Islamic rivals, including his condemnation of Western imperialism and Iranian 'Westoxication', the central position of Islam in Iranian identity, a rejection of clerical apoliticism, and, of course, uncompromising opposition to the Shah. In addition, Khomeini built bridges to other oppositional camps by picking up on their global value orientation. He, for instance, claimed that Islam stood for democracy and that Islam was for the benefit of the poor, in Shi'ite language, the 'disinherited'. Although these emphases may have been an example of Twelver Shi'a strategic dissimulation (*taqiyya*), the combination evidently convinced most of the non-clerical Islamic groups that he and his followers were trustworthy and sufficiently likeminded allies.

The other central condition for the victory of the Khomeinists was their strategic position in relation to the Iranian masses, especially those in the cities (see Kazemi, 1980; Farhi, 1990). It was to Islam that a great many migrants looked for continuity and meaning in the urban environment. It was to the Shi'a clerics that they looked for guidance and leadership. While the Shah was pursuing his development policies in isolation from the majority of Iranians, the *ulama* were maintaining their influence among them. In spite of the Shah's efforts to control and even displace the traditional clergy, the number of mosques in Iran increased significantly during the 1960s and 1970s. That vast network gave the clerics an organizational base that could be turned to political purposes and that was not easily controlled by the government. From his exile in Najaf (Iraq), Khomeini in particular was able to build up a strong and nationwide following among the clerics and, through them, among the mass of Iranians.

Moreover, although the Shah's government undermined traditional religious prerogatives, that policy actually brought many mullahs into modern sectors such as teaching in non-religious schools and journalism, situations that gave them some measure of independence from both the state and the traditional, quietist *ulama*; and that exposed them to the radicalizing currents prevalent among the secular Islamic intelligentsia. A great many clerics with such exposure became activists and followers of Khomeini (see Enayat, 1983). In the context of the late 1970s, the Khomeinists were thus logical allies of the other Islamic oppositional currents, as well as indispensable resources for the revolutionary mobilization of the urban middle and lower class population. All sides chose to ignore or underexpose the critical differences between the clerical and lay camps, in the interests of solidarity, because the reality of a genuine power struggle had not yet arrived, but also because many did not believe a clerical takeover was possible or actually intended.

In the period immediately after the fall of the Shah, the intent and the tactical superiority of the Khomeinists became evident. At the centre, they formed the clerical Islamic Republic Party and set up the Revolutionary Council as a deliberate rival to the existing governmental structures and the Provisional Government in particular. Along with their military arm, the Revolutionary Guards, these parallel power structures served as the bases from which the radical clerics, under Khomeini's leadership, gradually destroyed all their rivals. Locally, they controlled most of the revolutionary committees that quickly became the real foci of local power because they had the numbers and the guns. For the most part, the non-clerical factions had neither the broad grass-roots support and organization, nor the means of violence to compete effectively. The only real exception was the urban guerrilla group, the Mujahedin e-Khalq. This group managed to inflict significant damage before succumbing to the superior power of the Revolutionary Guards in 1982.[6]

In the present context, the conditions under which the radical Shi'a clerics came to power in revolutionary Iran has a double importance. On the one hand, the Khomeinists took advantage of both their long-standing influence among the mass of Iranians and the peculiar juncture of the late 1970s in Iran that permitted the revolution in the first place. As an organized and cohesive group of religious professionals, they engineered a deliberate takeover of political power in Iran. From this position, they could reestablish and enhance their performance positions in other domains, notably law and education. With these performance levers thus firmly under their control, they were in a position to enforce what they saw as pure Shi'a Islamic norms and values. On the other hand, the Iranian *ulama* pursued this project adapting the structures of an established modern state, and with more than passing appeal to global values. The revitalization of Iranian Shi'a particularity was to be accomplished using modern and globalized tools. Like Khomeini's theology, that process has implied the revolutionizing of Iranian Shi'ism itself (cf. Arjomand, 1988) and the transformation of Iran as a society. In different words, what we have here is not a traditionalist recovery of the past, and more than a defensive 'return to the Middle Ages'.

Ironically, considering the express goals of the clerical revolutionaries, but also typically in contemporary global society, the anti-modern and anti-global revolution in all likelihood is resulting in the further modernization of society in Iran and in the greater incorporation of Iran into global society. In Robertson's terms, the assertion of the Iranian Shi'a particularity in the face of globalization has been but another way of concretizing and spreading that global universal. Developments in Iran during the decade after the overthrow of the Shah illustrate how that could happen. It is to this matter that I turn in the following section.

Progress, Equality, and the Victory of Performance Pragmatism

As an event in contemporary global society, the Iranian revolution represents an effort to give a marginal, 'Third World' region greater access to the perceived material and cultural (such as prestige, recognition) benefits of globalized systems, but in such a way as to enhance the cultural particularity that hitherto has been associated with its marginalization. In other words, Iranians want to be richer, more powerful, and generally more influential through a *revitalization* of their cultural difference, not at the cost of it. It is an example of a general moment of the globalization process. In this case, movement participants have looked to religion (Twelver Shi'a Islam) both as an instrument for reaching this goal and as the name of the goal itself. Moreover, that goal has had a large this-worldly component and has been consistent with certain of the key values historically resonant with the global spread of the more prominent instrumental systems, above all, progress and equality.

Among the important things we can learn from the Iranian revolution, however, is that its religious nature, while a decisive mobilization strategy, also introduces certain characteristic difficulties. As has been the case for Latin American liberation theology, the religion involved has strong other-worldly tendencies, reflecting a high degree of functional differentiation and specialization of the religious system. This has led to a certain inner-religious tension which manifests itself in pressure to differentiate the revolutionary movement from that religious system. Correspondingly, while religious holism is precisely what makes religion suitable for framing the sort of identity question that informs the Iranian situation, it also runs counter to the fractionalization of goals attendant upon the structural dominance in global society of several functionally specialized societal systems, *including* the religious. The result of this latter consideration is that the revolution has come under pressure to differentiate its activity and translate it into the respective idioms of different systems, above all the political and legal, the economic, and the educational. That fractionalization, in turn, pushes the properly religious again in a differentiated and more privatized direction.

In the Iranian case, these theoretical predictions are particularly salient because, at least according to the victorious Khomeinists and their substantial following among the Iranian people, the revolution was to negate and reverse precisely these tendencies. Such differentiation or secularization was for them at the heart of the Western imperial threat. This was the evil that wished to obliterate Islam. Accordingly, the Khomeinists took a fairly consistently conservative religious direction. They emphasized the preservation of what they saw as the received 'fundamentals' of their Shi'a tradition, insisting that these must guide the formulation of solutions to contemporary problems. Everything that happens in society was to be judged according to traditional religious principles and, to the extent that it was not in accord with them, proscribed. There ought to be a specifically and traditionally warranted Islamic way of doing everything. Globalized values, so central to Shariati and his followers, were to be pursued only to the extent that they were also manifestly Islamic values. Not surprisingly, this Shi'a conservatism is also religiously particularistic. Khomeini and his followers have not only rejected all other religions as at best inferior; even their pan-Islamism is so strongly coloured in traditional Twelver Shi'a idiom as to make it difficult to export to otherwise sympathetic non-Shi'is (see Zonis and Brumberg, 1987). Correspondingly, for these revolutionaries, the explicit rejection of the relativizing implications of globalization meant that Iran would only be the beginning. From there, the Islamic revolution would spread to all Muslim lands and ultimately around the whole world, thereby inflicting a final defeat upon the evil that threatened them.

To a significant extent, the Khomeinists succeeded in implementing this vision, at least within Iran. As they defeated their erstwhile allies, they gradually dissolved the structures of revolutionary mobilization or absorbed them into the state power structures now firmly in their hands. One after another, the Revolutionary Council, the Islamic Republic Party, the revolutionary committees, and the Revolutionary Guard disappeared or were normalized. By the early to mid-1980s, the Islamic revolution had became the Islamic government. This was a rather different situation from mobilizing for the overthrow of the old order. Yet with this institutionalized power now under their control, they also faced the logic of its structures and the global context in which these had developed. Implementing Islam would have to occur under these conditions.

At the core of Khomeini's theology and practical aims was the dedifferentiation or integration of religious and other functional forms of authority. The most important doctrine in this regard was *velayat e-faqih,* the rule of the jurist. This was the 'line of the Imam [Khomeini]', adherence to which became the litmus test for loyalty to the Islamic revolution. One might expect that putting the doctrine into practice would create tension *vis-à-vis* the already specialized and highly developed political system that was the Iranian state. Where it ran into greater difficulty, however, was within the religious system itself. In Iran, as elsewhere in the world, differentiated religious institutions had existed for several centuries. As discussed above, that differentiation amplified during the nineteenth and twentieth centuries, spawning the relatively independent and influential class of religious professionals whose product the Khomeinists were. That influence and independence helped to make Islam a base for social mobilization, but also an internally problematic one.

A more minor instance of the problem occurred immediately after the overthrow of the Shah. As part of the effort to destroy the power of their erstwhile lay allies, Khomeini and his clerical activists also felt it necessary to deal with the potentially divisive counter-influence of those clerical leaders who favoured a less central role for the *ulama* in the state, and hence political authority differentiated from religious authority. The key figure in this regard was Ayatollah Mohammad Kazem Shariatmadari. He certainly favoured an Islamic state, but had problems with Khomeini's doctrine of 'rule of the jurist'. Already in 1979, the conflict between the radical and moderate positions sharpened: Khomeini's forces successfully silenced this chief inner-religious opposition even before they dealt thoroughly with their lay rivals (Rahnema and Nomani, 1990: 193–199).

In 1989, shortly before Khomeini's death, the problem attendant upon integrating political and religious authority in a differentiated context arose with far greater clarity. Ayatollah Hosain-Ali Montazeri, his officially designated successor, had fallen out of favour with Khomeini and been forced to resign largely because he had become increasingly outspoken in his criticisms of the regime. In response, Khomeini pushed for revision of the 1979 Constitution of the Islamic Republic so as to allow a lower-ranking cleric to succeed him in his political position: he was afraid that requiring a successor with his own high religious rank, as the Constitution foresaw, would narrow the field to more apolitical candidates than himself.[7] Ironically, therefore, Khomeini's last major act before his death was to ensure the redifferentiation of supreme religious authority from supreme political authority, something that his core doctrine of 'rule of the jurist' was expressly designed to negate (see Rahnema and Nomani, 1990). The point here, however, is not to accuse Khomeini of inconsistency, but to show that the very differentiation of religious and political authority which made a powerful and independent opposition figure like Khomeini possible in the first place also consolidated and enhanced religious systemic interests in the direction of more purely religious concerns. The leading *mujtahids* were highly trained and specialized professionals: the system that produced them was unlikely to generate too many Khomeinis. Even the 'government of God' could not easily undo that result.

These incidents of course do not present a complete picture of what has happened to the Khomeinist revolutionary Islamic ideal in practice. For the moment, however, I simply want to demonstrate that part of the problem with implementing it concerns the nature of a differentiated religious system itself, quite aside from what happens in other spheres of society and social life.

The sense in which this issue points to the globalizing context is also somewhat indirect: the revolutionary movement refers to it directly and, as a system of communication, Shi'a Islam and especially the *ulama* have to deal with that context in a variety of ways, including the extent to which they accept privatization. Yet, in contrast to, for instance, the global economic, political, or scientific systems, we do not have a relatively uniform global religious system that could set a prevailing pattern for all religions to follow. On the contrary, the variety of religious expression is, if anything, increasing in the wake of the global spread of the more dominant systems. To understand the more direct pressures of globalization on the Islamic revolution, we have to look at tensions between its religiousness and the secular systems in which the Khomeinists have attempted to institutionalize their vision. Here I confine my remarks primarily to what has happened with regard to the economic and political systems. Similar analyses are possible for other systems, notably the educational.

Above, I mentioned the extent to which the victorious Khomeinists in Iran insisted on the priority of traditional Islamic values and forms over global ones. Three central manifestations of this direction of the revolution can serve here as introduction to the kinds of changes that have happened as the policies confronted the globalized context.

The first concerns governmental (political and legal) structures. The 1979 Constitution set up what one can best describe as a mixed system of government. On the one hand, one sees globally common republican items like an appointed supreme court and a popularly elected president and legislature (Majles). While these do not contradict traditional Islamic laws and precepts, they are definitely Western in origin and form. Along with the elaborate bureaucracy built up under the Pahlavi shahs, the revolutionaries evidently kept these structures because of the political/administrative control they afforded over the country. Not to follow the dominant globalized pattern here would have been to doom the revolution and its theocratic turn to failure. That aspect of the matter, as I show below, has been critical. On the other hand, the constitution also erected three quite clearly Islamic offices: the Faqih or Jurist, who held ultimate 'rule' or authority; the Council of Guardians, whose specific task was to ensure that all governmental legislation and action was in accord with Islamic law; and the leaders of Friday prayer, who served as an official Islamic link with the people.

A second manifestation of the Islamic priorities of the revolution was the policy of exporting the revolution, of mobilizing the Iranian people for the purpose of spreading the Islamic impulse to other Muslim countries and eventually the whole world. What we have here is a direct and conscious attack on both the propensity in global society towards, as Robertson calls it, the relativization of particularisms, and correspondingly a clear favouring of Islamic values like martyrdom and *jihad* for the faith over secular global values like progress, equality, and inclusion. The major although not sole occasion for putting this policy into action was, during most of the first decade of the republic, the Iran–Iraq war. The devout disinherited were to forego material rewards and even sacrifice their lives and those of their children; but the reward would be a place in heaven and the triumph of Islam.

The third manifestation is more of a negative one: the lack of any clear economic direction. Although there now exist in the Muslim world numerous writings proclaiming an Islamic economics, it is unclear whether this amounts to more than the application of Islamic constraints on what is otherwise a modern market economy. A properly Islamic theory or mode of production and consumption seems to be missing. That ambiguity has been especially pronounced in Iran, where the very few contributions by thinkers like Sayyed Mohammad-Baqer Sadr and Abol-Hasan Bani Sadr do not even claim to provide such a theory (see Behdad, 1988; Katouzian, 1983). Overall, the situation is not that surprising since a differentiated economy about which one could build an independent theory is a peculiarly modern phenomenon. The discovery of an Islamic *economics* is therefore itself already an accommodation to the spread of the modern global economy. The Khomeinists, who have been concerned to do things in a fashion that is neither Western (capitalist) nor Eastern (socialist) but rather recognizably Islamic, have responded to the ambiguity by steering a path between these apparent options: by, for instance, nationalizing some industries and controlling foreign trade, while at the same time deliberately restricting the extent of state control in the name of Islam.[8] They have in addition put recognizably Islamic constraints on areas such as banking and contracts. One of the most notable aspects of this attempt to keep economic measures

Islamic, however, has been the failure to implement important items of economic policy proposed by the government precisely because they contradict Islamic norms.

Turning now to the fate of these attempts at Islamization over the first decade of the republic, it is important to recall that by no means everyone in Iran has had the same conception of the goals of the revolution, or of what Islam implies. Even among the clerics in power, there was a sharp difference of opinion on such central matters as the degree of state intervention in the economy, and how aggressively the revolution should be exported. In these and similar matters, a point at issue was whether, at root, 'Islam' meant 'progress and equality' or 'received tradition'; whether the revolution was essentially a modern nationalist one with Islamic details or one that implemented received Shi'a Islam, period. For a great many Iranians, of course, it was both; that, however, only begs the question of their degree of compatibility.

From the early years of the republic, this issue manifested itself as an ongoing battle between the Majles and the Council of Guardians, not accidentally between a principal modern structure and one of the key Islamic ones. Consistently between 1982 and 1988, the Council vetoed various pieces of legislation as contrary to Islamic law. These ranged from bills on foreign trade and taxation, to land reform and social welfare, all concerned with the extension of state power into non-traditional areas (Bakhash, 1990; Rahnema and Nomani, 1990). Although competing economic or class interests were quite evidently involved in these disputes, the sheer variety of measures vetoed on the basis of Islamic law and the fact that Khomeini, not specific interests, controlled appointments to the Council of Guardians indicates that religion was a prime, perhaps even the prime, consideration. What is important to realize is that the sticking issue for Shi'a law and therefore the Council was the broad powers typically claimed by the modern state and not directly the issues such as command versus market economies. The problem was that the Islamic revolution consisted precisely in taking over and using such a state to implement its Islamic vision. The logic of those modern structures combined with the strong presence among the revolutionaries of the globalized values that modern states typically pursue were however at odds with crucial aspects of Shi'a religion as they perceived it.

Khomeini's role in this ongoing conflict is instructive. As Faqih, he had ultimate authority under the constitution to decide these matters. Rather than simply taking one side or the other, he tried to find Islamic precedents which would allow the government to get around several Council objections. As an example, at one point he ruled that parliament could bypass the Council if it voted in response to 'overriding necessary conditions', a precept with Islamic precedent. Not surprisingly, the Council then began to veto on the basis that legislation exceeded those conditions. What Khomeini wanted was for the two centres of decision-making to resolve their differences; but received Islamic law quite clearly favoured the conservatives over the progressives, and yet the latter controlled the legislative and executive arms of the revolutionary state. Khomeini was faced with an impasse. Either the influence of Islamic law would have to be weakened or the state would. Khomeini tried to avoid choosing, because either option would strike at the heart of the revolution's purpose or power. He ended up clearing the path for the former: he declared that the Faqih exercised an absolute mandate, meaning essentially that the law-*making* power of the state superseded the law-*finding* power of traditional Shi'a jurisprudence; and he curbed the power of the Council of Guardians. The revised Constitution of 1989 formalized this trend: the Faqih, while no longer necessarily of the highest religious rank, nevertheless has the power of final decision in disputed matters. The state was henceforth free to pursue what it saw as the best interests of the republic.

Such political and legal changes were, of course, only part of the picture. While these disputes were going on, Iran was fighting a protracted and devastating war with Iraq. For years, Khomeini virtually identified the carrying on of this war with what the Islamic revolution was all about. Great masses of the 'disinherited' fought and died for the Islamic ideals that this attitude expressed. Yet here as well, the reliance on modern means to pursue religious ends itself worked against their accomplishment. To achieve victory Iran needed many highly motivated fighters; but it also needed money and technology. The fact that the war was fought in a global context where several outside powers were clearly interested in preventing an Iranian victory meant that Iran could not hope for victory on religious zeal alone. And yet the technology had to be obtained from those same outside powers, leading, among other things, to the Irangate affair which revealed to the Iranian people that their pious leaders, with Khomeini's approval, had dealt directly with the United States and indirectly with Israel, the prime incarnations of the evil against which the Iranians thought they were fighting.

Although other factors like Iran's worsening economic situation undoubtedly contributed to Iran's abandonment of the war effort, probably one of the more important was that the pool of zealous martyrs dried up in the wake of this revelation in Iran: Khomeini had given them a pure Islamic purpose that could take precedence over the improvement of their material conditions; and yet he compromised those ends by resorting to tainted means (Rahnema and Nomani, 1990). To be fair, he actually had little choice. In another of the ironies of this Shi'a Islamic revolution, to do otherwise would have meant, figuratively speaking, allowing a repetition of Karbala, when the root Islamic purpose of the revolution was to overcome that mytho-historical defeat. But to have a chance, the Imam had to negotiate with Yazid.[9]

The truce with Iraq in 1988 was more than a moral defeat for the Islamic republic. In effect, it allowed the secular global goals of the revolution the relative foreground. With the central Islamic goal on hold, the severe economic and political problems of the Iranian state and society came into much sharper profile. Now the Khomeinists had to show that Islam, as the complete way of life they claimed it to be, could actually run a country. Accordingly, the serious effort to solve the political impasse discussed above more or less coincided with the truce negotiations. The debate over how to solve the country's economic problems also took on new vigour. A key aspect of the debate centred on how much foreign involvement should be allowed, that is, how much Iran should permit itself to become further incorporated into the global economy. Reminiscent of arguments in the Latin American cradle of dependency theory, proponents of radical self-reliance like Prime Minister Mir-Hosain Musavi claimed that foreigners sought to invest in Iran only to make it dependent; while President Ali Khamane'i and Majles (parliament) Speaker Ali-Akbar Hashemi-Rafsanjani,[10] the leading proponents of the involvement option, contended that domestic resources were insufficient for the reconstruction effort. Rafsanjani in particular said 'that the people could not be asked to sacrifice and do without material necessities forever. *Islam is about construction and good management, as well as "martyr-seeking, crusade, and self-sacrifice"*' (Bakhash, 1990: 278; my italics). Khomeini, as usual in debates that did not touch the essentials of Islam as he saw it, took no clear side.

In the period after Khomeini's death in 1989, those who would promote the normalization, in the global sense, of Iran have, at least for a time, gained the upper hand. Relations with Western countries have normalized somewhat; foreign investment is welcome and increasing; the government has tried to entice skilled exiles back with material rewards and has even discussed abrogating the convictions and confiscations previously levelled at former supporters of the Shah. In the most recent elections, the radical faction was dealt a severe blow: many of its candidates were declared ineligible while many others suffered electoral defeat. Temporarily, at least, the 'purists' were relegated to the shadows. Even in the private lives of Iranians, the previously zealous enforcement of Islamic codes of behaviour eased for a time (Hepburn, 1992; but see *The Economist*, 1993). Iran is still very much an Islamic country, ruled by its religious elites. Nonetheless, in perhaps the greatest irony of the revolution, Islam may have served, not to establish a theocratic rejection of global incorporation, but to rid Iran of its neo-patrimonial heritage and pave the way for a uniquely Iranian particularization of the global universal. The revolution that Khomeini led eliminated the Shah; but the theocratic and anti-global impulse for which the Islamic Republic became famous does not seem to have outlasted its charismatic incarnation. At the moment – and I stress that qualification – it seems unlikely that this outcome will be reversed.

Religion under Globalization vs. Religion

The foregoing of course does not mean that the Islamic revolution has been a temporary aberration in some inexorable process; nor that its religious identity is similarly evanescent. In a manner comparable to the fate of the American New Christian Right, ardent movement supporters have had to compromise their religious goals; but in political and broadly cultural terms, they have succeeded in revitalizing the dominant religious worldview as a central (in the United States at least as a legitimate) element in public discourse and basis for public action. In the terms I am using here, the Shi'a clerics have managed to enhance the performance capacity of the system they represent and thus increase the public influence of religion in Iran and probably in other regions of the Muslim world. Nonetheless, as I stated at the beginning of this chapter, and as the above analysis of the Islamic Republic shows, that performance capacity seems to have some rather clear limits. In this concluding section, I address the extent to which these limits reflect globalization or simply tell us something about religion as a mode of communication.

Even though the dominance of functionally specialized societal systems has been central for the transition to a global society, functionally specialized institutional spheres have been a feature of many pre-modern societies as well. That is certainly the case for religion. Yet the social importance of religion does not just lie in its capacity for differentiation; it also lies in its ability to structure and lend meaning to the everyday, to the local world of interaction. In classic sociological terms, religion's strength is both communal and societal. That double character can be of advantage in the context of globalization. Communally, religion is very often a vital part of cultural particularities and, like ethnic culture in general, expresses what people are when faced with the seemingly external forces of globalization. Equally as important, however, is the societal manifestation of religion. Differentiated from local, interaction-based social formations and yet also rooted in them, it has been and still is an effective resource for mobilizing across other lines of social cleavage such as stratum, class, region, and local culture. As I discussed above in Chapter 2, religion is therefore both expressive and instrumental, both particular and universal. The combination makes for excellent mobilization, as the conjunction of *ulama* independence and rooted Shi'ism of the Iranian population showed in the revolution. It also reveals itself to have significant disadvantages under modern/global conditions.

Differentiation of religion in specialized modes of communication and institutions enhances the operation of religion, but also concentrates it on what is specific to it, namely the postulated transcendent or other-worldly. The this-worldly thereby tends to become less central; or central only to the extent that it verifies the transcendent. Nonetheless, as I argued in Chapter 3, if religion is to remain socially relevant it must still continue to have practical affects on the social world. Function presumes performance. That, as discussed in Chapter 4, is not a huge problem if the extent of functional specialization does not throw up whole legions of non-religious leaders and professionals who take over previous performances in everything from politics to healing. Even when such a characteristically modern situation does prevail, religious professionals retain the broad possibility of championing the problems that other systems do not address, that is, residual problems. In Iran, parallel to religious actors in the other movements I am examining here, the *ulama* did precisely that. The limits arrived when they switched from mobilization for dealing with the problems to running the Iranian state. As long as they could devote considerable energies to mobilization, essentially until the end of the Iran–Iraq war, their religious specialization was probably an advantage. Outside that context, it was at best neutral. The difference, however, was more than a matter of religious professionals trying to be political and economic professionals while lacking the experience. Instead, it refers chiefly to the fact of globalization.

Since the Iranian revolution was more a rejection of the *way* that Iran was being incorporated into global society than it was a movement toward principled isolation (as for instance in Hoxha's Albania, Ne Win's Burma, Pol Pot's Cambodia, or even Tokugawa Japan), it was eventually important for the Islamic Republic to show itself as a *better* way. That has meant working toward globalized goals like progress and equality, specifically through the development of those societal instrumentalities that have corresponded with those goals. Given that the effectiveness of the instrumental systems depends at least to some extent on their secularization, it should come as no surprise that the Islamic government has found ways of allowing its Islamic warrant to become less central and more flexible; or at least that it has become one theme of political contestation among others. If the current leadership has not adopted a Shariati-like liberalism, it has certainly moved toward a Bazargan-like modernism. Had the radicals carried the day after Khomeini's death, virtually the only way to preserve the Islamic purity of the revolution would have been to take the path of global isolation and constant, inevitably futile war with the devil at the gates.

A final point to complete the picture: it may well be that the moderation of the Islamic Republic will also work to the benefit of Islam as a religious system. Functional differentiation, after all, also means the development of specialized institutions and resources for pursuing religious goals as such. Iran is now, and will be for the foreseeable future, a country in which Islamic religion is very strong. If a certain amount of secularization is occurring at the level of societal systems, that does not mean a loss of vitality at either the individual or institutional levels. Indeed, the conscious identification of Iran as an Islamic Republic may allow its Shi'ism to take a less defensive posture *vis-à-vis* the world around it. Perhaps Shariati's vision of a dynamic yet authentic Islam may yet be realized. Whether it will then also retain its present level of public influence is of course an open question.

Notes

1 The declaration of *jihad* against the Russians in 1826, with disastrous consequences for the Iranians, would be one prominent example; see Algar, 1969: 82ff. To the degree that the

mid-century Babi movement was itself a response to social and economic dislocation brought on by Western influences, the clerical battle against it would be another; see Algar, 1969: 137ff.; Keddie, 1981: 48–51.

2 For analyses of Shariati's thought and role in the revolutionary mobilization of Iranians, see Abrahamian, 1982: 464–473; Akhavi, 1980: 143–158; 1983; Fischer and Abedi, 1990: 202–220; Rahnema and Nomani, 1990: 51–73; Richard, 1981: 215–230; Sachedina, 1983.

3 See the argument for the similar role of social Catholicism in Quebec's 'Quiet Revolution' of the 1960s in Beyer, 1989.

4 The most complete work in English on Bazargan and the LMI is Chehabi, 1990. This author also suggests an LMI–Christian Democratic parallel. Bazargan's moderately liberal religious position has its parallel in various other religious traditions faced with the challenge of relativizing globalization. The ideologues of Soka Gakkai as representatives of Japanese Buddhism and the Rashtriya Swayamsevak Sangh (RSS) as representatives of Hinduism provide further good examples. On the former, see Dator, 1969; Metraux, 1988; on the latter, Anderson and Damle, 1987: especially 71ff.

5 Important primary sources are in Khomeini, 1981. For analyses of Khomeini's thought, see Fischer, 1983; Fischer and Abedi, 1990: 128ff.; Rose, 1983.

6 For an excellent description of the mechanics of the clerical takeover, see Bakhash, 1990. On the Mujahedin, see Abrahamian, 1989.

7 See Bakhash, 1990: 281–286. The 1979 Constitution required that Khomeini's position, the faqih, be filled by a *marja e-taqlid*, a 'source of imitation'. The constitutional revision of 1989 changed this, allowing Ali Khamane'i, the lower-ranking cleric who had been Iran's President, to become the new faqih. For discussion of the *marja* title, see Lambton, 1964; Fischer, 1980.

8 As an example of this aspect of the policy, Khomeini said at one point that Iran 'is not a communist country where the state can do whatever it wants. Islam is for moderation . . . We must act according to Islam. As long as I am alive, I will not let the government deviate from the line of Islam.' Quoted in Rahnema and Nomani, 1990: 242.

9 In the first Islamic century (7th century CE), the Third Imam of the Shi'is, Husayn, son of Ali, died at the hands of the Sunni Yazid, thus effectively ending the claim of the Shi'is (partisans of Ali) that their leader was the legitimate successor of Muhammad. For the Shi'is, the event is of comparable mythic and ritual importance to Easter for the Christians, but without the happy ending.

10 The 1989 Constitution abolished the office of Prime Minister, strengthening the President and the Faqih, offices now held by Hashemi-Rafsanjani and Khamane'i respectively.

8
NEW RELIGIOUS ZIONISM IN ISRAEL

A not uncommon observation in the recent literature on Israel is that there is a serious danger that, in twenty to fifty years, this state will be either Jewish or democratic, but not both (see, for example, Jansen, 1987; Kimmerling, 1989; Lustick, 1988; Peleg and Seliktar, 1989; Thorsell, 1989). While the actual future is hard to predict on the basis of present trends, the current and recent tension between exclusive particularism and inclusive universalism in Israel provides a good illustration of some of the choices religious actors, elites, professionals, and organizations face in the context of a global society.

Given that this chapter represents the third case study of religious movements that take the conservative option, I deliberately focus on different aspects of the theoretical position presented in Part I. Above all, the treatment of religious Zionism that follows explores more closely the dynamic relationship between global inclusion and group exclusivity, a simultaneity that is both characteristic of modern and global society, and religiously most clear in those movements that reject the relativization attendant upon globalization. In carrying out this task, the presentation also touches on several other key issues, above all the importance of the social movement as a social-systemic vehicle for pursuing the goal of public religious influence, and the difficulties of translating the social movement impulse into the institutional forms of dominant instrumental systems, above all the political. In this latter context I analyse, among other factors, the specifically global constraints that operate.

Zionism as Inclusion and Exclusivity

Almost from its beginnings in the latter half of the nineteenth century, the European Zionist movement that eventuated in the founding of the State of Israel in 1948 expressed the ambiguous symbiosis of inclusion and exclusivity that has been so fundamental to the process of globalization. As a result of the progressive political, legal, and economic emancipation of Jews in much of Europe, the ghetto ceased to be the only alternative. A new Jewish intelligentsia formed. Espousing the modern Enlightenment ideals of equality, freedom, and the rational control of human destiny, they made a disproportionately large contribution to the rapidly expanding spheres of art and science especially.

Yet the civil inclusion of Jews was neither smooth nor complete. Among Jews themselves, there was the problem of continuity: what did it mean to be a Jew in this new situation?[1] Among non-Jews, the cultural habits of the past combined with modern discontents to reproduce nineteenth and twentieth century European anti-Semitism. Straightforward assimilation was problematic from both directions. Zionism was one – for our purposes here, the most important – response to this historical situation: like other nations, the Jews needed their own homeland both to contribute to the progress of the modern world and to benefit from it. Inclusion could only be brought about through the politically based nurture of exclusivity. The global orientation of this attitude was well expressed by David Ben-Gurion:

> In defining a new road toward a world of liberty, freedom, peace, justice, and equality, there is no monopoly to big powers. . . . Small states can nowadays guide humanity in scientific, social and spiritual progress. . . . With the establishment of our state we have become more than ever citizens of the world. *Our national independence has placed our world citizenship on a solid base.* Not because of unrootedness do we espouse these issues of humanity and are aware of its needs and problems but because we are equal partners in these needs and problems. (quoted in Rubinstein, 1984: 73; my italics)

From Theodor Herzl to Ben-Gurion, most Zionist leaders believed that their movement would establish Jews as a 'nation among the nations', as a group of people who would be recognized as worthy equals in a global society. The various factions within the Zionist movement disagreed on many things, but they all had two main concerns. First, the solution to the problem of inclusion for Jews in the modern world lay in establishing a Jewish homeland. Given that straightforward assimilation in Europe was impossible or undesirable, a particular territory was essential if Jews were to escape their excluded 'pariah' status.[2] From very early on, and with few exceptions, this territory had to be in Palestine. Second, a Zionist homeland would allow Jews to be true Jews who could make a unique contribution to the progress of the world. The point of inclusion was not to be like everyone else, but to allow the flowering of a globally beneficial exclusivity. The Jews were to be a 'nation among the nations' in order to be a 'light unto the nations'.

Varieties of Zionism

Within this general parameter, however, there was and is much disagreement. Before independence, most aspects of the basic Zionist idea were open to variation. On the question of territorial sovereignty, for instance, the political Zionism of Theodor Herzl or Leo Pinsker insisted on the creation of a nation-state to which Jews would emigrate *en masse*. Socialist Zionists like Ben-Gurion and A.D. Gordon placed more emphasis on economically-based redemption through the land than on political sovereignty, although they certainly did not exclude the latter. The cultural Zionism of Ahad Ha'am wanted only a small state which would act as a spiritual beacon for the world and for Jews. The greatest number of the latter would continue to live in the Diaspora. Most Orthodox Jews in the pre-World War II period rejected Zionism as the negation of Judaic religion; but a few religious Zionists, notably Rabbi A.I. Kook, saw in it the beginnings of the final Redemption. To these and other variations on the territorial theme corresponded different visions of what constituted Jewish exclusivity. I take a closer look at these below.

Two pivotal historical events radically recast the basic questions without in the least settling them. The Holocaust made many of the old options seem obsolete or hopelessly optimistic. It destroyed any remaining illusions about the gradual demise of anti-Semitism in Europe, making the Jewish national homeland that much more imperative. This renewed and indisputable urgency helped to bring about the second event, the establishment of the State of Israel in 1948. Territorial sovereignty, whatever its significance, became a reality. Followed as it was by the mass immigration of both European and Oriental Jews, independence altered the political picture. The population of the new state did not necessarily conform in its attitudes and social characteristics to how the secular leaders envisioned the inhabitants of the new state. And religious Jews came to Israel in much larger numbers not because they had now been converted to the Zionist vision, but because the European world had given them little choice. As a result, the ideological controversies about the inclusion and exclusivity of Jews were more radically transplanted to the specific territory of the state of Israel and became the inevitable stuff of Israeli politics and government programmes.

To be sure, independence did not magically create political directions that were not there before. With the departure of the British mandate authorities, however, Jewish institutions now had the power and responsibility to set policy for all people within Israel and for all aspects of their lives. Having been territorially and demographically determined by the historical events of the immediate post-war period, the state of Israel was henceforth at least as much a political reality to be governed as a national ideal to be debated. Ben-Gurion's socialist Zionists were the faction within Zionism clearly best positioned to take advantage of this transition. With their practical and flexible attitude toward the question of territory, they had succeeded more than other factions in establishing or dominating concrete Jewish institutions in Palestine during the pre-state period (cf. Migdal, 1989).

In consequence, the socialist Zionist political parties, especially Ben-Gurion's Mapai, formed the nuclei of successive Israeli governments from independence until 1977. Their particular ideology, revised to meet the practical exigencies of political power, informed much government policy and could even claim to be the dominant ideology in Israel during the first two decades of its existence. Nevertheless, Ben-Gurion's governments were always coalition governments, often with slim majorities, that included bourgeois elements and, above all, religious parties (cf. Wolffsohn, 1987: 44–46). Although Israel's system of proportional representation in itself encourages the survival of numerous small parties, it also allows the Knesset to reflect the country's actual political and ideological fragmentation. Correspondingly, the socialist vision of Israel was never sufficiently dominant to allow its representatives complete control of the government. As in the pre-state period, there were many competing visions. The most influential of these were those of the religious parties and the secular right.

Zionism and Orthodoxy

As already noted, most religious or Orthodox Jews in the nineteenth and much of the twentieth centuries opposed the Zionist project on religious grounds: it denied the religious identity of Jews and substituted secular nationalism for religious messianism. In other words, it desacralized the symbolic importance of the Land of Israel. Yet, from early on, there was a significant religious faction in the Zionist movement, founded in 1902 as Mizrachi (a Hebrew acronym for Spiritual Centre). The main anti-Zionist Orthodox faction split from Mizrachi and the World Zionist Organization in 1912 to form Agudat Israel. Both these factions became political parties after independence, the former to become the National Religious Party and the latter under its original name (see, for instance, Don-Yehiya, 1981; C. Liebman and Don-Yehiya, 1984; Oren, 1973; Schiff, 1977).

Israel's political system has therefore always had a religious wing as part of what is in fact a tripartite political spectrum (see Isaac, 1981). The other two wings are the more common 'left' and 'right' represented principally by the socialist/labour parties and the liberal nationalist parties. The fragmentation of the Israeli political system has ensured that, with their approximately 12–15 percent electoral support (see Wolffsohn, 1987: 22), the religious parties have consistently held the balance of power between the left and the right and have, accordingly, been coalition partners in every government until the present. This is not a mere political detail. It is an empirical expression of the persistent minority but ineluctable status of a religious self-conception of what Israel and Jewishness are all about, and of the ability of this vision to be practically compatible with either the secular left or right. Nevertheless, given the tendency of the Israeli left to stress global inclusion over exclusivity and the parallel tendency of the Israeli right to do the opposite, we should suspect that a left or right alliance of the religious parties is something more than inconsequential. In fact, the tension between inclusion and exclusivity in the global context, as well as the tension between religious function and performance, between privatization and public influence are clearly discernible in what has happened on the religious wing of the Israeli political spectrum since independence. Before we look at this question in more detail, however, we must examine the two main secular visions of Israel with which the religious option interacts practically and ideologically.

Socialist Zionism

In its earlier phases, socialist Zionism pursued more the goals of universal progress and inclusion than it did the creation of a nationalist state. The socialist ideal saw the solution to human problems in the overcoming of class distinctions, not in the establishment of national enclaves. The aim of the Zionist project was to allow Jews to make their contribution to this goal. Accordingly, emigration to Palestine to help establish a Jewish homeland was more than an escape from persecution. It was also an opportunity to work toward socialist ideals. In the new/old land, Jews would build the embryo of the classless society, one that would eliminate the exploitation of bourgeois capitalism and the anti-Semitism it engendered. Socialist Zionism was not, however, a matter of simple combination. Its adherents melded the socialist and Zionist programmes into a unique ideology that greatly influenced the historical shape of the Zionist enterprise; and that was in turn transformed by the concrete historical conditions in which it operated.

The advocates of socialism came mostly from among the Enlightenment Jews of Eastern Europe, in particular Russia. It was here that they learned their socialism and it was here that they formed their image of what it meant to be a Jew in the Diaspora. As Rubinstein (1984: 24; see also Diamond, 1957) points out, the socialism of these Jews was as much a rejection of the sectarian religious identity of their parents as it was a reaction to the crude and violent anti-Semitism of Eastern Europe. The rabbinical Judaism of the Diaspora was for the socialists a reflection of the oppressive conditions there. Migration to the Zionist homeland would allow Jews to create new conditions in which this religion would no longer be necessary. The self-conception of socialist Zionism therefore had little room for religious Jews. Yet these latter formed a significant portion of the future Israeli population; and they have usually held a measure of the political balance of power.

While the significant presence of religious Jews in Israel militated against its easy hegemony, socialist Zionism was nonetheless the prevailing self-conception among most of the state's government leaders for at least two decades after independence. Two reasons were central. To a large degree, the socialists could attain this position because they had concentrated their efforts in the pre-state period on the establishment or control of concrete institutions in Palestine, among others, the Assembly or Knesset Yisrael, the multifunctional labour union, the Histadrut, and, of course, the Kibbutzim. They therefore controlled key *in situ* organizational expressions of Zionism during the critical post-war years when historical conditions allowed the creation of a sovereign state. As practical incumbents, they acquired the status of founders.

The second main reason was their flexibility. From early in the twentieth century, socialist Zionists came to see agricultural labour as the essential and ideal activity for the new Jew (cf. Kimmerling, 1983). In this way, they reconciled the economic emphasis of socialism and the territorial emphasis

of Zionism: land was to be redeemed through labour and labour through
land. This secularized transformation of the traditional religious view of the
connection between the Land of Israel and Jews allowed socialists to pursue
their goal while more or less bracketing the question of the political status of
the land, much as the religious Jews of the pre-Zionist community in
Palestine had done for centuries. Hence the practical Zionism that
advocated gradual acquisition of land by Jews in Palestine without the
immediate aim of territorial sovereignty meshed well with the socialist idea
of Zionism. Their practical success gained the socialists the support of many
in the World Zionist Organization who did not share their ideology. And
when statehood was achieved, they could avoid an uncompromising
irredentism in favour of exercising sovereignty over what the historical
context delivered.

The flexibility of the socialists also became evident after independence.
Ideologically, Ben-Gurion and the Mapai leadership transformed their
pre-state socialism into a statist vision that emphasized identification with
the state and its institutions over the agricultural and socialist redemption of
the land (see C. Liebman and Don-Yehiya, 1983). In what must be seen as
the continuation of their practical Zionism, the socialists adapted their
socialist values to the new situation. Sovereignty changed the relation of the
Jewish leadership to the territory of Israel, making the state the prime locus
of power. Settlement as a method of establishing control over territory was
no longer necessary within the boundaries of the new state. Moreover, its
population was irrevocably pluralistic. Most Israelis were not socialists or
did not make their living off the land. The massive immigration in the years
after 1948 increased the demographic domination of those who would not or
could not fit the socialist Zionist image of the new Jew. Statism was the
practical ideology that responded to the new structural situation. It helped
Mapai and its successor parties maintain political power well beyond the
time when their earlier ideological impulse ceased to be an important factor
in the historical development of Israel.

Revisionist Zionism

Since the mid-1920s, the principal secular rivals to the socialists within the
Zionist movement have been the Revisionists and their nationalist successors. The emphasis of this group, as of its founder, Vladimir Jabotinsky, was
very much on the political status of the Land of Israel: the Jewish demand for
inclusion, for justice and equal rights, meant sovereignty over a specific
territory, namely that occupied by the Jews in ancient times (see Isaac,
1981: 135–141). It is perhaps one of the central ironies of Zionist history that
the party which most clearly insisted on political sovereignty as the central
goal of the movement was effectively frozen out of power until the eventual
state was almost thirty years old. The reasons lie in Revisionism's consistent
ideology and corresponding tactics.

The Revisionists shared several fundamental attitudes with their socialist rivals. Both saw in Zionism the solution to the problem of Jews living in the Diaspora: the new/old homeland would be the place for the cultural rebirth of Jewish particularity. Correspondingly, both rejected as inferior traditional Jewish life in the East European *shtetl* from which both drew their dominant following. Both were secular movements that nevertheless appropriated selected symbolic elements from pre-exilic and biblical times to help express the legitimacy and content of the Zionist enterprise. Beyond these general similarities, however, the two differed dramatically in specifics and priorities.

Even more than economic redemption was at the heart of the socialist agenda, political power was the key for the Revisionists. Sovereignty over a particular territory was not only the prime goal of Zionism, this power had itself to be gained through political, that is, military means. Strategic alliances with foreign powers could be of great advantage, but ultimately, the Revisionists believed that Jews would have to create and defend the state through force. The prime problem in the Diaspora had been that Jews could not or would not assert their particularity politically. To be included as an equal partner in the larger world system therefore required the creation of an exclusive and Jewish state; and the guarantee of that state, of that inclusion, had to be the threat or the reality of military power. With their concentration on the political system of modern global society, the Revisionists accepted completely the primacy of the nation-state as the central enabling institution.

The emphasis on a political definition of Jewish inclusion and exclusivity gave the Revisionists characteristic weaknesses and strengths. The matter of political boundaries was all-important; and military prowess was both the method of securing those boundaries and a prime mark of Jewish cultural renaissance. Revisionism therefore concentrated its pre-state efforts on battle. Its most successful institutional expression of that time was the underground fighting unit, the Irgun Zvai Leumi (National Military Organization), led initially by Jabotinsky and then by his successor, Menachem Begin. After independence, the Revisionists continued this emphasis. The founding document of their political party, Herut, reads in part:

> We must remind every man in Israel day and night that the target is the homeland and not a strip of its territory until the eternal yearning becomes living reality. Further one must tell the people: there is no liberty without the homeland. The partition statelet will give no freedom. . . . If we do not expand we will be thrown into the sea . . . (quoted in Isaac, 1981: 136)

Concentrating as they did on the matter of territorial sovereignty, the Revisionists did not compete effectively with the socialists for the establishment and control of practical Jewish institutions in pre-state Palestine. Whereas the socialist economic mode of redeeming the land was to a large degree attainable without first settling the sovereignty question, the Revisionist political mode was not. As a result, as Aronoff (1989: 2) puts it, the primary approach of the Revisionists was ideological and not organizational; and the socialists were able to freeze them out of power until after the death of Ben-Gurion.

A further corollary aspect of Revisionism's political emphasis was the insistence that Zionism not be diluted by foreign ideologies, most specifically socialism. For Jabotinsky and his followers, seeing class as a central line of social cleavage was counterproductive for the Zionist project because it detracted from the most important cleavage, namely Jew and non-Jew. Revisionist nationalism aimed at a maximal ingathering of the exiles, rejecting the selectivity that socialists, at least in the pre-state period, showed in this matter. Jabotinsky's 'monism' reinforced the exclusivism of Revisionist ideology because it insisted that Zionism devolve solely from what Jews were and not from the historical conditions of the modern world. This insistence opened Revisionism to a much more positive view of the Judaic religious tradition than was prevalent among the socialists. Indeed, Jabotinsky, but especially his successor, Begin, saw in religion an essential aspect of Jewish cultural revival intimately linked with the central political project. The Judaic tradition was not only the foundation of all that made Jews unique, but also the source of all that was good in the contemporary world (see Isaac, 1981: 137f.).

Given Revisionism's more positive attitude to the religious tradition, it would seem that the religious parties in Israel have in the parties of the secular right their more obvious political ally. Such an alliance had to wait until the 1977 elections, however. The reasons for this almost thirty-year 'delay' are, of course, complex. Much of it had to do with the ability of the Labour parties to occupy the political centre and thereby maintain their hold on power: religious party alliances with the secular right or even the more moderate liberals made little sense if the result was still too weak to form governments. Labour's institutional strength, discussed above, and the corresponding weakness of secular opponents also helped to perpetuate the power distributions of the initial years. Yet the policies of the religious parties were also a factor. And the eventual change of those policies in the aftermath of the 1967 Six-Day War was an important part of the reorientation of Israeli politics in recent decades. It is to an examination of the role of the religious parties before and after this redirection that I now turn.

The Religious Parties of Israel

As mentioned above, the problem that most Orthodox Jews have historically had with the Zionist project has been precisely the religious connotation of the Land of Israel. Jewish messianism has for centuries associated the end of exile and the return of the Chosen People to the Promised Land with the consummation of history and of divine creation. This return is political in the sense that pious Jews believe it will be physical; but it is much more purely religious both because divine agency brings it about and because the human portion of it is an act of return only in the sense of conversion to the divinely sanctioned life. Secular Zionism contradicted this messianic relation to the land in a double way. It proclaimed an end to the suffering of exile in the Diaspora and promised the redemption of Jews through their return to the Land of Israel, but as an essentially human enterprise. In so doing, it also denied the singular validity of Jewish piety as it had developed over the centuries in the Diaspora. In fact, for the more extreme secularists, the life of religious observance was a central manifestation of the exilic misery to be overcome (cf. Diamond, 1957). In short, by their project, the secular Zionists denied God and his sovereign power over human affairs. Little wonder, then, that few Orthodox Jews in Europe felt attracted to the movement.

Agudat Israel

The rejectionist response to Zionism received its strongest organizational expression among religious Jews in Agudat Israel, the Society of Israel. Founded formally in 1912, this clerically dominated and international association took an explicitly anti-Zionist stand during much of the pre-state period (see Schiff, 1977). Inasmuch as Zionism was a denial of Judaic law, its progress had to be opposed both in mandated Palestine and around the world. Agudat Israel represented the position that only a religious definition of Jewishness was valid; and that political nationalist conceptions were not only less important, but more than that, improper. Socio-structurally, this attitude reflected the condition of Jews in pre-modern Europe and in the Muslim countries of North Africa and the Middle East: Jews lived as recognized communitarian groups with their own internal, religio-legal authorities. To be a Jew was to live as a member of these groups. The larger secular – in the sense of temporal – political authorities were not Jewish, but either Christian or Muslim. Zionism, for the rabbis of Agudat Israel, was the Jewish manifestation of modernity, that broader threat to the public influence of religion of which the pressure towards universal inclusion is a symptom. Zionism represented privatization of Jewish faith.

Zionism, of course, did succeed; and the state of Israel was not founded on a religious basis. In addition, the more or less complete inclusion after World War II of the largest portion of Diaspora Jews, especially in North America, contributed further to the erosion of Orthodoxy as the dominant mode of being Jewish. Agudat Israel, as perhaps the most important international Orthodox organization, responded by retreating into sectarianism, or at least into a denominational form that, in analyses of Roman Catholicism, has been called pillarization (see, for instance, Coleman, 1979). In other words, rather than attempt to reestablish public religious influence on Jews in general and Israeli Jews in particular, Agudah promoted local enclaves of Orthodox Jews who would be served by Orthodox social institutions, thus filtering communication with the encompassing and largely secular society. This sectarian or pillarized response serves as the structural replacement of the old East European *shtetl*, although the comparison can only be carried so far because of the very different societal environments in which the two operate. More specifically, the modern sectarian response is a manifestation of the privatization of religion since adherence is optional in principle and in practice.

In Israel, Agudah's retreat tended much more in the direction of pillarized denominationalism.[3] Similar to the Roman Catholic pillars in Western Europe, this included the operation of Agudat Israel as a party in Israel's political system.[4] The policies of this party have reflected the overall response of Agudist Orthodoxy to modernity and Zionism. Between 1952 and 1977, Agudat Israel did not participate in the various coalition governments dominated by Mapai/Labour. What this long hiatus demonstrates is not so much that Agudat Israel hesitates to enter the compromising arena of political give and take, but rather that it will do this only with parties that are closer to its religious position, that is, in practical terms, Likud but not Labour. Agudat Israel has been concerned almost exclusively with securing state support for its institutions, that is, for its separatist option. Its involvement in government has, by and large, been as a lobby for a particular religious interest group. The party, no more than the religious Jews it represents, is therefore not an attempt to reassert public religious influence. That may be the desire and hope of Agudists, but it is not their political policy. Moreover, secularization among Jews in general, both in Israel and in the Diaspora, has meant the practical abandonment of the anti-Zionist battle. Agudat Israel is non-Zionist in that it does not see the state of Israel as an important sign of or contribution to the redemptive process; but it supports the state's existence and no longer considers it an affront to God.

The National Religious Party

An attempt to understand the difference between Agudat Israel and its main historical rival among the religious parties can begin by locating the two on scales of 'Orthodoxy' or 'Zionism'. Agudah, one can argue, is more Orthodox and less Zionist than the National Religious Party. While this strategy has the advantage of using relatively familiar words, it is at best a starting point because it looks at the matter only in terms of degrees and not in terms of qualitative differences.

We can take a step further by conflating the two scales into one of degree of separation: as discussed in the previous section, Agudat Israel seeks to separate its adherents from the largely secular influences around them. It does this through recognizable styles of dress, a distinct lifestyle, separate neighbourhoods, and separate institutions such as its own religious school system, and, of course, the Agudah organization itself. These constitute both its ultra-Orthodoxy and its non-Zionism. Followers and members of the NRP, by contrast, are more involved in the larger society. The political programme of this party is to influence that society, even to exercise dominant political control within it.

The logic of the NRP is churchly and not sectarian, in the Troeltschian sense of the terms. It seeks explicitly to establish public religious influence in society; and, like some other similarly intended movements in global society, it pursues this goal through the medium of the state. Its lack of separatism, its lesser Orthodoxy, and its positive Zionism are therefore also of a piece. Rather than retreating into the purity of religious function as does the ultra-Orthodox camp, the NRP compromises that purity for the sake of religious performance, first in the Zionist movement and then in the state of Israel. In so doing, it has been moderately successful at countering privatization in Israel, as I outline below. Yet that success has indeed been moderate. Religious Orthodoxy receives relatively high recognition in Israel; but faith is, for instance, only a very moderately advantageous resource for status attainment. The more dominant media such as education, wealth, political office, and technical expertise are much more effective. It should therefore not surprise us that, under favourable historical conditions, the NRP has spawned movements that pursue its root goal of public religious influence more aggressively.

Like Agudat Israel, the NRP and its predecessor, Mizrachi, have followed a varied course ranging between idealism and pragmatic compromise. Already in 1911, when those disenchanted with the World Zionist Organization's secular direction left to help found Agudat Israel, the religious Jews who stayed did so for pragmatic reasons: they wanted to maintain some religious influence within the movement. After World War I, however, Mizrachi adopted a more ambitious attitude that sought to institutionalize religious observance within the Palestinian Jewish community. Rabbinical courts with jurisdiction over personal matters such as marriage and divorce survived from the Ottoman millet system. The British mandate authorities not only kept this element of the old system, but also supported Mizrachi in the establishment of the chief rabbinate in 1921. Combined with the eventual formation of corresponding local religious councils and the earlier right granted by the WZO for Mizrachi to run its own independent school system, these institutions constituted the foundations of religious Zionist influence in the pre-state community and after independence (see Schiff, 1977: 46–49). Yet, with the exception of the rabbinical courts, none of these held binding authority over the general population or undermined the social position of those who chose to ignore them. In practice, respect for their decisions was voluntary.

In the light of the NRP's quite limited success at deprivatizing religion in Israel, the difference between the Zionist religious bloc and Agudat Israel during the first two decades of independence reduced in significance.[5] The qualitative difference between sacralizing Zionism or Israel and treating them as profane environment shrank to a quantitative difference of more or less separation, more or less participation. To be sure, the consistent presence of the NRP in the successive governments of this period assured

that past gains were preserved and even enhanced. Jewish dietary, sab-
bath, and personal status laws, and state support for the educational systems of both religious blocs have been strengthened as a consequence of
various coalition agreements (see Isaac, 1981: 59–90; C. Liebman and
Don-Yehiya, 1984: 15–40; Schiff, 1977: 151–221). Yet, while such successes
may amount to the equivalent of legal 'establishment' for Judaic Orthodoxy,[6] it falls far short of a generalized public religious influence in Israel.

Given the fact that religious Jews are no more than a sizeable minority in
Israel, the failure to achieve more than a mitigated privatization is hardly
surprising. The factors contributing to this limitation were, however, more
than demographic. Although, on purely religious issues, the NRP clearly
manifested its intention of creating a religious state, a 'Torah state', during
the first two decades of independence, it did not seek any significant extension of the range of issues on which it claimed a specifically religious
direction. Perhaps the most important area in which this manifested itself
was in the NRP's foreign policy.

Foreign policy in the modern global system is a primary way by which
states relate to that system directly. And, like all governmental action, it
has domestic repercussions. Religious incursion into this area would therefore be an important strategy for establishing public religious influence
domestically and globally. By sacralizing foreign policy, religious actors (in
particular religious leaders) attach religious significance to matters that are
not directly or purely religious. It is religion in a performance mode. The
central distinction introduced in Chapter 3, between liberal and conservative forms of religious performance, becomes operative here because it
indicates two fundamentally different directions, one emphasizing global
inclusion, the other local exclusivity. In the case of Israel, it takes on direct
salience because the Jewish claim to the Land of Israel is inherently embedded in the Judaic religious tradition; and the fact that Israel's neigh-
bours dispute that claim is what drives Israeli foreign policy.

Throughout the first two decades of Israel's existence as a state, the NRP
not only formed repeated alliances with the secular and, as I am using the
term here, liberal labour parties; it further advocated a consistently dovish
foreign policy. For instance, during both the 1955–6 Sinai–Suez crisis and
before the 1967 Six-Day War, NRP cabinet members opposed pre-emptive
strikes in favour of seeking international support in the conflict with the
surrounding Arab states (see Reiser, 1984: 19–33; 1988: 108f). This position may appear as an example of liberal performance, and possibly indicates the presence of such a tendency among the then dominant NRP
leadership. The overt reasons for the NRP position were not, however,
religious. NRP cabinet members like Moshe Shapiro and Yosef Burg felt
that unilateral Israeli military action was bad strategy, not that it violated
religious norms. The NRP took independent positions on foreign policy;
but it was not trying to sacralize Israel's political relations with other states.
Religious performance here was neither liberal nor conservative, it was
simply absent. In other words, until the 1967 Six-Day War, the NRP

accepted the situation of mitigated privatization and did not attempt to go further.

New Religious Zionism

The New Situation

The Six-Day War left Israel in control of a much larger territory stretching from the Suez Canal to the Golan Heights. Within the new sections were places of great religious significance in the Judaic tradition, such as Hebron, Nablus (Shechem), and Old Jerusalem. Moreover, the expanded area of occupation included important parts of the biblical land of Israel, above all large portions of biblical Judaea and Samaria now comprising the West Bank. The military results therefore had great potential religious significance. In combination with other developments within Israel proper, they recast some of the fundamental questions facing the Zionist project from the beginning, most particularly the relation between territorial sovereignty and religious tradition.

The period following the Six-Day War saw a significant shift in NRP policy in the direction of a sacralization of the question of state boundaries. A new, much more hawkish national religious position opposed, on religious grounds, any surrender of the newly occupied territories, especially those that were part of the biblical Land of Israel. Moreover, within a decade of the war, the perennially hawkish Revisionist-nationalist parties under Menachem Begin and the Likud alliance gained political ascendancy and formed the government after the 1977 national elections, thereby bringing thirty years of Labour party rule to an end. Likud could not have succeeded in this way without the support of the religious parties (Roumani, 1988: 83f); and for the NRP, this switch in alliance partners corresponded well with its new position on the matter of state boundaries.

Although the results of the Six-Day War were certainly a catalyst in bringing about these changes, it would be incorrect to see in them the only important pre-condition. Both the change in NRP direction and the electoral success of Likud also had a great deal to do with demographic changes in Israel. A new generation of NRP leaders challenged the policies of a party that was not national or religious enough for them. Zevulun Hammer and the Tze'irim youth faction had visions of turning the NRP into the dominant centre-right party in Israel by taking advantage of the significant shift to the right in Israeli public opinion (Reiser, 1984: 37f.; Sandler, 1981: 163f.). Religious influence was thus to be extended to all areas of state policy. If the NRP stood for a religious nation-state, then its goal must be to take control of the government.

The youthful ambition of a new generation within the NRP might have met with more success if the Revisionist Likud had not simultaneously occupied the growing centre-right of the political spectrum. It did this not simply through its emphasis on expanded boundaries, but on the basis of the support it received from Oriental Jews. By the late 1970s, this ethnic group had become the majority among Jews in Israel. They, but especially their second generation, had come to see in Likud the party that would help them to become equal or fully included citizens of Israel, and escape the socio-economic marginalization that had hitherto been their lot under successive Labour governments (see Lewis, 1984; Roumani, 1988; Wolff-sohn, 1987: 121f., 150f.).

As a group, the Jews of Asian and African origin also had attitudes more commensurate with Likud policy. They tended to be more nationalistic, more hawkish in matters of foreign policy, and religiously more traditional-istic: while on the whole less observant by Orthodox Ashkenazic standards, Oriental Jews also had more respect for religious authority than their secularistic European cousins. In more theoretical terms, they differen-tiated less between religious and political spheres, and therefore saw fewer and less sharp contradictions between the pure demands of religious function and applied exigencies of religious performance. Public influence for religion and especially for religious leaders was therefore also signifi-cantly less problematic for them than for the secular Ashkenazim. The result has been not only greater strength for the similarly directed Revisionist-nationalist parties, but also a larger, albeit different, potential support base for religious parties. Rather than being a boon for the NRP however, the new situation actually resulted in its weakening as a political party.

Gush Emunim and the Expansion of Public Religious Influence

Although the policy shift of the NRP had its origins in the late 1960s even before the Six-Day War, factional differences, pragmatic considerations and the continued influence of the more moderate old guard prevented a change of alliance until 1977. During the intervening decade, a segment of the party's youth faction became disenchanted with the practical limitations of action within a parliamentary political system and formed the nucleus of a social movement dedicated to making Israeli sovereignty over the occupied territories permanent. The principal strategy of the movement known as Gush Emunim, or Bloc of the Faithful, was to establish permanent Jewish settlements throughout the territories, thereby bringing about *de facto* annexation and making it difficult or impossible for any Israeli government to relinquish sovereignty over them. The ideology that informs this concerted mobilization has been a very pointed religious nationalism.[7]

A large number of Gush Emunim founders were products of Israel's state religious school system, the one controlled by the National Religious Party. Specifically, Gush leaders such as Moshe Levinger, Chaim Druckman, and Hanan Porat were graduates of a particular Orthodox *yeshiva* high school, Merkaz ha-Rav, whose spiritual leader was Rabbi Zvi Yehuda Kook, the son of the first Chief Rabbi of Palestine, Rabbi Abraham Isaac Kook. The latter had been a chief proponent of a religious Zionism that saw in Zionism the beginning of the final Redemption, and defended the cooperation of religious Jews with secular ones on the grounds that the Zionist project was itself a holy undertaking, even if many of its participants did not lead a holy life.

Rabbi Kook the younger carried this central idea one critical step further by arguing that the Land of Israel was itself holy: 'The Land was chosen even before the people. . . . The chosen land and the chosen people comprise one completed, divine unity, *joined together at the creation of the world and the creation of history*' (quoted in Lustick, 1988: 83). It was therefore incumbent upon Jews to establish sovereignty over the land as a religious duty. This 'commandment of conquest' (Liebman and Don-Yehiya, 1984: 75) combined with an emphasis, growing out of the experience of the Holocaust, on the irreconcilable chasm between Jews and Gentiles. The result was a virtual negation of the universalist, inclusive impulse that had always been present in most secular Zionism, and a corresponding assertion of radical religio-nationalist Jewish particularity. The Gush Emunim followers of Rabbi Z.Y. Kook emphasized exclusivity over inclusion: Israel was not to be a 'nation among the nations' but rather 'a people that dwells alone and that shall not be reckoned among the nations' (Numbers 23: 9). Esau hated Jacob and that was that.[8] Moreover, in sacralizing the Land of Israel as such, Gush Emunim also sacralized the question of state boundaries. Where the NRP before the 1970s had concentrated on seeking to institutionalize religious influence within the state, Gush Emunim sought to extend this to the state itself and thus to its foreign policy.

The import of Gush Emunim's founding ideology can only be appreciated in the light of its practical implementation. With its emphasis on religious performance, this could hardly have been otherwise. The founding meeting of Gush Emunim took place in 1974 at Kfar Etzion, a pre-independence kibbutz in the West Bank recaptured during the Six-Day War. The location was symbolic of the claim to the whole biblical Land of Israel, but it also pointed to Gush Emunim's specific strategy. Even before the founding meeting, future Gush members had been instrumental in establishing Kiryat Arba, a Jewish settlement near Hebron in the West Bank. This initially illegal settlement was eventually authorized by the Labour government of the day. The tactic of 'creating facts' in this way was repeated several times until Jewish settlement in even the heavily Arab portions of the occupied territories became government policy under Likud after 1977.

The technical illegality of Gush Emunim's settlement strategy in its earlier phases was indicative of its extra-parliamentary, social movement style. Gush Emunim began in 1974 as a faction within the NRP, but soon left the party in order to escape the actual and potential compromises that party politics and, indeed, coalition partnership in a Labour government entailed. Having left these strictures behind, it became a social movement with the express aim of establishing settlements. This conversion from political party faction to social movement allowed a more independent development of the Gush's religio-nationalist ideology, gave that ideology a more important role in reproducing the social system, placed the central emphasis on mobilization, and permitted the fuller flowering of an antisystemic thrust. In a way explicitly parallel to the settlement movement of pre-state secular Zionism,[9] Gush Emunim sought to transform the existing political realities in a radical way.

Since leaving the NRP, Gush Emunim has consistently avoided alliance with any one political party, keeping the movement free to garner support from sympathetic adherents of various political persuasions, from left to right, from religious to secular. Such independence has been compromised to a significant extent more recently, but this tendency is more indicative of the movement's success in helping transform the political agenda than it is of its cooptation by established political forces (cf. Sprinzak, 1988: 135–144). In keeping with Rabbi A.I. Kook's idea that secular Jews could be used by God to advance the redemptive process, Gush Emunim consistently oriented its message to the larger Israeli public, not just religious Jews.[10] The bulk of its followers are in fact from the latter camp, but they also include a significant segment of secular Israelis. These constitute an even larger proportion of those generally sympathetic to the Gush cause and of participants in its rallies and demonstrations.

Gush Emunim has succeeded in broadening its appeal beyond political party and religious cohorts not just by phrasing its public message in more inclusive ways; the very specific and concrete aim of its mobilization has also contributed. Establishing settlements in the territories gives Gush Emunim a visible focus that accomplished a number of things at once. It concretized the ideology in a fashion that is subject to a variety of interpretations,[11] from ultra-Orthodox and religious Zionist to secular nationalist and even economic.[12] It allowed Gush Emunim to influence and even determine Israeli foreign policy by incorporating the occupied territories – most importantly, the West Bank – into Zionist mythology physically and not just ideologically: that is, by 'creating facts' that foreign policy could not ignore (see Sprinzak, 1988: 140–144). It did this without forcing Gush Emunim back into actual governmental politics with its pressures toward conformity with the inclusive norms of the global political system.[13] Gush Emunim could thus maintain its antisystemic stand as long as further settlement remained unavowed or at least controversial government policy; that is, until the unlikely event that Israel formally annexes the occupied territories.

Looked at from the perspective of the secular nationalist government leaders in Likud and several other parties, Gush Emunim offered the reverse advantage: it created expansionist settlement in the occupied territories without this having to become overt government policy. What Gush Emunim has been doing accords very well with the fundamental Revisionist nationalist inspiration of the until recently governing Likud bloc. As a result, especially in the years from 1977–1984, the number of Jewish settlements in the West Bank and Gaza strip increased significantly, with Gush Emunim being responsible for the bulk of those strategic settlements in the heavily Arab parts of the territories (cf. Wolffsohn,

1987: xxvii–xxix). At the same time, the Gush supporters among the members of the Israeli Knesset increased steadily, by some estimates numbering at one time as many as 40 out of the possible 120 (Sprinzak, 1988: 142).

Peace Response as Inclusion and Privatization

Although Gush Emunim has been a significant success for religious Zionism and has done much to make aspects of the Judaic religious tradition a key determinant of the contemporary political reality in Israel, that success has not been unequivocal and may eventually prove to be ephemeral. Rather than simply supplant the greatly compromised, but nevertheless dominant, labour ideology of the decades before the 1970s, the new religious Zionism has succeeded at best in dividing Israel into opposing ideological camps. Some scholars, such as Liebman and Don-Yehiya (1983; 1984), have tried to make a convincing case for a succession of 'civil religions' in Israel in this regard. The evidence, however, points in another direction.

The rise of Gush Emunim, together with more or less related events such as the 1982 invasion of Lebanon and the Palestinian *intifada* that began in 1987, have generated reactions from other Israelis, both religious and secular, that explicitly counter the exclusivist direction of the new religious Zionism. The largest and best-known of the secular responses is Peace Now. Among religious Jews, small, but significant 'peace' movements have also formed, notably Oz ve-Shalom (Strength and Peace) and Netivot Shalom (Paths to Peace) (see Aronoff, 1989: 93–122). These have attempted to desacralize the issue of political sovereignty over the occupied territories by emphasizing Judaic ethical norms of peace and concern for human lives over the divine promise of the Land of Israel. In doing so, activists in these movements typically appeal for what amounts to a differentiation of religious and political concerns, and call for an inclusive respect for the equal rights of others in the world. Uriel Simon, a founder of Oz ve-Shalom, for instance, argues that religious Jews must 'distinguish clearly between our religious right to the land (which is effective in the spiritual sphere only), and the legal-political right (which can be immediately effectuated in practice)' (*Religious Zionism*, 1980: 23). And a 1975 Proclamation issued by Oz ve-Shalom states that 'in today's world . . . there is no chance for solutions which involve the negation of the national rights of one people by another' (quoted in *Religious Zionism*, 1980: 26).

Janet Aviad, a religious Jew and leading Peace Now activist, writes in a similar vein:

> The religious protest against Gush Emunim is against what is perceived of as a compromise of religious Zionism through the pursuit of secular goals and the use of secular means. It condemns a one sided concentration upon the political-territorial issue to the neglect of interior ethical, intellectual, and spiritual problems as a distortion of religious Zionism. (*Religious Zionism*, 1980: 30)

She goes on to attribute the success of Gush Emunim and the lack of a mass following for Oz ve-Shalom to various factors, including that 'a movement that speaks in the name of universal ethical values and the rights of the "other" is much less comfortable than one that asserts the unique and superior rights of the "family"' (*Religious Zionism*, 1980: 31). In terms of the theoretical analysis I am developing here, the religious peace movements have therefore responded to Gush Emunim and new religious Zionism with a programme of 'liberal' performance, but one without a concrete programme and one which in large measure accepts the effective privatization of religious concerns.

In taking its position, Oz ve-Shalom is also continuing the more moderate attitude of the pre-1967 NRP leadership. There is no denial of long-standing and persistent Arab hostility to Israel and Zionism; but there is denial that Jewish particularism means irreconcilable conflict with the non-Jewish world. Jewish exclusivism is consistent with inclusion in the world system and must be understood as implying such inclusion.

Political Fragmentation in Religious Zionism

Although the religious peace groups cannot be said to have developed an effective countermovement to Gush Emunim, it would be misleading to think that the new religious Zionism therefore dominates the religious wing of the Israeli political spectrum. Gush Emunim has managed to make its religio-political discourse salient in the political agenda of the country. Yet in seeking to extend its appeal beyond Orthodox Jewry, the Gush has also left its impetus open to appropriation by secular ultra-nationalists for whom religious duty as set out in Orthodox rabbinic tradition (*halacha*) is at best a secondary concern. The concrete result has not been a burgeoning of support for the NRP and other religious Zionist parties such as Morasha or the Sephardic Tami. Instead, the prime beneficiaries of the religious Zionist upsurge during the 1980s were, if anyone, Likud and secular nationalist parties to its right, such as Tehiya, Tzomet, and Moledet.[14]

Perhaps the most indicative, if ironic, trend of the 1980s on the Israeli religio-political scene was the replacement of the religious Zionist parties by religious non-Zionist parties as the dominant religious parties and hence those with that perennial balance of power in the Israeli Knesset. While Agudat Israel has not increased its support significantly, unlike the NRP, it has maintained something close to its historical strength. New ultra-Orthodox non-Zionist parties, in particular the Sephardic Shas (Sephardic Torah Guardians), have however split from Agudat Israel and garnered significant independent electoral support. At the moment (1993), Shas and United Tora Judaism, a non-Zionist religious bloc that includes Agudat Israel, hold between them ten Knesset seats, a number in tune with the previous strength of the NRP (Hadar, 1992). That situation was even clearer while the nationalist Likud was still in power after the 1988 elections (see Peretz and Smooha, 1989).

This greater support for non-Zionist religious parties probably has little connection with the fate of religious Zionism. Rather, much of it is apparently to be explained with an upsurge in political participation by ultra-Orthodox Jews in Israel, and with the switch of many Oriental Jews from Likud to the explicitly ethnic Shas. Be that as it may, the political behaviour of these parties is more in continuity with Agudah's past, namely a dominant concern with sectarian interests. Nevertheless, as the now strongest religious bloc and therefore potential coalition partners, their attitude to the other persistent issues in Israeli politics has been important. On the central issue of foreign policy, the parties are divided, incorporating both doves and hawks. Some are expansionist, but others do not rule out territorial compromise if it should lead to peace. Intriguingly enough, the latter justify relinquishing sovereignty over the occupied territories under certain circumstances in terms very similar to those of the religious Zionist peace groups, namely that the ethical demands of Judaism and the value of human life rule out maintaining political control at all costs (see Freedman, 1989: 417). Thus, the religious peace groups may have little mass following in Israel, but their theological logic has become effective within those religious parties that currently do.

The net result of the efforts of the new religious Zionism has therefore been equivocal in a way somewhat typical of the fate of successful conservative religio-political movements in contemporary global society. Gush Emunim did manage to help spawn a strong, local nationalist tendency in Israel, and to that extent reestablished public religious influence for a time. Yet, one has to ask whether this reestablishment was not, in the final analysis, merely another secularization of an originally religious impulse as has been the case in other parts of the globe such as Latin America and the United States. Religion in Israel remains in the quasi-privatized state that it has been in ever since the founding of the state. The religious minority has greater influence than in most other First World countries, but this does not amount to more than an inconvenience for secular Israelis. Few negative consequences result from ignoring religious precepts. The only real difference is that now the non-Zionist parties are fighting the battles that the Zionist religious parties fought under Labour governments of the past; and a strong and undeniable secular and exclusivist nationalism of the right has established itself alongside the older secular and inclusivist nationalism of the left.

Conclusions

The story of the new religious Zionism in Israel and Gush Emunim in particular thus illustrates well both the potential and the problems of public religious influence from the conservative option in contemporary global society. Much as in the cases of the United States and Iran, a certain juncture in recent history provided an opportunity for effective mobilization on a conservative basis. The result in all three cases was the possibility and even reality of significant effect on public policy and on the range of positions it was henceforth culturally legitimate to represent within those countries. Although more globally positive (i.e. liberal) trends currently again hold sway in all three areas, the conservative religious position remains a cultural and political force to be reckoned with. At the very least, the NCR, the Khomeinist radicals in Iran, and Gush Emunim provide precedents that may again be followed in more propitious circumstances, whether in these countries or elsewhere.[15]

On the other hand, the very partial, or even temporary success of these movements in implementing their particularistic and anti-global visions points to counterforces within global society, in terms of both global systems and global culture. The situation of Gush Emunim confirms observations I have made in previous chapters. Beyond a small core of genuinely religiously motivated followers, the Gush had to rely on the support of secular sympathizers: in government, as settlers for its central mobilizing task of creating facts in the occupied territories, and as voters that would keep sympathetic parties in power. Yet most Israelis, it appears, do not harbour a sufficient degree of exclusivism, valuing progress, security, and inclusion in the global order over belonging to the righteous few. Following Leon Hadar's (1992) analysis of the 1992 Israeli election results, when it came to choosing between involvement and acceptance in the global system and its presumed benefits, and following the sacrificial path of a people apart, the citizens of Israel, while anything but unanimous, chose the former. In that equivocal choice, they have followed a path similar to the Iranians, with the result that their conservative religious factions, while far from weak, have nevertheless become another part of the political and cultural landscape rather than the growing force they were less than a decade ago. We could make a similar observation about the New Christian Right in the United States.

What this may amount to is that the conservative option can under certain circumstances promise more direct public influence based on religious performance than can the liberal option: this, however, on a restricted, local, usually national scale. By contrast, liberal religion, while seemingly less visible, may in the final analysis be the religious direction with a greater chance of seeing its orientations institutionalized in global culture. It is to a consideration of this latter idea that I turn in the final chapter.

Notes

1 Aside from the obvious matter of what to do with the Jewish religious and cultural heritage, a question that was answered in different ways by movements ranging from Reform to Orthodox Judaism, the problem of continuity manifested itself in more subtle ways, as for instance in the very theoretical structures of such intellectual giants as Marx, Freud, and Durkheim. See Cuddihy, 1987; Lukes, 1975.

2 For a thorough treatment of precisely this question, see Kimmerling, 1983.

3 Edah Haredit, the Pious Community, consisting of about 1000 families living in the Mea Shearim district of Jerusalem, represents a truly sectarian direction. Among other things, its

existence helps profile the relative 'moderation' of Agudat Israel on matters of separation, justifying a term other than simply sectarian for the latter's approach. For an explicit comparison of Edah Haredit, Agudat Israel, and the National Religious Party on this basis, see Don-Yehiya, 1981: 55f.

4 For an analysis of points of similarity and difference between Christian Democratic parties and Agudat Israel (or the National Religious Party, discussed below), see Don-Yehiya, 1981: 59f.; Liebman and Don-Yehiya, 1984: 80–90.

5 See for instance, Don-Yehiya's (1981) attempt to distinguish Agudat Israel and the NRP as representing a 'confederative' and 'federative' approach respectively.

6 On the virtual absence in Israel of Reform and Conservative Judaism, see Abramov, 1976; Tabory, 1990.

7 The literature on Gush Emunim is growing rapidly. Among the core references in English are Aran, 1986; Aronoff, 1984; Don-Yehiya, 1987; Lustick, 1988; Newman, 1985; 1986; Sprinzak, 1981; 1988; 1991; Weissbrod, 1982.

8 A good summary of Gush Emunim ideology is in Lustick, 1988: 72–90.

9 On the basis of this parallel, Gush Emunim claims to be the contemporary successor to the original Zionist impulse, thereby enhancing its legitimacy. See, for instance, Sprinzak, 1981: 37; Rubinstein, 1984: 110f.

10 As an example of a defence of Gush Emunim on a purely secular nationalist basis, see Nisan, 1980.

11 From this perspective, the West Bank settlements function for Gush Emunim in a way similar to the way CEBs are the concrete focal point of the liberation theological movement in Latin America. See above, Chapter 6.

12 During the Likud regimes, Gush Emunim and the government, with some success, concentrated on attracting secular Jewish settlers to the occupied territories adjacent to Jerusalem by offering lower land prices, proximity to jobs in Israel proper, and better public services and lifestyle within these settlements. This policy came in the wake of the realization that the pool of religiously motivated recruits had been more or less exhausted and that therefore a new source of settlers had to be found if settlement was to continue. The apparently justified hope was that, once established in the West Bank, these non-ideological settlers would develop political attitudes reflecting their new material interests. See Aronoff, 1984: 80; Shafir, 1984: 819–821.

13 The Camp David peace accord with Egypt, which Gush Emunim resisted strongly, is one example of the reality of such pressure. Following Hadar's (1992) analysis, the victory of the secular centre-left in the 1992 elections is another.

14 From its perennial high of 12 Knesset seats in 1977, the NRP slipped to 6 in 1981, 4 in 1984, 5 in 1988, and 6 in 1992. Tami was temporarily successful in 1981 with 3 seats, but sank to 1 in 1984, after which it effectively merged with Likud. Morasha obtained 2 seats in 1984 and broke up thereafter. While Likud support at first stagnated around 40 seats after a 1981 high of 48, and then dropped to 32 in 1992, its rightist allies advanced from 3 seats in 1984 to 7 in 1988, and 11 in 1992. And more importantly in this last regard, the currently most powerful ultra-nationalist party, Tzomet, is anti-clerical; while Tehiya, the most religiously identified, failed to gain the necessary votes for a seat in 1992. See Hadar, 1992; Peretz and Smooha, 1989; Wolffsohn, 1987: 24–25.

15 In his more recent work, Sprinzak (1991: 107–166) argues for the continued existence, not only of the Gush Emunim ideology, but of an 'invisible realm' of Gush Emunim consisting largely of its control over local governmental structures in the occupied territories.

9

RELIGIOUS ENVIRONMENTALISM

The Recent Upsurge

Like most new social movements, those focusing on ecological issues have their practical origin in the 1960s. Already in this early phase, a number of religious actors, most often liberal Christian elites and church leaders, saw religious significance in environmental problems (see for example Barbour, 1972; Elder, 1970; Santmire, 1970). These received official mention in various Christian church documents and at various meetings (e.g. 'Justice in the World', [1971] in Walsh and Davies, 1984: 191; World Council of Churches, 1976: 120ff.). And individual churches passed resolutions formally stating the religious basis of their ecological concern.[1] In spite of the early entry into the arena, however, until the later 1980s environmentalism remained a secondary or marginal direction in most official religious circles, and even to that extent only among liberal bodies in the West. Instead, as exemplified in Latin American liberation theology, the 1970s witnessed a concerted turn on the part of the global liberal religious segment toward other kinds of residual problems, above all 'social justice' concerns centred on human progress and equality.

In recent years, by contrast, ecological issues have shifted from the margins, both in the religious system and in broader global society. The natural environment has become a mainstream concern, not only in rich countries, but in most corners of the world (see Gorrie, 1992). Matters like ozone depletion, habitat destruction, waste disposal, global warming, biodiversity, overpopulation, and a host of other problems are now the standard affair of everyone. from individual householders to government and business leaders. It has become rather normal to talk and act green.

The manifestations of this trend among liberal religious elites, leaders, and organizations are also unequivocal. In late 1989, for example, Pope John Paul II issued the statement, 'Peace with God the Creator, Peace with All of Creation' (1989), the first papal statement devoted exclusively to ecology. The following spring, the 307-member World Council of Churches (WCC) met in Seoul, Korea under the rubric of 'Justice, Peace, and the Integrity of Creation' (see WCC, 1990a), thereby signalling the elevation of ecological concern to a level comparable with peace and justice on its list of applied religious priorities. And in 1992, religious groups were heavily involved at 'Global Forum '92', the conference of non-governmental organizations that took place parallel to the United Nations Conference on Environment and Development (UNCED) in Rio de Janeiro. The same period has also been witness to a burgeoning of theo-ecological literature[2] and religio-ecological organizations.[3] As these examples show, the centre of gravity of religious environmentalism has been very much among Christians and Christian organizations, but certainly not to the exclusion of actors from other traditions.[4]

In contemporary global society, religious environmentalism and its recent upsurge are a prime illustration of how liberal religious actors are seeking to (re)insert themselves and the system they represent into the public domain. What we are witnessing here is a phenomenon similar to 'social justice' directions like liberation theology and its attendant movements: a social movement based in religious resources which applies these to perceived problems that result from the operation of global society and its dominant instrumental systems. There is in fact a close relation between large segments of the religious environmental movement and social justice thought and activism. Several of the observations I made about the Latin American liberation theological movement in Chapter 6 also apply here. Yet the two also exhibit some important differences, which point to the ambiguous position of religion under modern/global conditions. I discuss both the similarities and divergences below.

In contrast to the preceding chapters, there is a strong sense in which any analysis of contemporary religious environmentalism must as yet remain quite preliminary. We are dealing here with a new development and one which has neither been thoroughly institutionalized nor much researched. Little sociological research, for instance, exists on this topic, in contrast to the substantial literature on the broader secular movement and religious social justice directions like liberation theology. Of the very few studies that have been done, most are North American and concentrate on the microsociological connections between individual religious belief/involvement and environmental concern.[5] More macrosociological studies in terms of, for instance, social movements or organizations are only beginning to appear (see for example Kearns, 1990; 1991). What follows therefore depends on the results of my own research – still very much in its infancy – and the few secondary studies available at the time of writing. That insufficiency, however, affects primarily questions of extent and prognosis, and far less the suitability of religious environmentalism as a case study for the main theoretical theses of this book.

To show the connections, I divide the remainder of this chapter into four parts. The next section deals in a broad way with the logic of the religion/ecology relationship in the global/modern situation. I show why we should expect ecological issues under conditions of globalization to become a central concern of certain religious outlooks, if not all of them, and that the linking of these issues with those that fall under the 'peace and justice' rubric is just as likely. The section also discusses the inherent ambiguity of including environmental concerns among the central tasks of religion that reflects globalization and its core values. As such, the analysis concentrates on liberal religion, but not because more conservative religious orientations uniformly dismiss ecological problems. As is the case with the Latin

American liberation theological movement, there are strains in religious environmentalism that lean in an exclusivist, more conservative direction. On the whole, however, clearly liberal perspectives dominate.

The three final sections of the chapter then go on to look more concretely at some aspects of how the movement is manifesting itself. To this end, I examine recent developments in the World Council of Churches, and then analyse divisions within the larger phenomenon with a view to showing its diversity and differing emphases. The last section examines anew the questions of religious performance and public influence.

Globalization, Religion, and Ecology[6]

In some respects, environmental issues concretize the problematic effects of the global societal system more clearly than others. For instance, the degree to which Third World underdevelopment is a product of First World development may be a matter for debate; the radioactive fallout in Britain, Scandinavia, and elsewhere as a result of the Chernobyl disaster far less so. Ozone depletion is another of these globally extended, relatively incontrovertible manifestations. Less clear, but perhaps more far-reaching in their global implications, are the questions of global warming and over-population. These are interconnected problems of extent. Neither is the result only of specific destructive activity but of the quantity of human action everywhere in the world: even clean-burning automobiles, like people – and sheep, for that matter – still contribute simply because we have produced so many of them. The sheer volume of social communication, in other words, is as much at issue as the type. Moreover, both greenhouse gases and people affect the whole planet even though their most intense production is concentrated in different subglobal regions. Together with a whole host of other ecological issues, they raise on a global level the question of the consequences of human activity as such. There are always unintended effects, unforeseen results.

Historically, religions have concerned themselves with this root indeterminacy. They have postulated a way to circumvent the normal, the everyday, the profane, and communicate a transcendent realm that will ground and guarantee our choices 'in this world'. Whether it is remaining true to the ways of the ancestors, attaining mystical insights into the true nature of reality, living according to the true revelation, or any of a host of other forms, there exists for religion an essentially non-empirical way of knowing what is the *right way*. The unintended and unforeseen are in this mode indicators of both the necessity and the reality of the transcendent. Religion gives them meaning and promises the power to overcome them. The nature of environmental crisis is therefore just the sort of problem religion addresses: it is virtually religious.

Contemporary evidence of this relation is not hard to find. As I pointed out earlier, religious people – including theologians – have been concerned with environmental issues since their advent in the 1960s; and recently that concern has become a central issue for major religious organizations as well. Secular environmentalists, however, also make the connection. The publications of environmentalists and environmental organizations are replete with at least implicitly religious interpretations and explicit recognition that (some) traditional religions address this matter at the core of what they are all about.[7] Perhaps one of the clearest examples in this regard is the 25th Anniversary meeting of the World Wildlife Federation which took place in Assisi, Italy during 1986. The environmentalist WWF not only held its conference in the birthplace of the now Roman Catholic patron saint of ecologists (cf. John Paul II, 1989); it further invited leaders of five major world-religious traditions to the meetings to launch an environment and religion network that has since grown and publishes its own periodical (see Alyanak, 1991).

What one might call the 'theodicy' factor in environmental issues does not exhaust their virtual religiousness. Global environment issues in particular also point to the question of holism. One of the abiding themes of the overall environmental debate is the fact that all action is interconnected, that 'to pluck a flower is to trouble a star'.[8] From nuclear fallout and global warming to ozone depletion and waste disposal, local action creates problems that affect the planet as a whole. The holism of religious communication, discussed in previous chapters, offers a logical social perspective from which to address this aspect. Moreover, because global environmental problems are a result of the power of the globalizing functional social systems, they also point to the globalization of society and to the problem of conceiving that society. This again is a religious task: the meaning of the whole as immanence profiled by positing transcendence.[9] A direct result of this connection is that environmental theology will often contain a decidedly global thrust (see for example Ambler, 1990; Martin, 1990). It also means that prosystemic religion, especially if it also includes significant antisystemic elements, will in all likelihood take up environmental issues as a fundamental theological concern. We arrive here at the close relation among the liberal religious goals of, as the World Council of Churches phrases it, 'justice, peace, and the integrity of creation'.

Peace and justice have for some time been key terms for more liberal, especially Western, religion.[10] As religious concepts, they indicate both acceptance of the core values of modernity – equality, progress, and others – and rejection of what are deemed the negative consequences of modernity. We can describe the logic roughly as follows: More than the absence of open conflict, peace implies the existence of community, globally speaking, world community. The word points to a self-conception of a global society which harmoniously includes all people.[11] Justice is a strictly complementary term referring to the relations that must exist among people if community is to be realized. These ideal relations incorporate several core modern values, including equality, human rights, progress, individual and collective self-determination, and tolerance – even celebration – of diversity. Various forms of marginalization or exclusion are accordingly manifestations of injustice. Among these are racial/ethnic discrimination, poverty, political powerlessness, individual alienation, religious intolerance, sexism, and the vast disparities between rich and poor regions of the world. For there to be peace, there must be justice first.

Translated into the terms of the globalization debate used here, the continued elaboration of the global system depends on pursuing the cultural values that resonate with that system. The liberal religious concepts of peace and justice are not, however, simply an accommodating confirmation of emerging global social order. Contained within both notions is the assertion that the injustices are to a significant degree the result of the operation of the globalizing, instrumental systems.[12] The prosystemic/antisystemic combination discussed above manifests itself in this kind of religion. In Weberian terms, it is both priestly and prophetic. It attempts to conceive the global whole (peace) and does so by concentrating on the problems that the more dominant functional systems generate but do not solve (justice).

Global environmental issues are then a religiously logical complement to the peace/justice pair. Like peace, environmental issues point to the whole, in Abrahamic-faith terms, creation. Like justice, they also point quite specifically to the problems generated by the same globalization. The World Council of Churches rubric expresses the combination nicely: integrity (justice) of creation (peace). Indeed, beyond the logical parallel, religious actors in the field very often tie the two together explicitly. For example, in his recent message, the Pope (John Paul II, 1989) places part of the blame for the Third World's contribution to environmental problems on the injustices of the global economic system.[13] I discuss this connection in greater detail in the following two sections of this chapter.

Although peace/justice and environmental concerns thus seem to imply each other, there is also a certain amount of tension between the two. This derives from the prosystemic attitude of much liberal religion, namely that the cornerstone of injustice is the marginalization or oppression of the majority of people in the world by a minority, and that the solution lies in the elimination of these inequalities. Without going into the matter in great detail, simple redistribution of power and wealth will not work because the effectiveness of the major functional systems depends on a significant concentration of communicative resources. Continued growth of the same systems, on the other hand, even assuming that it will eventually spread the benefits to increasingly larger segments of the human population, carries with it the environmental problems typified by the issue of global warming. In this sense, solving the problem of injustice would imply exacerbating the problem of environmental degradation.

A few examples can illustrate the dilemma. In Canada, environmental activists were successful in effectively ending the hunting of harp seal pups. The brunt of the economic cost was borne by the chronically underemployed Maritime fishermen and, indirectly, various Native Canadian communities of the far north. Attempts to save virgin timber stands in various parts of

Canada constantly pit those wishing to preserve endangered jobs against those battling further environmental destruction. In Brazil, the desperately poor flock to the Amazon region in hopes of a better life, contributing to the destruction of the rainforest. Various Third World countries have at times been hesitant about cooperating in international environmental efforts for fear that their own development would be hurt and they would become even more dependent on First World capital, technologies, and expertise.

To be sure, each of these cases has its own complexities and one could argue that the core areas of the global system contribute far more to these problems than the peripheries. The point, however, is not who is to bear greater responsibility for both the mess and the clean up, both the injustice and the restitution; but rather that both the globalizing systems and the core values that resonate with them – in particular equality and progress – have spread to virtually all corners of the globe. And this implies the further growth or intensification of precisely the instrumentalities that are at the root of the environmental crisis.

Religious people concerned about both marginalization and the environment are, for the most part, aware of this tension (see Carmody, 1983: 39–52; Cobb, 1986; Hallman, 1989: 129ff.) The responses, of course, vary a great deal, but most call for some 'new understanding of who we are and how we fit in' (Daniel Martin quoted in McAteer, 1990; see also Cobb, 1986: 184ff.; McDaniel, 1986). Such vague formulations are indicative. They are a call to what, in effect, is a religious conversion, a change of heart, a *metanoia*. The purely religious content of this conversion, while important for a more detailed understanding, is of less interest here. More germane is the implicit attitude to the global system. Among various formulations of the supposedly proper religious responses to environmental problems, one often finds an ambiguous attitude that, in the light of the present analysis, we can see as typical of liberal religion with its combination prosystemic/ antisystemic outlook. In this regard, the following report of a debate at the 1975 World Council of Churches conference in Nairobi is worth quoting at length:

> . . . after a chillingly detailed analysis of the threats to human survival, . . . [Professor Charles Birch] asked what positively we could do, for if we cannot permit technology to have its head, we cannot do without it. Our goal, therefore, must be a just and sustainable society; and this demands a fundamental change of heart and mind about humankind's relation to nature. . . .
>
> Metropolitan Paulos Gregorios drew a sharp distinction between the Limits to Growth People (LGPs) and the Technological Optimism People (TOPs). They could, however, agree to put their best minds and efforts together to control the four elements of population explosion, resource depletion, environmental deterioration, and nuclear war. But success will depend on a new economics and a new science and technology; and these can only grow in a climate of thought and life which takes seriously the deep religious questions about our relationship with the Transcendent, with one another, and with nature. (WCC, 1976: 23f.)

The ambiguity is particularly clear in this quote. In the theological literature on this topic, however, 'LGP' (antisystemic) positions dominate (see, from among many, Berry, 1988; McDonagh, 1987). 'TOPs' (prosystemic), as such, seem not to be present at all. Environmental problems, after all, result from the unprecedented power of the globalizing systems, and not from their fragility. Global economy, polity, and science hardly need religious legitimation.

'Justice, Peace and the Integrity of Creation'

Like the broader environmental movement itself, religious environmentalism is a very diverse phenomenon, exhibiting various streams and camps along with their representative organizations, leaders, publications, activities, and followings. It is, moreover, difficult to draw a precise boundary around this movement – what belongs, what doesn't, especially because various portions of the secular environmental movement exhibit clear religious qualities. Certain centres of gravity are, however, quite evident. Most – but by no means all – institutional religious environmentalism has thus far arisen among Christians and Christian organizations, a reflection perhaps of the First World origins of the new social movements and the dominance of Christianity in those regions. And at the global, as opposed to local, national, or regional level the most visible example has thus far been the World Council of Churches. Beginning in the 1970s, but typically with much greater force during the last few years, this worldwide organ of mostly Protestant and Orthodox churches has made ecological concern a central part of its perceived overall mandate.[14] A closer look at how this has come about, some of the religious justifications involved, and the difficulties that this move has encountered within the organization can help to illustrate and elaborate further elements in the foregoing analysis. Above all, the WCC experience reflects well the ambiguities of the characteristic prosystemic/antisystemic liberal religious stand, but also the degree to which ecological issues stand out in their virtual religiousness.

The end of World War II ushered in a period of accelerated globalization, one prime symptom of which was the proliferation of international and worldwide organizations, both governmental and non-governmental.[15] The World Council of Churches formed in 1948. That phase also brought about the identification and inclusion of the 'Third World' as regions, countries, and cultures with, in principle, equal standing as actors in global society. The manifestly peripheral position of Third World countries henceforth became a problem of underdevelopment or oppression, depending on one's understanding of the causes and solutions. As the example of Latin American liberation theology shows, by the late 1960s, in a great many liberal religious circles, persistent or increasing Third World marginality became a prime instance of the dysfunctionality of the global system and a denial of the central values of equality, progress, and inclusion. Liberal religious people theologized the situation as a violation of the moral principles of peace and justice, and set for themselves and their organizations the religious performance task of pursuing social justice throughout the world. The WCC, in a functional sense a body dedicated to the ecumenical unity of world Christianity, followed this liberal trend: once the target of missionary expansion, Third World churches emerged as distinct but very much included member churches. The WCC had to provide an equal space for their perspective if it was to take its liberal ideals seriously. In consequence, the marginality of Third World regions, understood largely as the deleterious effect of global system operation, came to inform key items on WCC agendas. The situation of the poor and powerless in the world was religiously and morally unacceptable. A practical task of Christianity and the WCC was to address those problems.[16]

In the present context, the incorporation of a specifically Third World perspective into the heart of WCC identity is important not simply because it manifests the process of globalization within a religious organization, but because it more or less determined how the WCC would take up environmental issues in the early 1970s. Using the septennial WCC Assemblies as a guide, ecological issues first appear clearly on the agenda at the Nairobi Assembly in 1975 (see WCC, 1976: 120–141). It was at the previous Uppsala Assembly in 1968 that Third World priorities – what liberation theology would later call the 'preferential option for the poor' – first achieved prominence (see WCC, 1968: especially 39–73). Not surprisingly, when seven years later the question of 'sustainable development' appeared, it did so in the context of this already established social justice focus. Environmental degradation was a real problem; it was, however, but another manifestation of disordered and unjust human relations, the prime responsibility for which rested with those who benefited under these conditions. To take one example of this linking, the relevant report includes a statement under the heading 'Quality of Life' calling on the affluent

> to provide basic necessities for all the people of planet Earth, and to modify their own consumption patterns, so as to reduce their disproportionate and spiritually destructive drain on earth's non-renewable and renewable resources, excessive use of energy resulting in contamination of the sea and air, and urban concentration and rural poverty that are breeding grounds of starvation, crime, and despair. (WCC, 1976: 140)

The location of ecological issues within the WCC's performance mandate has not changed appreciably since the Nairobi Assembly. Successive assemblies in 1983 and 1991 have continued to produce reports that discuss environmental degradation strictly in conjunction with war and vast disparities in life chances (see WCC, 1983; 1991). What has changed is the relative weight or visibility of ecology as a practical concern but, perhaps more significantly, as a component in official theological reflection. Environmental problems have moved out from under the peace and justice umbrella to become a major focus alongside these two; and the WCC has begun to emphasize what is often called 'theology of creation' as a central component in its official religious mandate. What has become known as the 'JPIC process', the 1991 Canberra Assembly, and WCC meetings in conjunction with the UNCED conference at Rio de Janeiro illustrate these shifts.

'Justice, Peace and the Integrity of Creation', or JPIC, is one of several 'justice and service' programmes within the WCC, all of which centre on such liberal motifs as human rights, racism, refugees, and Third World development. Officially launched at the 1983 Vancouver Assembly, it expanded to become the topic of a WCC Convocation in Seoul during 1990 and a pervasive theme at the 1991 Canberra Assembly and the Rio conference.

Two aspects of this direction are of importance in the present context. First, JPIC puts ecological issues within the WCC on a par with the already established peace and justice emphases (cf. WCC, 1990a; 1991). It represents the institutionalization of ecological concern within the performance mandate of the WCC. Second, JPIC intensifies the specifically global as distinct from the worldwide orientation of the WCC. Making environmental issues a prominent focus has brought in its wake a renewed stress on holism, both religious and social. In its report to the Canberra Assembly, the WCC's Central Committee put the matter like this:

> Since Vancouver the WCC central and executive committees have deepened the understanding of JPIC as a *process* calling the churches to a new level of united response to the common threats opposing the wholeness of life. . . . Most fundamentally, JPIC is about drawing connections, about weaving together faith responses from the many particular contexts around the world into a diverse but unified whole. JPIC is about enabling and challenging churches and ecumenical groups working on particular issues to see the connections between their work and the larger struggles for survival and peace on the planet. (WCC, 1990b: 148)

The theological parallels to this practical holism are not difficult to find in official WCC publications. Some of the clearer examples stem from the 1991 Canberra Assembly, the official theme of which was 'Come, Holy Spirit – Renew the Whole Creation'. One can, for instance,[17] read the following statement:

> The divine presence of the Spirit in creation binds us as human beings with all created life. We are accountable before God in and to the community of life. . . . Yet, while the earth was created by God out of nothing . . . and the Spirit has never abandoned the creation or ceased sustaining it, the earth on which we live is in peril. Creation protests its treatment by human beings. It groans and travails in all its parts (Rom. 8:22). Ecological equilibrium has been severely broken. *Through misinterpretation of our faith and through collective and individual misbehaviour* we as Christians have participated in the process of destruction, rather than participating in the repentance that God requires. . . . The invitation is to return to God and call upon the Spirit to reorient our lives accordingly. (WCC, 1991: 55; my italics)

Immediately following this religious confession, the statement again makes the holistic justice/ecology connection:

> In the present international scene we confront two major problems: (a) the worldwide social justice crisis; and (b) the global ecological and environmental crisis. . . . A new vision will integrate our interdependent ecological, social,

economic, political and spiritual needs. We want to say as forcefully as we can that social justice for all people and eco-justice for all creation must go together. . . . Justice is truly indivisible, *not only as a matter of theological conviction but in practice*. The biblical concept of justice recognizes the need for healthy relationships in creation as a whole. This way of viewing justice helps us understand the linkage between poverty, powerlessness, social conflict and environmental degradation. (WCC, 1991: 55; my italics)

As the emphasized portions in these citations indicate, religious function in this vision serves as the basis for religious performance. Moreover, adding ecology to the already established social justice orientation noticeably allows a stress on holism of a kind that a more conflictual 'option for the poor' by itself does not encourage. The virtual religiousness of environmental problems is evident here. By the same token, these statements also point implicitly to problems with an ecological emphasis within the WCC, difficulties that have to do with the structure and dynamics of the global system, the values attendant upon the historical process, and the ambiguous place of religion in the context of globalization.

As I discussed above, the egalitarian, progressive, and inclusive values historically associated with globalization imply the intensification of the process and the continued development of the instrumental systems that have become so prominent in this global society. The theodical quality of many ecological issues is that they point to possible limitations inherent in the pursuit of these values: *sustainable* development may be a profound oxymoron. When WCC pronouncements insist that 'justice is indivisible', that is a liberal assertion of religious holism, formally analogous to a conservative connection between, say, sexual transgression and imperialism. But it is also a way of saying that ecological concern should not take priority over or conflict with the pursuit of social justice. Although – or perhaps just because – ecology meshes well with holism, it can also clash with social justice directions. This is a point I made in the previous section. It should not be surprising, therefore, that the introduction of ecological issues into the heart of the WCC agenda generated a certain amount of suspicion and even resistance on the part of those members for whom the most urgent performance problems centred on the gulf separating the powerful from the powerless.

As I mentioned at the beginning of this chapter, religious environmentalism first appeared in the late 1960s to mid-1970s but remained rather marginal until the mid-1980s. One important reason for that slow start was the simultaneous growth and prominence of egalitarian, inclusive, and progressive social justice agendas in many of the main liberal religious organizations, including the WCC. In the latter case, the evidence is quite concrete. When environmental issues first appeared on the agenda in the mid-1970s, the WCC attempted to launch a programme similar to what JPIC has now become. It was called the programme on a 'Just, Participatory, and Sustainable Society'. In 1979, the WCC abandoned it, to a large extent because many considered sustainability a false issue which would only block progress and equality for the marginalized.[18]

The successful launching of the JPIC programme after 1983 indicates that the polarization between justice and sustainability has been largely overcome or put aside. The tension, however, remains to some extent. Environmentalism after all, as one of the key new social movements, introduces a new globalized value to stand alongside inclusive equality and progress: quality of life or sustainability. As has been the case with the relation between progress and equality,[19] the pursuit of sustainability is not always simply consonant with these. In consequence, ecology has indeed become an equal priority within the WCC, but only as *eco-justice*, that is, the pursuit of environmentalism to the extent that it also addresses social justice issues. Put in a different way, the WCC formed and developed as a reflection of globalization and as a positive response to that process. To allow ecological thinking unrestricted leeway would raise the prospect of subordinating concern for humankind to the interests of Gaia, the planet earth conceived as a living being (cf. Lovelock, 1987). As we shall see in the next section, that possibility is a strong current within contemporary religious environmentalism. The ideological and organizational characteristics of the WCC have prevented it from rising to prominence there.

In the final analysis, then, JPIC expresses the liberal religious-holistic conviction within the WCC that addressing problems of global social marginalization cannot contradict the pursuit of global systemic sustainability and environmental integrity. The result is a position that constantly juxtaposes the different components. Statements on environmental problems almost invariably include references to justice considerations; although the reverse occurs relatively rarely (cf. WCC, 1990a: 22–33; 1991: 48–122). Sometimes one gets the sense that egalitarian inclusion is still the number one priority. Witness the following statement from the Seoul convocation:

> The three entry points of justice, peace and the integrity of creation into the one struggle have to take into account the fact that poverty, lack of peace and the degradation of the environment are manifestations of the many dimensions of suffering which have at their root the over-arching structures of domination, i.e. racism, sexism, casteism and classism. (WCC, 1990a: 22)

What this ordering in fact demonstrates is a typically liberal religious tension between antisystemic and prosystemic strains: the benefits of global systemic development must be apportioned to all, but that same global systemic development is also at the root of great problems. Somehow, for the prevailing view in the WCC, working toward global community, that is enhancing and improving the global system, must be the way to resolving the problems. That is a statement of religious faith as much as it is a practical call to action.

Styles of Religious Environmentalism

The eco-justice emphasis that dominates in the World Council of Churches is a strong current in the broader phenomenon of religious environmentalism, but it is not the only one. At least two other directions of eco-religiosity are currently also well developed. The three very often appear together, especially in eco-theological literature. They are not so much independent types as a matter of differing stress, different centres of gravity. A brief look at these and some of their manifestations on the basis of recent work by Laurel Kearns will carry the analysis further at this point.

Focusing on the American case, Kearns (1990; 1991) has suggested a threefold typology of religious environmentalism. Reflecting the Christian-centredness of most such activity, she calls the three types 'creation spirituality', 'eco-justice', and 'stewardship'. They accurately label the three dimensions I have just mentioned and can serve as a good point of departure for looking more closely at how religious environmentalism relates to the issues of religious function/performance and the liberal or conservative options in the context of globalization. The exercise also contributes to a deeper understanding of the inherent ambiguity of religion's role in global society, and especially the problem of public influence.

The main distinguishing feature of creation spirituality is its focus on holistic continuity between the human and natural worlds. Humankind loses its privileged position to become a feature in a larger organic and cosmic whole. A clearer label for this direction might be *eco-spirituality* (cf. Cummings, 1991; McDaniel, 1990) to reflect the degree to which an ecological orientation informs the religious vision. If we think of the eco-justice perspective as one that treats environmental problems more strictly in the context of concerns with inequality and marginalization of humans in society, then formally speaking, eco-spirituality reverses the order. In this case, the holistic, interconnected, and continuous meanings embedded in the notion of ecology shape the theology. Examples are not hard to find. Jay McDaniel, one prominent representative includes the following in what he means by an 'ecological spirituality':

> It springs from a deep-seated hope, not for utopia, but for a more just, sustainable, and spiritually satisfying world. It is shaped by a distinctive way of thinking and feeling: one that emphasizes the interconnectedness of all things, the intrinsic value of all life, the continuity of human with non-human life, and the compassion of God for life. . . . It employs a pan*en*theistic way of imaging the divine mystery, which means that it images the divine mystery as the mind or heart of the universe, and the universe as the body of God. (1990: 182f.)

Similar statements are to be found in most of the eco-spiritual literature (e.g. Berry 1988; Conlon, 1990; Fox, 1988).

The above discussion of the JPIC programme within the WCC says enough about what distinguishes the *eco-justice* perspective. In that context, however, one additional point needs stressing. Eco-justice is less a separate way of theologizing ecological issues than it is a practical strategy. It seeks to reconcile a theology informed by the pursuit of egalitarian inclusion with one that draws its inspiration from the value of sustainability or harmony. It would not at all be going too far to say that the eco-justice perspective marries liberation theology and creation spirituality in the interests of a broader religious performance than either alone can envisage (cf. Birch et al., 1990; Hessel, 1992).

Moreover, the antisystemic/prosystemic tension within both eco-spirituality and eco-justice finds its echoes in differing emphases within contemporary feminism, another of the most significant new social movements. Here the tug is between a quest for equal female access to the power of dominant systems and the development or assertion of antisystemic, purportedly female, and often local-oriented alternatives to the global system.[20] The manifest attempt to pursue both goals at the same time lends the globally extended women's movement a comparable ambiguity to that of environmentalism, whether religious or not.[21] Indeed, feminism as a global movement is another strong current within the WCC and liberal religion in general. It could have served as another case study of public-influence-oriented liberal religion in a global context; this aspect of the analysis of religious environmentalism shows part of that parallelism.

In the light of this comparison, then, eco-spirituality is not somehow the more antisystemic dimension of religious environmentalism with the eco-justice perspective as the more prosystemic. As I pointed out in the analysis of the Latin American liberation theological movement, social justice concern, while pursuing access for the marginalized to systemic power, also contains its own antisystemic stress. That is especially evident in view of approaches which, inspired by dependency theory, recommend withdrawal from the global system as the only way of dealing with the negative consequences of its operation. Eco-spirituality does indeed tend toward emphasizing a restrained and simple lifestyle in a local communitarian context. Yet its vision is almost always global as well, usually wishing to preserve global links and often celebrating the cultural diversity that these currently imply (see Conlon, 1990; Hallman, 1992).[22]

What Kearns labels the 'stewardship' direction in religious environmentalism distinguishes itself primarily by the greater theological conservatism of its proponents. Ecological crisis here is not a cause for creating a new religious vision so much as it is a reason for affirming the old one. According to this point of view, environmental problems have reached their current proportions because we have strayed from the traditional religious message. In relation to the other two and for the sake of parallelism, one might call it *eco-traditionalism*. Yet what we are dealing with here is not at all the enlisting of ecological problems in the service of the conservative religious option, as I am using that term in this book. It is rather the attempt to liberalize (Christian) religious groups that are generally more theologically conservative. Accordingly, as Kearns points out (1990), 'stewards' are usually representatives from more conservative denominations such as those in the Christian Reform or Eastern Orthodox branches of Christianity (cf. Bhagat, 1990; DeWitt, 1987; Granberg-Michaelson, 1988). But their message is not the assertion of particularistic withdrawal and the unique value/truth of their own religious/cultural tradition. Instead it amounts to a call for the revitalization of traditional religion in the light of ecological crisis.

Here is how Wesley Granberg-Michaelson, one of eco-traditionalism's more well-known representatives, sees the task:

> The church's theology has failed to provide modern culture with an integrated vision of life. Evangelical theology has stressed personal conversion. More liberal theology has emphasized the movements in history to liberate people from oppression. Both have largely neglected the biblical emphasis on redeeming the creation. And neither has set forth an alternative vision for modern culture's understanding of humanity's relationship to creation, technology, and values in the light of God's place as Creator of the heavens and the earth. (1988: 25)

What is most evident in this quote is the insistence that traditional religious symbols and sources – here God and the Bible – contain the religious answer to ecological crisis: this is not a condemnation of modernity and globality so much as it is a claim that received religion already contains the ethical resources for addressing the problematic results.

The differences among these three directions within contemporary religious environmentalism are therefore much more a matter of emphasis than of fundamentally opposed points of view. Eco-spirituality, eco-justice, and eco-traditionalism do have their different leading representatives and different organizations. Thus, for example, the official ecological arms of the North American liberal mainline Christian churches tend strongly to represent eco-justice positions; eco-spirituality has its representative institutions like the Institute in Culture and Creation Spirituality in the USA or the Holy Cross Centre for Spirituality and Ecology in Canada. One of the better-known North American eco-traditional institutes is the AuSable Institute in the state of Michigan. The followers of the three directions do also clash on occasion: eco-justice types will accuse eco-spiritualists of 'hugging trees' while children starve; and for many eco-traditionalists, the other directions may not be Christian enough (see Kearns, 1991). Yet, these divergent manifestations and disagreements do not amount to concerted opposition as between, for instance New Christian Rightists and American liberal mainliners, or the followers of Khomeini and Shariati.

Religious environmentalism, in spite of internal strains between more liberal and more conservative tendencies, is at the moment a predominantly liberal expression of religion. The chief reason for this tendency is undoubtedly the unavoidably global scope of many ecological problems, leading directly or indirectly to cooperation among the ecologically concerned representatives of different religious groups, and hence to a level of pluralistic tolerance and even valorization of religious/cultural pluralism that is antithetical to the conservative option. In this regard, it is perhaps not surprising that, although eco-justice dominates, all three directions are well represented within the World Council of Churches.[23] Similarly, the Roman Catholic branch of Christianity counts among its adherents many of the leading proponents of eco-spirituality; many of its social justice organizations are heavily involved in environmental action; and the current

Pope himself addresses ecological issues in the typical manner of an eco-traditionalist.[24]

Environment, Religious Performance, and Public Influence

The different directions or emphases within religious environmentalism are not, however, merely an incidental curiosity. The tensions among them, while not that severe, point immediately to the relation between religious function and performance, and from there to the issue of public influence.

As I indicated earlier in this chapter, environmental problems present a clear performance possibility for religion and religious professionals in particular: threats to the ozone layer or to species habitats are results of the operation of the more dominant global instrumental systems. Religion, it would seem, might be able to provide a message that addresses the root causes of these problems. Ecological crisis, once recognized, may be that which brings even the non-believers to hear the new religious message or the revitalized old one. And unlike the ambiguous case of the social justice direction, here it might be argued that the purely religious, the functionally religious, is a necessary component for solving the problems. This idea is very common in the eco-theological literature (see from among many Bhagat, 1990; Hallman, 1989; McDaniel, 1990). Defending what he believes to have been a more than marginal role for religious representatives at the Rio summit, Granberg-Michaelson expresses this idea as follows:

> It is easy to be apologetic about spirituality. Many, perhaps, find it more comfortable to write documents, reports, and analytical papers which set forth the correct political positions of the churches and the ecumenical movement on pressing issues. All that is necessary and of value. But those at the Earth Summit expected and even asked the religious communities to give something more – to share the power of their spirituality and to nurture this as a foundation for overcoming the deep causes which destroy the earth and consign millions to desperate poverty. (1992: 38)

We might interpret this task as that of providing a viable self-conception for global society. The global implication of environmental issues again points to the essentially religious task of lending meaning to the whole in terms of its relation to a posited transcendent. It is with these possibilities in mind that the arguments among religious environmentalists gain their relevance.

Each of the three directions discussed above has its own typical approach to the problem of tailoring contemporary liberal religion to meet this presumed opportunity. Eco-spirituality offers what amounts to a new religion, albeit using a great deal of extant religious symbolism. Eco-traditionalism, its clearest opponent, seeks to reform traditional religious messages in the light of ecological issues, and thereby to revitalize the received traditions. Both concentrate on religious function. Eco-justice, by contrast, is more nearly the pragmatic compromise that offers little additional theology as such, seeking instead to enhance the performance capacity offered by social justice concerns. Not surprisingly, the most visible disagreements occur between the new spirituality and the old traditions (cf. Kearns, 1991, for an American example). Yet these are of a more purely functional or theological nature; they have had few if any repercussions outside the circle of religious adherents.

The question, however, becomes: do these differing ways of appropriating ecological concern for religious revitalization actually point to the possibility of renewed public influence for religion and specifically for religious authorities? Again Granberg-Michaelson offers a succinct formulation of the problem:

> If economic systems are to be geared toward sustainability, . . . how is this to be accomplished? . . . What political mechanisms are needed to constrain resource depletion? How are equity and justice to be established without relying on unlimited economic growth? . . . Guiding ethical principles are necessary to help answer such questions. . . . Churches have been empowered in their ability to denounce the reigning powers of injustice and destruction. But the next step has been more difficult: what counsel and guidance can be offered to societies searching for new alternatives? What advice and wisdom do the churches have to offer regarding ethical values that would clarify political programmes and economic choices facing societies? (1992: 44)

Twice in this statement, we hear about the dominant global systems: economy and polity; twice we are told that religion's role is to provide ethical principles or values. The question of public influence would ask: are these ethical principles or values required? Can they influence the operation of economic, political, and other global systems? But above all, if so, is the provision of these guiding principles the kind of service for which religious professionals and authorities can successfully claim unique qualification?

Provisorily, we can answer in the affirmative to the first two questions. Insofar as the global cultural values of progress, equality, and inclusion have been driving forces in the history of modernization and globalization, sustainability or quality of life seems at the moment to be institutionalizing itself as another. On this score and in the matter of translating that value into the codes and programmes of global systems for economy, polity, health, science, and education, the new social movements in general and the environmental movement in particular are having a clear and public influence. There is also little doubt that religious actors and organizations have played meaningful roles in these movements, as the descriptions in this chapter illustrate.

Nonetheless, as with all performances, one has to ask what is characteristically religious here. In terms of the concept of religion I am using in this book, is communication with a posited transcendent dimension, realm, or being an unavoidable component in isolating and addressing environmental problems? The straightforward answer, in the absence of evidence to the contrary, is no: such communication is optional, whether through the typically religious mode of professionally controlled ritual or through less systemic forms. To approach the matter from a slightly different angle, the production and elaboration of the ethical principles necessary for meeting the problem of environmental degradation may be accomplished via the complex of beliefs, practices, social networks, and organizations that historically constitute differentiated and institutionalized religion; but they need not be.

Conclusions

The ambiguity inherent in at least much liberal religious response to environmental issues illustrates an important aspect of the dilemma of religion in globalizing society. Religion is a relatively diffuse mode of human communication that in many respects thrived better in smaller, more clearly bounded societies lacking the potent functional specialization of instrumentally oriented systems. As the contemporary world shows, however, this feature does not mean a crude form of secularization in which religion simply declines, inevitably to disappear. In the globalization theory terms used here, it is unlikely that religion can become a specialized system as powerful and clearly defined as, for instance, the global economy or polity; but a functionally differentiated system it can become and to a great extent is. Nonetheless, the characteristic disadvantages of religion *vis-à-vis* other systems, rooted as they are in the very nature of religious communication, point to a different, more indirect way of making its influence felt in global society. The response of religion to environmental issues illustrates this.

Religion cannot do anything direct about environmental problems. It can offer the just-discussed ethical principles of sustainability and living in harmony with the constraints of the extra-human world. Its professionals and adherents can posit the efficacy of religious ritual, belief, and ethics in the hoped-for solution to the problems. And many individuals may approach these issues through specifically religious interpretations and as adherents to religious traditions and institutions. As with peace and justice issues, many religious people and organizations will become deeply involved in the problems; but the preferred solutions are going to be political, educational, scientific, economic, and medical – assuming, of course, that the global system does not collapse along with its biological environment. Put slightly differently, as with other negative effects of the global system, religion can offer significant organizational, ideological, and motivational resources which primarily religious, but also non-religious, people can use to conceptualize 'residual' problems and mobilize to deal with them.[25] The temples and the synagogues, the churches and the holy places, however, are not going to be filled to overflowing as a result. Nor even, one might hazard, are significant numbers of us going to relocate to bioregional communes or lead a small, beautiful, and harmonious life. That conclusion may seem unduly pessimistic and even premature to some; but in the absence of evidence or contemporary precedents to the contrary, it may be the only scientifically justifiable one.

Notes

1 See, for instance, the 'Resolution on Pollution' passed by the General Synod of the Anglican Church of Canada in 1969, reprinted in Hamel, 1990; and 'A Social Statement on the Human Crisis in Ecology' adopted by the Lutheran Church in America in 1972 (Lutheran Church in America, 1972).

2 See, as representative examples, Berry, 1988; Birch et al., 1990; Conlon, 1990; Cummings, 1991; Fox, 1988; Hallman, 1989; McDonagh, 1987; Moltmann, 1989.

3 To mention only prominent international groupings, there are the 'Justice, Peace and Integrity of Creation' (JPIC) programme within the World Council of Churches (which I discuss below), the World Wildlife Federation's International Conservation and Religion Network, and the International Coordinating Committee for Religion and the Earth. Many more operate on a national or regional basis.

4 From the literature, see for example Badiner, 1990; Dwivedi and Tiwari, 1987; Hargrove, 1986; Khoury and Hünermann, 1987.

5 See Eckberg and Blocker, 1989; Hand and Van Liere, 1984; Kanagy and Willits, 1991; Shaiko, 1987; Woodrum and Davison, 1992. These studies, moreover, all refer to Lynn White's thesis (1967) that posits a causal relation between features of Judaism and Christianity and environmental problems. For the most part, they either confirm or at least do not falsify White's thesis; but they operate with a conception of religion that equates greater religiosity with more conservative religiosity, thus effectively blocking out that segment of the religious spectrum in which religious environmentalism has taken hold.

6 This section essentially reproduces portions of Beyer, 1992, but with a number of additions and amendments.

7 As examples of the former, see many of the contributions in Greenpeace, 1990. Some examples can also be found in *Probe Post*, 1989, although far fewer, reflecting perhaps the less 'anti-systemic' orientation of this publication and its parent organization, Pollution Probe. See also Mowat, 1990. As regards the latter, the works just cited include several examples of the appeal that particularly non-literate religion has for many environmentalists. This attraction probably has more to do with the fact that these religions have not de-socialized the non-human environment than some inherently greater sensitivity to the deleterious effects of humans on the world around them. On this point, see Luckmann, 1970. For an environmentalist's assessment of various religions in this regard, see the series of articles by Timmerman in *Probe Post* (1989; 1990).

8 From the title of McAteer, 1990 which includes a report of a letter by eminent scientists calling for cooperation between science and religion: 'Efforts to safeguard and cherish the environment need to be infused with a vision of the sacred, said the scientists, who acknowledged the power of religion to motivate.' From the religious end of this science/religion connection, see for example Hallman, 1992.

9 Self-conception of society is, of course, not exclusively a religious task. The globalization debate outlined in Chapter 1 also has this as part of its agenda. See Robertson, 1992a; 1992b; Luhmann, 1984a; 1990c. Even here, however, the results are often virtually religious, as exemplified in the function of 'socialism' among the Wallersteinians. See Wallerstein, 1979: 269–282.

10 Here cannot be the place for a detailed proof of this assertion. Beside the clear case of liberation theology discussed in Chapter 6, see, as typical examples, Walsh and Davies, 1984; J. Williams, 1984; World Council of Churches, 1976; 1983. These sources also exemplify the interpretation in the text that follows.

11 Recall Roland Robertson's categorization of such conceptions of global order, particularly as manifested by the Roman Catholic church, as *Global Gemeinschaft 2*: above Chapter 1; Robertson, 1992b: 78ff.

12 As just one example, see the critique of 'capitalism' (globalizing functional system) in John Paul II's encyclical, 'Laborem exercens' in Walsh and Davies, 1984: 271–311.

13 See also Hallman, 1989: 129–142. Among more secular environmentalists, the connection is even more explicit. Animal rights advocates, for instance, as the name implies, trace environmental problems to injustice (denial of 'human' rights) toward animals. One also encounters the wider argument that the environment itself has rights. See Stone, 1988. For potential problems with such a simple extension of rights to non-humans, this time from a philosophical perspective, see Paul Taylor, 1986: 219ff.

14 The other large and obvious worldwide Christian organization, the Roman Catholic Church, has to date been somewhat more hesitant about adopting ecology as a key and differentiated focus. This does not mean that Roman Catholics and Roman Catholic organizations do not make up an important segment of the broader religious environmental movement; only that the official worldwide church has demonstrated a certain caution, the reasons for which are probably complex, having more directly to do with Rome-centred 'raison d'église' (Coleman, 1989) than a disapproval of birth control. For one Catholic viewpoint that looks at the matter from a different angle, see Development and Peace, 1990.

15 On the growth of the latter, see Boli, 1992.

16 As discussed in Chapter 6, similar shifts were taking place in the Roman Catholic church at the same time, reflecting again the worldwide extent and liberalization of that organization.

17 See, as a further clear example, the statement to the Assembly by Hans Joachim Held, moderator of the WCC: WCC, 1991: 134.

18 See Granberg-Michaelson, 1992. Internal opposition to JPSS also centred on the 'Just and Participatory' aspects, these implying for some far too unequivocal support for various radical political movements around the world, movements which often had no intrinsic connection with Christianity. As one example, see Lefever, 1987.

19 See above, Chapter 2.

20 For an explicit comparison of environmentalism and feminism as new social movements, see Rucht, 1988. Rucht, however, tries to see environmentalism as basically prosystemic and feminism as more antisystemic. My point here is that each of these movements, whether in its religious or secular wings, tends in both directions simultaneously.

21 The tension here is in fact quite similar to and perhaps an instance of the contemporary dilemma of antisystemic movements about which Wallerstein writes, and also refers to the problematic status of these in Wallerstein's world-system theory. See Wallerstein 1976; 1988b.

22 The global/local dialogic tension is of course central to Roland Robertson's vision of the central dynamic of globalization. See Robertson, 1992b; and the section on Robertson in Chapter 2 above.

23 See Birch et al., 1990; Breuilly and Palmer, 1992 as two collections with strong WCC ties and in which representatives from all three types participate. The latter is one in a series of volumes in the 'World Religions and Ecology Series' sponsored by the World Wide Fund for Nature of the World Wildlife Federation. See also the report of debates within the WCC in WCC, 1990a; 1991.

24 Both Matthew Fox and Thomas Berry are Roman Catholics; the heavy involvement of official Brazilian Roman Catholic Church organs at the religious parallel gatherings to the UNCED conference in Rio de Janeiro is documented in Granberg-Michaelson, 1992; and see John Paul II, 1989.

25 James Beckford comes to a similar conclusion on the basis of a very different analysis:

> The partial freeing of religion from its points of anchorage in communities and natural social groupings has also turned it into a resource which may be invested with highly diverse meanings and used for a wide variety of purposes. Religion can now be put to varied uses both within and outside the framework of religious organizations. . . . Health care, movements for the protection of the environment or the promotion of peace, and the institutions of human rights are . . . spheres in which religious symbolism is increasingly being appropriated. (1989: 171)

CONCLUSION

Throughout this volume, I have concentrated overwhelmingly on systemic religion, on the institutionalized, organized, and specialized forms of religion that generally – but not always – have religious professionals associated with them. The definition of religion that I have used, however, does not preclude religious communication, structured around the immanent/transcendent polarity, from being non-systemic. That is, religion can be simply cultural, part of an ecology of themes and usages that informs a variety of social systems not specialized as religion. This possibility is implicit in how I have framed the whole question of public influence: under conditions of modernization and globalization, the prime way for religion as societal system to gain this is to emphasize its status as cultural resource for other systems. That is, it can do so through performance, just as specialized religion has done before the current era. Yet now that performance occurs in a more problematic context dominated by globalized and mostly secularized instrumental systems. Nonetheless, the pressure to take that route to public influence does not mean that religion's primary social manifestation is now or will increasingly be as cultural resource rather than societal system.

To understand religion as societal system in global society, I have relied heavily on the notion of privatization. Modernity and globality do not result in the disappearance of religion either in terms of importance for the conduct of social life or in terms of visibility on the social landscape. Like morality, religion is a constantly present mode of communication, but, on the level of society, a 'deregulated' one (Beckford, 1989: 172). Unlike morality, however, religion continues to inform a broad, and even global, societal system. Internally segmented into 'traditions' or 'religions', this system constitutes itself through a particular mode of communication on the basis of recursively structured and often professionally controlled codes. The system and its internal structure have been as much a product of modernization/ globalization as any of the others, like the global economy or polity. The difference is in the comparative difficulty religion has in exercising its influence, and especially that of its leaders or professionals, outside the sphere of those voluntarily associated with it, and in many cases even within it.

The distinction between religion as societal system and religion as culture raises three interrelated questions: Does the comparative lack of public influence simply point to a transitional state *within* the religious system? Does the globalized context mean the gradual erosion of the religious system as system, to be replaced by a highly diverse ecology of religious culture? And, are we heading toward the development of a broadly cultural 'religion of humanity' as the typical religion of the future? The first question asks about a revitalization of the religious system; the second about its dissolution; the third about its replacement.

Among several others, the American sociologists of religion, Rodney Stark and William Bainbridge (1985; 1987) have argued that religion around the globe has always been and is now in a state of flux: religions arise, flower, and eventually decline to be replaced by others more in tune with changed social contexts. Slightly adapting their hypothesis, one could ask whether I have not posed the question of public influence incorrectly. Is that problem perhaps really only a symptom of the decline of 'decadent' religion? If so, then the future of religion in global society rests with new, possibly not yet fully formed religions that will eventually be able to exercise public influence more easily and consistently.

In the context of the cases I examined in Part II, this line of questioning might be particularly appropriate in Chapter 9 on religious environmentalism. There the religious quality of much in the secular environmental movement – for instance deep ecology, eco-feminism, or the syncretic effort that revitalizes above all elements from oral religious traditions – combined with the evident broader effect of this movement could lead one to speculate that a new religion is forming that resonates closely with the structures and values of global society. While that may eventually happen, it is difficult to imagine how this new religion could escape the typical difficulty of liberal religion in general: the problems it points to are perhaps real enough; but the *religious* solutions do not attract more than another minor group of voluntary adherents. Only the breakdown of the dominant instrumental systems could yield a different result.

Accepting that prognosis leads to the second question. Will religion increasingly become a matter of culture with the gradual fading of its systemic form? Here environmentalism could again serve as an example. Like equality, progress, human rights, or inclusion, the value of 'sustainability' may bring with it a widespread cultural conception that there are cosmic constraints on what human beings can do, leading perhaps to ritual or quasi-ritual action such as periodically communing with nature or pilgrimages in the form of eco-tourism. Quite evidently, however, such a development and others, like various 'civil religions', would not detract from the continued vitality of the systemic form of religion. People may well be and become religious in a cultural way, but this does not preclude their – albeit often selective – participation in specific religions. The market economy model of religion (see for example Berger, 1967; Bibby, 1987; Luckmann, 1967) suggests itself as appropriate in this case. People 'consume' what they want from various religious 'producers' without any necessary loyalty to one 'company' and including the possibility of 'home-brew'. In addition, for the foreseeable future at least, a great many people in global society, perhaps the majority, will continue as almost exclusive adherents and practitioners of the traditional systemic forms, a fact that the abiding vitality of conservative religion only serves to underscore.

The final question asks the system vs. culture question in a different way. A global society has to include all human beings in some structural way, for instance, through a Wallersteinian class system, as citizens of states, or by way of societal system/life-world distinctions. The matter of what self-descriptions are to operate in this society is of corresponding importance. Given the religious modality's holistic base, it seems likely that most offerings will have a virtual religious quality and some will be expressly religious. Is it possible that the result of this search for self-description will lead to a global religious culture, a kind of 'global civil religion' that still permits subglobal and particular systemic religion and religious culture? From a Wallersteinian viewpoint, this is where the socialist ideal would enter, albeit with the tacit assumption that other religions would, as it were, wither away. For Robertson, such 'humanitic concern' is a key pole in the global field, but a highly contested one, not likely to yield a single solution in the near future, if ever. For Luhmann, self-descriptions are useful, but a dominant one is highly unlikely so long as global society continues to have functional subsystems as its dominant structures.

All in all, then, we might provisorily conclude that 'global civil religion' is both possible and likely; but there will be more than one of them and these will simply be more religious offerings beside others, both systemic and cultural. As the analyses above have shown, the perspective of the whole is not a privileged one in our society. We live in a conflictual and contested social world where the appeal to holism is itself partisan. That paradox alone is enough to maintain the religious enterprise, even if with more risk and less self-evidence.

BIBLIOGRAPHY

Abercrombie, Nicholas, Hill, Stephen and Turner, Bryan S. (1980) *The Dominant Ideology Thesis*. London: George Allen & Unwin.

Abrahamian, Ervand (1982) *Iran between Two Revolutions*. Princeton, NJ: Princeton University.

Abrahamian, Ervand (1989) *Radical Islam: The Iranian Mujahedin*. London: Tauris.

Abramov, S. Zalman (1976) *Perpetual Dilemma: Jewish Religion in the Jewish State*. Rutherford, NJ: Fairleigh Dickinson.

Adorno, Theodor W. and Horkheimer, Max (1972) *Dialectic of Enlightenment*. Tr. John Cumming. New York: Seabury.

Adriance, Madeleine (1986) *Opting for the Poor: Brazilian Catholicism in Transition*. Kansas City, MO: Sheed and Ward.

Ahlemeyer, Heinrich W. (1989) 'Was ist eine soziale Bewegung? Zur Distinktion und Einheit eines sozialen Phänomens', *Zeitschrift für Soziologie*, 18: 175–191.

Akhavi, Shahrough (1980) *Religion and Politics in Contemporary Iran: Clergy–State Relations in the Pahlavi Period*. Albany, NY: SUNY.

Akhavi, Shahrough (1983) 'Shariati's Social Thought', in Nikki R. Keddie (ed.), *Religion and Politics in Iran: Shi'ism from Quietism to Revolution*. New Haven: Yale University. pp. 125–144.

Al-e Ahmad, Jalal (1982) *Plagued by the West*. Tr. Paul Sprachman. New York: Caravan.

Algar, Hamid (1969) *Religion and State in Iran, 1785–1906: The Role of the Ulama in the Qajar Period*. Berkeley & Los Angeles: University of California.

Alves, Rubem (1969) *A Theology of Human Hope*. St Meinard, IN: Abbey.

Alyanak, Leyla (1991) 'The New New Road', *The New Road*, No. 20 (October-November).

Ambler, Rex (1990) *Global Theology: The Meaning of Faith in the Present World Crisis*. London & Philadelphia: SCM/Trinity.

Ammerman, Nancy Tatom (1987) *Bible Believers: Fundamentalists in the Modern World*. New Brunswick, NJ: Rutgers University.

Ammerman, Nancy Tatom (1990) *Baptist Battles: Social Change and Religious Conflict in the Southern Baptist Convention*. New Brunswick, NJ: Rutgers University.

Anderson, Walter K. and Damle, Shirdhar D. (1987) *The Brotherhood in Saffron: The Rashtriya Swayamsevak Sangh and Hindu Revivalism*. Boulder, CO: Westview.

Appignanesi, Lisa, and Maitland, Sara (eds) (1990) *The Rushdie File*. Syracuse, NY: Syracuse University.

Aran, Gideon (1986) 'From Religious Zionism to Zionist Religion: The Roots of Gush Emunim', *Studies in Contemporary Jewry*, 2: 116–143.

Arjomand, Said Amir (1984) *The Shadow of God and the Hidden Imam: Religion, Political Order, and Societal Change in Shi'ite Iran from the Beginning to 1890*. Chicago: University of Chicago.

Arjomand, Said Amir (1988) *The Turban for the Crown: The Islamic Revolution in Iran*. New York: Oxford.

Aronoff, Myron J. (1984) 'Gush Emunim: The Institutionalization of a Charismatic, Messianic, Religious-Political Revitalization Movement in Israel', in Myron J. Aronoff (ed.), *Religion and Politics. Political Anthropology, Vol. 3*. New Brunswick, NJ: Transaction. pp. 63–84.

Aronoff, Myron J. (1989) *Israeli Visions and Divisions: Cultural Change and Political Conflict*. New Brunswick, NJ: Transaction.

Arrighi, Giovanni, Hopkins, Terence K., and Wallerstein, Immanuel (1989) *Antisystemic Movements*. London & New York: Verso.

Assmann, Hugo (1976) *Theology for a Nomad Church*. Tr. Paul Burns. Maryknoll, NY: Orbis.

Azevedo, Marcello deC. (1987) *Basic Ecclesial Communities in Brazil: The Challenge of a New Way of Being Church*. Tr. John Drury. Washington, DC: Georgetown University.

Badiner, Allan Hunt (ed.) (1990) *Dharma Gaia: A Harvest of Essays in Buddhism and Ecology*. Berkeley: Parallax.

Bakhash, Shaul (1990) *The Reign of the Ayatollahs: Iran and the Islamic Revolution*. Rev. ed. New York: Basic Books.

Barbour, Ian G. (ed.) (1972) *Earth Might Be Fair: Reflections on Ethics, Religion, and Ecology*. Englewood Cliffs, NJ: Prentice-Hall.

Barker, Eileen (ed.) (1983) *Of Gods and Men: New Religious Movements in the West*. Macon, GA: Mercer University.

Barker, Eileen (1991) *New Religious Movements: A Practical Introduction*. London: HMSO.

Bashiriyeh, Hossein (1984) *The State and Revolution in Iran 1962–1982*. London & New York: Croom Helm & St. Martin's Press.

Baum, Gregory (1975) *Religion and Alienation: A Theological Reading of Sociology*. New York: Paulist.

Baum, Gregory and Cameron, Duncan (1984) *Ethics and Economics: Canada's Catholic Bishops on the Economic Crisis*. Toronto: Lorimer.

Baum, Rainer C. (1980) 'Authority and Identity: The Case for Evolutionary Invariance', in Roland Robertson (ed.), *Identity and Authority*. New York: St. Martin's Press. pp. 61–118.

Beckford, James A. (1987) 'The Restoration of "Power" to the Sociology of Religion', in Thomas Robbins and Roland Robertson (eds), *Church–State Relations: Tensions and Transitions*. New Brunswick, NJ: Transaction. pp. 13–37.

Beckford, James A. (1989) *Religion and Advanced Industrial Society*. London: Unwin Hyman.

Beckford, James A. (1990) 'The Sociology of Religion and Social Problems', *Sociological Analysis*, 51: 1–14.

Behdad, Sohrab (1988) 'The Political Economy of Islamic Planning in Iran', in Hooshang Amirahmadi and Manoucher Parvin (eds), *Post-Revolutionary Iran*. Boulder, CO: Westview. pp. 107–125.

Bellah, Robert N. (1970a) 'Religious Evolution', in *Beyond Belief: Essays on Religion in a Post-Traditional World*. New York: Harper & Row. pp. 20–50.

Bellah, Robert N. (1970b) 'Civil Religion in America', in *Beyond Belief: Essays on Religion in a Post-Traditional World*. New York: Harper & Row. pp. 168–189.

Bellah, Robert N. (1975) *The Broken Covenant: American Civil Religion in Time of Trial*. New York: Seabury.

Bellah, Robert N. (1976) 'The New Consciousness and the Berkeley New Left', in Charles Y. Glock and Robert N. Bellah (eds), *The New Religious Consciousness*. Berkeley: University of California. pp. 77–92.

Bendix, Reinhard (1977) *Nation-Building and Citizenship*. Rev. ed. Berkeley: University of California.

Berger, Peter L. (1967) *The Sacred Canopy: Elements of a Sociological Theory of Religion*. Garden City: Doubleday.

Berger, Peter L. (1977) *Facing Up to Modernity: Excursions in Society, Politics, and Religion*. New York: Basic Books.

Berger, Peter L. (1979) *The Heretical Imperative: Contemporary Possibilities of Religious Affirmation*. Garden City: Doubleday.

Berger, Peter L. and Luckmann, Thomas (1966) *The Social Construction of Reality: A Sociological Treatise in the Sociology of Knowledge*. Garden City, NY: Doubleday.

Berger, Peter L., Berger, Brigitte, and Kellner, Hansfried (1973) *The Homeless Mind*. New York: Random House.

Bergesen, Albert (ed.) (1980) *Studies of the Modern World System*. New York: Academic.

Bergesen, Albert (ed.) (1983) *Crises in the World System*. Vol. 6, Political Economy of the World-System Annuals, Immanuel Wallerstein (ed.) Beverly Hills: Sage.

Bergesen, Albert (1990) 'Turning World-System Theory on Its Head', *Theory, Culture and Society*, 7(2–3): 67–82.

Bergesen, Albert and Schoenberg, Ronald (1980) 'Long Waves of Colonial Expansion and Contraction, 1415–1969', in Albert Bergesen (ed.), *Studies of the Modern World-System*. New York: Academic. pp. 231–277.

Bergmann, Werner (1987) 'Was bewegt die soziale Bewegung? Überlegungen zur Selbstkonstitution der "neuen" sozialen Bewegungen', in Dirk Baecker (ed.), *Theorie als Passion: Niklas Luhmann zum 60. Geburtstag*. Frankfurt: Suhrkamp. pp. 362–393.

Berry, Thomas (1988) *The Dream of the Earth*. San Francisco: Sierra Club Books.

Berryman, Phillip (1984) *The Religious Roots of Rebellion: Christians in Central American Revolutions*. Maryknoll, NY: Orbis.

Berryman, Phillip (1987) *Liberation Theology: The Essential Facts about the Revolutionary Movement in Latin America and Beyond*. New York: Pantheon.

Beyer, Peter F. (1989) 'The Evolution of Roman Catholicism in Quebec: A Luhmannian Neo-Functionalist Interpretation', in Roger O'Toole (ed.), *Sociological Studies in Roman Catholicism*. Lewiston/Queenston: Edwin Mellen. pp. 1–26.

Beyer, Peter F. (1990) 'Privatization and the Public Influence of Religion in Global Society', *Theory, Culture and Society*, 7(2–3): 373–395.

Beyer, Peter F. (1992) 'The Global Environment as a Religious Issue: A Sociological Analysis', *Religion*, 22: 1–19.

Bhagat, Shantilal P. (1990) *Creation in Crisis: Responding to God's Covenant*. Elgin, IL: Brethren Press.

Bibby, Reginald W. (1987) *Fragmented Gods: The Poverty and Potential of Religion in Canada*. Toronto: Irwin.

Birch, Charles, Eakin, William, and McDaniel, Jay B. (eds) (1990) *Liberating Life: Contemporary Approaches to Ecological Theology*. Maryknoll, NY: Orbis.

Boff, Clodovis (1987) *Theology and Praxis: Epistemological Foundations*. Tr. Robert Barr. Maryknoll: Orbis.

Boff, Leonardo (1978) *Jesus Christ Liberator: A Critical Christology for Our Time*. Tr. Patrick Hughes. Maryknoll, NY: Orbis.

Boff, Leonardo (1979) *Liberating Grace*. Tr. John Drury. Maryknoll, NY: Orbis.

Boff, Leonardo (1986) *Ecclesiogenesis: The Base Communities Reinvent the Church*. Tr. Robert R. Barr. Maryknoll, NY: Orbis.

Boff, Leonardo and Boff, Clodovis (1987) *Introducing Liberation Theology*. Tr. Paul Burns. Maryknoll, NY: Orbis.

Boli-Bennett, John (1979) 'The Ideology of Expanding State Authority in National Constitutions, 1870–1970', in John W. Meyer and Michael T. Hannan (eds), *National Development and the World System: Educational, Economic, and Political Change, 1950–1970*. Chicago: University of Chicago. pp. 222–237.

Boli-Bennett, John (1980) 'Global Integration and the Universal Increase of State Dominance, 1910–1970', in Albert Bergesen (ed.), *Studies of the Modern World-System*. New York: Academic. pp. 77–107.

Boli, John (1992) The World Polity Dramatized: Global Rituals. Paper presented to the conference on 'Religion, Peace, and Global Order: The Contemporary Circumstance', Washington, DC.

Bonacich, Edna (1972) 'A Theory of Ethnic Antagonism: The Split Labor Market', *American Sociological Review*, 37: 547–559.

Bonino, José Míguez (1975) *Doing Theology in a Revolutionary Situation*. Maryknoll, NY: Orbis.

Bourricaud, François (1981) *The Sociology of Talcott Parsons*. Tr. Arthur Goldhammer. Foreword, Harry M. Johnson. Chicago: University of Chicago.

Bousquet, N. (1980) 'From Hegemony to Competition: Cycles of the Core?' in Terence K. Hopkins and Immanuel Wallerstein (eds), *Processes of the World-System*. Beverly Hills: Sage.

Bradstock, Andrew (1987) *Saints and Sandinistas: The Catholic Church in Nicaragua and its Response to the Revolution*. London: Epworth.

Brannen, Noah S. (1968) *Soka Gakkai*. Richmond, VA: John Knox.

Brass, Paul R. (1988) 'The Punjab Crisis and the Unity of India', in Atul Kohli (ed.), *India's Democracy: An Analysis of Changing State/Society Relations*. Princeton: Princeton University. pp. 169–213.

Breuilly, Elizabeth and Palmer, Martin (eds) (1992) *Christianity and Ecology*. London: Cassell.

Bromley, David G. and Shupe, Anson (1984) *New Christian Politics*. Macon, GA: Mercer.

Bruce, Steve (1988) *The Rise and Fall of the New Christian Right: Conservative Protestant Politics in America 1978–1988*. Oxford: Clarendon.

Bruneau, Thomas C. (1974) *The Political Transformation of the Brazilian Catholic Church*. New York: Cambridge University Press.

Bruneau, Thomas C. (1981) 'Basic Communities in Latin America: Their Nature and Significance (especially in Brazil)', in Daniel H. Levine (ed.), *Churches and Politics in Latin America*. Beverly Hills, CA: Sage. pp. 225–237.

Bruneau, Thomas C. (1985) 'Church and Politics in Brazil: The Genesis of Change', *Journal of Latin American Studies*, 17: 271–293.

Burman, Bina Roy (1979) *Religion and Politics in Tibet*. New Delhi: Vikas.

Carmody, John (1983) *Ecology and Religion: Toward a New Christian Theology of Nature*. New York: Paulist.

Chase-Dunn, Christopher (1981) 'Interstate System and World-Economy: One Logic or Two?' in W. Ladd Hollist and James N. Rosenau (eds), *World System Structure: Continuity and Change*. Beverly Hills: Sage. pp. 30–53.

Chase-Dunn, Christopher and Rubinson, Richard (1979) 'Cycles, Trends, and New Departures in World-System Development', in John W. Meyer and Michael T. Hannan (eds), *National Development and the World System*. Chicago: University of Chicago. pp. 276–296.

Chehabi, H.E. (1990) *Iranian Politics and Religious Modernism: The Liberation Movement of Iran under the Shah and Khomeini*. Ithaca, NY: Cornell University.

Chirot, Daniel (1986) *Social Change in the Modern Era*. Chicago: Harcourt Brace Jovanovich.

Chirot, Daniel 'and Hall, Thomas D. (1982) 'World-System Theory', *Annual Review of Sociology*, 8: 81–106.

Cleary, Edward L. (1985) *Crisis and Change: The Church in Latin America Today*. Maryknoll, NY: Orbis.

Cobb, John B., Jr (1986) 'Christian Existence in a World of Limits', in Eugene C. Hargrove (ed.), *Religion and Environmental Crisis*. Athens, GA: University of Georgia. pp. 172–187.

Coleman, John A. (1979) *The Evolution of Dutch Catholicism*. Berkeley: University of California.

Coleman, John A. (1989) '*Raison d'Eglise*: Organizational Imperatives of the Church in the Political Order', in Jeffrey K. Hadden and Anson Shupe (eds), *Secularization and Fundamentalism Reconsidered. Religion and the Political Order*, Vol. III. New York: Paragon. pp. 252–275.

Conlon, James (1990) *Geo-Justice: A Preferential Option for the Earth*. Winfield, BC & San Jose, CA: Wood Lake Books/Resource Publications.

Cuddihy, John Murray (1987) *The Ordeal of Civility: Freud, Marx, Lévi-Strauss, and the Jewish Struggle with Modernity*. Boston: Beacon.

Cummings, Charles (1991) *Eco-Spirituality: Toward a Reverent Life*. Mahwah, NJ: Paulist.

Dator, James Allen (1969) *Soka Gakkai, Builders of the Third Civilization*. Seattle: University of Washington.

de Kadt, Emanuel (1970) 'JUC and AP: The Rise of Catholic Radicalism in Brazil', in Henry A. Landsberger (ed.), *The Church and Social Change in Latin America*. Notre Dame, IN: University of Notre Dame. pp. 191–219.

Development and Peace [Canadian Catholic Organization for Development and Peace] (1990) *Environmentalism and Development*. Montreal: CCODP.

DeWitt, Calvin B. (1987) *A Sustainable Earth: Religion and Ecology in the Western Hemisphere*. Mancelona, MI: AuSable Institute.

Diamond, Stanley (1957) 'Kibbutz and Shtetl: The History of an Idea', *Social Problems*, 5 (2): 71–99.

Dobbelaere, Karel (1984) 'Secularization Theories and Sociological Paradigms: Convergences and Divergences', *Social Compass*, 31: 199–219.

Dobbelaere, Karel (1985) 'Secularization Theories and Sociological Paradigms: A Reformulation of the Private–Public Dichotomy and the Problem of Societal Integration', *Sociological Analysis*, 46: 377–387.

Dobbelaere, Karel (1988) 'Secularization, Pillarization, Religious Involvement, and Religious Change in the Low Countries', in Thomas M. Gannon (ed.), *World Catholicism in Transition*. New York: Macmillan. pp. 80–115.

Dodson, Michael and O'Shaughnessy, Laura Nuzzi (1990) *Nicaragua's Other Revolution: Religious Faith and Political Struggle*. Chapel Hill, NC: University of North Carolina.

Don-Yehiya, Eliezer (1981) 'Origins and Development of the *Agudah* and *Mafdal* Parties', *Jerusalem Quarterly*, 20: 49–64.

Don-Yehiya, Eliezer (1987) 'Jewish Messianism, Religious Zionism, and Israeli Politics: The Impact and Origin of Gush Emunim', *Middle Eastern Studies*, 23: 215–234.

Douglas, Mary (1970) *Natural Symbols: Explorations in Cosmology*. New York: Vintage.

Douglas, Mary (1975) 'Self-Evidence', in *Implicit Meanings: Essays in Anthropology*. London: Routledge & Kegan Paul. pp. 276–318.

Driedger, Leo (1989) *The Ethnic Factor: Identity in Diversity*. Toronto: McGraw-Hill Ryerson.

Dumont, Louis (1970) *Homo Hierarchicus: The Caste System and Its Implications*. Rev. ed. Tr. Mark Sainsbury, Louis Dumont, and Basia Gulati. Chicago: University of Chicago.

Durkheim, Emile (1933) *The Division of Labor in Society*. Tr. George Simpson. New York: Free Press.

Durkheim, Emile (1965) *The Elementary Forms of the Religious Life*. Tr. Joseph Ward Swain. New York: Free Press.

Dussel, Enrique (1981) *A History of the Church in Latin America: Colonialism to Liberation*. Grand Rapids, MI: Eerdmans.

Dwivedi, O.P. and Tiwari, B.N. (1987) *Environmental Crisis and Hindu Religion*. New Delhi: Gitanjali.

Eagleson, John (ed.) (1975) *Christians and Socialism: Documentation of the Christians for Socialism Movement in Latin America*. Maryknoll, NY: Orbis.

Eckberg, Douglas Lee and Blocker, T. Jean (1989) 'Varieties of Religious Involvement and Environmental Concerns: Testing the Lynn White Thesis', *Journal for the Scientific Study of Religion*, 28: 509–517.

Economist, The (1993) 'One too many', 127(7809) (1–7 May): 41–42.

Egerton, John (1974) *The Americanization of Dixie: The Southernization of America*. New York: Harper & Row.

Elder, Frederick (1970) *Crisis in Eden: A Religious Study of Man and Environment*. Nashville: Abingdon.

Elias, Norbert (1978) *The Civilizing Process: The History of Manners*. Tr. Edmund Jephcott. New York: Urizen.

Elias, Norbert (1982) *Power and Civility: The Civilizing Process* Volume II. Tr. Edmund Jephcott. New York: Pantheon.

Ellul, Jacques (1964) *The Technological Society*. Tr. John Wilkinson. New York: Alfred A. Knopf.

Ellul, Jacques (1967) *The Political Illusion*. Tr. Konrad Kellen. New York: Random House.

Ellul, Jacques (1983) *Living Faith: Belief and Doubt in a Perilous World*. Tr. Peter Heinegg. New York: Harper & Row.

Enayat, Hamid (1983) 'Revolution in Iran 1979: Religion as Political Ideology', in Noel O'Sullivan (ed.), *Revolutionary Theory and Political Reality*. New York: St. Martin's. pp. 197–200.

Esposito, John L. (1987) *Islam and Politics*. Rev. 2nd ed. Syracuse: Syracuse University.

Falwell, Jerry (ed.) (1981) *The Fundamentalist Phenomenon: The Resurgence of Conservative Christianity*. With Ed Dobson and Ed Hindson. Garden City: Doubleday.

Falwell, Jerry (1986) *Strength for the Journey: An Autobiography*. New York: Simon & Schuster.

Farhi, Farideh (1990) *States and Urban-Based Revolutions: Iran and Nicaragua*. Urbana, IL: University of Illinois.

Featherstone, Mike (ed.) (1990) *Global Culture: Nationalism, Globalization, Modernity*. London: Sage. Reprint of *Theory, Culture and Society*, 7(2–3).

Fenn, Richard K. (1978) *Toward a Theory of Secularization*. Storrs, CT: Society for the Scientific Study of Religion.

Ferm, Dean William (1986) *Third World Liberation Theologies: A Reader*. Maryknoll, NY: Orbis.

Fischer, Michael M.J. (1980) *Iran: From Religious Dispute to Revolution*. Cambridge, MA: Harvard.

Fischer, Michael M.J. (1983) 'Imam Khomeini: Four Levels of Understanding', in John L. Esposito (ed.), *Voices of Resurgent Islam*. New York: Oxford. pp. 150–174.

Fischer, Michael M.J. and Abedi, Mehdi (1990) *Debating Muslims: Cultural Dialogues in Postmodernity and Tradition*. Madison, WI: University of Wisconsin.

Foroohar, Manzar (1989) *The Catholic Church and Social Change in Nicaragua*. Albany, NY: State University of New York.

Foucault, Michel (1978) *The History of Sexuality*. Vol. I. New York: Pantheon.

Fox, Matthew (1988) *The Coming of the Cosmic Christ: The Healing of Mother Earth and the Birth of a Global Renaissance*. San Francisco: Harper & Row.

Francou, François (1988) *L'Eglise au Nicaragua: L'escalade de la violence*. Paris: Aide à l'Eglise en détresse.

Frankl, Razelle (1987) *Televangelism: The Marketing of Popular Religion*. Carbondale, IL: Southern Illinois University.

Freedman, Robert O. (1989) 'Religion, Politics, and the Israeli Elections of 1988', *Middle East Journal*, 43: 406–422.

Garrett, William R. (1986) 'Religion and the Legitimation of Violence', in Jeffrey K. Hadden and Anson Shupe (eds), *Prophetic Religion and Politics*. New York: Paragon. pp. 103–122.

Garrett, William R. (1988a) 'Liberation Theology and the Concept of Human Rights', in Anson Shupe and Jeffrey K. Hadden (eds), *The Politics of Religion and Social Change*. New York: Paragon. pp. 128–144.

Garrett, William R. (1988b) 'Liberation Theology and Dependency Theory', in Richard L. Rubenstein and John K. Roth (eds), *The Politics of Latin American Liberation Theology: The Challenge to U.S. Public Policy*. Washington, DC: Washington Institute Press. pp. 174–198.

Geertz, Clifford (1966) 'Religion as a Cultural System', in M. Bainton (ed.), *Anthropological Approaches to the Study of Religion*. London: Tavistock. pp. 1–46.

Gellner, Ernest (1983) *Nations and Nationalism*. London: Basil Blackwell.

Giddens, Anthony (1987) *The Nation-State and Violence*. Volume Two of *A Contemporary Critique of Historical Materialism*. Berkeley: University of California.

Giddens, Anthony (1990) *The Consequences of Modernity*. Stanford, CA: Stanford University.

Giddens, Anthony (1991) *Modernity and Self-Identity: Self and Society in the Late Modern Age*. Stanford, CA: Stanford University.

Gorrie, Peter (1992) 'Environment now a worry around the globe, Gallup says', *The Toronto Star* (October 31): D6.

Granberg-Michaelson, Wesley (1988) *Ecology and Life: Accepting Our Environmental Responsibility*. Waco, TX: Word Books.

Granberg-Michaelson, Wesley (1992) *Redeeming the Creation. The Rio Earth Summit: Challenges for the Churches*. Geneva: WCC Publications.

Greenpeace (1990) 'How We Can Save It', *Greenpeace*, 15(1) (January/February).

Gutiérrez, Gustavo (1988) *A Theology of Liberation: History, Politics, and Salvation*. Rev. ed. with new introduction. Tr. Sister Caridad Inda and John Eagleson. Maryknoll, NY: Orbis. (1st ed. 1973.)

Habermas, Jürgen (1981) 'New Social Movements', *Telos*, 49 (Fall): 33–37.

Habermas, Jürgen (1984) *The Theory of Communicative Action. Vol. I: Reason and the Rationalization of Society*. Tr. Thomas McCarthy. Boston: Beacon.

Habermas, Jürgen (1987) *The Theory of Communicative Action. Vol. II: Lifeworld and System: A Critique of Functionalist Reason*. Tr. Thomas McCarthy. London: Polity.

Hadar, Leon T. (1992) 'The 1992 Electoral Earthquake and the Fall of the "Second Republic"', *Middle East Journal*, 46: 594–616.

Hadden, Jeffrey K. (1970) *The Gathering Storm in the Churches*. New York: Doubleday.

Hadden, Jeffrey K. (1987) 'Religious Broadcasting and the Mobilization of the New Christian Right', *Journal for the Scientific Study of Religion*, 26: 1–24.

Hadden, Jeffrey K. and Swann, Charles E. (1981) *Prime Time Preachers: The Rising Power of Televangelism*. Reading, MA: Addison-Wesley.

Hallman, David G. (1989) *Caring for Creation. The Environmental Crisis: A Canadian Christian Call to Action*. Winfield, BC: Wood Lake Books.

Hallman, David G. (1992) *A Place in Creation. Ecological Visions in Science, Religion, and Economics*. Toronto: United Church Publishing House.

Hamel, Peter (1990) 'History of the Anglican Church's Involvement in Environmental Issues'. Typescript, Toronto.

Hammond, Phillip E. (1983) 'Another Great Awakening?' in Robert C. Liebman and Robert Wuthnow (eds), *The New Christian Right: Mobilization and Legitimation*. New York: Aldine. pp. 207–223.

Hand, C. and Van Liere, K. (1984) 'Religion, Mastery-over-Nature, and Environmental Concern', *Social Forces*, 63: 555–570.

Hannigan, John A. (1990) 'Apples and Oranges or Varieties of the Same Fruit? New Religious Movements and New Social Movements Compared', *Review of Religious Research*, 31: 246–258.

Hannigan, John A. (1991) 'Social Movement Theory and the Sociology of Religion: Toward a New Synthesis', *Sociological Analysis*, 52: 311–331.

Hargrove, Eugene C. (ed.) (1986) *Religion and Environmental Crisis*. Athens, GA: University of Georgia.

Harper, Charles L. and Leicht, Kevin (1984) 'Explaining the New Religious Right: Status Politics and Beyond', in David G. Bromley and Anson Shupe (eds), *New Christian Politics*. Macon, GA: Mercer. pp. 101–110.

Hechter, Michael (1978) 'Group Formation and the Cultural Division of Labor', *American Journal of Sociology*, 84: 293–318.

Hepburn, Bob (1992) 'Farewell to Fury: Rafsanjani puts Iran on a more moderate course', *The Toronto Star*, (May 31): F1–F2.

Hessel, Dieter T. (ed.) (1992) *After Nature's Revolt: Eco-Justice and Theology*. Minneapolis, MN: Fortress.

Hewitt, W.E. (1989) 'Origins and Prospects of the Option for the Poor in Brazilian Catholicism', *Journal for the Scientific Study of Religion*, 28: 120–135.

Hewitt, W.E. (1990) 'Religion and the Consolidation of Democracy in Brazil: The Role of the Comunidades Eclesiais de Base (CEBs)', *Sociological Analysis*, 51: 139–152.

Hewitt, W.E. (1991) *Base Christian Communities and Social Change in Brazil*. Lincoln, NE: University of Nebraska.

Hewitt, W.E. (1992) 'Brazil's Progressive Church in Crisis: Institutional Weakness and Political Vulnerability', in Edward Cleary and Hanna Stewart-Gambino (eds), *Conflict and Competition: The Latin American Church in a Changing Environment*. Boulder, CO: Lynne Rienner.

Hill, Samuel S. and Owen, Dennis E. (1982) *The New Religious Political Right in America*. Nashville: Abingdon.

Hooglund, Eric J. (1982) *Land and Revolution in Iran, 1960–1980*. Austin, TX: University of Texas.

Hoover, Stewart M. (1988) *Mass Media Religion: The Social Sources of the Electronic Church*. Newbury Park, CA: Sage.

Houtart, François (1989) 'Jean-Paul II à Managua: L'échec de la reconquête d'un espace social hégémonique', *Social Compass*, 36: 327–336.

Hunter, James Davison (1983) *American Evangelicalism: Conservative Religion and the Quandary of Modernity*. New Brunswick, NJ: Rutgers University.

Ibrahim, Saad Eddin (1986) 'Egypt's Islamic Militancy Revisited', in Jeffrey K. Hadden and Anson Shupe (eds), *Prophetic Religions and Politics. Religion and the Political Order*, Volume 1. New York: Paragon. pp. 353–361.

Innis, Harold A. (1972) *Empire and Communication*. 2nd. ed. Toronto: University of Toronto.

Isaac, Rael Jean (1981) *Party and Politics in Israel: Three Visions of a Jewish State*. New York: Longman.

Jansen, Michael (1987) *Dissonance in Zion*. London: Zed Books.

John Paul II, Pope (1989) 'Peace with God the Creator, Peace with All of Creation'. Message of Pope John Paul II for World Day of Peace, 8 December 1989. *Osservatore Romano* (English Edition), No. 51–52 (1120) (18–26 December): 1–3.

Johnson, Stephen D., Tamney, Joseph B., and Burton, Ronald (1989) 'Pat Robertson: Who Supported His Candidacy for President', *Journal for the Scientific Study of Religion*, 28: 387–399.

Jorstad, Erling (1981) *Evangelicals in the White House: The Cultural Maturation of Born Again Christianity 1960–1981*. Lewiston, NY: Edwin Mellen.

Jorstad, Erling (1987) *The New Christian Right 1981–1988: Prospects for the Post-Reagan Decade*. Lewiston, NY: Edwin Mellen.

Kanagy, Conrad L. and Willits, Fern K. (1991) 'Religion and Environment: Evidence from a Sample of Pennsylvania Residents', Paper presented at the Society for the Scientific Study of Religion Annual Meeting, Pittsburgh, PA.

Kapur, Rajiv (1986) *Sikh Separatism: The Politics of Faith*. London: Allen & Unwin.

Katouzian, Homa (1983) 'Shi'ism and Islamic Economics: Sadr and Bani-Sadr', in Nikki R. Keddie (ed.), *Religion and Politics in Iran: Shi'ism from Quietism to Revolution*. New Haven: Yale University. pp. 145–165.

Kazemi, Farhad (1980) *Poverty and Revolution in Iran: The Migrant Poor, Urban Marginality and Politics*. New York & London: New York University.

Kearns, Laurel (1990) 'Redeeming the Earth: Eco-Theological Ethics for Saving the Earth', Paper presented at the Association for the Sociology of Religion Annual Meeting, Washington, DC.

Kearns, Laurel (1991) 'Saving the Creation: Stewardship Theology and Creation Spirituality', Paper presented at the American Academy of Religion Annual Meeting. Kansas City, MO.

Keddie, Nikki R. (1980) 'The Economic History of Iran 1800–1914 and Its Political Impact', in *Iran: Religion, Politics and Society. Collected Essays*. London: Frank Cass. pp. 119–136.

Keddie, Nikki R. (1981) *Iran: Roots of Revolution*. New Haven: Yale University.

Kelley, Dean (1972) *Why Conservative Churches Are Growing*. New York: Harper & Row.

Khomeini, Ruhollah (1981) *Islam and Revolution: Writings and Declarations of Imam Khomeini*. Tr. Hamid Algar. Berkeley: Mizan.

Khoury, Adel T. and Hünermann, Peter (eds) (1987) *Wie sollen wir mit der Schöpfung umgehen?* Freiburg i.B.: Herder.

Kimmerling, Baruch (1983) *Zionism and Territory: The Socio-Territorial Dimensions of Zionist Politics*. Berkeley: Institute of International Studies, University of California.

Kimmerling, Baruch (1989) *The Israeli State and Society: Boundaries and Frontiers*. Albany, NY: SUNY.

Klandermans, Bert and Tarrow, Sidney (1988) 'Mobilization into Social Movements: Synthesizing European and American Perspectives', in Bert Klandermans, Hanspieter Kriesi, and Sidney Tarrow (eds), *From Structure to Action: Comparing Social Movement Research Across Cultures*. International Social Movement Research: A Research Annual. Volume 1. Greenwich, CT: JAI. pp. 1–38.

Kriesi, Hanspieter (1988) 'Local Mobilization for the People's Petition of the Dutch Peace Movement', in Bert Klandermans, Hanspieter Kriesi, and Sidney Tarrow (eds), *From Structure to Action: Comparing Social Movement Research Across Cultures*. Greenwich, CT: JAI. pp. 41–81.

Küng, Hans and Ching, Julia (1989) *Christianity and Chinese Religions*. New York: Doubleday.
LaHaye, Tim (1980) *The Battle for the Mind*. Old Tappan, NJ: Fleming Revell.
Lambton, Ann K.S. (1964) 'A Reconsideration of the Position of the *Marja' Al-Taqlid* and the Religious Institution', *Studia Islamica*, 20: 115–135.
Langguth, Gerd (1989) *Wer regiert Nicaragua? Geschichte, Ideologie und Machtstrukturen des Sandinismus*. Stuttgart: Bonn Aktuell.
Leaf, Murray J. (1985) 'The Punjab Crisis', *Asian Survey*, 25: 475–498.
Lechner, Frank (1987) 'Modernity and its Procontents: Societal Solidarity in Comparative Perspective', Paper presented at the American Sociological Association annual meetings, Chicago.
Lechner, Frank (1989) 'Cultural Aspects of the Modern World System', in William H. Swatos (ed.), *Religious Politics in Global and Comparative Perspective*. Westport, CT: Greenwood. pp. 11–27.
Lefever, Ernest W. (1987) *Nairobi to Vancouver: The World Council of Churches and the World, 1975–1987*. Washington, DC: Ethics and Public Policy Center.
Levenson, Joseph R. (ed.) (1967) *European Expansion and the Counter-Example of Asia 1300–1600*. Englewood Cliffs, NJ: Prentice-Hall.
Levine, Daniel H. (1981) *Religion and Politics in Latin America: The Catholic Church in Venezuela and Colombia*. Princeton: Princeton University.
Levine, Daniel H. (ed.) (1986) *Religion and Political Conflict in Latin America*. Chapel Hill: University of North Carolina.
Lewis, Arnold (1984) 'Ethnic Politics and the Foreign Policy Debate in Israel', in Myron J. Aronoff (ed.), *Political Anthropology, Vol. 4: Cross-Currents in Israeli Culture and Politics*. New Brunswick, NJ: Transaction. pp. 25–38.
Liebman, Charles S. and Don-Yehiya, Eliezer (1983) *Civil Religion in Israel: Traditional Judaism and Political Culture in the Jewish State*. Berkeley, CA: University of California.
Liebman, Charles S. and Don-Yehiya, Eliezer (1984) *Religion and Politics in Israel*. Bloomington, IN: Indiana State University.
Liebman, Robert C. (1983) 'Mobilizing the Moral Majority', in Robert C. Liebman and Robert Wuthnow (eds), *The New Christian Right*. New York: Aldine. pp. 49–73.
Liebman, Robert C. and Wuthnow, Robert (1983) *The New Christian Right: Mobilization and Legitimation*. New York: Aldine.
Lipset, Seymour Martin and Rabb, Earl (1978) *The Politics of Unreason*. 2nd ed. Chicago: University of Chicago.
Lovelock, J.E. (1987) *Gaia: A New Look at Life on Earth*. Oxford: Oxford University.
Luckmann, Thomas (1967) *The Invisible Religion: The Problem of Religion in Modern Society*. New York: Macmillan.
Luckmann, Thomas (1970) 'On the Boundaries of the Social World', in Maurice Natanson (ed.), *Phenomenology and Social Reality: Essays in Memory of Alfred Schutz*. The Hague: Mouton. pp. 73–100
Luhmann, Niklas (1970) *Soziologische Aufklärung 1: Aufsätze zur Theorie sozialer Systeme*. Opladen: Westdeutscher Verlag.
Luhmann, Niklas (1971) 'Die Weltgesellschaft', *Archiv für Rechts-und Sozialphilosophie*, 57: 1–35. Reprinted in Luhmann, 1975, pp. 51–71.
Luhmann, Niklas (1975) *Soziologische Aufklärung 2: Aufsätze zur Theorie der Gesellschaft*. Opladen: Westdeutscher Verlag.
Luhmann, Niklas (1977) *Funktion der Religion*. Frankfurt/M: Suhrkamp.
Luhmann, Niklas (1978) 'Soziologie der Moral', in Niklas Luhmann and Stephan H. Pfürtner (eds), *Theorietechnik und Moral*. Frankfurt/M: Suhrkamp. pp. 8–116.
Luhmann, Niklas (1980–81) *Gesellschaftsstruktur und Semantik: Studien zur Wissenssoziologie der modernen Gesellschaft*. 2 vols. Frankfurt/M: Suhrkamp.
Luhmann, Niklas (1981) 'Wie ist soziale Ordnung möglich?' in *Gesellschaftsstruktur und Semantik: Studien zur Wissenssoziologie der modernen Gesellschaft*. Vol. 2. Frankfurt/M: Suhrkamp. pp. 195–285.

Luhmann, Niklas (1982) *The Differentiation of Society*. Tr. Stephen Holmes and Charles Larmore. New York: Columbia University.

Luhmann, Niklas (1984a) 'The Self-Description of Society: Crisis Fashion and Sociological Theory', *International Journal of Comparative Sociology*, 25: 59–72.

Luhmann, Niklas (1984b) *Soziale Systeme: Grundriss einer allgemeinen Theorie*. Frankfurt: Suhrkamp.

Luhmann, Niklas (1984c) *Religious Dogmatics and the Evolution of Societies*. Tr. Peter Beyer. Lewiston, NY: Edwin Mellen.

Luhmann, Niklas (1985) 'Society, Meaning, Religion – Based on Self-Reference', *Sociological Analysis*, 46: 5–20. Reprinted in Luhmann, 1990a: 144–164.

Luhmann, Niklas (1986) *Love as Passion: The Codification of Intimacy*. Tr. Jeremy Gaines and Doris L. Jones. Cambridge, MA: Harvard University.

Luhmann, Niklas (1987a) 'Die Unterscheidung Gottes', in *Soziologische Aufklärung 4: Beiträge zur funktionalen Differenzierung der Gesellschaft*. Opladen: Westdeutscher Verlag. pp. 236–253.

Luhmann, Niklas (1987b) 'The Evolutionary Differentiation between Society and Interaction', in Jeffrey C. Alexander, et al. (eds), *The Micro-Macro Link*. Berkeley: University of California. pp. 112–131.

Luhmann, Niklas (1989a) *Gesellschaftsstruktur und Semantik: Studien zur Wissenssoziologie der modernen Gesellschaft*. Vol. 3. Frankfurt: Suhrkamp.

Luhmann, Niklas (1989b) 'Die Ausdifferenzierung der Religion', in *Gesellschaftsstruktur und Semantik: Studien zur Wissenssoziologie der modernen Gesellschaft*. Vol. 3. Frankfurt: Suhrkamp. pp. 259–357.

Luhmann, Niklas (1990a) *Essays on Self-Reference*. New York: Columbia University.

Luhmann, Niklas (1990b) 'The World Society as a Social System', in *Essays on Self-Reference*. New York: Columbia University. pp. 175–190.

Luhmann, Niklas (1990c) 'Tautology and Paradox in the Self-Descriptions of Modern Society', in *Essays on Self-Reference*. New York: Columbia University. pp. 123–143.

Lukes, Steven (1975) *Emile Durkheim: His Life and Work*. Stanford: Stanford University.

Lustick, Ian S. (1988) *For the Land and the Lord: Jewish Fundamentalism in Israel*. New York: Council on Foreign Relations

Lutheran Church in America (1972) *A Social Statement on the Human Crisis in Ecology*. Waterloo, ONT: Institute for Christian Ethics.

Lynch, Edward A. (1991) *Religion and Politics in Latin America: Liberation Theology and Christian Democracy*. New York: Praeger.

Mainwaring, Scott (1986) *The Catholic Church and Politics in Brazil 1916–1985*. Stanford, CA: Stanford University.

Mainwaring, Scott (1989) 'Grassroots Catholic Groups and Politics in Brazil', in Scott Mainwaring and Alexander Wilde (eds), *The Progressive Church in Latin America*. Notre Dame, IN: University of Notre Dame. pp. 151–192.

Mainwaring, Scott and Wilde, Alexander (1989) 'The Progressive Church in Latin America: An Interpretation', in Scott Mainwaring and Alexander Wilde (eds), *The Progressive Church in Latin America*. Notre Dame, IN: University of Notre Dame. pp. 1–37.

Markoff, John and Regan, Daniel (1987) 'Religion, the State and Political Legitimacy in the World's Constitutions', in Thomas Robbins and Roland Robertson (eds), *Church–State Relations: Tensions and Transitions*. New Brunswick, NJ: Transaction. pp. 161–182.

Marsden, George M. (1980) *Fundamentalism in American Culture: The Shaping of Twentieth-Century Evangelicalism: 1870–1925*. New York: Oxford University Press.

Marsden, George M. (1983) 'Preachers of Paradox: The Religious New Right in Historical Perspective', in Mary Douglas and Steven Tipton (eds), *Religion and America: Spiritual Life in a Secular Age*. Boston: Beacon. pp. 150–168.

Martin, David (1990) *Theological Reflections on the Ecological Crisis*. Waterloo, ONT: Institute for Christian Ethics.

Martin, Vanessa (1989) *Islam and Modernism: The Iranian Revolution of 1906*. London: Tauris.

Mathisen, James A. (1989) 'Twenty Years after Bellah: Whatever Happened to American Civil Religion?' *Sociological Analysis*, 50: 129–146.

McAteer, Michael (1990) ' "To Pluck a Flower is to Trouble a Star" ', *The Toronto Star* (June 30): M15.

McDaniel, Jay (1986) 'Christianity and the Need for New Vision', in Eugene C. Hargrove (ed.), *Religion and Environmental Crisis*. Athens, GA: University of Georgia. pp. 188–212.

McDaniel, Jay (1990) *Earth, Sky, God and Mortals: Developing an Ecological Spirituality*. Mystic, CT: Twenty-Third Publications.

McDonagh, Sean (1987) *To Care for the Earth: A Call to a New Theology*. Santa Fe: Bear.

McGovern, Arthur F. (1989) *Liberation Theology and Its Critics: Toward an Assessment*. Maryknoll, NY: Orbis.

McGuire, Meredith (1983) 'Discovering Religious Power', *Sociological Analysis*, 44: 1–10.

McLoughlin, William G. (1978) *Revivals, Awakenings, and Reform: An Essay on Religion and Social Change in America, 1607–1977*. Chicago: University of Chicago.

Melucci, Alberto (1985) 'The Symbolic Challenge of Contemporary Movements', *Social Research*, 52: 789–816.

Metraux, Daniel (1988) *The History and Theology of Soka Gakkai: A Japanese New Religion*. Lewiston, NY: Edwin Mellen.

Meyer, John W. (1980) 'The World Polity and the Authority of the Nation-State', in Albert Bergesen (ed.), *Studies of the Modern World System*. New York: Academic. pp. 109–137.

Meyer, John W. (1987) 'Self and the Life Course: Institutionalization and Its Effects', in George Thomas, et al. (eds), *Institutional Structure: Constituting State, Society and the Individual*. Beverly Hills: Sage.

Meyer, John W. and Hannan, Michael T. (eds) (1979a) *National Development and the World System: Educational, Economic, and Political Change, 1950–1970*. Chicago: University of Chicago.

Meyer, John W. and Hannan, Michael T. (1979b) 'Issues for Further Comparative Research', in John W. Meyer and Michael T. Hannan (eds), *National Development and the World System*. Chicago: University of Chicago. pp. 297–308.

Meyer, John W., Boli-Bennett, John and Chase-Dunn, Christopher (1975) 'Convergence and Divergence in Development', *Annual Review of Sociology*, 1: 223–246.

Meyer, John W., Hannan, Michael T., Rubinson, Richard and Thomas, George M. (1979) 'National Economic Development, 1950–1970: Social and Political Factors', in John W. Meyer and Michael T. Hannan (eds), *National Development and the World System*. Chicago: University of Chicago. pp. 5–116.

Michael, Franz H. (1982) *Rule by Incarnation: Tibetan Buddhism and Its Role in Society and State*. Boulder, CO: Westview.

Migdal, Joel S. (1989) 'The Crystallization of the State and the Struggles over Rulemaking: Israel in Comparative Perspective', in Baruch Kimmerling (ed.), *The Israeli State and Society: Boundaries and Frontiers*. Albany, NY: State University of New York. pp. 1–27.

Miranda, José (1974) *Marx and the Bible*. Maryknoll, NY: Orbis.

Moberg, David O. (1972) *The Great Reversal: Evangelism and Social Concern*. Philadelphia: Lippincott.

Moltmann, Jürgen (1989) *Creating a Just Future: The Politics of Peace and the Ethics of Creation in a Threatened World*. London: SCM.

Moore, Wilbert E. (1966) 'Global Sociology: The World as a Singular System', *American Journal of Sociology*, 71: 475–482.

Morris, Henry (1984) *History of Modern Creationism*. San Diego: Master Books.

Mowat, Farley (1990) *Rescue the Earth!* Toronto: McClelland & Stewart.

Nayar, Kuldip and Singh, Khushwant (1984) *Tragedy of Punjab: Operation Bluestar and After*. New Delhi: Vision Books.

Nelson, Benjamin (1968) 'Scholastic *Rationales* of "Conscience", Early Modern Crises of Credibility, and the Scientific-Technocultural Revolutions of the 17th and 20th Centuries', *Journal for the Scientific Study of Religion*, 7: 157–177.

Nelson, Benjamin (1969) *The Idea of Usury: From Tribal Brotherhood to Universal Otherhood*. 2nd ed. Chicago: University of Chicago.

Nettl, J.P. and Robertson, Roland (1968) *International Systems and the Modernization of Societies: The Formation of National Goals and Attitudes*. London: Faber & Faber.

Newman, David (ed.) (1985) *The Impact of Gush Emunim: Politics and Settlement in the West Bank*. London: Croom Helm.

Newman, David (1986) 'Gush Emunim between Fundamentalism and Pragmatism', *Jerusalem Quarterly*, 39: 33–43.

Nisan, Mordechai (1980) 'Gush Emunim and Israel's National Interest', *Viewpoints* 9 (January), Jerusalem Institute for Federal Studies; reprinted in Mordechai Nisan, Janet Aviad, and Mervin F. Verbit, *Gush Emunim, Shalom Achshav and Israel's Future*. Jerusalem: Jerusalem Institute for Federal Studies.

Norton, Augustus Richard (1987) *Amal and the Shi'a: Struggle for the Soul of Lebanon*. Austin: University of Texas.

Nuñez, Emilio A. (1985) *Liberation Theology*. Tr. Paul E. Sywulka. Chicago: Moody.

O'Brien, David J. and Shannon, Thomas A. (eds) (1977) *Renewing the Earth: Catholic Documents on Peace, Justice and Liberation*. New York: Doubleday Image.

O'Shaughnessy, Laura Nuzzi and Serra, Luis (1986) *The Church and Revolution in Nicaragua*. Monographs in International Studies. Latin American Series, No. 11. Athens, OH: Ohio University Center for International Studies.

Offe, Claus (1985) 'New Social Movements: Challenging the Boundaries of Institutional Politics', *Social Research*, 52: 817–868.

Oren, Stephen (1973) 'Continuity and Change in Israel's Religious Parties', *Middle East Journal*, 27: 36–54.

Parsons, Talcott (1951) *Religious Perspectives of College Teaching in Sociology and Social Psychology*. New Haven: Hazen Foundation.

Parsons, Talcott (1960) 'Some Comments on the Pattern of Religious Organization in the United States', in *Structure and Process in Modern Societies*. New York: Free Press.

Parsons, Talcott (1966) 'Religion in a Modern Pluralistic Society', *Review of Religious Research*, 7: 125–146.

Parsons, Talcott (1967) 'Christianity and Modern Industrial Society', in *Sociological Theory and Modern Society*. New York: Free Press. pp. 385–421.

Parsons, Talcott (1971) *The System of Modern Societies*. Foundation of Modern Sociology Series, Alex Inkeles (ed.). Englewood Cliffs, NJ: Prentice-Hall.

Parsons, Talcott (1974) 'Religion in Postindustrial America: The Problem of Secularization', *Social Research*, 41: 193–225.

Peleg, Ilan and Seliktar, Ofira (eds) (1989) *The Emergence of a Binational Israel: The Second Republic in the Making*. Boulder, CO: Westview.

Peretz, Don and Smooha, Sammy (1989) 'Israel's Twelfth Knesset Election: An All-Loser Game', *Middle East Journal*, 43: 388–405.

Pipes, Daniel (1990) *The Rushdie Affair: The Novel, the Ayatollah, and the West*. New York: Birch Lane.

Poggi, Gianfranco (1967) *Catholic Action in Italy: The Sociology of a Sponsored Organization*. Stanford: Stanford University.

Poggi, Gianfranco (1978) *The Development of the Modern State*. Stanford: Stanford University.

Probe Post (1989) 'The Environment and Environmentalism: Our Progress, Problems and Prospects', *Probe Post*, 11 (4): 10–39.

Rahnema, Ali and Nomani, Farhad (1990) *The Secular Miracle: Religion, Politics and Economic Policy in Iran*. London & New Jersey: Zed Books.

Ramirez, Francisco O. and Meyer, John W. (1980) 'Comparative Education: The Social Construction of the Modern World System', *Annual Review of Sociology*, 6: 369–399.

Reiser, Stewart (1984) *The Politics of Leverage: The National Religious Party of Israel and Its Influence on Foreign Policy*. Harvard Middle East Papers, Modern Series, No. 2. Cambridge, MA: Center for Middle Eastern Studies, Harvard University.

Reiser, Stewart (1988) 'The Religious Parties and Israel's Foreign Policy', in Bernard Reich and Gershon R. Kieval (eds), *Israeli National Security Policy: Political Actors and Perspectives*. Westport, CT: Greenwood. pp. 105–121.

Religious Zionism: Challenges and Choices (1980) Jerusalem: Oz ve-Shalom.

Richard, Yann (1981) 'Contemporary Shi'i Thought', in Nikki R. Keddie, *Roots of Revolution: An Interpretative History of Modern Iran*. New Haven: Yale University. pp. 202–228.

Robbins, Thomas (1988) *Cults, Converts and Charisma: The Sociology of New Religious Movements*. London: Sage.

Robertson, Pat (1986) *America's Dates With Destiny*. Nashville: Thomas Nelson.

Robertson, Roland (1970) *The Sociological Interpretation of Religion*. New York: Schocken.

Robertson, Roland (1977) 'Individualism, Societalism, Worldliness, Universalism: Thematizing Theoretical Sociology of Religion', *Sociological Analysis*, 38: 281–308.

Robertson, Roland (1986) 'Liberation Theology in Latin America: Sociological Problems of Interpretation and Explanation', in Jeffrey K. Hadden and Anson Shupe (eds), *Prophetic Religion and Politics*. New York: Paragon. pp. 73–102.

Robertson, Roland (1987a) 'Church–State Relations and the World System', in Thomas Robbins and Roland Robertson (eds), *Church–State Relations: Tensions and Transitions*. New Brunswick, NJ: Transaction. pp. 39–52.

Robertson, Roland (1987b) 'Latin America and Liberation Theology', in Thomas Robbins and Roland Roberston (eds), *Church–State Relations: Tensions and Transitions*. New Brunswick, NJ: Transaction. pp. 205–220.

Robertson, Roland (1987c) 'Globalization and Societal Modernization: A Note on Japan and Japanese Religion', *Sociological Analysis*, 47 (S): 35–42.

Robertson, Roland (1989a) 'Internationalization and Globalization', *University Center for International Studies Newsletter*, University of Pittsburgh, (Spring): 8–9.

Robertson, Roland (1989b) 'Globalization, Politics, and Religion', in James A. Beckford and Thomas Luckmann (eds), *The Changing Face of Religion*. Beverly Hills: Sage. pp. 10–23.

Robertson, Roland (1990a) 'Mapping the Global Condition: Globalization as the Central Concept', *Theory, Culture and Society*, 7 (2–3): 15–30.

Robertson, Roland (1990b) 'After Nostalgia? Wilful Nostalgia and the Phases of Globalization', in Bryan S. Turner (ed.), *Theories of Modernity and Postmodernity*. London: Sage. pp. 45–61.

Robertson, Roland (1991) 'Social Theory, Cultural Relativity and the Problem of Globality', in Anthony D. King (ed.), *Culture, Globalization and the World System*. New York: Macmillan.

Robertson, Roland (1992a) 'Globality, Global Culture and Images of World Order', in Hans Haferkamp and Neil Smelser (eds), *Social Change and Modernity*. Berkeley: University of California.

Robertson, Roland (1992b) *Globalization: Social Theory and Global Culture*. London: Sage.

Robertson, Roland, and Chirico, JoAnn (1985) 'Humanity, Globalization, and Worldwide Religious Resurgence: A Theoretical Exploration', *Sociological Analysis*, 46: 219–242.

Robertson, Roland and Lechner, Frank (1985) 'Modernization, Globalization, and the Problem of Culture in World-Systems Theory', *Theory, Culture and Society*, 2 (3): 103–118.

Roof, Wade Clark (1986) 'The New Fundamentalism: Rebirth of Political Religion in America', in Jeffrey K. Hadden and Anson Shupe (eds), *Prophetic Religions and Politics. Religion and the Political Order*, Volume 1. New York: Paragon. pp. 18–34.

Roof, Wade Clark and McKinney, William (1987) *American Mainline Religion: Its Changing Shape and Future*. New Brunswick, NJ: Rutgers University.

Rose, Gregory (1983) '*Velayat-e Faqih* and the Recovery of Islamic Identity in the Thought of Ayatollah Khomeini', in Nikki R. Keddie (ed.), *Religion and Politics in Iran: Shi'ism from Quietism to Revolution*. New Haven: Yale University. pp. 166–188.

Rostow, W. W. (1960) *The Stages of Economic Growth: A Non-Communist Manifesto*. Cambridge: Cambridge University Press.

Roth, John K. (1988) 'The Great Enemy? How Latin American Liberation Theology Sees the United States and the USSR', in Richard L. Rubenstein and John K. Roth (eds), *The*

Politics of Latin American Liberation Theology: The Challenge to U.S. Public Policy. Washington, DC: Washington Institute Press. pp. 225–246.

Roumani, Maurice M. (1988) 'The Ethnic Factor in Israel's Foreign Policy', in Bernard Reich and Gershon R. Kieval (eds), *Israeli National Security Policy: Political Actors and Perspectives.* Westport, CT: Greenwood. pp. 79–103.

Rubinstein, Amnon (1984) *The Zionist Dream Revisited: From Herzl to Gush Emunim and Back.* New York: Schocken.

Rucht, Dieter (1988) 'Themes, Logics, and Arenas of Social Movements: A Structural Approach', in Bert Klandermans, Hanspieter Kriesi, and Sidney Tarrow (eds), *From Structure to Action: Comparing Social Movement Research Across Cultures.* International Social Movement Research: A Research Annual. Volume 1. Greenwich, CT: JAI. pp. 305–328.

Sachedina, Abdulaziz (1983) 'Ali Shariati: Ideologue of the Iranian Revolution', in John L. Esposito (ed.), *Voices of Resurgent Islam.* New York: Oxford. pp. 191–214.

Salehi, M.M. (1988) *Insurgency through Culture and Religion: The Islamic Revolution of Iran.* New York: Praeger.

Sandler, Shmuel (1981) 'The National Religious Party: Towards a New Role in Israel's Political System?' in Sam N. Lehman-Wilzig and Bernard Susser (eds), *Comparative Jewish Politics: Public Life in Israel and the Diaspora.* Jerusalem: Bar-Ilan University. pp. 158–170.

Santa Ana, Julio de (1981) *Towards a Church of the Poor.* Maryknoll, NY: Orbis.

Santmire, H. Paul (1970) *Brother Earth: Nature, God, and Ecology in Time of Crisis.* New York: Thomas Nelson.

Schennink, Ben (1988) 'From Peace Week to Peace Work: Dynamics of the Peace Movement in the Netherlands', in Bert Klandermans, Hanspieter Kriesi, and Sidney Tarrow (eds), *From Structure to Action: Comparing Social Movement Research.* Greenwich, CT: JAI. pp. 247–280.

Schiff, Gary (1977) *Tradition and Politics: The Religious Parties of Israel.* Detroit: Wayne State University.

Scholz, Frithard (1981) *Freiheit als Indifferenz: Alteuropäische Probleme mit der Systemtheorie Niklas Luhmanns.* Frankfurt/M: Suhrkamp.

Segundo, Juan Luis (1984) *Faith and Ideologies.* Tr. John Drury. Maryknoll, NY: Orbis.

Shafir, Gershon (1984) 'Changing Nationalism and Israel's "Open Frontier" on the West Bank', *Theory and Society*, 13: 803–827.

Shaiko, Ronald G. (1987) 'Religion, Politics, and Environmental Concern', *Social Science Quarterly*, 68: 265–281.

Shibley, Mark A. (1991) 'The Southernization of American Religion: Testing a Hypothesis', *Sociological Analysis*, 52: 159–174.

Shortridge, James R. (1977) 'A New Regionalization of American Religion', *Journal for the Scientific Study of Religion*, 16: 143–153.

Shupe, Anson (1986) 'Militancy and Accommodation in the Third Civilization: The Case of Japan's Soka Gakkai Movement', in Jeffrey K. Hadden and Anson Shupe (eds), *Prophetic Religions and Politics. Religion and the Political Order*, Volume 1. New York: Paragon. pp. 235–253.

Shupe, Anson and Stacey, William A. (1982) *Born Again Politics and the Moral Majority: What Social Surveys Really Show.* Lewiston, NY: Edwin Mellen.

Sigmund, Paul E. (1990) *Liberation Theology at the Crossroads: Democracy or Revolution?* New York: Oxford.

Simmel, Georg (1959) *Sociology of Religion.* Tr. Curt Rosenthal. New York: Philosophical Library.

Simmel, Georg (1971) 'How is Social Order Possible', in *On Individuality and Social Forms: Selected Writings.* Donald N. Levine (ed.). Chicago: University of Chicago. pp. 6–22.

Simpson, John H. (1983) 'Moral Issues and Status Politics', in Robert C. Liebman and Robert Wuthnow (eds), *The New Christian Right: Mobilization and Legitimation.* New York: Aldine. pp. 187–205.

Simpson, John H. (1985) 'Status Inconsistency and Moral Issues', *Journal for the Scientific Study of Religion*, 24: 155–162.

Simpson, John H. (1987) 'Globalization, the New Religious Right, and the Politics of the Body', *Psychohistory Review*, 15(2): 59–75.

Simpson, John H. (1991) 'Globalization and Religion: Themes and Prospects', in William Garrett and Roland Robertson (eds), *Religion and Global Order*. New York: Paragon. pp. 1–17.

Simpson, John H. and MacLeod, Henry (1985) 'The Politics of Morality in Canada', in Rodney Stark (ed.), *Religious Movements: Genesis, Exodus, Numbers*. New York: Paragon. pp. 221–240.

Skocpol, Theda (1977) 'Wallerstein's World Capitalist System: A Theoretical and Historical Critique', *American Journal of Sociology*, 82: 1075–1090.

Smith, Anthony D. (1981) *The Ethnic Revival*. Cambridge: Cambridge University Press.

Smith, Anthony D. (1986) *The Ethnic Origins of Nations*. London: Basil Blackwell.

Smith, Brian H. (1982) *The Church and Politics in Chile: Challenges to Modern Catholicism*. Princeton: Princeton University.

Smith, Christian (1991) *The Emergence of Liberation Theology: Radical Religion and Social Movement Theory*. Chicago: University of Chicago.

Smith, Wilfred Cantwell (1981) *Towards a World Theology*. Philadelphia: Westminster.

Snow, David A. and Benford, Robert D. (1988) 'Ideology, Frame Resonance, and Participant Mobilization', in Bert Klandermans, Hanspieter Kriesi, and Sidney Tarrow (eds), *From Structure to Action: Comparing Social Movements Research Across Cultures*. Greenwich, CT: JAI Press. pp. 197–218.

Sprinzak, Ehud (1981) 'Gush Emunim: The Tip of the Iceberg', *Jerusalem Quarterly*, 21: 28–47.

Sprinzak, Ehud (1988) 'Extremist Inputs into Israel's Foreign Policy: The Case of Gush Emunim', in Bernard Reich and Gershon R. Kieval (eds), *Israeli National Security Policy: Political Actors and Perspectives*. Westport, CT: Greenwood. pp. 123–146.

Sprinzak, Ehud (1991) *The Ascendance of Israel's Radical Right*. New York: Oxford.

Stark, Rodney and Bainbridge, William Sims (1985) *The Future of Religion: Secularization, Revival and Cult Formation*. Berkeley: University of California.

Stark, Rodney and Bainbridge, William Sims (1987) *A Theory of Religion*. Toronto Studies in Religion, Vol. 2. New York: Peter Lang.

Steinberg, David I. (1990) *The Future of Burma: Crisis and Choice in Myanmar*. New York & Lanham, MD: University Press of America and The Asia Society.

Stone, Christopher D. (1988) *Earth and Other Ethics: The Case for Moral Pluralism*. New York: Harper & Row.

Swanson, Guy E. (1986) 'Immanence and Transcendence: Connections with Personality and Personal Life', *Sociological Analysis*, 47: 189–213.

Tabory, Ephraim (1990) 'Reform and Conservative Judaism in Israel', in Calvin Goldsheider and Jacob Neusner (eds), *Social Foundations of Judaism*. Englewood Cliffs, NJ: Prentice-Hall. pp. 241–258.

Taylor, Paul W. (1986) *Respect for Nature: A Theory of Environmental Ethics*. Princeton: Princeton University.

Taylor, Peter J. (1985) *Political Geography: World-Economy, Nation-State and Locality*. London & New York: Longman.

Telford, Hamish (1992) 'The Call for Khalistan: The Political Economy of Sikh Separatism'. MA thesis, McGill University, Department of Political Science, Montreal.

Thomas, George M. and Meyer, John W. (1980) 'Regime Changes and State Power in an Intensifying World-State System', in Albert Bergesen (ed.), *Studies of the Modern World-System*. New York: Academic. pp. 139–158.

Thorsell, William (1989) 'Future for the Promised Land Looks Far from Promising', *The Globe and Mail* (November 4), Toronto.

Tilly, Charles (1975) *The Formation of National States in Western Europe*. Princeton: Princeton University.

Timmerman, Peter (1989) 'God is Closer to You Than Your Jugular Vein', *Probe Post*, 12(1): 24–26.

Timmerman, Peter (1990) 'Holding the World Together', *Probe Post*, 12(3–4): 26–29.

Tönnies, Ferdinand (1963) *Community and Society*. Tr. C.P. Loomis. New York: Harper & Row.

Torres, Sergio and Eagleson, John (eds) (1982) *The Challenge of Basic Christian Communities*. Maryknoll, NY: Orbis.

Touraine, Alain (1981). *The Voice and the Eye: An Analysis of Social Movements*. Tr. Alan Duff. Cambridge & Paris: Cambridge University Press & Editions de la Maison des Sciences de l'Homme.

Touraine, Alain (1985) 'An Introduction to the Study of Social Movements', *Social Research*, 52: 749–787.

Tully, Mark R. and Jacob, Satish (1985) *Amritsar: Mrs. Gandhi's Last Battle*. London: Cape.

Vallier, Ivan (1972) 'The Roman Catholic Church: A Transnational Actor', in Robert O. Keohane and Joseph S. Nye (eds), *Transnational Relations and World Politics*. Cambridge, MA: Harvard University.

Van Vugt, Johannes P. (1991) *Democratic Organization for Social Change: Latin American Christian Base Communities and Literacy Campaigns*. New York: Bergin & Garvey.

Wald, Kenneth D., Owen, Dennis E., and Hill, Samuel S., Jr (1989) 'Evangelical Politics and Status Issues', *Journal for the Scientific Study of Religion*, 28: 1–16.

Wallace, Paul (1986) 'The Sikhs as a "Minority" in a Sikh Majority State in India', *Asian Survey*, 26: 363–377.

Wallace, Paul (1988) 'Sikh Minority Attitudes in India's Federal System', in Joseph T. O'Connell, et al. (eds), *Sikh History and Religion in the Twentieth Century*. Toronto: South Asian Studies, University of Toronto. pp. 256–273.

Wallerstein, Immanuel (1974a) *The Modern World System: Capitalist Agriculture and the Origins of the European World-Economy in the Sixteenth Century*. New York: Academic.

Wallerstein, Immanuel (1974b) 'The Rise and Future Demise of the World Capitalist System: Concepts of Comparative Analysis', *Comparative Studies in Society and History*, 16: 387–415. Reprinted in Wallerstein, 1979: pp. 1–36.

Wallerstein, Immanuel (1976) 'Semi-Peripheral Countries and the Contemporary World Crisis', *Theory and Society*, 3: 461–483.

Wallerstein, Immanuel (1979) *The Capitalist World-Economy*. Cambridge: Cambridge University.

Wallerstein, Immanuel (1980) *The Modern World-System II: Mercantilism and the Consolidation of the World Economy 1650–1750*. New York: Academic.

Wallerstein, Immanuel (1983) 'Crises: The World-Economy, the Movements, and the Ideologies', in Albert Bergesen (ed.), *Crises in the World-System*. Beverly Hills: Sage. pp. 21–36.

Wallerstein, Immanuel (1984a) 'Long Waves as Capitalist Process', *Review* (of the Fernand Braudel Center), 7: 559–575.

Wallerstein, Immanuel (1984b) *The Politics of the World-Economy: The States, the Movements and the Civilizations*. Cambridge: Cambridge University.

Wallerstein, Immanuel (1987) 'World-Systems Analysis', in Anthony Giddens and J. Turner (eds), *Social Theory Today*. Stanford, CA: Stanford University. pp. 309–324.

Wallerstein, Immanuel (1988a) 'The Ideological Tensions of Capitalism: Universalism versus Racism and Sexism', in J. Smith, et al. (eds), *Racism, Sexism, and the World-System*. Westport, CT: Greenwood. pp. 3–9.

Wallerstein, Immanuel (1988b) 'Typology of Crises in the World-System', *Review* (of the Fernand Braudel Center), 11: 581–598.

Wallerstein, Immanuel (1989) *The Modern World-System III: The Second Era of Great Expansion of the Capitalist World-Economy, 1730–1840s*. New York: Cambridge.

Wallerstein, Immanuel (1990) 'Culture as the Ideological Battleground of the Modern World-System', *Theory, Culture and Society*, 7(2–3): 31–55.

Walsh, Michael and Davies, Brian (eds) (1984) *Proclaiming Peace and Justice: Documents from John XXIII to John Paul II*. London: Collins/CAFOD.

Weber, Max (1946) 'Religious Rejections of the World and Their Directions', in H. H. Gerth and C. Wright Mills (eds), *From Max Weber: Essays in Sociology*. New York: Oxford. pp. 323–359.

Weber, Max (1958) *The Protestant Ethic and the Spirit of Capitalism*. Tr. Talcott Parsons. New York: Scribner.

Weber, Max (1978) *Economy and Society: An Outline of Interpretative Sociology*. 2 vols. Guenther Roth and Claus Wittich (eds). Berkeley, CA: University of California. (1st edn, 1968.)

Weber, Philip Robert (1983) 'Cyclical Theories of Crisis in the World-System', in Albert Bergesen (ed), *Crises in the World-System*. Beverly Hills: Sage. pp. 37–55.

Weisburd, David (1989) *Jewish Settler Violence: Deviance as Social Reaction*. University Park, PA: Pennsylvania State University.

Weissbrod, Lily (1982) 'Gush Emunim Ideology: From Religious Doctrine to Political Action', *Middle Eastern Studies*, 18: 265–275.

White, Lynn (1967) 'The Historical Roots of Our Ecological Crisis', *Science*, 155: 1203–1207.

Wilcox, Clyde (1989) 'Evangelicals and the Moral Majority', *Journal for the Scientific Study of Religion*, 28: 400–414.

Williams, John R. (1984). *Canadian Churches and Social Justice*. Toronto: Lorimer.

Williams, Philip J. (1989) *The Catholic Church and Politics in Nicaragua and Costa Rica*. London: Macmillan.

Wilson, Bryan R. (1976) 'Aspects of Secularization in the West', *Japanese Journal of Religious Studies*, 3/4: 259–276.

Wilson, Bryan R. (1982) *Religion in Sociological Perspective*. Oxford: Oxford University.

Wilson, Bryan R. (1985) 'Secularization: The Inherited Model', in Phillip E. Hammond (ed.), *The Sacred in a Secular Age: Toward Revision in the Scientific Study of Religion*. Berkeley: University of California. pp. 1–20.

Wilson, John (1973) *Introduction to Social Movements*. New York: Basic.

Wolffsohn Michael (1987) *Israel: Polity, Society, Economy 1882–1986. An Introductory Handbook*. Atlantic Highlands, NJ: Humanities Press International.

Woodrum, Eric and Davison, Beth L. (1992) 'Images of God and Environmental Concern', Paper presented at the Society for the Scientific Study of Religion Annual Meeting, Washington, DC.

World Council of Churches (1968) *The Uppsala Report 1968: Official Report of the Fourth Assembly of the World Council of Churches*. Norman Goodall (ed.). Geneva: World Council of Churches.

World Council of Churches (1976) *Breaking Barriers, Nairobi 1975. The Official Report of the Fifth Assembly of the World Council of Churches, Nairobi, 23 November–10 December, 1975*. David M. Paton (ed.). London & Grand Rapids, MI: SPCK/Eerdmans.

World Council of Churches (1983) *Gathered for Life. Official Report of the VI Assembly, World Council of Churches, Vancouver, Canada, 24 July–10 August, 1983*. David Gill (ed.). Geneva & Grand Rapids, MI: World Council of Churches/Eerdmans.

World Council of Churches (1990a) *Now is the Time. Final Document and Other Texts, World Convocation on Justice, Peace and the Integrity of Creation, Seoul, 1990*. Geneva: WCC Publications.

World Council of Churches (1990b) *Vancouver to Canberra 1983–1990. Report of the Central Committee of the World Council of Churches to the Seventh Assembly*. Thomas F. Best (ed.). Geneva: WCC Publications.

World Council of Churches (1991) *Signs of the Spirit. Official Report Seventh Assembly. Canberra, Australia, 7–20 February 1991*. Michael Kinnamon (ed.). Geneva & Grand Rapids, MI: WCC Publications/Eerdmans.

Wuthnow, Robert (1987) *Meaning and Moral Order: Explorations in Cultural Analysis*. Berkeley: University of California.

Yinger, J. Milton (1970) *The Scientific Study of Religion*. New York: Macmillan.

Yinger, J. Milton (1985) 'Ethnicity', *Annual Review of Sociology*, 11: 151–180.

Yinger, J. Milton and Cutler, Stephen J. (1983) 'The Moral Majority Viewed Sociologically', in David G. Bromley and Anson Shupe (eds), *New Christian Politics*. Macon, GA: Mercer University. pp. 68–90.

Zald, Mayer N. and McCarthy, John D. (1987) 'Religious Groups as Crucibles of Social

Movements', in *Social Movements in an Organizational Society: Collected Essays*. Intro. William A. Gamson. New Brunswick, NJ: Transaction. pp. 67–95.

Zolberg, A.R. (1981) 'Origins of the Modern World System: A Missing Link', *World Politics*, 33: 253–281.

Zonis, Marvin, and Brumberg, Daniel (1987) *Khomeini, the Islamic Republic of Iran, and the Arab World*. Harvard Middle East Papers. Modern Series, Number 5. Cambridge, MA: Center for Middle Eastern Studies, Harvard University.

INDEX